THE RISE OF
THE NEW MODEL
ARMY

THE RISE OF
THE NEW MODEL
ARMY

MARK A. KISHLANSKY

Department of History, University of Chicago

CAMBRIDGE UNIVERSITY PRESS

Cambridge

London   New York   Melbourne

109450

Published by the Syndics of the Cambridge University Press
The Pitt Building, Trumpington Street, Cambridge CB2 1RP
Bentley House, 200 Euston Road, London NW1 2DB
32 East 57th Street, New York, NY 10022, USA
296 Beaconsfield Parade, Middle Park, Melbourne 3206, Australia

© Cambridge University Press 1979

First published 1979

Printed in the United States of America
Typeset, printed and bound by Vail-Ballou Press, Inc.,
Binghamton, N.Y.

Library of Congress Cataloging in Publication Data
Kishlansky, Mark A
The rise of the New Model Army.
Includes bibliographical references.
1. Great Britian – History – Civil War, 1642–1649.
2. Great Britain. Army – History – 17th century.
I. Title.
DA415.K52   941.06′2   79–4285
ISBN 0 521 22751 8

For
CHARLOTTE KISHLANSKY
and the memory of
MORRIS KISHLANSKY

CONTENTS

PREFACE

Qui s'excuse, s'accuse – still, a word about method and organization is necessary. Sources for the study of politics in the period preceding the English Revolution are plentiful but perplexing. Besides the efforts of contentious authors to portray only one side of an issue, men who lived through the upheavals of the midcentury spent some of their declining years justifying their own conduct and vilifying that of others. Thus any attempt to provide an account of what happened during the 1640s is fraught with difficulty. I have sought to observe two rules of evidence that may seem unimaginatively rigid, but that I believe have saved me from error: to ignore the assertions of obviously biased informants unless otherwise supported and to prefer contemporary accounts to retrospective ones. In the first instance, I have made little use of Baxter, Edwards, and the religious disputants, of the Clarendon Mss. (a most tempting source), and the ambassadorial intrigues of Sabran and Montreuil. Baillie, on whom I have relied for the Scottish point of view, occasionally falls into the same category. The tendency of these men to polarize and exaggerate the situations they observe should be apparent to any who have attempted to substantiate their accounts. In the second category, I have made sparing use of Clarendon, Whitelocke, Ludlow, Holles, Hutchinson, and other memorialists who, though participants in the events they describe, wrote their recollections through the distorting glass of hindsight. This is a most complicated problem, for some, like Clarendon and Whitelocke, relied upon notes made at the time or on collections of newsbooks. Nevertheless, all these authors assess the causes of events by their consequences, hopelessly muddling their unfolding. In these accounts men who benefit from developments are accused of plotting them, a determinism one would hardly expect from such a "providential" generation.

Likewise, but for different reasons, I have tried to avoid the historiographical wars that have devastated study of this period. My method has been to develop the narrative from the sources alone and only later to compare my accounts with those of other historians. As my focus and interpretive emphasis differs markedly from those who have come before me, this has not been as difficult as might be imagined. Where I have borrowed, or at places where matters of fact are at issue, I hope I have supplied full citations. That there are substantive and interpretive differences between this work and that of others who have covered much of the same period will be obvious to anyone who makes the comparison. I hope that these differences will reopen examination of the sources rather than initiate another round of theoretical skirmishing.

I have organized my narrative around two principal themes, the disintegration of the parliamentary cause and the rise of the New Model Army. These themes are fundamentally intertwined and can, I believe, be explicated only by a precise narrative – day to day at crucial moments. Narrative history, no longer the staple it once was, is now thought difficult and "boring" for it relies on the willingness of readers to familiarize themselves with intricate detail before they can understand the argument being presented. I have tried to summarize the argument at both the beginning and end of the work and to preview the major events and issues at the start of each chapter. Moreover, I have kept my focus directly upon Parliament and the Army so as to give greater coherence to the story. Chapter 4, which strays from this intention by studying two extraparliamentary bodies, is a critical component in the breakdown of parliamentary unity. The narrative of the City petitioning campaign was made possible by my discovery of Thomas Juxon's journal, a unique source for understanding London politics.

The focus of the narrative has also led me to give scant attention to developments in the counties and to the history of religious and political radicalism during this period. County history is best treated in its own integrity: generalizations are risky and frequently out of place. Clearly the mood in the country was an important element in parliamentary decision making although, I would contend, less so in this period than in the one immediately succeeding it. The decision to exclude the so-called Levellers was a more difficult one. The absence of Leveller penetration in the Army will, I hope, be recognized from my account of the soldiers' radicalization. The source materials leave little impression of radical infiltration or leadership, but recent historiography has raised the Levellers to fantastic heights. They are nothing less than the deus ex machina in explanations of the Revolution. I have attempted to deal more explicitly with this problem in a separate essay elsewhere.

Preface

This work began as a study of the officer corps of the New Model Army. It was originally my intention to provide a biographical composite of the Army leaders in the belief that their common political and religious objectives might be explained by their formative experiences. This, I had hoped, would lead to an understanding of revolutionary radicalism and tie together the Army and the Leveller movement. The period I set out to examine was from the summer of 1647 to the execution of the King. It was shortly after I began collecting material for this prosopography that I discovered the diversity of the Army's composition. The disintegration of the original New Model in the spring of 1647, no less than the extraordinary pattern of withdrawal among regimental commanders, first alerted me to the problematic nature of my assumptions. Moreover, investigation of the great outpouring of materials from the Army during the first half of 1647 led to the inescapable conclusion that the officers and soldiers were undergoing a process of politicization and radicalization, a process that I assumed superfluous.

What began as a study of background, then, took on new proportions. The events of the spring and summer of 1647 became the very crux of the Army's revolutionary radicalism (such as it was), and rather than go forward to find its ultimate meaning, I was led backward to origins, to an uncovering of the Army's creation and its interrelationship with its creators. Despite the euphoria that accompanies fresh historical understanding, I had not yet accepted the results of my preliminary work. Although I was now sensitized to material that would demonstrate the nonradical character of the Army (even now the extent of radicalism remains the unavoidable measure), I retained both my original predilections and the deep-rooted historical interpretation I had been taught. Study of the Army's creation was, thus, alternately exhilarating and deeply disturbing. To discard the notion that the New Model Army was a radical Army was also to undercut the belief that a struggle between Presbyterian and Independent parties (with their accompanying "middle group") dominated Long Parliament politics. For diverse reasons such a challenge was not a course I welcomed.

If my study of the Army was backward looking, beginning with its disintegration, my examination of parliamentary politics moved inexorably forward. The work of modern revisionists pointed to intensive study of diaries, letters, state documents, and private correspondence. Although I remained primarily interested in the interrelationship between Parliament and Army, the transformation of parliamentary practice was too clear to be ignored. Through the polarization of parliamentary politics and politicians after the war ended I finally understood the intensity of the Army's response to Parliament's plans for its disbandment. The accusation made by the soldiers that parliamentarians were self-interested and factious, charges I had long discounted as hollow phrases that insisted upon an impractical ideal, became haunting. If the soldiers really eschewed and feared faction and self-interest in Parliament the actions that they defended as reasonable and necessary – even the seizure of the King – became coherent and explicable. The Army's radicalization, which I knew could not be explained by either puritan extremism or Leveller infiltration, now had a motive force.

In the research and writing of this book I have incurred numerous debts to both institutions and individuals. The staffs of the British Library, House of Lords Record Office, Corporation of London Record Office, Dr. Williams' Library, and the Bodleian have all showed me the greatest kindness. The patience of the staff in the students room of the British Library was Penelopean, especially in producing the first 700 volumes of the Harleian Manuscripts for my inspection. Mr. David Thomas of the Public Records Office was extremely helpful in sorting out my frequent difficulties at Chancery Lane; Leslie Montgomery at Worcester College Library cheerfully duplicated sections of the Clarke Mss. and shared her knowledge of the College's pamphlet collection with me. In America, I was assisted by the staffs of the Rockefeller and Hay Libraries at Brown University; Widener and Houghton Libraries at Harvard; Sterling and Bienecke Libraries at Yale; and the Regenstein Library at the University of Chicago, where Howard Dillon was most kind in helping me to obtain microfilms and in cutting red tape to make them promptly available.

My gratitude to the Institute of Historical Research, its staff and facilities, is unending. Not only is the library a treasure trove for historical studies, but the seminars and informal exchange of ideas that the Institute makes possible were extraordinarily stimulating. It provides a most necessary environment for scholarly endeavors.

Funds from the graduate school of Brown University made possible my initial stay in England; the Social Science division of the University of Chicago defrayed the cost of purchasing films and of reproducing the various drafts of the manuscript.

Preface

The intellectual debts that preceded the completion of this project are of equal value to those that accompanied it. Karl Bottigheimer, Tom Kranidas, and Bernard Semmel nurtured my interest in English history during most difficult times. The members of the Department of History at Brown University, especially Tom Gleason, Stephen Graubard, Anthony Molho, and Gordon Wood, gave encouragement and inspiration as well as training.

A number of scholars have generously read this work in its various forms and provided most useful criticisms and corrections: Jerald Brauer, Ted Cook, L. P. Curtis, Jr., Barbara Donagan, Dave Dyer, Christopher Hill, Stan Katz, Emmet Larkin, Conrad Russell, and Lawrence Stone. My obstinacy in refusing to accept some of their most incisive objections will be plain. It is a constant source of joy and worry that each part of my argument has found supporters and detractors from among this group. John Morrill read the work twice, saving me from errors of expression and fact, and provided the plan for condensation. His frank assessments and commentaries went beyond the call of scholarly assistance.

That this work has a life at all is mostly owing to the efforts of David Underdown. He suggested the topic, supervised the research, and sorted through my first painful efforts at explication. Both by precept and example he has taught me the skills of scholarship. His friendship and generosity have been a constant well from which I have drawn the perseverance and enthusiasm necessary to bring this study to conclusion. Though a pale shadow, this work aspires to the standards he set in *Pride's Purge*.

I wish to thank the following publishers for permission to use copyrighted material: The University of Chicago Press for "The Emergence of Adversary Politics in the Long Parliament," *Journal of Modern History*, 49 (1977); and The Past and Present Society for "The Case of the Army Truly Stated," *Past and Present*, 81 (1978).

Finally, the sacrifices of my family cannot go unrecorded. My parents' financial support during the long years of my education and my wife's interruption of her own career to travel to England greatly eased many burdens. At Jeanne's unfailing good humor during what must have seemed an interminable process of research and writing I can only marvel.

Chicago, Illinois   M. A. KISHLANSKY
January, 1979

ABBREVIATIONS

Abbott	W. C. Abbott, ed., *The Writings and Speeches of Oliver Cromwell*, 4 vols. (Cambridge, Mass., 1937–47)
Add. Mss.	Additional Manuscripts
Baillie	David Laing, ed., *The Letters and Journals of Robert Baillie*, 3 vols. (Edinburgh, 1841–2)
Bodl.	Bodleian Library
B.L.	British Library
Clarendon	W. D. Macray, ed., *Clarendon's History of the Rebellion*, 6 vols. (Oxford, 1888)
Clarke Mss.	The Clarke Manuscripts, Worcester College, Oxford
Clarke Papers	C. H. Firth, ed., *The Clarke Papers*, 4 vols. (London, 1891–1901)
C.J.	*Journals of the House of Commons*
Common Council Journal	Journals of the Common Council of London, The Corporation of London Record Office
C.S.P.D.	*Calendar of State Papers, Domestic Series*
D'Ewes	Journal of the Parliament begun November 3, 1640
E.	The Thomason Tracts
Gardiner, *Great Civil War*	S. R. Gardiner, *The History of the Great Civil War*, 4 vols. (London, 1893)
Harl.	Harleian Manuscripts
H.L.R.O.	House of Lords Record Office
H.M.C.	*Historical Manuscripts Commission Reports*
Juxon	The Journal of Thomas Juxon
L.J.	*Journals of the House of Lords*
Luke	H. G. Tibbut, ed., *The Letterbooks of Sir Samuel Luke 1644–45* (Streatley, Bedfordshire Historical Records Society Publications, vol. 42, 1963)
O.P.H.	*The Parliamentary or Constitutional History of England*, 24 vols. (London, 1751–62)

P.R.O.   Public Record Office
Rushworth   John Rushworth, *Historical Collections*, 8 vols.
                  (London, 1721)
S.P.   State Papers
Whitacre   Proceedings in the House of Commons
Whitelocke,   Bulstrode Whitelocke, *Memorials of English
  Memorials   Affairs*, 4 vols. (London, 1853)
Yonge   Journal of Proceedings in the House of Com-
                  mons

All dates are given in old style with the year reckoned to begin on January 1. Spelling and punctuation have been modernized to make the meaning of quotations clear.

PART I

Parliament Triumphant

Behold how good and how pleasant it is for brethren to dwell together in unity.

Psalm 133:1

Chapter 1

THE PARLIAMENTARY CAUSE

The Lords and Commons in this present Parliament assembled according to the duty and trust which lies upon them, for prevention of these great mischiefs and preservation of the safety of His Majesty's person, the peace of the Kingdom and the defense of the Parliament resolved and ordained that an Army be forthwith raised.[1]

From Civil War to Revolution – the progression is unmistakable. Fundamental authority, first in the person of the King and then in the institution of Parliament, was under attack. The King's power eroded slowly over decades, victim of both long-term forces and of his own policies and personality. Parliamentary legitimacy collapsed spectacularly in the year between the end of the war and the Army's march to London. It too gave way before a combination of factors not all of its own making. Royal defeat and parliamentary collapse were the antecedents to military rule. The images of change are vivid: Charles defiantly raising his standard at Nottingham; fleeing to Newcastle in the guise of a servant; seized unceremoniously by Cornet Joyce; and finally executed in the name of the people. The Houses of Parliament successively violated: by the King in search of the five members; by the mob of apprentices forcing Lords and Commons to recall their votes; by Colonel Pride's clumsy purge; and by Cromwell's file of musketeers, who neatly dissolved the Rump. Even in these symbolic episodes the war and revolution are distinguished, as political maneuvering gave way to action and finally a new order. Incrementally, reform and the safeguards necessary to maintain it brought the nation from internecine strife to political upheaval.

Though it became increasingly unavoidable, neither King nor Parliament consciously sought the war. The King's concessions in the face of a united parliamentary reform movement did little to rebuild the trust necessary to ensure constitutional safeguards. Although the first session of the Long Parliament achieved a near constitutional "revolution," Charles's past conduct, particularly his

3

willful disregard of the Petition of Right, had not been expiated.[2] In part, this was due to his own indecision in the critical months after the first session. Plans to coopt the reform leaders, the "official country," alternated with a hard line against further change; the sacrifice of Strafford, a personal tragedy for the King, was publicly recanted; and, slowly, the parliamentary reform movement was breaking up, with influential members deserting to the "King's party."[3] After so much had been resolved, and in a parliamentary way, a permanent settlement still hinged on Charles's unpredictable inclinations and the ingrained distrust parliamentary leaders had of him. The Irish rebellion brought out the worst in each: Charles's determination to end the escalation of demands and the diminution of his power coupled with Parliament's decision to usurp his military prerogatives ended the stalemate.

Neither side took the steps necessary to prevent it, but there was little enthusiasm for the war. Outside London, where the political atmosphere was electrified by the attempt on the five members and the governmental apparatus was seized by a solid group of reformers, the nation remained remarkably calm in the face of the declaration of war.[4] Initially most communities remained studiously neutral, appealing to King and Parliament for an immediate recomposition. Others raised forces with the express intention of inhibiting "strangers" from entering their counties in support of either side. Treaties, like the Yorkshire pacification, sought to prevent individual extremists from dividing the county.[5] In other places the drift toward war was accelerated by the opportunity to resolve long-standing personal and familial hostilities.[6] As neither side had very clear war aims, the nation's disinclination toward fighting was only gradually overcome. Armies raised for self-defense proliferated and inevitably came to clash. But mixed feelings and mixed motives predominated in the first, tentative year of war.

The disinclination for war was not only to be observed in the counties. Within Parliament a large group of those who remained at Westminster, and who accepted the necessity of self-defense, urged an immediate pacification. They foresaw with the utmost clarity that the fighting would escalate the conflict beyond the areas of disagreement that then existed. Obviously the war would create suffering, outrages, and acts of vengeance that would be justified by raising particular issues to general principles. A civil war would quickly take on a logic of its own. Moreover, resort to arms would commit the combatants to a decisive and one-sided resolution of their disagreements. A balance between prerogatives and privileges, which both King and Parliament intended to maintain, could not be aided by military conquest or defeat. Nor, with very few exceptions, did those who supported the war seek to use it as an end in itself. It was fought in defense of the reforms that had been achieved; an extreme demonstration of purpose that, it was thought, would restrain the King in future by fear of its recurrence. Until they were palpably in danger of losing it, the men at Westminster were never intent on winning the war.

The underlying absence of purpose compounded the institutional difficulties Parliament faced in waging war with the monarch. Despite its centuries-old tradition and the heightened expectations many had for its success, even as late as 1642 Parliament was without executive or administrative capacities. The Houses had no formal leaders and most of those who had directed legislative programs in the past departed with the King. The committee system, which would eventually expand into an administrative apparatus, was still in its infancy, used mainly for internal purposes. Although the concept of "representative" was expanding, Parliament had no institutional means of carrying the will of the Houses to the communities of the nation. Local government, despite the presence at Westminster of leading justices, Lords, and Deputy Lieutenants, was still the King's government. Procedures to define relations between the Houses were also inchoate and the withdrawal of the larger part of the peerage was a further complicating factor. As befitted an institution that counseled and legislated, Parliament's privileges, procedures, and powers were defined by precedent and were thus an uncertain guide to action in an event as unparalleled as civil war.

Finally, those who remained to guide the war differed little from those who left to support the King. Lawyers, country gentlemen, aristocratic heirs, wealthy merchants – these were men who had a solid stake in society, who felt aggrieved by aspects of Charles's rule, but who were little inclined to disturb fundamental order.[7] It is of no little significance that each side accused the other of essaying to raise the rabble and steadfastly denied each other's accusations. Though the reformers had capitalized on the crowds of Londoners who screamed for Strafford's blood, once the war broke out popular demonstrations were quickly curtailed. The armies were formed, on both sides, through the old noble and gentry networks. Professional soldiers with continental military experience complained bitterly of being passed over for promotion in favor of the sons of gentlemen.[8] Impressment from the lower orders was unavoidable, especially as the war ground on, but the only genuine popular risings of the Civil War were those of the clubmen – conservators of local order and advocates of peace.[9]

Opposition among parliamentarians to innovation in military affairs was mirrored by their hostility to changes in the political realm. The rationale that they fought in the name of the King – for the "preservation of the safety of His Majesty's person, the peace of the Kingdom and the defense of Parliament" – to separate him from his councillors and reunite him to his Parliament was crucial.[10] It allowed for the continuation of the session and, more or less, its normal activities: levying taxes, raising and supplying forces, creating and regulating law. But it also placed severe limits upon those novelties that were absolutely necessary for survival. It made self-deception necessary, the constant search for incidents in the past that would legitimate present actions. Members of Parliament kept precedent books, which were constantly updated as their legislation diversified. Walter Yonge cited statutes for Parliament's appointment of military officers, councillors, and Lord-Lieutenants. Under the heading of "Parliament" he recorded precedents from the reign of Henry VI that justified parliamentary rule without the monarch, placing his symbol of especial importance beside the notation, "Parliament made an ordinance without the King which was binding."[11] The need for cautious, painstaking deliberation before each necessitous decision characterized parliamentary government during the fighting.

Thus the war progressed. If Parliament possessed all the logistical advantages – control of the fleet; the large London population from which to recruit; easy access to treasure and supply; a more compact area to defend – the King had strategic superiority, for only he had a clearly defined purpose: the reoccupation of his capital. Charles fought against a rebellion and his aim was to suppress it. Parliament fought in the name of the King and as long as there remained a literal sense to this justification an offensive war was impossible. So, too, as the campaigns of 1642 and 1643 demonstrated, was an indefinite holding action. As the advocates of an immediate cessation predicted, the war assumed its own shape. Charles's recruitment among the Irish was answered by the parliamentary treaty with the Scots, which brought a large Army into the royalist north. The prolongation of hostilities meant burdensome taxation, siege and occupation, death and destruction. The summer soldiers did indeed shrink away from the armies on both sides and increasingly those who answered the call for each new campaign were men of determined purpose and bitter experience. By 1644 the war was being fought to justify the war. The decimation of the parliamentary armies in the campaign of that year initiated a reexamination of what had by then become the parliamentary cause.

The soul searching was serious and intense but not even in desperation would the men at Westminster abandon the limited goals that had carried them into the conflict. During the autumn of 1644 another effort at peace was undertaken. Though it was, perhaps, doomed from the start by Charles's military reinvigoration, Parliament worked hard at producing the Uxbridge proposals, examining yet again its members' ultimate desires, and baring yet again the diversity of opinion within the Houses. The process, though occasionally divisive, reemphasized the overriding unity parliamentarians shared, the sense of purpose that united godly divines, constitutional reformers, and those who simply sought resolution of the conflict. Their examination of parliamentary misfortunes gave rise to the movement for self-denial, a controversial solution to interrelated military, political, and religious problems. But little reformist zeal touched the reestablishment of Parliament's southern forces, the creation of the New Model Army. "This Army, under God, is the principal means to preserve us in safety," Speaker Lenthall observed, and its creation and intended service affirmed his theme of defense.[12] If the aristocratic generals were removed from the fighting, they still made the strategic decisions. The debate between an active and passive pursuit of the war was not resolved by the formation of the New Model and its triumph was as unexpected – "the success is hardly imaginable which accompanies Sir Thomas Fairfax's Army" – as it was puzzling.[13]

Paradoxically, military victory did not end the war. It served rather to reveal the bankruptcy of the assumption that the King would yield to Parliament's terms after his armies had been crushed. Instead of succumbing to the verdict of battle, Charles sought refuge in the Scottish Army, where his intrigues to bring foreign forces into England were balanced by overtures of a separate peace with the Scots. Parliamentary proposals, tendered after its military victory, were again rejected and the fear of renewed war heightened. The King's offer to come to London was as frightening to Parliament as it was welcome to many war-weary citizens: "And indeed many wise and good men are of this opinion to wish the King here," thought Thomas Juxon, a London militia captain, "that thereby men might be taken off from pursuing their several interests and from seeking to devour each other and to mind the common good."[14]

United in war, the parliamentary cause could not withstand the pressure of the unresolved peace. Even before the King's rejection of the Newcastle propositions divisive issues such as the church establishment and the sale of royalist estates had threatened parliamentary unity. The sacrifices demanded by the war led those who had made them to expect a role in determining the shape of the ultimate settlement. This was especially true of the Scots, whose clamor for a rigid presbyterian establishment became even louder in the months preceding the King's flight to their Army. Unable to influence the Houses in a parliamentary way, the Scots launched an appeal to public opinion, openly accusing M.P.s and Army leaders of encouraging the growth of heretical and profane religious practices. Though not as vociferous as their brethren, the City of London joined the call for a presbyterian church establishment. In a series of petitions that challenged parliamentary privileges, the London government also demanded the expansion of its civil jurisdiction and a massive demobilization of Parliament's military forces. Fearful of religious and political extremism, Scots and City were intent upon a speedy resumption of constitutional government.

The disintegration of the parliamentary cause made the institution vulnerable to these attacks from its constituents as well as to innovations by groups of its members: "In all ages those who sought their own greatness have always sought to diminish the powers of Parliament," a group of radical Londoners declared in urging the Houses to resist such assaults.[15] But the need to legislate a settlement without the King's prior approval and the danger that powerful elements would desert Parliament made it necessary to abandon the methods that had maintained unity within the institution. By the winter of 1647 the House of Commons came to be dominated by a political party led by Denzil Holles that received support from groups within and outside the Houses. With his overwhelming majority Holles developed a program to reunite King and Parliament by eliminating the areas of disagreement between them. This involved securing the return of the King and the withdrawal of the Scottish Army, supporting the diluted presbyterian establishment already erected, suppressing the Irish rebellion, and reorganizing the military forces. Thus Holles sought the middle ground between those ready to settle with Charles on any terms and those who despaired of an accord with the dissembling monarch.

To secure his objectives Holles seized the reins of government and spurred a transformation of parliamentary practice. An insignificant standing committee was reorganized into a new executive body, the Derby House Committee. There the policy of the military disestablishment was formulated and implemented. To avoid delay, important decisions were shunted off the floor of the Commons to Derby House and then presented to the House as resolutions that were decided in an increasing number of divisions. Ad hoc committees were all but eliminated from the parliamentary process and sharp tactics and maneuvers were employed to aid Holles's program. Means were sacrificed to ends and Holles's opponents could no longer participate in parliamentary government. "The Presbyterians now carry all things with a high hand," one of Clarendon's correspondents assessed at the end of the winter.[16]

Holles's power within Parliament, however, was not alone sufficient to carry through his plans. To suppress the Irish rebellion it was necessary for him to recruit an invasion force from among the idle regiments of the New Model Army. Learning of the impending military disestablishment (besides those recruited for Ireland some of the forces would be garrisoned throughout England and the rest disbanded) the soldiers of the New Model drew up a petition outlining their material complaints, which they intended to present to Sir Thomas Fairfax. When news of the subscription campaign reached Parliament it was interpreted not as a lawful expression of just grievances but as a mutinous attempt to sabotage the Irish venture. In the Commons Holles drafted a savage declaration branding promoters of the petition "enemies to the state," and

Parliament ordered senior New Model officers to London for examination of their role in the agitation. With their right to petition denied and their officers under attack, the soldiers of the scattered New Model regiments sought means to reassert their legitimate grievances and to defend their hard-won honor. "Who would have thought that so modest an address as the late petition drawn up to be subscribed by the Army, to be presented to the General, would have raised so much dust?"[17] By May 1647, the soldiers had elected representatives and were rapidly developing a radical political consciousness. Holles's efforts to disband the Army at the end of the month failed, undermining all his plans for reconciliation with the King.

The Army's gradual radicalization broke the deadlock between King and Parliament. The soldiers came to realize their own part in settling the kingdom's future, a role that involved delimiting the power of Parliament as well as monarch. "And always men may see it," one of the Army's manifestos asserted, "that Parliament privileges, as well as royal prerogative, may be perverted and abused, or extended to the destruction of those greater ends for whose protection or preservation they were admitted or intended."[18] The Army identified the perversion of parliamentary privilege with the transformation of political practice that had occurred over the past year and had resulted in factionalism and the pursuit of self-interest. They impeached Holles and ten of his party followers and kept up pressure on Parliament until they withdrew. The Army also leveled charges against the conduct of the City's militia committee and it was these charges that induced the confrontation whereby the Houses of Parliament were invaded and the Army marched to London to restore parliamentary freedom.

Thus was the conflict that had begun between King and Parliament transformed. The rise of the Army and its assault upon Parliament made constitutional recomposition along the old lines impossible. The Army's insistence upon parliamentary reform and the King's continued refusal to come to terms necessitated the constitutional experiments of Commonwealth and Protectorate. The revolution that the Army made was not unrestrained for it grew directly from the goals that served to justify the Civil War – freedom from tyranny (royal or parliamentary) and the defense of native liberties – but it gave an increasingly radical interpretation to what was necessary to secure and safeguard the nation's future.

Where Parliament had sought to avoid decisions that would alienate those who had opposed it, the Army sought programs to reward those who had supported it. Where Parliament's free debate and cautious decision making had checked the course of change, the Army's experience of decisive action against an unequivocal enemy led, in the end, to fundamental alteration. The symbol of the Army's revolution was not the King executed, but the Parliament eclipsed.

The inherent conservatism of those members of Parliament who remained to direct the war, their "gentry constitutionalism," was strengthened by the procedures and practices of their institution. Though its roles varied according to the demands placed upon it by the King, Parliament was, as William Prynne declared, "the greatest council of the Kingdom."[19] Its central function was to do the King's business: each Parliament was called into existence for a specific purpose laid before it by the crown. The guiding principles of the parliamentary method were unencumbered debate and the quest for unanimous resolution. Free debate, though not the equivalent of free speech, was persuasive discussion, reasoned argument among men uncommitted to predetermined positions. Debate revealed the strengths and weaknesses of the measures presented to the Houses and initiated the committees that reshaped bills in light of arguments offered by the speakers. Debate was designed to convince, not to conquer, and during debate the members of the socially stratified House of Commons acted as equals. Great rhetoricians and cunning lawyers as well as aristocratic heirs were not to have an overbearing influence upon the House, and the rule that no member could speak twice to an issue was strictly enforced.[20]

As debate was framed to persuade, it was also intended to perfect rather than to oppose the King's business. Indeed, parliamentary practice left little place for opposition. A member who spoke against the body of a bill could not be named to the committee which considered it: "For by being [of] a committee it is supposed he liketh the bill for matter, but disliketh the form only, which is the office of committees to amend."[21] Such rules favored the passage of all bills and led to what one parliamentarian condemned as "policies in Parliament." " 'Tis a common policy in Parliament if any man be against a bill but would not seem to be so, to speak for it and by way of objections to show such matter against it as may not be answered."[22] The necessity for such circuitous techniques is one indication that opposition was not an integral part of parliamentary experience. This can also be seen in relations between the Houses, where it was a general rule that one House would not reject a bill presented to it by the other. Bills could be amended, although not to negate their intention, or they could be withdrawn, generally as the result of a conference between the Houses. "If the two Houses cannot agree," wrote William Hakewill, "then sometimes the Lords, sometimes the Commons, require a meeting of some of each House, whereby information may be had of each others' mind for the preservation of a good correspondency between them, after which meeting for the most part (though not always) either part agrees to the Bill in question."[23] When the House of Lords protested against the self-denying ordinance, this procedure was still followed. The Commons insisted that the peers' objections be submitted as amendments, but as they comprised a negation of the bill, the Lords were forced to substitute an ordinance of their own for that of the Commons.[24] In general, however, matters that aroused opposition or required excessive time or energy were "allowed to sleep" by the Speakers or the members of the House, who could refuse commitment.[25] Rejection of a measure was uncommon and acceptance so routine that the Speaker would accumulate a half-dozen or more bills before presenting them, one after another, for final resolution.[26]

The procedural prejudice in favor of the King's business is also exemplified by the method of putting questions. Although the Speaker was at liberty to end debate by accepting a call for the question, he could only present a motion for the passage of a bill, never for its rejection. "If upon the second reading of the Bill the[y] cry away with it, the speaker may not make that the question, but must put it to the question whether it shall be committed or no; if the greatest voice be no, the speaker must put the question for the engrossing, which is always denied, if it be denied a committee by a negative, but the speaker is notwithstanding to make the question so."[27] Moreover, questions were put first in the affirmative, a factor that allowed undecided members to abstain when the negative vote was taken.

Unanimity rather than diversity was the goal of parliamentary procedure. The committee system was intended to deflect opposition, and committees were appointed after debate so that any exceptions raised there could be considered. It was the committee's prerogative to amend the bill, and this was another method of providing a compromise course when opposition or disinclination persisted. Committees were eager to achieve consensus, and, as Wallace Notestein observed of the committees in the parliamentary session of 1604–10, "to gain agreements they would put forward amendments and provisos until the final form of the measure was burdened with exceptions."[28] Once a bill was reported by the committee and returned to the House, its chances for unanimous approval could easily be determined, for any opposition to its final form had to be expressed before its engrossing. Then an effort might be made "to have the question deferred till the next day or some longer time ... especially if it be a matter they desire should either pass with unanimous consent or not at all."[29] Even after the vote was taken, moves might still be afoot to achieve unanimity: "And if upon putting the question in the negative there be but one that is heard to say no it hath been seen that he being a man of special note hath been desired by the House to discover to them the reason of his differing in opinion from the whole House."[30]

That parliamentary procedure eschewed opposition is not to say that none existed, but it is a reminder that opposition was not the normal course of affairs and that it explicitly violated one of the Houses' underlying principles.[31] Two striking illustrations of this point can be found among the descriptions of parliamentary procedure. In a chapter entitled "Concerning Cases and Judgments Which Are Hard," Hakewill relates how the most difficult judgments "Between the King and some nobleman" or a complicated legal case "before the Chancellor" could be resolved by Parliament. A committee of twenty-five Lords and Commoners was appointed to study the matter. If disagreement was present in that body, it would select half its number to consider the case, and this contraction was continued to its logical conclusion: "If the King consent to three, these three may condescend to two, and may descend to another, and so at length his ordinance shall stand above the whole Parliament, and so condescend from twenty and five persons to one only person, unless the greater number will agree and ordain, at the length, one person, as is said, shall agree for all, who cannot disagree from himself."[32]

The second example is found in an examination of the division, the House of Commons' single institutionalized form of opposition. The division, like the poll in an election, enabled the Speaker to determine which side held a majority. Like the poll, it was rarely necessary, and it was generally related to private rather than public business. Two of its characteristics, however, are worth noting. Divisions occurred on issues seen to have a conservative and an innovative side. It was the innovators who were required to leave the House, a distinct disadvantage both because of the competition for seats and the strong conservative bent of the Commons' members. "If the question be for the passing of a bill, those of the affirmative part do always go forth, and those of the negative part sit still (which privilege of sitting is given to them, because they are against innovation, which every new bill brings in though it be never so good in appearance)."[33] The innovators had raised the issue, which in normal practice should not have come to the vote without the opposition to it being cleared or the entire matter deferred, and the onus was on them to prove the worthiness of their cause. If they did, however, those who had opposed them customarily withdrew from their seats, "thereby to acknowledge their consent to it, and their error in being against it," and together both sides reentered the House and presented the bill to the Speaker as the sense of the unified membership.[34] As opposition was rare the methods of dealing with it were also unusual.

The distinction between precedent and innovation in the mechanics of the division suggests one dimension of the innate conservatism that characterized the House of Commons. Two groups, country gentlemen and lawyers, tied to the past by experience and inclination, dominated the Commons' membership. For the great county families a parliamentary seat was an inheritance and an affirmation of their status almost as important as their estate. Many of these families, represented in Parliament from one generation to another, were interrelated, with noble kinsmen in the House of Lords and as part of vast regional cousinages. As county leaders their training grounds for parliamentary service were the commissions of the peace and the deputy lieutenancies where they administered the King's law and organized the crown's defenses. In these arenas, if not in the Inns of Court or at the manor court, they met at first hand the common law, with its emphasis upon the past as a guide to the present. To the country gentlemen, the House's

largest occupational group, were added the lawyers, whose insistence upon precedent and custom was a principal cause of the
formalization of parliamentary procedure. Their professional skills
made them indispensable in the drafting of private bills and as
members of committees of all kinds: "the articles, or principal
points of the bill as they are agreed upon, which being read and
allowed, are committed to some lawyer commonly of the company
to be drawn into form."[35] Although Parliament's methods were
never as routinized as the lawyers or the authors of parliamentary
handbooks desired, precedent had its place in procedure, not only
as custom, but also in the reverence shown to "ancient Parliament
men" who were given preference in debate and whose memories
were, until well into the seventeenth century, guides to the Houses'
common practice.[36]

Parliament's practices as well as its composition were suited to
maintaining the unity of its cause. Although there were differing
tactical and philosophical preferences within the Houses, initially,
"parties" were a cultural and structural impossibility.[37] Contemporary commentators were not merely slipshod when they employed
the word but rather during the course of the war the meaning of
party underwent a redefinition. During the early part of the
century party did not have a political sense – it simply meant a part
of the whole. In its legal usage it was synonymous with a side, but
only as an expression of a group or individual in a suit. Its military
meaning, which first appeared during the war, denoted a group of
soldiers, as in "the Lord Goring's party." In an organic political
structure there was hardly much place for such a term, and it
continued to express groupings in a neutral way throughout the
war. Thus Whitelocke spoke of "Cromwell's party," Juxon of the
"Stapletonian party," Ludlow hailed the "Commonwealth party,"
and Baillie reviled the "party of worldly profane men"; when the
war began the royalists were called the "King's party."[38] Dozens
of similar descriptions, usually preceded by the name of a leading
"grandee," abounded, as did the less frequent but equally general
identifications like the "godly party." In this sense, parties were not
structures in the political system but groupings of politicians: the
House of Commons was never divided into Independents, lawyers,
and worldly profane men except as Baillie viewed the opposition to
the *jure divino* Presbyterian settlement. In modern parlance this
meaning of party is best equated with group, because it is an iden-

15

tification of loose and transitory political configurations and an expression of an amorphous political system.

After the outbreak of war, party began to lose its neutral connotations and came to be an expression of political practice. It is impossible to date such a change in meaning precisely, and the older sense was never wholly replaced, but by the mid-1640s another meaning was clearly taking shape. It became synonymous with words that described political structure and practice, the three most usual being "cabal," "faction," and "junto." Baillie expressed the confusion of meanings when he wrote in 1646, "there are here four or five juntoes, all of diverse and somewhat contrary cabals, but those who are little acquainted with the designs of any of them are the greatest, strongest, and honestest party."[39] But D'Ewes, who recorded the proposal to censure Chillingworth in 1641 "for his scandalous speeches against this House, in saying there were parties or sides in the House of Commons," began referring to an "Independent party" by 1645.[40] "The leading men or grandees first divided themselves into two factions, or juntoes of presbyterian and independent," Clement Walker observed of this same period when writing in 1647.[41] In this sense, party came to describe a new method of political action, one that implied a corruption of the old political system – more explicitly, the pursuit of self-interest against the common good. This is what Edmund Ludlow meant when he explained why he was ousted from his command of the Wiltshire forces: "Observing me not fit to promote a faction and solely applying myself to advance the cause of the public, they combined against me." This was what Whitelocke meant when he exhorted his children, "Learn my children of your father, so to carry yourselves in public business that you may be esteemed of all parties and believed that you follow your own conscience and no faction." Sir William Waller, who had much time to reflect on it, wrote: "In the multitude of my thoughts within me, this comfort hath refreshed and delighted my soul; that after that way which others are pleased to call faction and party, I have walked in the singleness and integrity of mine heart, according to the principles upon which I first engaged."[42] This use of party is best equated with faction, expressive of its pejorative connotations and of the personal rivalries that generated its appearance.

When contemporaries came to use terms like Presbyterian party and Independent party they were thus assimilating two different meanings of the word, expressing both a part of the whole and the corrupt methods employed by members of these groupings. By the end of the first Civil War the political system had adopted this oppositional structure, which was first identified as faction, and political alignments had stabilized into coherent and durable bodies. The intervention of the Army and its impeachment of its opponents accelerated this process, as did the subsequent events of the Revolution. The unitary parliamentary cause was fragmented into opposing political parties, with leadership, organization, ideology, and constituency – that is, the modern notion. In this sense party again became a neutral term, for it expressed the oppositional political structure and its coherent organization. When memorialists spoke of the Presbyterian party or the moderate party they now meant not only a group of individuals but one with an explicit ideology opposed to another ideological grouping. Whether or not the development was lamented, party lost its unsavory connotations and became descriptive of both organization and structure.[43] So Rushworth could write in the introduction to his *Historical Collections*, "I have heartily studied to declare myself unbiased and to give an instance, that it is possible for an ingenuous man to be of party and yet not partial."[44]

The successive stages of political development were masked both by the continuous use of a single word and because that word's new meaning became its permanent modern one. Preparty politics could only be defined in party terms and because so many of the contemporary accounts of the revolution were retrospective ones the political structure that emerged became the model of explanation for all preceding events. Parties, in the modern sense, did appear at the end of the Civil War, but the inconsistent use of the term made it seem that they had existed from its beginning or even, in Clarendon's account, earlier.

The transilience of party is one element in the transformation of political practice that occurred during the course of the Revolution. During the early years of the war parliamentarians attempted to practice consensus politics – decision making characterized by unencumbered debate and, wherever possible, unanimous resolution. It was a political scene dominated by "the greatest, strongest and honestest party" of men uncommitted to predetermined positions, swayed by debate, and used to compromise. This was the principle Lucy Hutchinson defended when she exonerated those noncommitted members who supported the "Independent faction": "the rest believed to adhere to them only out of faction, as if those who did not vaingloriously lay out themselves without necessity, but chose rather to *hear and vote* had no understanding of right and wrong."[45] "To hear and vote" was the parliamentary way; to follow faction was its corruption. "To resign a man's judgement to the opinion of another man's is but a silly trust and confidence," Clement Walker declared in an effort to persuade honest parliamentarians to desert the leaders of the juntoes.[46] Even Denzil Holles conceived of the political process in this fashion, claiming that in 1647 the Independents lost their support because they were "now a known, engaged faction."[47]

Across the spectrum of political opinion a single concept of politics prevailed, even after it had fallen into disuse. Colonel Hutchinson, his wife declared, "was as ready to hear as to give council, and never pertinacious in his will when his reason was convinced." "They knew him very little that could say he was of any faction, for he had a strength of judgement able to consider things himself and propound them to his conscience."[48] "Nothing should be done," Cromwell told the agitators in July 1647, "but with the best reason and with the best and most unanimous concurrence."[49] The eleven members impeached by the Army sounded the same theme, proclaiming "that they detest the maintaining of a faction, or carrying on of any design other than the common good."[50] Indeed, when the self-proclaimed agitators presented the Agreement of the People at Putney, Cromwell objected to it on the grounds that predetermined propositions could not be debated as befitted "a company of men that really would be guided by God." "But if any come to us tomorrow only to instruct us and teach us," he warned the radicals, "I refer to every sober spirited man to think of and determine how far that will consist with the liberty of a free deliberation or an end of satisfaction. I think it is such a preengagement that there is no need of talk of the thing."[51] The search for God's guidance was an effort to humble individual will to the good of the public, and extraordinary fasts and humiliations were frequent during political crises.

Such methods of decision making preserved the traditional practices of the House of Commons and maintained parliamentary unity. When the first important political difference between supporters of war and advocates of peace appeared in Parliament, the contending proponents did not simply struggle for ascendancy. As neither side could be convinced of the opposite course, both policies were pursued. While new armies were erected, peace propositions were drafted. It was not a middle group but a middle way that John Pym mastered in the winter of 1643–4, and this preference for contradictory policies that would maintain unity endured beyond his death and even the succession of political crises of the following year. In both the winters of 1644–5 and 1645–6 peace propositions would accompany new military developments. The other great issue of the war's early years was handled in much the same manner. A committee of accommodation was appointed to find a middle ground in the religious dispute between presbyterians and independents. It was revived in 1645 and even the declaration of April 1646, after the passage of the presbyterian establishment, promised toleration for tender consciences. Members of Parliament who supported these opposing viewpoints were included on committees, perhaps on occasion even purposely balanced, and heard in debate. Not until the autumn of 1646 would such practice alter.

The canker of civil war and the festering religious dispute inevitably weakened consensus decision making. The self-denying ordinance that accompanied the creation of the New Model Army was an attempt to unify the parliamentary cause that had the opposite effect. The ouster of Parliament's old generals and Oliver Cromwell's exception from self-denial produced a factionalism that encouraged political participation from agencies outside Parliament. The defense of parliamentary privilege, which was a defense of the political process, weakened as the factional leaders became intent upon pressing their political solutions to the exclusion of their opponents'. This was the genesis of adversary politics, the emergence of permanent political parties in opposition to each other. Parliamentary procedure, under the impact of factional rivalry, was gradually transformed. By the autumn of 1646 parties dominated the political process, and by the winter of 1647 Denzil Holles was the undisputed leader of a majority within and outside of Parliament.

The erosion of unity was seen in the application of party labels. The ideals of consensus were preserved in theory though violated in practice. Thus party ascriptions were used to denigrate men who combined in faction. Such terms were always opprobrious, like "Leveller," which was most effective because it conjured fears of the most extreme social and political radicalism – the leveling of hedgerows on a man's estate. Religious terms like "erastian" and "sectary" were used much like "Brownist" and "puritan" in an earlier day. D'Ewes's epithet "the violents" is particularly illuminative in this context because it not only implied a political stance, but an immoderate tenacity not at all consonant with the unimpassioned search for reason and judgment that was characteristic of the parliamentary way. As consensus politics gave way to adversary practice, men at Westminster were caught between two different modes of behavior. Sir William Waller's case was typical, for he was later accused of playing both ends, of "having at first sided with that party which is *now* declared independential, and since with the other known by the name presbyterian." He claimed to belong to neither, stressing the integrity of his own judgment: "the change was not in me but in others . . . I changed my company but not my mind."[52] Bulstrode Whitelocke, against whom such charges had more grounds, attempted to be friendly to all parties and a member of none. As the political process changed, men labeled their opponents as factious and denied their own self-interested conduct. Holles could describe his followers as moderates while heaping every title of political opprobrium upon his opponents. The erosion of consensus was best expressed in the frustration of Roger Hill. The quest for unanimous resolution was behind his blasphemous assertion that "if the Devil came to the House he would find some advocates."[53]

The war absorbed the work of the Houses. Despite their efforts to avoid innovations, the men at Westminster created an entire administrative superstructure to regulate the fighting. Initially, Parliament depended upon traditional local forces, the London trained bands, the county militias, even the tenantry of prominent nobles and gentlemen. In order to coordinate the activities of such diverse participants it was necessary to erect a series of overlapping authorities. Lord-Lieutenants were appointed in place of those who left to support the King; governors were chosen for the parliamentary garrisons; and committees were selected from among the leading parliamentary gentry to oversee county affairs. The county committees were responsible for raising and maintaining local forces and for carrying out Parliament's military directives.[54] In some shires the committee spearheaded the war effort; in others it was its chief obstacle. Although an imaginative response to Parliament's logistical problems, the county committees were never mature organs of administration.[55] Their relations with military governors and commanders of combined county forces depended more on the initiative of individual committeemen than on an explicit demarcation of powers.[56] Local officials were jealous of their own treasure and manpower and conscious of hedging their bets, especially if their country was actively contested. Like the quasi-independent armies raised by nobles, the county committees were a mixed blessing.

The difficulty of implementing war strategy in the separate localities was a principal cause of the creation of the regional associations. The artificiality of county jurisdictions was immediately apparent once the fighting began. The disinclination of commanders and committees to send their forces into other counties gave local skirmishes the character of border raids and made pitched battles extremely difficult.[57] Local forces were generally small bodies hastily called to service when fighting threatened. In contrast, the combination of county forces could create a large Army, more easily trained and equipped and battle-ready. The most successful regional scheme was that of the Eastern Association, which combined the forces of the counties of Cambridge, Essex, Hertfordshire, Huntingdonshire, Lincolnshire, Norfolk, and Suffolk.[58] This produced an Army of 14,000 men under the command of the Earl of Manchester. As established, the Army was raised for the defense of the Association, with a committee appointed to supervise its maintenance and direct its activities.[59] But as the military importance of Manchester's Army increased, the Association's control over its forces diminished. Payment and supply remained centered at Cambridge whereas strategic direction shifted to Westminster, a development bitterly resented. In imitation of this organization, Parliament created the Southeastern Association, combining the forces of Hampshire, Kent, Surrey, and Sussex to provide 4,700 men under the command of Sir William Waller.[60] Like Manchester's Army, military control of Waller's forces was exerted from Westminster, but unlike the Eastern Association, the Southeastern organization was unable to raise and maintain its forces.

The Army had been launched by a large recruiting effort in London and then had to receive frequent injections of men and money from the central government to remain viable.

The Association experiments solved some of the difficulties of coordination at the local level, but by no means all. The tangled lines of command among individual counties, the association committees, and the generals who were prominent members of Parliament created delay and obstruction. Only Parliament's national Army, commanded by its Lord General, the Earl of Essex, surmounted the difficulties of locally raised forces. When fully recruited it had an establishment of 10,500 men and was unique among all parliamentary forces in having no local basis. Two-thirds of its monthly pay was derived from revenue collected by the excise and all of its funds were distributed and controlled by the national government.[61] Its manpower came largely from the capital and the ranks were refilled by impressment in the counties through which the Army passed. It was Essex's Army that bore the brunt of fighting in the first years of war, participating in campaigns on the outskirts of London and as far west as Gloucester.

Besides these three forces, a fourth Army was in Parliament's employ by the opening of the campaigning season in 1644. This was the 20,000-man Scottish Army commanded by the Earl of Leven. The Scots, whose disputes with Charles antedated the English fighting, had been brought south the previous year as part of a mutual defense pact. In return for Scottish military assistance Parliament undertook to pay their forces and to provide a small fleet to protect the Scottish coast. The English also pledged to send an Army into Scotland in the event of a foreign invasion. To these military provisos was attached the promise that a reformed Protestant church on the Scottish model would be established in England. This obligation was contained in an oath from which the agreement derived its name – the Solemn League and Covenant.[62]

The entry of the Scottish Army into the war necessitated coordinating the commands of the various English forces with those of the Scots. Although from the beginning they displayed an inclination to besiege and garrison towns on their borders, there was every expectation that the Scots would enter the main arena of war in the south. Thus a common protocol, if not a mutual strategy, needed to be developed. From this need, and also out of a desire to find a smaller and more active body to direct the war, came the

Committee of Both Kingdoms. Organized like the defunct Committee of Safety, the Committee of Both Kingdoms was composed of prominent Parliament men of both Houses and a number of Scottish Lords and commoners who would permanently reside in London. Whatever the political significance of its composition, the fundamental elements in the Committee's membership were soldiers and lawyers.[63] Lawyers were the ubiquitous element of all parliamentary committees and soldiers the logical choice for a committee devoted to directing the war.[64]

In common with all parliamentary committees, the Committee of Both Kingdoms was strictly controlled by the two Houses at Westminster. It handled the day-to-day business of communicating with officers in the field and suggested to Parliament alternative courses of military action. As often as not, however, policy was created by the Houses and given to the Committee of Both Kingdoms to implement. The need for swift military decision making was not resolved by the creation of the Committee of Both Kingdoms, for although its role was greater than the simple implementation of policy it stopped short of its formulation. The Committee's unique position, apart from its Scottish members and its role as a conduit for communication with the Scots, lay in the influence its members held within the political structure at Westminster. In fact, the Committee was only one of several that held responsibility for military affairs.

Two permanent standing committees had responsibility for the necessities of the Earl of Essex's Army. First was the Committee to Reform the Lord General's Army, chaired by Zouch Tate, which dealt exclusively with personnel and regimental composition.[65] The second was the Army Committee, chaired by Robert Scawen, whose purview was the administrative details of accounts and supply.[66] Distinct from these committees, four parliamentary Commissioners resided in Essex's Army and acted as liaison between it and Parliament.[67] This cumbersome structure had resulted from the parliamentary proclivity for layering new mechanisms upon old, of superseding rather than eliminating unsatisfactory administrative devices. The Committee of Both Kingdoms thus became another conduit, and the nerve that connected the Earl of Essex's Army to the brain center at Westminster had four separate endings, each sending only part of a larger message. Parliament remained the sole originator and controller of policy, leaving all its committees without the defined responsibilities that would ease the burden on the already-overworked Houses.

From this fragmentation of parliamentary responsibility problems were bound to arise in managing the war. Not the least of these were differences in the general philosophies that underlay the war's conduct. A split had developed at Westminster on the question of peace almost as soon as the fighting began. Many M.P.s supported an immediate cessation of war and the dispatch of peace proposals to the King. This position was consistently advocated in the House of Commons by a group led by Denzil Holles and Sir Philip Stapleton. They argued that the divisive causes of the war would only be exacerbated by prolonged fighting. A cessation and accommodation was in the best interests of King and Parliament. Their position was most attractive to the full House at the beginning of the fighting and produced the Oxford proposals, the first formal attempt to come to terms with Charles. It also received more support, naturally, at moments of military uncertainty. Rebels who opposed a King and lost were usually hanged, whereas rebels who fought and found agreement might be able to secure their places for the future. But accommodation was dependent upon the King's willingness to compromise, and throughout the first years of war Charles remained obdurate.

The weakness of the program for an immediate peace was, of course, its reliance upon the King for success. The strength of those who advocated a vigorous pursuit of the war was in self-reliance. They based their policies upon the belief that military victory would force the King to accede to Parliament's terms and guarantee his adherence to them. Immediate peace, even on favorable terms, would neither settle the causes of the war nor assure the King's future compliance. For the advocates of war, men such as Sir Henry Vane, Jr., Oliver St. John, and the military leaders like Cromwell, the secret of success was to avoid defeat. Although the House of Commons heard advocates of both positions, it was by no means divided into two camps. The traditional local outlook of most M.P.s made their adherence to policies of war or peace more dependent upon the military situation in their counties than on general philosophies. Since the outbreak of hostilities in 1642, the full House had shown itself reluctant to embrace either position consistently, preferring to react to military and political circumstance.[68] Because peace could not be achieved without the King, and because Parliament's military weaknesses made full-scale fighting impossible, a commitment to continue the war or to make an immediate peace was never arrived at.

Rather, although they were incompatible, the Commons was inclined to accept the alternatives proposed by both groups of its members. At the beginning of 1643 the Lower House agreed to an initiative from the House of Lords to present peace proposals to the King. Simultaneously, the groundwork was being laid for an efficient military establishment. The peremptory rejection of the Oxford proposals by Charles in January 1643 left few options to those who supported and advocated accommodation. Although they still believed that continued fighting, especially if successful, would make settlement more difficult, along with the rest of the House they were forced to accept the necessity of self-defense. Their hope was that a military stalemate would present a new opportunity for negotiations and they prayed that the King would then be more pliant. Indeed, a stalemate was not a course to be shunned by a House of Commons unable to choose between war and peace. Even the supporters of an active war effort were incapable of remedying either the inefficiency of their armies or the unwillingness of their generals to risk full-scale battle. Parliament rarely acted with one voice in deciding any course of action, and when it did it was usually to retrieve a military disaster.

Thus encumbered, Parliament faced the campaign of 1644. Each year that the war progressed the methods that had held together the parliamentary cause weakened; each season that ended without military progress or prospect of peace increased the rancor among parliamentarians. With the Scots poised for a full campaign, with the Armies better recruited than ever, with their options again foreclosed, the men at Westminster readied for war.

Chapter 2

THE CREATION OF THE
NEW MODEL ARMY

This Army, under God, is the principal means to preserve us in safety.[1]

———

Another year had passed and Parliament's hope that its conflict with the King would be resolved in 1644 had faded with the leaves. "The harvest is past; the summer is ended and we are not saved," Thomas Hill drew from Jeremiah in his fast-day sermon "The Season for England's Self-Reflection."[2] Through spring and summer Parliament's armies had been triumphant, relieving York and defeating the royalists in battle at Marston Moor. But the seeds of victory had yielded no crop. In September, after an ill-advised march into Cornwall, the Earl of Essex had surrendered his entire infantry to the King at Lostwithiel. A month later the regrouped parliamentary forces had engaged in a reluctant battle at Newbury. This encounter proved indecisive but was followed by the humiliation of Charles's unopposed relief of Donnington Castle. With the autumn rains the military campaign yet again had ended in a stalemate. The collapse of its armies ensured Parliament another winter of discontent.

At Westminster the military failures precipitated a twofold reevaluation of the parliamentary cause. To men who equated earthly failure with heavenly wrath the Lord's judgment was unmistakable. The Assembly of Divines spent three days in September examining the meaning of Essex's defeat, "searching the cause of God's displeasure...which they divide in four sorts: (1) their own sins; (2) the Parliament's sins; (3) the Army's sins; (4) the sins of the people."[3] To those who looked to secondary causes the signs were equally clear: understaffed armies, bickering commanders, and Parliament's own vacillation between continuing and ending the hostilities. While the Earl of Essex had requested reinforcements for his march to Cornwall his plea initiated a full-scale debate in the House of Commons concerning the conduct and financing of the

26

war.[4] When, after Essex's defeat, the Earl of Manchester had been ordered west it was the turn of the Eastern Association Committee at Cambridge to argue strategy with the Committee of Both Kingdoms.[5] Parliament's divided counsels and its alternation between effort and apathy were mirrored in the conduct of the war, where victory and defeat were so often coupled. Reform to extirpate the sins and errors that were as manifest in Parliament as in its armies was now most necessary.

This reforming spirit resulted in the movement for self-denial, a psychological and religious response to the events of the autumn. The self-denying ordinance was put forth as a solution to the interrelated problems of reversing God's judgment against the parliamentary cause and of settling the disputes among its Army commanders. The abandonment of all civil and military office was a worthy sacrifice that could be shared by both Houses and by all groups of Parliament men; subsequent events would emphasize the military, to the exclusion of the civil, aspects of the ordinance. Moreover, self-denial embraced all the conflicting alternatives posed by the military leaders, eliminating "all the quarrels which were betwixt Manchester and Cromwell; all the obloquies against the General" at a stroke.[6] Yet as a method of reconciliation it failed. It was, first, too radical a solution for the taste of many parliamentarians, who argued simply for retention of the old commanders and reform of their armies. To them self-denial was a judgment that fell unevenly and unfairly. Orignating in the Commons the ordinance also created conflict between the Houses. Self-denial struck hard at the peerage, abolishing its ancient military rights and implicitly censuring the conduct of the aristocratic generals. The dissension it occasioned would sear deep into the parliamentary political process.

Although the New Model Army also emanated from the movement for reform it was created from military necessity rather than religious zeal. Despite the legends that arose in the wake of its triumphs it marked no great break with Parliament's past, no ascendancy of a "win-the-war" policy, and no feat of administrative genius. If some parliamentary members were more determined to fight to the finish, and others more fearful of the war's outcome, none had any insights into military conduct that differed from those that had produced three years of stalemate. "No way of safety now but the sword," the diarist D'Ewes recorded bitterly after the failure of the Uxbridge proposals.[7] Nor did the spirit of reform affect the new Army's establishment. It was organized almost entirely on the model provided for the Earl of Essex's Army without overcoming even its greatest deficiencies. It was recruited from the old armies, financed through the old assessment scheme, and run by Parliament's administrative committees. After the furor created by the self-denying ordinance the Army was established in accordance with the conservative tradition of parliamentary decision making.

Monday, December 9, 1644, was not a day of great expectations. The House of Commons began its session with perfunctory debate on a number of insignificant administrative orders: to take a collection for "the poor captives of Algiers"; to empower the London Militia Committee to search for deserters; and to have a new seal made for the Newcastle customs house.[8] The chief business of the day was to be a report from the committee assigned to examine the accusations made by Oliver Cromwell and Sir William Waller against the Earl of Manchester for his role in the debacle at Newbury. On November 24 they had charged that Manchester had refused to prosecute the war and that he had persistently and intentionally disobeyed Parliament's commands. Cromwell contended that Manchester's inaction and disobedience derived from his belief that the war could not be won: "that this war would not be ended by the sword . . . but it would be better for the Kingdom if it were ended by an accommodation."[9] For two weeks this business had been considered by Zouch Tate's committee for the reformation of the Army, and the passions surrounding the military disputes were given full vent. Manchester provided a point-by-point refutation of the imputations, asserting that after his rendezvous with the forces of Waller and Essex "I never did anything without a joint consent of the rest of the commanders-in-chief."[10] Violation of the secrecy of the committee's debates and absenteeism, perhaps designed to discredit its proceedings, had already marred the investigation. Manchester's countercharges against Cromwell, accusing him of fomenting divisions with the Scots and impugning the dignity of the peerage, further embittered the committeemen and their work. Balanced and objective as it might be,

Tate's report was bound to fan the flames of the officer's contentions.[11]

The Speaker left his chair and a committee of the whole House was formed to hear whether the accusations against Manchester would be sustained or rejected. But Zouch Tate, who now held the floor, did not address his remarks to the seemingly intractable disputes of the Army officers. Instead he issued an animadversion against the "pride and covetousness" that had invaded the parliamentary cause, giving rise to the lack of charity and harmony that his committee's investigation had revealed.[12] Rather than air the sordid details of innumerable squabbles, Tate proposed "that during the time of this war, no member of either House shall have or execute any office or command, military or civil, granted or conferred by both or either of the Houses of Parliament."[13]

After some silence and reflection, Oliver Cromwell, the protagonist in the affair, rose to speak. He, too, set aside the specific charges and countercharges to address the issue of "pride and covetousness." "For what do the enemy say? Nay, what do many say that were friends at the beginning of the Parliament? Even this, that the members of both Houses have got great places and commands, and the sword into their hands, and what by interest in Parliament, and what by power in the Army, will perpetually continue themselves in grandeur and not permit the war to speedily end, lest their own power should determine with it."[14] Calling for an end to the divisive inquiry that his own report had fostered, Cromwell concluded: "Let us apply ourselves to the remedy which is most necessary: and I hope we have such true English hearts, and zealous affection towards the general weal of our Mother country, as no members of either House will scruple to deny themselves and their own private interests for the public good."[15] Another (unknown) member spoke to the same effect, disparaging any further examination of the commanders' charges but attesting, " 'Tis apparent that the forces being under several great commanders, want of good correspondency among the chieftains, has oftentimes hindered the public service."[16] When the Speaker resumed the chair Tate formally offered his resolution, which was seconded by Sir Henry Vane, Jr., and presented to an eight-man committee to be drafted into an ordinance.[17]

Thus submitted, the self-denying ordinance took observers by surprise. "A very unexpected vote," Colonel John Lambert wrote on December 10 amid generally favorable reactions.[18] The *Weekly Intelligencer* thought that by the ordinance "equal justice is done"; whereas the conservative *Scottish Dove* exalted that "by this vote the Parliament do clearly free themselves of all imputations of covetousness."[19] Although perplexed, Robert Baillie saw that the ordinance eliminated the cankerous disputes with which the Scots themselves had been afflicted. Nearly three weeks after the presentation of Tate's resolution he offered his balanced assessment in a public letter to Edinburgh. "They have taken all office from all members of both Houses. This was done on a sudden, in one session, with great unanimity; is still more and more admired by some as a most wise necessary and heroic action; by others as the most rash, hazardous and unjust action as ever Parliament did. Much may be said on both hands but as yet it seems a dream and the bottom of it is not understood."[20] Self-denial presented little ambiguity to Thomas Juxon, captain in the City's militia: "Herein they clearly vindicated themselves, that they do not seek themselves, or desire the continuance of the war for their own particular advantage," he recorded in his journal. "Now and never till now have they acted like the Commons of England and as such who (de jure) are to take care of the Kingdom and revive the almost obsolete motto 'salus populi.' "[21]

Although those outside Parliament were caught unawares by Tate's motion, the self-denying ordinance was firmly rooted in the events of the autumn, nourished by the reactions to the military failures. As Tate's jeremiad suggested, the ordinance was a response to the belief that military defeat was a sign of divine wrath that members of Parliament had to strive to reverse. Efforts to reform Parliament had focused on places and profits, beginning in mid-November with a heated debate on the appointment of John Lisle as a master of St. Cross's Hospital. Before the House would agree to Lisle's preferment it had established a committee chaired by Robert Reynolds to examine all civil offices held by its members in order to determine what part of the profits of their offices could be turned to the public use.[22] Besides its pecuniary aspects, office holding contributed to the decline in attendance at Parliament. With many M.P.s disabled, deceased, or employed upon military matters, the two Houses faced a serious shortage of manpower. Since mid-October the Commons had been considering plans for recruitment through the issuance of warrants to return permanent members from unrepresented boroughs.[23] This was a complex matter, for writs were issued only under the King's seal through chancery. If Parliament could order its own writs, then it could sanction its own sessions. These considerations had produced inconclusive debates and postponements, although the Commons continued to mull over the possibility of recruitment.

Reform of Parliament also entailed reform of its armies, and as a result of the collapse in the autumn this work had been most intense. In November the Eastern Association Committee had again informed Parliament of its inability to finance Manchester's large establishment.[24] On November 19 the Commons had ordered the Committee of Both Kingdoms to examine the state of all the parliamentary armies, an order that was extended four days later "to consider a frame or model of the whole militia."[25] For the next two weeks, while Tate's committee examined the charges of military misconduct, the Committee of Both Kingdoms scrutinized military organization. Its first task was to ensure that Parliament's line of defense would hold against any further royalist assaults, and the committee had recalled all its army members on November 25 to devise a concerted plan.[26] A meeting to discuss the southern military situation had been scheduled for December 4, but on that day the Committee had been burdened with investigating Manchester's countercharges against Cromwell. Two days later the first plans for reorganization had probably been aired, for on December 7 Henry Vane, Jr., had reported a plan to the full House that would provide £31,000 per month for maintenance of the Scottish Army.[27]

Tate's resolution spoke to all three issues: offices and places would be taken from M.P.s; the Houses would be refilled by all those who were engaged in other employments; and the new frame for the Army could be established by thorough reorganization. Above all, the bitter military disputes would come to an end. "The Lord heal our breaches, reconcile our differences and knit our hearts together in more strong brotherly love through Christ," Manchester's chaplain, Simeon Ashe, had pleaded in recounting his perception of the relief of Donnington Castle.[28] Tate's resolution was an answer to Ashe's prayer. It was also a response to the necessary reforms advocated by the author of "The Six Secondary Causes of the Spinning Out of This Unnatural War." Three advantages would accrue from reformation: the end to division and contention, an improvement in the methods of fighting, and renewed perseverance.[29] Thus self-denial cut a Gordian knot, and it would be naïve to think that it was not worked out in advance to address these particular problems.[30] Yet if it was a solution, it was not a "policy," an orchestrated plan to supplant one political faction by another. The critical component was *self*-denial, the puritan emphasis on individual reformation that was shared by the Presbyterian Tate and the Independent Cromwell. This was the point emphasized by the three ministers selected to preach at the special fast on December 18. Parliament, they contended, must "preserve that opinion the nation had of their honesty and integrity, and be without any selfish ends, of seeking their own benefit and advantage."[31]

Tate's proposal was made on the 9th and committed for drafting. Two days later, after a motion had been made to appoint an extraordinary fast on December 18 so that the M.P.s could "humble themselves for their particular and parliamentary sins and failings whereby they may hope to obtain God's blessing in a better measure upon their endeavors in the future," it was read for the first time.[32] Two debates on the ordinance were held during the next week, with the House in grand committee. On December 17 after general approbation was expressed for the motion, Robert Reynolds moved that the Earl of Essex be excepted from its provisions.[33] This cut to the heart of the problem, for Essex remained a military hero in an age susceptible to such prowess. Even his cowardly retreat from Lostwithiel had not fully tarnished his reputation for risking his life and fortune in the service of Parliament. Yet the point of Tate's motion had been the avoidance of individual cases and the establishment of a standard that would circumvent rather than judge merits and faults. Debate lasted all day and into the night before a division was called. Denzil Holles and Sir Philip Stapleton, two officers who had served under Essex, appeared as tellers in favor of his exception. By only seven votes in a House of nearly two hundred they were defeated in their bid.[34] Before the lengthy session could adjourn, Sir John Potts reintroduced the religious element into the deliberations, moving that those who were to receive civil and military office be required to take the covenant and to adhere to the future religious establishment. His motion was postponed to the next consideration of the ordinance.[35]

The creation of the New Model Army

In the week following the introduction of Tate's resolution, then, self-denial had entered the stormy waters of parliamentary decision making. As revealed in the motions on the 17th, numerous objections could be raised to this radical reform. Beyond Essex's employment and the religious controversy, other questions loomed. Members of Parliament had sacrificed the care of their estates, and their civil offices were a necessary source of income for their families' well-being.[36] There was also the issue of local power, the offices in the counties through which the members confirmed their status and standing. Would these, too, go to new men, some perhaps unworthy of public trust? These concerns motivated Bulstrode Whitelocke's opposition to self-denial. He responded to arguments that the ordinance would fill the House of Commons by urging the issuance of writs, countered claims that it would benefit the reform of the Army by pointing to the chaos that would result from the displacement of so many loyal commanders, and rejected the notion that those not of Parliament would more readily obey Parliament's commands.[37]

With the ordinance thus opposed the members of the House of Commons attended their extraordinary fast. The three preachers, Stephen Marshall, Thomas Hill, and Obadiah Sedgwick, were undoubtedly chosen in the spirit of unity that the self-denial implied.[38] "No wonder there was division among them in their counsels," Clarendon reported from one of the sermons, "when there was no union in their hearts."[39] "God would take his own work into His hand; and if the instruments He had already employed were not worthy to bring so glorious a design to a conclusion, that He would inspire others more fit."[40] The preachers' call to unity and reform sealed the inclination the House had already expressed for the ordinance. On the afternoon of December 19 the Commons again addressed Tate's resolution, rejecting Potts's amendment, probably as divisive, but accepting the exclusion of all local offices including the Lord-Lieutenancies. Then, without division, the Commons passed the ordinance.[41]

Fully debated in four sessions of the House of Commons, the self-denying ordinance was not a spontaneous suggestion thrust upon an unwitting House. The fervor for reformation was strong throughout the autumn and rather than playing upon it, self-denial was a product of it. The quest for "union in their hearts" was the motive of Tate's resolution, shared as a matter of principle in all quarters of the House of Commons. But the unity the ordinance might bring to the Lower House was offset by the division it was likely to create among the Lords. The Commons' recent investigation of the Earl of Denbigh's war record and Cromwell's attack upon Manchester preceded this vote, which struck at the traditional privilege of the peerage to command the King's Armies. The earlier controversies had centered on individuals, but self-denial was a rejection of an entire stratum of the social order – Lords, by definition, were to be excluded from civil and military office. Was this an extension of the class warfare that Manchester had conjured in his report of Cromwell's speeches? Despite the vote that clearly excluded Essex, the Lord General did not believe that self-denial would be accomplished.[42] The Commons, too, anticipated opposition. On December 21 the full House accompanied the bill into the Lords' chamber, a procedure reserved for only the most important matters.[43]

The Lower House expected prompt action. Three days later it reminded the Lords of the ordinance and requested expedition.[44] Although the bill was read on the 26th, it was not until the 30th that the Lords finally debated its merits and appointed a committee, significantly including Essex, Manchester, Warwick, and Denbigh, to prepare the House's objections.[45] By January 6 no further action had been taken, although it seems clear that this committee had met. Again the impatient Commons, ready to re-cast its Armies, demanded expedition.[46] This came the following day when the Lords produced a lengthy statement of their reasons for objecting to the ordinance. They believed that it would injure the parliamentary cause, eradicate the ancient rights of the peerage, and place an unjust disability upon the members of the Upper House.[47]

When this response reached the Lower House the call for a conference was immediate. At the meeting of the representatives of the two Houses the Commons' managers, William Pierrepont, Bulstrode Whitelocke, Edmund Prideaux, and William Ellis, rejected the Lords' statement as a breach of privilege, instructing the peers that "when any bill or ordinance hath been sent from one House to the other, that in case of disagreement upon alteration or amendment they have ever sent down the bill or ordinance with the particular amendment or alteration."[48] The Lords had not amended the bill and thus the Commons were incapable of responding to their objections. They therefore requested that the Lords pass the bill, it being "of so high a concernment for the public good."[49] Clearly the managers were attempting to bully the Lords into accepting self-denial. The day after the conference another call for expedition came from the Lower House. The Lords then responded with a most precise definition of their procedure. They agreed that they had not amended the bill and admitted that they could not amend it without nullifying its intent. Their objections, then, must be taken to imply a rejection of the bill, but one that according to precedent came with a full explanation of motive. If the Commons was to insist upon punctilious adherence to procedure, then the Lords desired that such procedure be firmly established and recorded. But when the Commons, incredibly, again insisted upon action from the Lords, the ordinance was unceremoniously rejected and a committee of peers appointed to draw a new ordinance for the exclusion of all members of Parliament from civil office.[50]

The Lords' rejection of the first self-denying ordinance presented deeper problems than the caustic exchanges between the Houses. The suggested compromise that only civil places should be yielded did not address the rebuilding of the armies. On December 9, in the afternoon after Tate's resolution, the Committee of Both Kingdoms held its first full-scale debate on the reform of the entire military structure. The preliminary discussion pointed to a two-part solution to the military situation: the use of the Scottish forces in the northeast and the reorganization of the major parliamentary Armies in the south.[51] The role of the Scottish Army in the plan was central. It had successfully stormed Newcastle in October 1644, providing the single bright spot in Parliament's autumn fortunes, and its 20,000-man establishment, although not fully recruited, was large enough to guard the northern approaches to the Eastern Association. Along with the Scots in this region was the army of the north commanded by Ferdinando Lord Fairfax, and his son Sir Thomas, and the strong Lincolnshire regiment raised by Colonel Edward Rossiter. The local character of these forces was to be preserved, and with the Scots near the forces of the Association Parliament had a strong base of power. The £31,000 monthly assessment for the Scottish Army, already proposed on December 7, was thus an essential element in the overall military picture. The

35

Scottish Army gave Parliament a reserve and stable force to offset the anticipated experimentation in reorganizing the Southern Armies.[52]

The passage of the self-denying ordinance through the Lower House provided the first direction to the Committee of Both Kingdoms' search for a southern establishment. Reform was imperative, although the shape it was to take was difficult to discern. The contentious commanders all sat on the Committee of Both Kingdoms, which was charged with proposing the New Model and, until the Lords finally accepted or rejected self-denial, only administrative decisions could be made. Indeed, the plan evolved slowly, for the Committee was also faced with the problem of presenting the Uxbridge proposals to the King and the necessity of staging a holding operation in the west.[53] As late as the 24th it revealed that a thorough reorganization was not yet contemplated when it urged the Eastern Association Committee to prepare its forces for an early campaign. "We need not remind you of the advantages secured last year by our forces going so early into the field," the Committee wrote. "We therefore desire you . . . to put forward the recruiting of horse and foot for Manchester's army."[54] On December 27 the Committee met with all the Eastern Association M.P.s, probably to urge their cooperation in raising money for recruitment. The first debate on reorganization was to be held on the 28th, but both Cromwell and Essex were absent from that session and it is unknown whether or not the debate was held.[55]

By December 30, however, the first frame had been sketched: "16,000 foot, 8,000 horse and 1,500 dragoons . . . the pay to be according to the last establishment of the Lord General's Army."[56] All the Committee's military commanders were appointed to the subcommittee that was to make the first decisions on regimental organization, and a separate committee was selected to resolve the details of military finance.[57] That these discussions remained preliminary could be seen in the inflated size first proposed – the 25,500 men would soon be trimmed by 3,500 – and in Lord Wharton's report of the progress that had been made by the 31st: "our business concerning the armies and officers depending yet betwixt the Houses upon great uncertainties, and all things in the interim lying very loose."[58]

These "uncertainties" ensured that the administrative reform of the Army would hew to the most traditional lines possible. When the subcommittee appointed to establish military finance made its report on January 6, it was clear that the new Army would be founded upon old principles. The experimental assessment scheme, which had proved inadequate as a source of funding for both the Earl of Essex's Army and the Army of the Eastern Association, was, nevertheless, to finance the New Model. The county-by-county assessments were not even reevaluated but simply combined to provide £53,000 a month for the payment of 22,000 officers and soldiers.[59] Like the assessment scheme, the schedule of pay was also copied from that of Essex's Army, eightpence per diem for an infantryman up to £1 per diem for the general.[60] All officers ranked at captain or above were to have half their pay deducted on the public faith. The decision to reduce the Army's size to 22,000 men was the only departure from form, but the three old Armies that contained 29,000 men were rarely at full strength and the reduction was an obvious economy measure.[61]

This plan for the New Model was submitted to Parliament on January 9. There was nothing in either its organization or finance to delay its passage. Votes two days later reduced its size to 14,000 foot, 6,000 horse, and 1,000 dragoons. On January 13 a Commons committee consisting of John Maynard, Thomas Lane, and Lawrence Whitacre was appointed to draft the Committee of Both Kingdoms' report into an ordinance. No element of this ordinance was to differ from those that established the old armies.[62] One Army it was, rather than two associated forces and Essex's national Army, but it was only one part of an overall military organization that would eventually grow into four separate Armies and innumerable local brigades and companies. Its regiments were to be orderly and its chain of command precise, but these were paper considerations that applied equally to the old armies. On the surface there was no reason to expect better recruitment or more obedient commanders than had been experienced during the past three years of fighting. Nor had the "New Model" been carefully planned. From the decision on its size and pay to the second reading of the bill on January 18 only twelve days had elapsed, days filled also with preparations for the Uxbridge proposals and with the execution of Archbishop Laud.

While the Committee of Both Kingdoms was defining the administration of the new Army, a separate committee was examining the question of new commanders. This was Tate's committee, and its appointment was further indication that with or without the Lords' consent self-denial would be implemented in military commands. On January 21 a list of commanders was completed that included every senior colonel of the old Armies who was not a member of Parliament.[63] At the head of the cavalry regiments as senior colonel of horse was Sir Thomas Fairfax, general of the Northern Army and the only parliamentary general not excluded by the ordinance.[64] In fact, Tate's committee did not choose any generals for the new Army. This was a politically charged issue, for the Earl of Essex, although refused an exclusion from self-denial, remained the Lord General. The committee may have found it presumptuous to recommend a new Lord General and injudicious to reappoint Essex after the Commons' vote. There was certainly nothing sinister about leaving the question of chief command to the House.

When debate began on the officer list it was clear that the appointment of Fairfax as senior horse colonel provided a solution to the problem of eliminating the aristocratic generals. As Whitacre, the only diarist present at the debate, recorded: "Sir Thomas Fairfax being named for the first colonel of horse, it was afterwards upon debate resolved that he should be commander in chief over the whole Army of which the model was made and it being from thence inferred that the Lord General Essex must be laid aside."[65] Indeed the motion for Fairfax to be commander of the New Model resulted in a division, carried in his favor, 101–69.[66] As soon as Fairfax's appointment was confirmed, the Commons similarly elevated Philip Skippon, who had been named senior colonel of foot, to Sergeant-Major-General of the Army. This aroused no apparent opposition, nor did the rapid appointment, without demur, of the entire list of horse and foot colonels submitted by Tate. At the conclusion of this debate Tate's committee was appointed "to consider of, and present to the House, some mark of honor to be set upon [the] Lord General, the Earl of Essex."[67]

The selections of Fairfax and Skippon to lead the new Army had a soothing effect upon both the military and religious contentions that had erupted in the autumn. Both were men of sound military reputation who had avoided the officers' disputes, and neither was known to hold strong religious views other than a desire for godly reformation. The religious issue was becoming particularly important ever since Manchester's accusation against Cromwell reopened the animosities between presbyterians and independents in the Eastern Association Army. Efforts to compose these differences were well known and even the royalist newsbook, *Mercurius Aulicus*, could comment: "The rebels are now busy upon their new militia ... the committee must be such as are indifferently disposed to the several moulds of church discipline lest their particular zeal to presbytery or independency should engender factions and retard the plot."[68] On January 27 the New Model ordinance and the bill naming Sir Thomas Fairfax commander in chief passed through the Commons and was sent to the Lords. Fairfax's appointment and the selection of the colonels, none of whom was a member of the Houses of Parliament, made clear that the Commons had ignored the Lords' opposition to the self-denying ordinance. Would the Lords now refuse the Army establishment?

The conservative framework of the New Model damped much of the opposition that was expected to come from the Lords. Yet, despite rejection of the self-denying ordinance, the military reorganization adhered to the principle that no member of Parliament would hold military command. If the Lords had been displaced, they had not abdicated their military responsibilities. Besides the blow at their status, the "new modeling" threatened to remove the restraining influence they had exerted upon the conduct of the war. Their fears of social and religious anarchy roused in Manchester's accusations against Cromwell ensured careful scrutiny of the Commons' plans. The Lords would not be "bamboozled."[69]

The ordinances for the establishment of the New Model and for Fairfax's command were sent to the peers on January 28. Busy with the Uxbridge proposals and the details for the church establishment the Lords did not appoint the first reading of the bills until three days later. On that morning Sir Christopher Yelverton came from the Commons with a request to expedite the ordinance and the next morning Sir Anthony Irby reiterated the plea.[70] "The King's Army is drawing into a body," Yelverton advised the Lords, and "the time of year draws on for the Army to be in the field."[71] On February 3 the recorder of London, John Glyn, also urged expedition upon the peers and finally on the following day the New Model ordinance was debated and returned to the Commons.[72] The Lords had made three changes in the Commons' draft, stipulating that all officers would be chosen by both Houses of Parliament, that officers and soldiers alike would take the covenant, and that they would also agree to conform to the church government established by Parliament.[73]

These three provisos were read in the Commons on February 5 and sent to two separate committees for consideration. On the 7th the first amendment, that the two Houses appoint the Army's officers, was debated. Any attenuation of Fairfax's powers was strongly resented and only after long discussion and a division was it agreed, as a compromise, that both Houses would approve Fairfax's selections. As the Commons had already passed the list of Army colonels it was thought that this applied only to the lower echelons of the officer corps, which, by the terms of the ordinance, were to be drawn from the three old armies.[74] On the next day compromise was also achieved on the amendments pertaining to religious conformity. The Commons could agree to the requirement that all take the covenant, but it was successfully argued that men could not be expected to adhere to a church government not yet in existence. Again debate was lengthy, lasting from 10 A.M. to 6 P.M., before the compromise that accepted the second proviso and rejected the third was reached.[75] If the issue was to force men's consciences, as many thought it was, the Lords had missed their mark. The taking of the covenant was a requirement for service in the old armies, and as Sir Oliver Luke observed, "few of them will stick at the covenant as long as they can be their own interpreters."[76] On February 17, almost three weeks after the initial ordinance was submitted by the Commons, and after thorough debate and cautious compromise, Fairfax's command and the New Model establishment passed into law.[77]

These delays left little more than a month before the new Army would be required to take the field. The Commons had already made this point on January 31 and the Lords' insistence upon the clauses for uniformity and the time expended on compromise ensured that the remainder of the work would be completed under great pressure. With the passage of the New Model ordinance only the delicate task of selecting the Army's officers remained uncompleted. This was, according to the compromise reached by the Houses, delegated to Sir Thomas Fairfax, who was to name all senior officers below the rank of colonel. Fairfax's service in the north had kept him free from the contentions among the southern military commanders, but also ignorant of the personnel in their armies. Indeed, Sir Thomas had his own misgivings about accepting command of the New Model. He would later recall, "Had I not been urged by the persuasion of my nearest friends, I should have refused so great a change."[78]

Once in London Fairfax paid a visit to the Earl of Essex, doubtless to seek his blessing in the operation and his counsel in the selection of officers. The Earl's opposition to the new Army was well known and he held strong veiws on how it should be composed. It would be surprising had he not communicated these to Fairfax during their meeting. Essex believed that wherever possible whole regiments should be chosen, that regimental colonels should approve the choice of their own officers, and that none who had faithfully served Parliament should be excluded.[79] These were sound principles and would ensure that Fairfax's own unfamiliarity with the old armies would not cause delay in the appointment of the officer corps. Whether Essex gave this advice and whether Fairfax followed it can only be surmised. Sir Thomas did dispatch urgent requests to the appointed colonels for regimental lists of officers down to the rank of captain and he did incorporate full regiments into his scheme. But important exceptions to these rules were also made. Eight days after his first appearance in London Sir Thomas Fairfax had completed his list of New Model officers.[80]

While the two Houses considered his choices, the Committee of Both Kingdoms and Scawen's Army Committee were busily preparing the groundwork that would enable the Army to take the field once its commanders were chosen. On February 5 the Earl of Essex's Army, Manchester's forces at Farnham, and the remains of Waller's troops had been provided with two weeks' pay.[81] Once the New Model ordinance passed the Lords these troops were ordered to be recruited into the new Army. The latest musters were to be examined by still another committee headed by Scawen, and the ranks of the New Model were to be filled from these lists.[82] Simultaneously, M.P.s from the counties assessed for the Army were directed to devise a plan that would ensure regular pay for the soldiery.[83] Finally, on March 4 a delegation of Lords and Commoners was sent to the City of London to relate the failure of the Uxbridge negotiations and to request an advance of £80,000 upon the New Model ordinance. This was necessary to supply and equip the new troops and of such importance that the House of Commons adjourned its sessions on March 7 and 8 to entreat the City's financiers to provide the loan.[84]

In an atmosphere of impending military crisis, for the royalist forces were already gathering, the list of officers presented by Sir Thomas Fairfax was debated in Parliament. In the Commons discussion lasted three days, although only the session on February 28 was lengthy.[85] This debate was also acrimonious, for members of the House chose to reexamine the list of colonels that had been passed upon in January. The appointment of Colonel John Pickering, who had given a deposition highly critical of the Earl of Manchester's conduct at Donnington, occupied almost an entire day's discussion before it was finally confirmed.[86] On March 1, Nathaniel Rich's appointment was reconsidered. This debate, however, went beyond the recent feuds of the generals. Although Rich had also deposed against Manchester, he had been appointed to command a regiment raised and maintained throughout the war by Sir Robert Pye. It was argued that if Rich were given preeminence over Pye, this regiment and two other troops Pye had raised would be lost to parliamentary service. For this reason D'Ewes argued against Rich's colonelcy, claiming that as he was young his appointment as major would still be a great honor.[87] This argument persuaded the House, which replaced Rich with Pye. In all, the Commons eliminated three officers and referred three others back to Fairfax, one of whom, Colonel Ayloff, was known not to desire a New Model command. Pye was the only specific suggestion for replacement that the Commons made.[88]

These votes were sent to the Lords on March 2. The peers hurriedly dispatched a copy of the officer list to the Earl of Essex, and probably one to the Earl of Manchester, for their comments.[89] On March 10 the Lords returned Fairfax's list to the Commons with fifty-one emendations. Two whole regiments, Crawford's and Pickering's, were displaced, and two others, Crawford's original Scottish regiment and Lord Robartes's regiment, put in their place. Four colonels – Pickering, Montague, Rainsborough, and Okey – were also excluded.[90] Although they were both religious radicals, Pickering and Montague were almost certainly set aside for their parts in the Manchester accusation. Rainsborough and Okey more likely lost their places because of radical religious opinion.

The majority of alterations made by the Lords, however, should not be seen as religiously motivated. The largest number of changes involved patronage and preferment: in ten regiments the most junior captain was replaced by an officer not included in the establishment. The second largest category of exclusions followed Essex's principle that whole regiments should be incorporated whenever possible. Five such changes were made in regiments formerly under Essex's command, and the two entire regiments that were replaced also followed this principle.[91] Finally came the alterations based upon religious considerations. It can be safely assumed that the two colonels, Rainsborough and Okey, Major Richard Cromwell, and Captains Bush and Rainsborough were all put out for their beliefs.[92]

But there was another side to this coin that demonstrated that religious persuasion may have been only a secondary factor even in these displacements. Lieutenant Colonel Thomas Pride, a known religious extremist, was excluded on the Commons' list but *included* by the Lords on the principle of maintaining complete regiments. The relationship between religious affiliation and inclusion or exclusion on the officer list is, finally, impossible to unravel. Of course subsequent behavior is no indication of belief at the time of the reorganization, and the accusations of Baxter and Edwards are less than useful on this count. Only one historian has made careful study of the Earl of Manchester's Army before the creation of the New Model, and Professor Holmes is unconvinced that a campaign to cashier presbyterian officers existed in the summer of 1644. Several of the officers he identifies as known independents – Beaumont, Margery, and Nevill – were on Fairfax's list and not removed by the Lords. Nor was Fleetwood or Harrison, although the latter was demoted to captain. At least two others, Holcroft and Moore, who were allegedly cashiered for being presbyterians, may have found their way back into the New Model by April.[93] Moreover, in the eighteen troops of horse that Cromwell raised and commanded, the heart of so-called independency in the Army, only three changes were made: Bush, already noticed; Captain William Packer, a religious extremist, but also the most junior captain in his regiment; and Major Christopher Bethell, whose exclusion may have been designed to balance a Cromwellian colonel with a Manchesterian major.

That such balancing underlay some regimental composition is to be seen in the disposition of Cromwell's three regiments. As they were reputed to be the most extreme tolerationists, composed of all varieties of sectaries, and as Cromwell's quarrel with Manchester continued to seethe, it could be expected that these regiments received the closest scrutiny. Byond the fact that only three changes were made among the eighteen, the selection of colonels and majors is interesting. Only one of the original colonels remained, Edward Whalley. The two new colonels were the Dutchman, Vermuyden, and Sir Thomas Fairfax himself, both religiously "safe." In the regiments Vermuyden and Fairfax commanded, the original majors were retained, including John Desborough, who kept his command after having given a deposition against Manchester.[94] In the regiment Whalley commanded, however, the major was set aside by the Lords. Could this have been a coincidence? Balance was certainly part of Sir Simonds D'Ewes's argument in the Pye–Rich debate. Pye was a well-known supporter of the presbyterian settlement whereas Rich was thought to hold radical religious opinions. Although the debate centered upon Pye's individually raised troops, in rebutting the arguments made in Rich's favor by the "violents" D'Ewes claimed that a major, always present in the field, would have more influence upon his men than a colonel. D'Ewes's argument for the inclusion of both Pye and Rich and his point that Rich would have more influence upon the troops was an attempt to satisfy both points of view. Was D'Ewes admitting the necessity of a quid pro quo?

It will never be established with certainty whether or not senior New Model officers were deliberately balanced between the contending religious viewpoints. There are strong reasons to suggest that this was the case in several regiments but it is, perhaps, *une question mal posée.*[95] The principles of inclusion enunciated by Essex and, in a large degree, followed by Fairfax stressed military considerations above all others. Full regiments were already organized and disciplined and had passed the acid test of battle. Allowing regimental commanders to choose their subordinates produced the same advantages. Moreover, the New Model's composition was dictated by practical necessities. The cavalry regiments came almost entirely from the Eastern Association Army and the foot from that of the Earl of Essex. This was so because both Manchester's horse and Essex's foot had been recruited and equipped at the end of the autumn campaign and again in the first months of 1645.[96] Two other regiments were strictly local units: Rossiter's

44

from Lincolnshire and Weldon's from Kent. These came whole, with only the slightest scrutiny of their officers; indeed, Fairfax's list for Weldon's regiment did not name a single officer other than the colonel, and this spectral band was passed upon by the Lords without comment.[97]

In the first place, then, military considerations predominated and the inclusion or exclusion of senior officers was in large part dictated to Fairfax by these necessities. Second, for all the immediate concern over religion – the worst of which was brought out in the Manchester–Cromwell affair – there remained considerable difference between independency and sectarianism. To the Scots, and the most rigid presbyterians, no such subtle distinctions could be drawn, but to most others, accommodation was to be a part of the nation's future religious estabilshment. That both Tate and Cromwell could participate in the formulation of self-denial was an expression of the middle ground that continued to be shared. That Maynard and Whitacre could draft the New Model ordinance and Yelverton, Irby, and Glyn could press it upon the Lords were measures of Presbyterian support for the reorganization. The winter of 1644–5 was the last moment when compromise on religious issues was possible, and the New Model was the final achievement of consensus decision making.

Thus the majority of the Lords' exceptions to the officer list was not doctrinally motivated and the Commons' rejection of their changes not the manifestation of a radical spirit. The compromise that was struck at the passage of the New Model ordinance now proceeded to unravel. Unlike the Commons, the Lords had not exercised a right of approval, but a right of nomination. For every man excepted from the list the Lords appointed a replacement. Their fifty-one emendations involved ninety-odd persons: a major reconstruction of the Army. On March 11, while the Commons considered these changes, the Army committees moved to complete the military establishment. Sir Thomas Fairfax was ordered to select all officers from lieutenant down without the approval of the two Houses as long as they were drawn from the three armies.[98] An ordinance for placing all soldiers of the old armies under his command was drafted, read three times, and passed all on the same day. The four regiments to which the Lords had raised no objections were ordered, commissioned, recruited, and readied for service.[99]

In conference with the Lords the Commons repudiated the peers' alterations for three reasons: that the list was Fairfax's own nominations and elimination of his choice might discourage his service, that debate over the numerous exceptions and additions would consume far too much valuable time and inevitably shatter parliamentary unity, and that the Lords had presented no compelling reasons for the changes to be made. Only the Lords could prevent an impasse that would "make the difference endless, and the ordinance ineffectual," the Commons' conference managers warned.[100] On March 17 the Lords held their third debate on the New Model officers. Twice the list had been considered and twice it had been rejected. Now the third vote ensued and twenty-two Lords divided evenly.[101] Hastily Viscount Say and Sele produced the proxy of the old Earl of Mulgrave, Sir Thomas Fairfax's grandfather. The opposition was caught off guard and the House thrown into confusion. A tacit agreement not to use proxies when questions were called had apparently existed in the Upper House, which Say, for the sake of the officer list, had violated. But a tacit agreement was not black-letter law, and when he was accused of heavy-handed practice a search of the Lords' records to determine if there was any rule preventing the use of proxies was demanded. No such prohibition could be found, and the officer list passed the Lords by one vote, but with ten Lords entering formal dissents.[102]

The passage of the officer list left only Sir Thomas Fairfax's commission to be completed. Like the Army itself, this was modeled upon the commission granted to the Earl of Essex when he was made Lord General. It was a commission of appointment, setting forth the general's powers and responsibilities, but it was also an expression of the fundamental parliamentary philosophy toward the war, empowering the general to defend King and Parliament and enjoining him to protect the person of the King. In the early days of the war this latter dictum had been taken literally, and parliamentary forces would withdraw from the field rather than engage in battle where the King was physically present. But soon even the most weak-willed of the parliamentary generals saw the impracticality of such an injunction, and the notion of protecting the King's person came to mean protecting him from those of his followers who would place him in grave danger by opposing his Parliament. In Fairfax's commission this phrase was omitted – a sign of resolve and a warning to the King.[103] Charles's cavalier attitude toward the Uxbridge negotiations was one cause of this hardening of feelings; fear of military disaster, probably another. For whatever reasons, Fairfax's commission engendered little interest and no opposition in the House of Commons until the Lords made it the object of renewed confrontation.

On March 27 the Lords read the ordinance for Fairfax's commission twice and appointed a committee, marginally in favor of the "new modeling," to consider objections that had been made in debate.[104] They proposed two amendments, one relating to Fairfax's powers over local forces and the other restoring the clause for protection of the King's person. These were sent down to the Commons, where the latter was rejected and a conference between the Houses called for. The clause "seems rather a mockery, than a reality," the Commons told the Lords on March 29, and it might set confusion amongst the soldiery should the King appear at the head of his army. Moreover, it would suggest that the King was fighting for the defense of true religion rather than in opposition to it.[105] Thus they asked that the Lords accept the commission without the clause "to protect the person of the King." The Commons' adherence to their vote produced the same division in the Upper House that had occurred over the New Model ordinance, only this time Mulgrave's proxy, rather than deciding the issue, deadlocked it.[106] This worked in favor of those who opposed the Commons' ordinance for, although it was not rejected, it could not pass.

Then the Lower House attempted to apply additional pressure upon the peers, communicating letters that detailed mutiny and confusion among the parliamentary soldiers. "The Army is in mutiny and disorder and that they know not who to obey: and until this ordinance is passed Sir Thomas Fairfax has no power to do anything," the Lower House warned the Lords; "they [the Commons] have done their parts; therefore, if any inconveniency come upon the stay of it, they conceive it will not lie upon them."[107] On April 1 the Commons again pressed for passage, but now in the Upper House only eighteen Lords were present, and the three absentees were all from the side that opposed the commission. D'Ewes thought that the Earl of Bolingbroke had defected to break the deadlock; in any case by the morning of April 1 the deadlock no longer existed.[108] By then the Earl of Essex and his supporters seem to have decided to yield. No protests were entered to the vote and on the following day both Essex and Manchester delivered up their commissions. Even in his bitter disappointment Essex offered moderate advice to his colleagues: "I know that jealousies cannot be avoided in the unhappy conditions of our present affairs, yet wisdom and charity should put such restraints thereto, as not to allow it to become destructive."[109] On April 3 the self-denying ordinance received the unanimous consent of the peers – a fait accompli gracefully accepted.[110] Finally, five months after the order for the Committee of Both Kingdoms to prepare a new frame for the militia, the New Model was completed.

The completion of the legislation, however, was not the equivalent of building the new Army. As the Lords and Commons debated the philosophy of his command, Sir Thomas Fairfax was faced with more practical problems. Four senior colonels – Middleton, Holborn, Barclay, and Crawford, all Scots who had fought in the English Armies – resigned their posts.[111] They may have left in anger over the exclusion of some loyal Scottish regiments from the New Model, although, as their Commissioners on the Committee of Both Kingdoms well knew, the Scottish Army was to have a major role of its own in the new war effort. More likely it was the threat of Montrose in the Highlands that precipitated the exodus of the Scottish officers. By the end of March Montrose's power was at its height and those Scotsmen who had come to fight royalists in England now had a theater of war closer to home. Two other colonels chosen to command New Model regiments also refused service: Edward Aldriche and Algernon Sidney. Aldriche was disturbed by the composition of the regiment he was to command, for his was one of the few to combine troops from both the armies of Manchester and Essex. On March 28 he wrote to Fairfax requesting that the regiment be reconstituted. "I much marvel at the nomination of the list of my regiment; I shall humbly desire if possible my former list might stand . . . for having made inquiry I perceive some to be put to me of weak resolution so I conceive it to be both dishonorable for me to engage with them as also may prove prejudicial to the cause and service we undertake." Aldriche concluded this appeal by stating his alternatives: "If not rightly stated I shall humbly desire (though my resolution be to proceed) to desist rather than engage with dishonor." Fairfax took Aldriche at his word and replaced him.[112] Sidney submitted his resignation, suffering from a leg wound that he claimed made him unfit for service.[113] He would soon recover sufficiently to become governor of Chichester. He, too, preferred men of unquestionable zeal.[114]

The loss of six colonels at the beginning of April was a severe blow to hopes for an orderly transition to the new Army command. The departing colonels left their former regiments intact and a hurried search for replacements was initiated, making promotions inevitable. The heated debate over Nathaniel Rich's position in the Army was made superfluous by the sudden dearth of commanding officers: Rich replaced Sidney. Lieutenant Colonel Walter Lloyd, who had served in Essex's Army, was promoted to colonel and given command of Adlriche's regiment. The replacements for the Scottish officers were Sir Hardress Waller (Holborne), Robert Hammond (Crawford), Edward Harley (Barclay), and John Butler (Middleton).[115] The resignation of senior officers compounded the problem of organizing the soldiery into the new regiments. A mutiny of Essex's troops in February when placed under Sir William Waller's command highlighted the danger of change in midstream and many, like Sir Oliver Luke, believed that Essex's troops and officers would not fight under other commanders. "Many expected a great mutiny upon this regulation of the old army; but it came off better than it was expected," Whitelocke recalled.[116] It was Major General Philip Skippon, general of the foot, who accomplished the successful assimilation of Essex's forces into the New Model. His speech to the officers and soldiers was reported to have been so persuasive that "all sergeants and corporals which were formerly employed are willing to serve as common soldiers."[117] Although Skippon's efforts were of great importance, the presence of the City of London's £80,000 loan played no small part in the Army's smooth recruitment. Fourteen days advance pay was given to those who took up their posts.

In two weeks a large part of the New Model was recruited and equipped. After initial uneasiness the soldiers poured into the ranks, believing that the regular pay assured them by their new commanders would be forthcoming. By the end of April all fully recruited regiments received a further two weeks' pay. They were specifically prohibited from taking free quarter, another indication that their wages would remain regular. By the end of the month much of the Army was ready for service.

In creating the New Model Army both Houses followed their traditional methods of decision making and their conservative military principles. The new Army was an amalgamation, not a fresh beginning – "I call it the new Army not because any new officers are to be chosen, for there are only such . . . who are already in the service."[118] In its composition, its form, and its finance, the New Model Army differed little from its predecessors. It was drawn by Parliament's traditional military leaders and refined slowly by the full membership of both Houses. The resolve to reform the parliamentary cause had been spent in the movement for self-denial and by the time military reorganization began in earnest the members of the Houses had had more than enough of radical solutions. It was no subtle design sprung upon a depressed and unsuspecting Parliament and it was to have no independent life of its own. As before, overall military policy was to come from Westminster. The Committee of Both Kingdoms, with the ousted generals, their supporters, and the Scots constituting a majority, was to devise strategy, the Army Committee to secure supplies, and the treasurers in London to collect revenue. Army administration had not been centralized any more than the assessment scheme had been reformed, and there was little reason to think that the plaguing problems of the past did not still exist in epidemic proportions.

Yet for all that was traditional and uncontroversial about the Army's creation, it left a residue of rancor. Relations between the two Houses had deteriorated badly during the winter, a carryover from the incessant bickering about commands and strategies, no doubt, but raised to a new height. The Lords, individually and collectively, resented their exclusion from military affairs, and the necessity of the change, which evoked the support of a bare majority, could not remove the sting of rejection. The Earl of Essex, especially, had been a national hero unceremoniously discarded. The emendations to the officer list had been the last chance for Essex and Manchester to reassert their rightful role in military affairs, and it had been a dismal failure. The cumulative effect of a summer's feuds and a winter's discontents was to be the growth of personal faction in the two Houses – political controversy that

50

centered upon individuals and interests rather than visions of the common good. Expectation of an impending military disaster would lead the Earl of Essex and his allies in the Commons to embrace the Scottish party at Westminster and their Army in the north. The unexpected triumph of the New Model would harden animosity into permanent opposition. In less than a year the new Army would become a political issue; in less than two years a political participant. The spirit that evoked self-denial and the compromise and caution that created the New Model Army would then be forgotten.

Chapter 3

THE TRIUMPH OF THE
NEW MODEL ARMY

The success is hardly imaginable which accompanies Sir Thomas
Fairfax's army.[1]

The campaign of 1645 dawned darkly. The reorganization of Parliament's southern forces was barely completed before the royalists
were in the field. Hopes that the spirit of reform that resulted in
self-denial would spread to military matters quickly dimmed. "I
pray God this poor Kingdom pays not too dear for this New
Model," one of the discarded parliamentary commanders wrote.[2]
At the Committee of Both Kingdoms the philosophical and personal differences that had stamped the first years of fighting weighed
heavily in debates over strategy. Plans for war were formulated,
reformulated, and changed again as the weakness of Fairfax's forces
and the refusal of the Scots to move south became apparent. Scottish obduracy was particularly galling, for Leven's men represented
the safeguard upon which the Committee had relied in deciding to
recast the English armies. When the Scots declined to join Association forces raised by Cromwell, the twin beacons of reform – the
unification of the English armies and the elimination of recriminations – were put out. Detachments of the New Model were sent
west to relieve Taunton and east to guard the Association, and its
core was ordered to blockade Oxford. On June 1 Parliament suffered its worst defeat yet, the siege and sack of Leicester.

The failure of reform initially to reverse Parliament's military
fortunes, and thus God's judgment reflected in that failure, heightened the disputes that new modeling essayed to dispel. After the loss
of Leicester charges of betrayal rang out at Westminster, where the
strategy of the Oxford siege was discredited and its formulators
attacked. An accusation by James Cranford against a subcommittee
of the Committee of Both Kingdoms threatened to undermine the
authority of Parliament's military administration. Concurrently the
conduct of members of Parliament at the recent negotiations at

Uxbridge was also examined on the basis of information provided by the turncoat, Lord Savile. With the military prospects uncertain and the rancor created in the winter revived, factional dispute soon came to dominate the proceedings of Parliament. "Could we agree here and attend the public good we might hope, God blessing us, to see an end of much of our miseries," the disheartened Robert Scawen believed.[3] Fearful that the loss of Leicester presaged disaster, the leading opponents of military reorganization entered a political alliance with the Scots that would ensure their cooperation in the fighting. Determined to risk all, the supporters of the new Army demanded decisive action. Despite the military successes that began with the victory at Naseby, tensions between the factions escalated throughout the year.

Contentions between parliamentary factions and the hostility of the Scots had little effect on the English forces now under Fairfax's command. After an inactive spring the Army was ordered into battle and its first test was the decisive encounter at Naseby. At a stroke the King's chief army was annihilated and the tactics of war were shifted from defense of London and the east to a vigorous campaign to clear the West Country. In July the Army was divided again into brigades to lay sieges, and throughout the summer and fall royalist strongholds fell. In its first year of existence the New Model was occupied with military affairs. Its concerns centered on recruitment, supply, and the maintenance of discipline. The separate brigades and detachments exhibited little sign of political awareness despite the controversy that soon developed in London over the Army's religious diversity. If the soldiers saw the hand of God guiding their work, it was no cause for self-righteousness; "let's not be overconfident in the arm of flesh," they and the nation were repeatedly admonished.[4] As long as the King was in the field and his hope for foreign intervention high, the soldiery and its commanders were concerned only with winning the war.

Reorganization of the Army had little effect upon military decision making. The Committee of Both Kingdoms was still charged with devising strategy and the two Houses continued to debate the Committee's decisions. If some, like Peregrine Pelham, the merchant M.P. from Hull, believed "that as long as Essex and Manchester were managing the war it could not prosper," others soon realized that it was the imprecision and delay in the decision-making process that undercut the military effort.[5] Planning for the campaign of 1645 was a case in point. Parliament's strategic objectives were the relief of Taunton, the renewal of the siege of Chester, and the prevention of an attack by the King upon the Eastern Counties. The Committee of Both Kingdoms decided to send the partially recruited New Model west and the Scottish Army to Chester, forcing the King's main body to follow one or the other.[6] But with Montrose threatening their homeland the Scots declined a long-term siege and the Committee was forced to revise its thinking. It was now proposed that the Scots send a smaller contingent of troops south to join Cromwell, who was raising men in the Association.[7] This force still might be strong enough to prevent the King's advance on Chester. Again the Scots balked: "we conceived, for divers reasons, it would not be for the good of the service that Lieutenant General Cromwell should command those forces who were to correspond with the Scottish army."[8]

The Scots' refusal to move south – indeed several of their cavalry regiments returned home in May – led to the abandonment of the siege of Chester and left only a small force to protect the Association. The plan to draw the King westward had failed and the Committee was forced to detach 3,000 men from Fairfax's army for the relief of Taunton.[9] With the New Model divided it was now necessary to formulate a design that would keep the King from either attacking in the east or turning upon Fairfax's weakened force in the west. The Committee struck upon a brilliant plan: the New Model would besiege Oxford. This would prevent the King from attacking the Association from fear of losing his capital and would give the new Army time to fill its ranks. Not coincidentally, this plan would also satisfy the contrasting preferences for an active or passive pursuit of the war of the Committee's members. To those fearful of the new Army's abilities and uncertain that military success would improve Parliament's negotiating position, the siege would provide respite from the dangers of battle. To those who urged victory, the fall of the King's capital was a welcome prospect. Moreover, among these men a plan to gain Oxford by betrayal was secretly being tested.[10]

On May 17 the Committee of Both Kingdoms presented its decision to the Commons. Sir Philip Stapleton explained the strategic advantages of the siege and requested supplementary finance for it.[11] The House quickly agreed to the proposal, resolving to borrow £20,000 more from the City of London for its execution. Fairfax was ordered to take up positions around the royalist stronghold and £6,000 was sent to the Army for its preparations.[12] Despite its subsequent repudiation on all sides, the siege of Oxford was supported unanimously in the House of Commons. Scawen's committee devoted an entire week at the end of May to raising the money from the City. Parliament reassessed its military strategy on the assumption that the New Model would remain at Oxford. Colonel Edward Massey was voted to command the western forces, which were to be composed of the regiments of Waller's and Essex's army that had participated in the winter expedition to the west. Two weeks later an ordinance was brought in to associate the Northern Counties, ordering 10,000 men raised for its protection.[13] The military landscape returned to its familiar features: the major national Army would draw off the large royalist forces and local armies would secure their areas for the cause.

The plan was a good one and might have succeeded if the King had followed the role that the Committee's strategists had assigned to him. But rather than follow the New Model toward Oxford to assure provisions for his capital, the King struck boldly east. With Cromwell raising forces in Ely, Major General Richard Browne at Abingdon, and the Scots retreating ever northward, only Colonel Vermuyden's regiment lay immediately east of the royalist force. Under cover of darkness Prince Rupert outflanked Vermuyden's lines and arrived unopposed before the city of Leicester. After a brief but ferocious struggle, the city fell.[14] The tales of pillage and mayhem that reached London on June 1 had no parallel since the Ulster massacre. But the sack of Leicester was only insult added to injury of its loss. This was indeed the gravest defeat suffered by Parliament since the beginning of the war. With its untested Army far off, the King threatened to bring the war to the east with startling success. At Westminster the loss of Leicester was received with recriminations and cries of betrayal. No atmosphere was better suited for factional strife.

In the House of Commons the inevitable investigation began to determine the cause of another military setback. The Scots were the first target. Their failure to march into Lincolnshire at the beginning of April had encouraged the royalists, and their refusal to send troops to follow the King had left Vermuyden alone to defend Leicester. Even the pacific D'Ewes was astounded by the strategy that left Cromwell idle: "For we are sure that the first error was the calling back of Colonel Cromwell and now it be fit to know where Colonel Vermuyden is and whether the Scots' forces be advanced."[15] The Scottish Commissioners, too, realized that the key to their influence lay in the contributions of their army: "For no man here doubts, but if once our Army was in such a condition as easily, if we were diligent, it might be, all these clouds would vanish, and we would regain this people's heart."[16] By failing to support Vermuyden Scottish prestige sank. But the Scots could not bear the entire blame – the emphasis of new modeling after all had been on self-reliance.

Nor would the Scottish Commissioners accept responsibility that could easily be shared. On June 11, Thomas Adams, Mayor of London, reported to the Commons that James Cranford, a leading presbyterian minister in the City, had accused several parliamentary leaders of a design to betray the cause to the King by surrendering all of Parliament's garrisons.[17] As the House was already examining charges that Leicester had been betrayed, Cranford's denunciations, delivered at the Royal Exchange, had grave implications.[18] That afternoon he was summoned to the bar of the Lower House and questioned. There Cranford divulged that a secret committee had been formed by leading members of the Committee of Both Kingdoms with the intention of making a separate peace with the King. He identified Lord Savile, who had recently defected from the royalist camp, as the parliamentary go-between, and Lord Digby as the royalist agent. Cranford also claimed that this committee designed the Oxford siege to facilitate its secret and illicit communications with the royalists.[19] These charges concerning parliamentary members made in a public place constituted a breach of privilege for which Cranford was arrested, although a committee was appointed to examine the information.[20]

Immediately following Cranford's appearance at the Commons' bar, Denzil Holles requested that Savile be examined. Holles contended that Savile had made private accusations against Holles's conduct at Uxbridge.[21] Thus a second, separate investigation was initiated. Although Savile became the focus of both, the charges remained distinct: Cranford accusing the Committee of Both Kingdoms' subcommittee of betraying its trust, and Savile making similar charges against Holles. Cranford's accusations proved of interest to the Commons only as they related to the Oxford siege. As that strategy had clearly backfired it was likely that the Commons would investigate its formulation at the Committee of Both Kingdoms. Here Cranford, in accusing Sir Henry Vane, Jr., Oliver St. John, and Viscount Say and Sele of forming a secret subcommittee, a charge that was true with certain qualifications, placed the entire Committee in further disrepute. Although the positions of leadership enjoyed by the three accused members might have precipitated a factional free-for-all in any case, a more basic consideration ensured support for Cranford. Essex and Stapleton had reasons of their own for pressing the charge. Both were members of the Committee and Stapleton had proposed the Oxford siege to the full House and had pressed for its acceptance. Essex, Manchester, and Waller, to whom the Houses necessarily looked for military guidance, had offered no opposition. It was now necessary for them to dissociate themselves from the discredited strategy.

Beyond the political logic that gave them substance, Cranford's accusations were completely fantastic. There is no doubt but that they were fomented by the Scots, to whom Cranford was directly connected through Baillie.[22] They exhibit what had long been apparent, that the Scots could see English politics only in religious categories. Convinced that the aim of their religious counterparts in Parliament would be the elimination of their tolerationist opponents, they devised charges that were so politically naïve as to be transparent. The activist leaders, who had continuously opposed a diluted peace settlement, were accused of secret negotiations leading to a treaty. Moreover, their terms involved moderating their own insistence upon Parliament's control of the militia in exchange for the King's acceptance of some form of religious toleration. In 1645, this was a settlement that might have been embraced by a majority of both Houses.

In fact, the establishment of the subcommittee and the contacts with Savile had a goal more consistent with political reality. The activists' leaders, as they had on several occasions, saw the opportunity to gain a military advantage through royalist duplicity. Savile's hasty departure from the King's ranks, owing, many believed, to an irreversible loss of favor at court, seemed a plausible cause of his desire to aid Parliament. When the plum he dangled before Say proved to be the very goal of Parliament's strategy –

the surrender of Oxford – Say informed Vane and St. John and negotiations were earnestly begun.[23] The increased factional conflict may have influenced the three to keep Essex and Stapleton in the dark, but more likely they believed, as Savile revealed to them, that the royalists received detailed information of parliamentary proceedings from Holles and his supporters. If this were true, advising Essex and Stapleton of the plot would be the same as announcing it to the King.[24] In negotiating secretly with Savile, Say may have violated the letter but not the spirit of the parliamentary order prohibiting secret contacts with the enemy.

The Cranford affair had more significant consequences than its details might suggest. By actively supporting the Scots' trumped-up charges, Holles, Essex, and Stapleton moved into an alliance that the Scots had eagerly sought since the first parliamentary attempt at religious accommodation in the autumn of 1644. In December they had tried to forge these ties by an equally rash accusation against Cromwell. At that time Essex, who was present at a meeting that evaluated the Scots' allegations, was able to resist their pressure.[25] In the intervening months, however, the Scots continued their overtures, doubtlessly supporting the siege of Oxford on the grounds that it would minimize the fighting. In return for support on the presbyterian settlement the Scots could offer the cooperation of their army. In devising and revising the plans for the spring campaign, Essex and Stapleton learned that Scottish opposition to the New Model was so intense that the Scots' Army could not be counted upon to participate in the fighting. Whatever its shortcomings, however, the Scottish Army was an essential part of the military plans. Its loss was directly attributed to the policies and personalities of the men who had rejected the old armies. However active Holles may have been to secure peace at Uxbridge, a royalist victory would make traitors of them all. Thus, in rejecting the Oxford siege and supporting Cranford's charges, they made their alliance. They did not run to the Scots so much as they ran from the New Model.

Closely allied to Cranford's charges against Vane, St. John, and Say were accusations made by Lord Savile against Denzil Holles and Bulstrode Whitelocke. Savile's appearance in London had thus resulted in two separate examinations. The first, relating to Cranford's charge that negotiations had been secretly undertaken for the surrender of Oxford, was mitigated by the victory at Naseby. The dramatic reversal of fortune made the investigation of military failures superfluous. The second inquiry concerned the conduct of Holles and Whitelocke when they were commissioners to the peace negotiations at Uxbridge. The victory at Naseby heightened interest in these charges, for the King's captured correspondence revealed that the parliamentary Commissioners had been divided on the terms of peace. Savile possessed a letter that detailed secret meetings between Holles and Whitelocke and several of the royalist negotiators.[26]

Echoing the revelations in the King's captured correspondence, Savile's charges received thorough examination. A committee led by Samuel Browne, who had directed the prosecution of Archbishop Laud, was chosen to examine both accuser and accused. Although Browne's questioning of all of the principals was intense, the Commons deemed the committee's report unsatisfactory.[27] On July 17 the House decided to examine Holles and Whitelocke itself. This inquiry revealed, beyond doubt, that both defendants had had communications contrary to their instructions. The content of these talks, however, remained obscure. After initially refusing to identify his source, Savile finally produced the incriminating letter he had received from the Earl of Lindsay, but he could not provide corroboration of its authenticity.[28] Consequently, the two M.P.s stood charged only by Savile, whose own credibility was now under attack. The Scots, in taking Carlisle, captured correspondence that they insisted, revealed Savile's continued adherence to the royalist cause.[29] Although these letters were doubly inadmissible, lacking identification as well as corroboration, they cast doubts upon Saville's character. With both sources of evidence so unreliable, the House of Commons, after long debate, decided to lay the matter aside.[30]

Neither the judicial technicalities nor the Scots' revelations explain the Commons' decision to sidestep the issues involved in Savile's charges. The principal reason for the Commons' resolve "to meddle no further in it" was that it was degenerating into a factional fight.[31] Self-serving as Whitelocke's account is, it makes clear that the attack on Holles had deeper roots than his conduct at Uxbridge. With Cranford's accusations as yet unresolved, Savile's charges provided a neat counterbalance. Nor did Holles and Whitelocke bare their souls before the examiners. The investigating committee was carefully chosen by "Mr. Elsynge, the clerk of the

Parliament, my kind friend and a friend to the Earl of Essex his party," who "took orders about the names of those that were friends to us," Whitelocke recalled.[32] Their testimony was carefully coordinated "to omit any thing in my narrative which might differ from what Mr. Holles had before delivered."[33] During Holles's interrogation runners kept Whitelocke informed of both questions and answers, and for an extra measure of caution "Mr. Osbaldston and some others of our friends were attending at the doors of the House and were thereabouts to solicit the members, our friends, to return to the House."[34] Factionalism was fed by committee packing, collaborated testimony, and the use of "whips." But for the moment such activity remained an aberration, designed only to secure the acquittal of Holles and Whitelocke in a matter "which so much concerned us."[35]

However much light Whitelocke's account of the Savile charges throws upon factional development, it also reveals that the factions had not yet come to dominate the House of Commons or to command the unqualified allegiance of those sympathetic to the factional leaders. Whitelocke relates, for example, that on the morning of his first appearance to answer the charges many of his friends, notably the conservative presbyterian Robert Reynolds, ignored him in Westminster Hall.[36] As the examination proceeded these rebuffs continued and Whitelocke "wondered at the strangeness of some of them and did forbear to trouble them."[37] The reluctance of some of his friends to consort with him demonstrated both the gravity of the charges and the survival of the evenhandedness with which the House traditionally made its decisions.

It was this evenhandedness that finally accounted for the resolution of Savile's charges. Reluctant to fuel the factional contentions, the House refused either to convict or to exonerate the two members. Successive motions to put the question of their guilt or innocence were defeated by the full membership.[38] As it had done in the preceding week when Sir Arthur Haselrig's charges of assault and breach of privilege against the Earl of Stamford were heard, the full House refused to act.[39] In both cases the accusations had been substantiated, and the Commons, concerned about the precedents it was creating, turned its wrath upon its nonparliamentary accusers. James Cranford was fined and imprisoned, as was John Lilburne, who had leveled an unsubstantiated allegation against Denzil Holles.[40] Both Holles and Whitelocke, after a decent face-saving period, requested leave to go into the country.[41] The charges, unresolved, would continue to cause Whitelocke sleepless nights and would eventually serve as the technical basis for Holles's expulsion from the House in 1647. But for the moment the House of Commons remained in control of its factions and proceeded to the more important business of settling its dispute with the King.

The succession of New Model victories in the year after Naseby did little to change its structure or composition. As always, innovation was resisted at Westminster and necessities were adapted to in the field. The Army's basic logistical problems became insoluble once the well of finance ran dry, and its tactics, after the battle of Langport, were limited to the storming of garrisons. In only one aspect did parliamentary conservatism and military circumstance combine to produce a departure from the structure intended for the New Model. This was the realization that the Army must be divided into detachments rather than fight as a unit if it were to accomplish an early end to the war. Colonel Edward Rossiter's regiment, which already had a quasi-independent status, was the first to be severed from the New Model, becoming the nucleus for the forces that attempted several sieges of Newark. Next, Colonel Charles Fleetwood's regiment was assigned to remain in Buckinghamshire, centering its operations at Aylesbury. Along with Browne's supernumerary forces this regiment maintained pressure on the eastern side of Oxford. In the west, the main body of the Army was also divided. Cromwell and a cavalry detachment were ordered eastward, where they captured garrisons at Devizes and Winchester. Commissary General Henry Ireton led three regiments northward to the western side of the royalist capital at Oxford. Their positions there prevented the King's forces in Hereford and Oxford from joining up. Concurrently, Fairfax took Exeter and then marched west into Cornwall.[42]

The division of the Army had the unintended effect of inhibiting its institutional growth. The Council of War, which might have provided such coherence, operated effectively only between June and September 1645, from the battle of Naseby to the siege of Bristol. After the loss of Leicester the Committee of Both Kingdoms had granted Fairfax control over military decision making, which enabled the Council of War to take on a more permanent character.[43]

In the next three months its meetings were frequent. The Council was composed of the senior officers, the Army colonels or their representatives, and the administrative staff. Four parliamentary Commissioners sat in on the proceedings and acted as liaison to the Houses.[44] Council deliberations were free and uninhibited, but in its decisions unanimity was sought. This is suggested by the request to have a commission granted to Cromwell prior to the battle of Naseby. The Council's debate revealed considerable opposition to Cromwell's exception from self-denial. Colonel Edward Montague, in particular, opposed the move, but once it was resolved to make the request his signature along with those of all the Council's members was appended to the Army's petition to Parliament.[45] Although Cromwell's place in the Army was also a political issue, the Council's action was based on military considerations. Its work, almost without exception, centered on campaign strategy, supply and recruitment, and the administration of justice.[46]

The tripartite division of the New Model in September marked the end of the Council's coordinated activities. In the new branches of the Army occasional strategy sessions called into existence smaller councils, but the New Model was no longer represented by a single institution. With Fairfax remained the general administrative officers of the Army who formed the general's headquarters, including John Rushworth, the Army's secretary. From headquarters requests for pay and recruits, which applied to all the scattered elements of the New Model, were sent to Parliament, but Cromwell and Ireton issued applications to cover the necessities of their own detachments. Institutionally, the New Model functioned much as had the old armies and the occasional reappearance of the Council of War, at times when large segments were reunited, was insufficient to provide unification.

The exigencies of war that necessitated the division of the Army and in large part dictated the initial use of the Council of War also accounted for a number of changes within the Army's officer corps. These alterations refute contentions that during this period officers were cashiered for their support of presbyterianism. Within the horse regiments, where compositional changes among the officers can be carefully traced, not a single colonel and only one major was killed during the 1645 campaign.[47] This was Major Christopher Bethell, who died at Bristol and was replaced by the regiment's senior captain, Robert Swallow.[48] Only six captains of horse fell in service between the battle of Naseby and the siege of Oxford.[49] They were normally replaced by the troop's own lieutenant. In addition, only three horse captains voluntarily left the New Model during this period. One, John Horseman of Whalley's regiment, left in the spring of 1645 before fighting was underway, and the other two, both in Rich's regiment, left in the spring of 1646 after the fighting was over.[50] These comprise all the changes made in the senior officer corps in the New Model's cavalry regiments.

The infantry presents a more complicated problem, for here the evidence does not permit so precise an analysis as can be made for the cavalry. Two colonels of foot, John Pickering and Walter Lloyd, were killed in service.[51] Pickering was replaced by his lieutenant colonel, John Hewson, and Lloyd's regiment was given to William Herbert.[52] Two other colonels, Edward Montague and Ralph Weldon, left service voluntarily during this period. Weldon departed the New Model when he was chosen governor of Plymouth in December 1645 and subsequently assumed command of a local regiment in Kent.[53] Montague withdrew from the Army shortly after he was elected to Parliament in October 1645. In Cromwell's accusation against the Earl of Manchester Montague had testified in Cromwell's behalf against his cousin and he was one of the colonels the House of Lords attempted to purge from the Army list.[54] On the other hand, he was an opponent of Cromwell's re-entry into the New Model. Although his military career is perplexing, it is difficult to attribute his withdrawal to pressure from the Independents. Weldon and Montague were replaced by Colonels John Lambert and Robert Lilburne, appointments that seem to be a manifestation of Fairfax's own influence and the increasing importance of a group of northern M.P.s. Lambert had initially been touted for a New Model regiment, but as he had not fought in any of the three old armies he was excluded.[55] Neither can be identified as religious extremists. Besides the colonels, five lieutenant colonels and one major of foot were killed in action during 1645–6.[56] In each case they were replaced by the officer ranking immediately beneath them. This process was complicated in Colonel Richard Fortescue's regiment, where three successive lieutenant colonels fell in service. The foot regiments also lost no fewer than sixteen captains, and at least one, Michael Bland, became disabled after he was wounded in battle.[57]

Brief as this reconstruction is, it points to two complementary aspects of the history of the New Model officer corps. First, the small number of officers who left service voluntarily does not support contentions of cashiering or widespread religious disaffection among the Army's officers. On the whole, the sparse number of replacements demonstrates a remarkable stability among the Army's ranking officers. Secondly, promotion was almost certainly determined by the seniority system. This is clearly documented in the case of lieutenant colonels and majors, where not a single example of irregular promotion exists. The nomination of Army colonels was controlled by the Houses of Parliament as it had been at the Army's creation. This is attested to by the delays in filling vacancies. The principle governing the selection of captains is more difficult to establish because of the obscurity of the officers below them. Many of those promoted to fill vacant captaincies can be identified as the lieutenants of their troops. In Whalley's regiment, where changes can be definitely traced, both Henry Cannon and William Evanson, who filled the regiment's only two vacancies, had been lieutenants at the time of their promotions.[58] Clearly Fairfax believed that when changes were made seniority preceded merit, and both excluded patronage. Responding to a request from his father that he find a place for a Captain Hoyle, Fairfax wrote, "I shall do what I can for him but when places fall in this Army they are presently claimed by antiquity or merit as it is hard to place any strangers in it."[59]

Insistence upon "antiquity or merit" rather than patronage and privilege was a characteristic feature of the New Model's procedure. Fairfax resisted pressure to stock the Army with his former colleagues from the north. Even Lambert, who had been his principal agent in the Northern Army, had to wait for his appointment until the northern front was controlled by the parliamentary forces under Poyntz. In addition, Fairfax established equality among all the Army's regiments. Joshua Sprigge, who followed the Army on its western campaign, related that during long marches the general's own regiment took its turn marching in the rear rather than insisting on the privilege of setting the pace.[60] This trivial concession to regimental equality was supplemented by the manner in which Fairfax disregarded the traditional claims of the lifeguard. In the early years of war lifeguard officers were chosen on the basis of social prestige and they quickly stepped into vacant combat commands. Many New Model colonels began their military service in the Earl of Essex's lifeguard. Fairfax, however, abandoned this practice in favor of strict seniority, and in January 1646 he reduced the lifeguard to a single regiment of flintlocks.[61]

The equal treatment accorded the regiments did not carry over to equality of command. As long as the New Model detachments fought under Fairfax, Cromwell, and Ireton the problem of precedence, which had plagued the old armies, was not at issue. However, with the further fragmentation of the New Model in January 1646, the question of precedence was again revived. The *Moderate Intelligencer* claimed that "They never stand upon that, who shall be chief? But sometimes it is agreed upon the youngest, sometimes the eldest and sometimes the middle Colonel to command the party or brigade."[62] In fact, strict seniority was followed, and the House of Commons recognized and approved this procedure. In sending orders to the three colonels at the Oxford siege the Committee of Both Kingdoms reminded them "that it is a constant order of Sir Thomas Fairfax that when brigades are abroad from the Army they are commanded by the eldest Colonel."[63]

The selection of the eldest colonel to command New Model brigades as well as promotion by seniority were typical solutions to the traditional problems the Army faced. In spite of the accolades the Army received for its exemplary conduct, its real success was in maintaining discipline rather than in eliminating offenders against it. At the end of April 1645 the debauchery exhibited by some of the New Model officers led to orders that Fairfax should execute the "discipline of war" upon malefactors.[64] In May the conduct of New Model horse troops in Lincolnshire provoked many gentry, friend and foe, to transport their valuables to the royalist garrison at Newark.[65] Sir Samuel Luke described drunkenness and debauchery within the New Model with the same disgust he showed when it appeared within his own forces: "These new modellers knead all their dough with ale."[66] The several well-publicized examples of Fairfax's strict disciplinary measures, as in November 1645 when a swearer had a hole bored through his tongue, or when several plunderers were hanged, were warnings designed to inhibit widespread pillage of the countryside.[67] Indeed, the soldiers themselves were increasingly concerned with the legality of their conduct during the war. One of their primary demands in the winter of 1647 would be for an act of indemnity that would free them from prosecution when they returned to their homes. Although they had legitimate reasons for this desire, the doubtful legality of some of their actions was also a strong motivation.[68] Sir Charles Firth astutely characterized New Model conduct and discipline as having developed over the years of war rather than as being the product of the character of those who composed the Army.[69]

Discipline was a function of control by field officers rather than of the general policies established by Fairfax at Army headquarters. The officers for the most part were responsible for the conduct of their own troopers, with senior regimental officers accountable for their subordinates. Few specific examples of officer misconduct in this period have been found, besides the complaints of religious diversity. But Army officers were still liable to the same degree of absenteeism as their predecessors had been. In February 1646 the governor of Abingdon found it necessary to send to London in an attempt to locate officers of Rainsborough's regiment, which was quartered there. "I desire you will be pleased to order the officers of Colonel Rainsborough's regiment to come down to look to their charge," he wrote, "there being here but four of ten commanders."[70] For many reasons, London remained an attractive alternative to the field, especially during the winter months, and officer absenteeism remained a problem that periodically evoked threats of cashiering from both Fairfax and Parliament. At the end of the western campaign absenteeism was so vexing that it was suggested that the Army no longer appoint married men to fill officer vacancies.[71]

Desertion, especially by the large number of impressed soldiers, was a far greater problem than absenteeism. Robert Baillie certainly overstated the case when he claimed "this new-modeled army consists for the most part of raw, unexperienced pressed soldiers."[72] If the experience of Norwich is typical, many deserted from their gangs after receiving their new suits of clothing, leaving the community responsible for finding replacements and outfitting them again. No wonder so many were completely unfit for service, as the undersheriffs and bailiffs who enlisted them were well aware.[73] The number of men pressed into service was considerable and the Army was constantly under strength. Men to press into service, though drawn from among a community's transient or impoverished populations, were difficult to find by 1645.[74] Paradoxically, the Army's successes made it more difficult to recruit the ranks, for as the danger to the nation receded localities were less willing to make costly expenditures.

This reluctance could also be seen in the difficulty of collecting the monthly assessments. By the end of the western campaign Parliament was forced to borrow from the City or charge against other sources of income to provide for the Army's maintenance. In September £50,000 was sent from the parliamentary coffers to the west, in October £40,000 was borrowed from the City, and in November £30,000 was diverted from other parliamentary revenue. This signaled the beginning of the collapse of the assessment scheme, victim of overburdened taxpayers, local troop costs, and the Army's victories.[75] The £120,000 disbursed over these three months, provided in installments that diminished by £10,000, effectively terminated the New Model's financial self-reliance. At the end of September Sprigge sadly reported that the Army had taken free quarter in the west for the first time.[76] There is no doubt that the monthly assessment followed the excise in becoming a source of local rather than national expenditure.[77]

The state of Army finance during 1645–6 presents a most intricate problem. There can be no doubt that the soldiers never received full pay and that arrears accumulated quickly, more among cavalry than infantry. Yet the evidence demonstrates that the soldiery regularly received some pay, one or two weeks in almost every month. The pay was sufficient to satisfy a soldier's immediate necessities and to avoid long periods of free quartering. Indeed the critical factor in assessing the state of Army finance is the length of time between disbursements rather than the cumulative state of arrears.[78] The absence of seven or fourteen days pay each month, although amounting to three months over a year, might not be as significant as two consecutive months without pay. Moreover, aggregate arrears were subject to seasonal fluctuations, as the Army was better paid in the spring than in the winter. This resulted from the willingness of communities to pay their assessments only during the campaign, although as the ranks were generally depleted during winter fewer disbursements went further.

Analyzing those infantry regiments for which sufficient records survive, it is apparent that the foot soldiers received regular, but not full, pay during the fifteen months of war.[79] Inasmuch as the entire Army went unpaid in September 1645, twenty-eight days was the base period a regiment was without salary. Only three regiments endured a longer hiatus: Pickering's, whose regiment's forty-two days' lapse occurred in April–May 1645 before the entire regiment had been raised; Harley's, which went two months without pay; and Skippon's, which went three. (There is a strong possibility that the warrants for Skippon's regiment may be missing. In the three months in which there are no records for this regiment it was detached from the rest of the Army and in service around the Welsh border.) The aggregate state of arrears was also surprisingly good in the foot regiments. The artificial arrears claims accepted by Parliament for this period establish the foot regiments to have been eighty-four days behind during fifteen months of service, whereas calculations based on the pay warrants find an average regiment less than two months in arrears.[80] In general, the foot soldier received four-fifths of his total pay and went little longer than one month without a disbursement of wages.

The horse regiments and Okey's dragoons were more seriously underpaid than were the infantry. Considering aggregate arrears in June 1646, cavalrymen received little more than half their total pay. The Army committee accepted an artificial estimate of cavalry arrears at 189 days, which closely resembles the figures that can be reconstructed from the pay warrants. Significantly, only one regiment went longer than twenty-eight days without pay, Graves's men, who endured two months without salary.[81] The time over which horse regiments were unpaid is particularly important in comparing their arrears with the infantry. Because the cavalryman received a generous daily allowance, he was able to survive on half pay as long as that pay was regular. Foot soldiers, recompensed at eightpence a day, received little more than a laborer's wage and thus needed a larger proportion of their full pay in order to survive and pay their debts.

The system by which soldiers and their officers borrowed from each other during the intervals they went unpaid is not sufficiently documented to allow for generalizations.[82] It is clear from scanty evidence that officers occasionally supported their troops when times were particularly difficult. It is also true that free quarter was resorted to once the Army's payment lapsed for a month or longer.[83] In calculating the cost of quartering, Parliament estimated that three-fourths of a foot soldier's pay and one-half of a cavalry trooper's would be so expended.[84] Calculations of arrears demonstrates that in the first fifteen months the Army received sufficient funds for subsistence maintenance. In general, a soldier's arrears became his savings.[85]

During its years of battle the material condition of the Army depended upon recruitment and supply as well as its pay. Here again the picture remains incomplete. It is doubtful if the New Model ever reached the 21,000-man strength authorized for it. The battle of Naseby and the western campaign, although not inflicting heavy casualties upon the Army, took a toll in illness and desertion. By August 1645 depletion of the ranks had become acute and led the Army to delay the siege of Sherborne to await reinforcements from London.[86] In the event, only 1,200 of an expected 4,000 arrived, evoking numerous protests from the Army.[87] Fairfax, whose *Memorials* are not always to be trusted, recalled that the Army was "made so inconsiderable for want of fit and necessary accommodations that it rather seemed that we were sent to be destroyed than to do any service to the Kingdom."[88] Indeed, the want of "fit and necessary accommodations" in the form of reinforcements prompted Fairfax to request a full recruitment of the Army following the siege of Bristol. This led to a renewed call throughout the nation, and more especially in London, for men to join the New Model. On October 1 the Committee of Both Kingdoms authorized 1,465 men to be raised and equipped.[89] But the approach of winter and the cost of raising the men conspired to nullify the Committee's intention. In November the House of Lords voted to delay all further recruitment of the Army, feebly arguing that its ranks were full.[90] Fairfax settled for double pay for men already in service and 6,000 suits of clothes.[91] By February 1646 knowledgeable estimates of Cromwell's brigade showed it to be short 200 troopers in five cavalry regiments, and the strength of seven regiments of foot was estimated at 5,200, 1,800 short of full strength.[92]

Similarly, insufficient supplies vexed the western campaign. One reason for the shortage was the constant action in which the Army was engaged. Scawen's committee found it impossible to handle the streams of requests for clothing and munitions that came from the three separate New Model detachments situated in Devon and Oxfordshire. As early as July the Army Committee was overwhelmed by the logistical problems posed by the Army's success. "Consider what we have had to do since you left us," Scawen wrote to Sir John Potts, "the more victories we have, the more trouble to us how to get supplies."[93] In fact, the absence of supplies at Sherborne caused Rushworth to complain somewhat petulantly, "the Army when we come before a place should not stay an hour for materials."[94] But on the whole the Committee acquitted its task admirably and earned the accolades of the London newsbooks: "that Honorable committee for [the] army who though divers of [them] are taken off upon other public affairs yet some few attend so constantly that the Kingdom owes them very much."[95]

Unlike men, supplies were more easily obtained in the field. These included food, except cheese and biscuits, which were contracted for in London, provender for the horses, and, of course, housing. Carts, ladders, shovels, and picks necessary for sieges were also acquired locally, and the Army's prompt payment for such necessities astounded local inhibitants.[96] Most importantly, fresh horses were procured in the communities through which the Army passed. In the months between April 1645 and June 1646 the Army bought 6,410 horses, an average of 427 a month. These were either purchased outright or with the exchange of a trooper's old mount. The three months in which horses were most heavily purchased were April 1645, when 1,100 horses were bought to equip the newly formed regiments; July 1645, after the battle of Naseby and before the long march to the west, when 830 horses were acquired; and May 1646, when 940 new mounts were provided for the expected spring offensive. Characteristically, the fewest purchases took place in the autumn of 1645, when in the four months between August and November only 402 horses were bought. In October, with the Army unpaid the previous month, only 18 horses were obtained.[97]

Thus in its composition and organization as much as in its material condition of pay and supply, the New Model was very like the old armies. In the first fifteen months of its existence the Army was continuously engaged in battle or siege and its military concerns were paramount. The most frequent statements from the Army, Rushworth's letters to Parliament, or the reports of victories by various messengers focused on the Army's logistical problems. Hugh Peter, after relating the victory at Winchester to Parliament, requested the establishment of resident treasurers with the Army to facilitate pay, and John Lilburne's report after Langport included an urgent request for a supply of shoes and stockings.[98] It was these missives that were most characteristic of the Army's concerns and consciousness.

Peter and Lilburne are thought to have been connected to the Army in ways other than as occasional messengers. Indeed, for many who have stressed the radical character of the New Model, Peter and Lilburne represent the two sides of its coin: radical religion and radical politics. Whether Hugh Peter was characteristic of radical religion as it developed during the Civil War is an unresolvable question. Although the King would later be surprised by Peter's moderation, he has become a symbol of the "New Blazing Stars" who were the radical Army chaplains. Peter's stature derives from his prominence in delivering messages of New Model victories and preaching sermons to soldiers and townsmen in the west. His role as an Army chaplain is more obscure, as only Sprigge has so identified him, placing him as chaplain to the artillery train.[99] No pay warrants to him survive as they do for other Army chaplains, and by January 1646 John Saltmarsh was chaplain to the artillery train.[100] In fact, in April 1646 the House of Commons debated Peter's reappointment as a parliamentary messenger with a yearly salary, suggesting that this had been his role since the New Model's creation.[101]

Beyond this problem, only nine "Saints in Arms" have been identified, two of whom, Edward Bowles and Richard Baxter, were clearly presbyterians, and a third, Robert Ram, served in the conservative presbyterian regiment of Edward Rossiter.[102] The others were Peter; William Dell and John Saltmarsh, who were attached to the general's headquarters at different times; Henry Pinnell, chaplain to Pickering's regiment; William Sedgewick, and William Erbury.[103] How effective so few men were or could be in trumpeting radical religion to the truncated brigades of the New Model is impossible to estimate, but their roles have certainly been overplayed. Actually it was the shortage of chaplains, of whatever persuasion, that provided contemporary observers with explanations for some of the Army's religious diversity. The New Model had great difficulty in attracting ministers, as camp life and uncertain pay were unable to compete with the plethora of vacancies, "it being a time to wait for good livings."[104] In mid-May the *True Informer* reported that only four ministers were currently employed in the Army and Parliament turned to the Westminster Assembly of Divines to provide men of God for the New Model.[105] How many of these Assembly-approved ministers besides Baxter took posts in the Army remains unknown. Cromwell, for one, insisted that his regiment would accept any minister recommended by the Assembly, and the numerous regiments officered by presbyterians should have provided positions for ministers whose religious preference was similar to Baxter's and the majority of the Assembly.[106] Nevertheless, complaints of the dearth of godly ministers continued throughout the war. In defending the Army in 1647 the author of "Vox Militaris" stressed "the want of honest, able and Godly ministers in our Army," reminding Army opponents that they had not come forward to preach to the soldiers.[107]

The lack of ordained ministers to preach in the Army furthered the lay preaching that was characteristic of some independent churches. In April 1645, as the Army's regiments were being formed, Parliament passed an order prohibiting lay preaching.[108] This was supposedly occasioned by a sermon preached by Colonel John Pickering to his newly assembled troops. The royalist news-book *Mercurius Aulicus* spitefully reported that "the great edge against this preaching Colonel was because he taught against the Scots."[109] Whatever the truth of the matter, the presbyterian ministers in London had long advocated a ban on lay preaching, which was far more common in City parishes than in the ranks of the recently disbanded armies. The Scottish presbyterian George Gillespie took pains to explain the underlying cause of the order against lay preaching: "The Parliament has made an ordinance for restraining popular preaching, an abuse which was beginning in their armies and that through want of ministers as a principal occasion."[110] Debate over lay preaching was one of the central conflicts between presbyterians and independents. In the Army it was defended both as a substitute for the lack of ministers and because some of the preachers were university-educated men.[111]

Radical chaplains and mechanic preachers did exist within the New Model. They were supported by groups within the Army that held to independent and sectarian doctrines. Their existence, however, should not imply that the Army as a whole espoused or supported such viewpoints. Both existed in far greater profusion in London and had little success in spreading radical theology. "Q. Why is there such envy between the Independents and Presbyterians in the City and garrisons of the Parliament and yet they agree so well in Sir Thomas Fairfax's Army? A. Because in the Army they are free from self-ends and join together in love to have the work done and therefore lay aside all base ends."[112] The Army was continually characterized as a peaceful mixture of diverse religions, a description that certainly applies to its officer corps. If

72

religious radicals looked to the Army for support it was because they could find it nowhere else. The faithful service performed by independents and sectaries raised hope that they would be accommodated in the final religious settlement, but these were hopes that did not emanate from the Army. Richard Baxter and Thomas Edwards, who complained loudest about the Army's religious diversity, were expressing their fears that dissenting opinion would spread throughout the nation – they were not estimating the numbers of Army adherents to these opinions. This was the meaning of Edward's metaphor of gangrene: its danger was to the unaffected parts of the body.

Nor is it accurate to find a connection between the radical religion that did exist within the Army and radical political activity. Indeed it is difficult to find any traces of Army involvement in politics during this first year of its existence. "We protest that we have no other end than to discharge the trust imposed upon us," a letter from the Army proclaimed in response to rumors that the New Model would force a religious settlement upon the kingdom.[113] Although many in the City were gripped with such fears the Army did nothing to enhance them. In this regard the general's attitude is revealing. Although there is nothing to suggest a connection between Fairfax and radicalism, the respect and honor shown him by the soldiers makes plausible that his views were typical of Army politics. In September 1645 he summoned Bristol with a letter to Prince Rupert that encapsulated the Army's war aims. "The Crown of England is and will be where it ought to be, we fight to maintain it there. . . . The King in supreme acts concerning the whole state is not to be advised by men to whom the law takes no notice, but by his Parliament where he hears all of his people, as it were, at once."[114] In November, when Lord Goring proposed that the New Model join with the King to achieve a settlement of the war, Fairfax refused to treat with him on any but military matters.

In light of the constant military pressure placed upon the New Model during its first year it would be unnecessary to examine its political role were it not for the belief that the Army was the extra-parliamentary support of the Independent M.P.s. This connection has placed a political burden upon the Army, especially in relation to the important recruiter elections that occurred in the wake of the Army's success. Denzil Holles would later claim that royalist control of the west was simply replaced by Army domination.[115] But like so many charges against the Army, these were not contemporaneous, coming rather after the tumultuous events of 1647. In essence, New Model involvement in the western elections rests upon the potential influence of prominent men connected with the Army like Sir Thomas Fairfax and Hugh Peter. To examine their roles it is imperative to separate the men from their officers. Sir Thomas's father, Ferdinando Lord Fairfax, was an inveterate electioneer who viewed his son's newly won acclaim as an asset to be capitalized upon during the recruitment. He wrote a series of letters requesting help for Sir William Selby and James Chaloner, one of which elicited Rushworth's cryptic comment, "No place so likely to have a burgess obtained for Sir William Selby as here [Tiverton], the General being present."[116] But neither Selby nor Chaloner procured places through Army influence. Fairfax's influence was personal rather than military and, above all else, local, confined to Yorkshire. It was this personal interest that prompted Sir Thomas's inquiries at Tiverton rather than any attempt to secure friends for the Army, and it was the lack of personal influence that caused the failure to secure the desired places. Indeed, it is difficult to see how the localities could have resisted a concerted effort by the Army to influence elections. Whatever Hugh Peter's affiliation to the Army may have been, the numerous accusations about his electioneering have been seriously undermined by recent research, and it need only be added that a preacher's presence at an election was commonplace, as a sermon normally preceded the poll.[117]

The picture of the New Model that emerges from this examination is far different from that usually drawn. The presupposition, basic to diverse historical interpretations, that the New Model was radical at its creation and continued to be dominated by those who espoused radical religion and politics, cannot be supported. Although unified by its opponents, the Army did not develop a singular identity. It was physically separated into brigades and detachments, financially distinguished as infantry and cavalry, and ideologically diverse. The physical dispersal retarded the growth of the Council of War, which might have provided institutional coherence to the New Model, and also deterred ideological confronta-

tion among the mixture of religious viewpoints. Most of all, in its
first months the Army was occupied with winning the war, not
securing the peace. It was more concerned with its material condition than with religion or politics and its infrequent public pronouncements centered on pay, recruitment, and supply. Its material
condition precluded serious economic grievances and the plaudits
of the nation resounded to its victories. It had begun as an amalgamation of the old Armies and nothing in the first fifteen months of
its history substantially changed its composition, character, or conduct.

To understand the dimensions of the political revolution that
loomed beyond the horizon of June 1646 it is essential to understand the character of the New Model. The factors that maintained
its stability and encouraged its victories would soon disappear; its
regular pay would turn into unredeemable debts, its public acclaim
into accusations and disgruntlement. The essentially apolitical military organization that was the New Model would then be transformed into a truly radical Army. But the Army's politicization
awaited the failure of Parliament to secure the peace that the New
Model's victories made possible. Not until Parliament itself was
tarnished by attacks from outside pressure groups and the emergence of its own political parties would the soldiers come to see
themselves as peacemakers rather than warriors.

Chapter 4

THE ASSAULT ON
PARLIAMENTARY POLITICS

And indeed, many wise and good men are of this opinion to wish
the King here; that thereby men might be taken off from pursuing
their several interests and from seeking to devour each other and
to mind the common good.[1]

The year 1646 was a time for decisions. In years crowded with unprecedented events since the beginning of "these unnatural wars,"
1646 promised to be denser still. Preparations for another campaign
proceeded smoothly in contrast to the disarray of the King's forces.
The noose of New Model regiments around Oxford was being
drawn tighter and few believed the war would last much longer.
With its military victory, Parliament's vacillating course between
war and peace was over – peace alone remained to be settled. Since
the previous September the two Houses had been studying proposals for a final accommodation. The issues to be resolved were
those that had initiated the fighting: religion, control of the militia,
and the Protestant ascendancy in Ireland. The King's duplicitous
conduct at Uxbridge, no less than Parliament's decisive military
triumph, eliminated the possibility of negotiated settlement.[2] The
terms that were set by the Houses were to be presented as bills to
be signed into law.

Although negotiations would not take place between King and
Parliament, the men at Westminster would not settle the future
course of government alone. The war had developed a momentum
and a logic of its own. The parliamentary cause was a conglomerate
of interests, at best held together by principled opposition to royal
tyranny, at worst by fear of defeat and retribution. The financial
and military support provided by the City of London and the Scots
gave these allies the expectation that their desires would form part
of Parliament's proposals. In the autumn and winter of 1645–6 the
City and the Scots had presented demands for the establishment of
a rigorous *jure divino* presbyterianism to a Parliament increasingly

76

concerned with finding a new *via media*. Support for Parliament had come from radical puritans as well as from presbyterians, and the two Houses again sought accommodation for "tender consciences that differ not in fundamentals." Moreover, religious recomposition, like the reunification of government, entailed a settlement that would not disenfranchise the King's supporters. If episcopacy had been abolished, there was much in doctrine and practice that might make anglicans, presbyterians, and independents all conformists. In April 1646 Parliament produced a lengthy declaration promising a political and religious settlement that would reunite the nation.[3]

Divisions in the parliamentary cause, particularly over religion, enhanced Charles's options. His efforts to secure foreign troops, as hopeful as they were unsuccessful, did not preclude an alliance with his Scottish subjects. In Scotland there remained a strong royalist party that, if joined to Leven's army, would make a considerable force. In May, after overtures to the Estates in which the King dangled a presbyterian establishment for the two nations, Charles fled his capital at Oxford for the shelter of the Scottish Army in England. His presence there reinvigorated both the Scots, whose fidelity or treachery now meant war or peace, and the City, whose coffers and manpower were the central support for another war effort. Both now used their political leverage to resuscitate their separate campaigns to influence parliamentary decision making. The self-confidence with which the peace propositions began turned sullen by the time they were presented to the King at Newcastle in July.

The pressure applied upon Parliament by the City, the Scots, and groups of London citizens opposed to the presbyterian establishment slowly eroded the ability of the two Houses to settle their conflict with the King. The breakup of the parliamentary alliance certainly provided Charles with a straw at which to grasp, but, of far deeper significance, it further divided the members of the Houses. The factional disputes, which had become embittered after self-denial and the Cranford and Savile affairs, deepened over issues of religion and Scottish participation. Efforts to achieve a broad-based coalition between political conservatives, religious presbyterians, the City government, and the Scots were not successful, but they were devisive. City petitions and Scottish appeals to public opinion repeatedly attacked Parliament's procedures of unencumbered debate and unpressured decision making and finally politicized the questions of parliamentary privilege that, as a barrier between reason and force, had even withstood a civil war. The development of outside pressure groups and the sophistication of political organization and tactics began the process that resulted in the demise of Parliament.

On November 19, 1645, Alderman William Gibbs headed a delegation of aldermen and common councillors of the City of London that appeared at the doors of the House of Commons. They had come to present a petition to Parliament from the London government. Periodically delegations from the City had arrived at Westminster with petitions on behalf of the citizens. Ever cognizant of the services rendered the parliamentary cause by Londoners, the Houses of Parliament were attentive to their needs. The presence of the delegation would be announced to the full House of Commons and their spokesman ushered to the bar where, after a customary speech attesting the affection between City and Parliament, the sheaf of parchment he had come to deliver would be presented to the Speaker. On this November morning Alderman Gibbs informed the members of the dangerous increase of religious schism and heresy within the City's boundaries. He detailed the myriad abuses that had derived from the lack of a permanent religious establishment. His petition included the objections of a large group of City ministers to decisions on the church already passed by Parliament and the suggestions of many honest citizens for a speedy establishment of presbyterianism. They desired that Parliament would, without delay, establish church government according to the word of God. So saying, Gibbs withdrew, leaving the House to consider his words and the documents he had presented.[4]

The November petition was the culmination of efforts by both London citizens and the City government to contribute their views on central public issues. Although petitions from London did not originate with the crisis of war, it was not until 1645 that the City government began a prolonged effort to influence parliamentary decision making. The crowds of citizens that had converged on the Houses in 1641–2 spurring the members to action were not a pleasant precedent for the substantial burghers who sat on the Common Council and the aldermanic bench.[5] During the first years of

78

fighting the government of London had restricted its appeals to issues that directly affected its own jurisdiction. In June 1645, after the fall of Leicester, the City fathers again took notice of public affairs, modifying a petition submitted to them and presenting it to Parliament. That petition expressed fears of a royalist advance on London and, among other suggestions, desired a commission for Oliver Cromwell to command the Eastern Association forces.[6] As the citizens' program touched on debates and votes pending before the Lower House it violated Parliament's right to unpressured decision making. But, as Sir Simonds D'Ewes recorded, although it was agreed that the petition was a breach of privilege, "Since the affairs of Parliament were now in such a doubtful position, it was decided to give them thanks."[7] After the Commons' favorable response the City had secured leave to present its petition to the Lords, thereby assuring a hearing in both Houses of Parliament.[8]

The acceptance of the City's June petition encouraged Londoners to petition Parliament through the Common Council. In September, another group of citizens had begun a petitioning campaign to express dissatisfaction at the lack of progress made in settling church government. To give force to their desires they had launched a drive to gain the signature of every Londoner who had taken the covenant. The petition was circulated within the London parishes and each subscriber was requested to state his "quality."[9] When the House of Commons had learned of this activity the citizens' petition was voted scandalous and the lord mayor ordered to suppress its circulation.[10] This precipitous rejection, so unlike Parliament's response in June, led to demands for more direct action. On the morning of September 23 the pillars of the Royal Exchange and the walls of the City had been covered with handbills stating that "Most damnable doctrines being broached daily to the scandal of our religion and without controls it is desired by divers Christians that no man hereforth pay any taxes till the promised government of the church be settled according to our covenant."[11]

Nor had Parliament's attempt to reassert its privileges proved successful. In October the House of Commons had passed a controversial ordinance for the election of elders to the presbyterian church and later that month had revived the Committee for Accommodation, which was again directed to find a settlement acceptable to presbyterians and independents.[12] In the City reactions to these votes had been swift. At the end of the month the Commons again heard news of a petitionary campaign.[13] By then, however, not only the citizenry was aroused by the parliamentary program for the church. A large group of London ministers, informed of the Commons' intentions, had presented the Common Council with five specific objections to the proposed ordinance for the election of elders.[14] They desired that the City government present these complaints in the form of a petition to Parliament. After hearing the ministers' contentions the Common Council had appointed a largely presbyterian committee to study the proposal for a petition.[15] Two weeks later the London citizens, having revived their September campaign and "deeply apprehensive of the many woeful divisions touching matters of religion," had presented their own petition to the Common Council.[16]

When these appeals were presented to Parliament on November 19 by Alderman Gibbs, affairs were no longer in a "doubtful position" and the House of Commons was determined to reassert its privileges. In a precise statement of its institutional prerogatives the Commons declared that "they found the proceedings of Parliament misrepresented and mistaken ... that in things depending in Parliament, their proceedings may neither be prejudged nor precipitated, nor any sense put upon them than the Parliament itself shall declare."[17] These uncompromising observations were directed to the ministers and citizens who issued the petitions rather than to the Common Council, which formally presented them. Hoping to avoid controversy with the City government the Commons added in a postscript that, "having so great a testimony of your good affection to the public, and in particular to this House, [we] do interpret this to proceed from the good intentions of the Common Council."[18] Despite the rebuff that the petitions had received from the Commons, the representatives of the Common Council fulfilled the procedure they had established in June, presenting the same documents to the Lords the following day. This, Thomas Juxon observed, "was extremely ill taken of the Commons looking upon it as that which might make the two Houses clash and that they would have their wills one way or another."[19]

One month later, preceding the elections for aldermen and common councillors, another petition was launched in the City. Its organization and distribution imitated the citizens' initial campaign in September. A curt three-point document, "all drawn by the same hand," was sent to every parish in the City.[20] On the morning of the wardmote elections sermons were preached in its favor, and aldermen were canvassed for their support. Though extensive, and doubtless designed to influence the elections, the movement was not uniformly successful: "in many wards it was cried up, and in many not."[21] It took the organizers another two weeks before they were ready to press their desires upon the Common Council. Following Simeon Ashe's provocative sermon "Religious Covenanting Directed and Covenant Keeping Persuaded" on January 14, the London government debated presenting the wardmote petition, commonly known as the Farringdon-Within Petition, to the House of Commons.[22] It advocated the speedy settlement of a church government "which is agreeable to the word of God and the example of the best reformed churches," and that Parliament not tolerate "popery, prelacy or schism."[23] Although shorn of the ministers' objections to the votes on ordination, the Farringdon-Within Petition challenged Parliament's desire for religious accommodation.

On January 15 Alderman Gibbs again led the City delegation to Westminster. Again he informed the Commons of the intolerable practices that increased daily within the City and emphasized the role of women preachers and the continuation of private meetings on the Lords' day.[24] After his speech he delivered a petition from the Common Council as well as the Farringdon-Within Petition. If Gibbs expected a storm he was quickly relieved. The Speaker expressed the House's sincere thanks, observing that their concern for the religious establishment was "full of piety, Godliness, and weight." The Commons took the opportunity to declare "that notice be taken of the seasonableness of this their petition."[25] On the following day the House of Lords was as effusive with praise. After complimenting the City on its affection toward the church, the Speaker urged "the Lord Mayor and such as are in office in the City to suppress and prevent such great offenses by you mentioned," assuring the Aldermen that "wherein you shall find yourselves wanting in power, the Lords will be ready to contribute their authority for your encouragement and assistance."[26]

This was a remarkable *volte face* in Parliament's attitude to City petitions. Like the ministers' demands, the Farringdon–Within Petition violated parliamentary privilege by attempting to influence pending legislation, "by precipitating parliamentary decisions." The explanation of Parliament's perplexing response is to be found in the petition's language. The Brevity of the petition allowed the City's own paper to elucidate the petitioners' desires. In a lengthy preamble the Common Council expressed regret for its actions in November. Gibbs proclaimed "that they resolved according to their duty to have a tender respect for the privileges of Parliament whereby the liberties of the City and the Kingdom are preserved."[27] This even extended to their desires for the establishment of the church. Although the clauses of their petition were explicit, the City amended some wording to allow Parliament its primacy. They desired "that church government may speedily be settled according to the Solemn League and Covenant in such manner and form as to your wisdom shall seem most agreeable."[28] Such deferential expressions made this petition acceptable to the two Houses. In September when the Commons had ordered the mayor to suppress the citizens' petition it was the method of petitioning to which the members objected; in November when the citizens' and ministers' petition had been rejected it was their content that gave offense. Now, in January 1646, by accepting the Farringdon-Within Petition and the City's preamble to it, Parliament displayed a willingness to place form above both method and content. This shift provided another important precedent to the City and firmly established its propriety in petitioning on matters of state.

Parliament's acceptance of the January petition reinvigorated the role of the Common Council in public affairs. In the following month the Scottish Commissioners made a formal appeal to the City government to remain steadfast in support of true religion.[29] Then, at the beginning of March, the City government was again called upon to act as agent for a petition. On March 9 a document was presented to the Common Council containing the signatures of more than one-hundred prominent citizens. It was directed against Parliament's establishment of the lay commissioners who were appointed to regulate the expulsion of church members by their ministers.[30] The petitioners requested the City to renew its plea for the establishment of religion "according to the word of God," arguing that the power placed by Parliament in the hands of lay commissioners should instead be exercised by the presbyteries. Such innovation, they concluded, "was pleasing to the opponents of presbyterianism."[31] Keeping with custom, the Common Council accepted this petition and sent it to a committee for consideration. Two days later, when it was agreed to present the petition, the government broke with precedent by determining to proceed first to the House of Lords.

Thomas Juxon astutely cited two reasons for this change. The ordinance to establish the lay commissioners had already passed the Commons and was now pending before the Upper House. More importantly, "They judged the peers to be their best friends in it, and the rather because they had courted each other several times."[32] The belief that the House of Lords would be more receptive to the petition derived from its handling of the City's earlier presentations. Both in November 1645 and in January its replies had been more favorable than those of the Commons and the Lords had recently taken the City's side in a dispute over the jurisdiction of its militia.[33] Fears of common councillors that the petition would breach parliamentary privilege and provoke a confrontation were overridden by the knowledge that the Lords had never resorted to claims of privilege when it had received the City's previous supplications.

Despite these supposed tactical advantages, the Lords did vote the petition a breach of parliamentary privilege because it undertook to influence the votes of Parliament on legislation immediately under consideration; it interpreted votes already passed by Parliament, contending that they aided the enemies of true religion; and it most emphatically attempted to divide the Houses of Parliament against each other. Yet although the petition constituted a clear breach of privilege, the peers were not unanimous in their decision. Juxon recorded that ten Lords took the City's part and entered dissents to the vote on privilege. Thus by only a slim majority of three was the petition rejected, a fact that encouraged the aldermen to test the will of the House of Commons on the following day.[34]

When the City representatives arrived at Westminster the next morning they were not ushered into the House of Commons as usual. Instead, John Glyn, the City's recorder and a prominent M.P., came outside to confer with them.[35] He advised the delegation that the Commons had already been informed of the content of their petition and was ready to declare it a breach of privilege. Warning the citizens that they would only provoke a confrontation by insisting on presenting desires that were offensive to the House, Glyn suggested that they not proffer their petition.[36] His advice was accepted by the leaders of the delegation, who agreed to return to the Common Council without submitting the petition. Not all the delegates or those among the throng that had accompanied them to Westminster, however, understood or acquiesced in this decision. As the aldermen and their followers retraced their steps, rumors preceded them that the Commons had refused to accept the City's petition.[37] In these tense moments Juxon recorded, "they came to so great a heat in the business that some said [the Parliament] taxed them with breach of privilege but they would let [the Parliament] know it was they that had broke their privilege."[38]

The City's attempts to challenge parliamentary legislation on the church and the misconceptions it generated were cause for concern at Westminster. Such conflict threatened Parliament's alliance with the City government at the moment that men and money were being sought for the expected spring offensive. A few days after the City delegation had been persuaded not to present its petition to the Commons, a parliamentary committee from both Houses appeared at the Common Council.[39] Led by Samuel Browne, this committee engaged in a frank discussion of the votes on church government. They informed the common councillors and aldermen that the Westminster Assembly of Divines had been convoked only as an advisory body and that Parliament alone was entrusted with legislating the government of the church. The Commons had not accepted the Assembly's claim that the presbyterian church was established by the word of God and was awaiting answer to several questions put to the Assembly on this point.[40] The petition that the City presented to the Lords, the parliamentarians asserted, had attempted to divide the two Houses, and they now demanded that the original petition containing the London citizens' signatures be given over for Parliament's inspection. The councillors, "their judgments being fully informed . . . what danger and evil consequence their opposing the House might be," agreed to this request. They apologized for their conduct, admitting "that they were sensible it was a great breach, but not intended by them." They entreated that all mention of the City petition and the Lords' vote of privilege be removed from the parliamentary journals, assuring the committee "that as they had covenanted, so had they resolved to maintain with their lives the privileges of Parliament."[41]

Although the City government backed away from a confrontation with Parliament, this petition marked another advance in the development of pressure techniques. Conscious of where its support lay, the City had first presented their demands to the House of Lords. Although it had failed to gain acceptance for its petition, it was able to divide the Lords on the issue of privilege, seriously undermining Parliament's institutional prerogatives. Privilege was not a question of policy but a necessity of procedure. By forcing those Lords who supported them to choose between the two, and to choose in favor of policy, the City successfully politicized the appeal to privilege. This could also be seen when the parliamentary committee had come to explain their votes on the church. The discussion had been on content rather than on procedure. When Browne had claimed that the Parliament "did not except against the matter but the reason" of the petition, he had added that they "did not believe they [the City] had any evil design in the petition and that it was ignorance in them."[42] This had been the impression the meeting made on Thomas Juxon, although the topics the Commons had intended to have discussed were much less ambiguous, emphasizing the inviolability of their institutional privileges.[43] Browne's conciliatory stance was reminiscent of the response given to the City the previous November. In both instances Parliament was willing to rely upon the City's "good affections" and to smooth over conflict. The consequences of the failure to end, firmly and completely, the City's violation of parliamentary privilege were too soon to appear.

By the beginning of May the national crisis reached its height. The King's departure from Oxford to the Scots' Army dissipated hopes for peace, yet Parliament was no closer to finding an equitable solution for church government. The continuing religious contentions led to a new movement from within the City. At a meeting of the Common Council on April 14 notice had again been taken of the unabated growth of heresy in the kingdom.[44] After this debate the Common Council appointed a committee to prepare its own petition to Parliament. Soon, this resolution gave way to a more radical solution. With their previous appeals ignored or voted breaches of privilege, some citizens urged that a remonstrance be prepared by the Common Council.[45] This suggestion may even have come from City supporters in Parliament: "The party in the City having their instructions from Sir Philip Stapleton by Colonel Copley and Colonel Harley put them to a desperate resolution to petition no more but to put forth a remonstrance and pay no taxes and excise."[46] Even as they learned of the King's flight, the Common Council heard the first proposals to present a remonstrance to

Parliament. Opposition from leading aldermen who were uncommitted in the religious controversy was swept aside by pressure from the parliamentary Presbyterians.[47]

Early in May the Common Council began consideration of two separate remonstrances to be presented to the Houses of Parliament. Debate was fierce and acrimonious. When a councillor began his remarks with the phrase "My Lords, this Court deals unjustly with the Parliament," he was called to the bar for explanation.[48] Indeed the remonstrances aroused such controversy that discussion had to be limited to facilitate votes on specific clauses.[49] When the Council approved the first remonstrance eleven aldermen and councillors desired to enter dissents to the resolution, an unprecedented demand that renewed the bitter dispute.[50] Finally, on May 22 the remonstrances were approved and, as Juxon claimed, "Captains Jones and Bellamy went to the Lords' House and spake with My Lord General to know what day it should be delivered: who ordered it to be on Tuesday following."[51]

On Tuesday, May 26, two delegations simultaneously presented separate remonstrances to the Houses of Parliament. Alderman Kendricke brought a seventeen-point document to the House of Commons.[52] It reiterated the requests made by previous petitions that church government "according to the word of God" be established and that the sectaries and schismatics, now indiscriminately identified as independents, be repressed. Parliament's April declaration promising consideration for tender consciences was assailed for encouraging "the sectaries to expect a toleration which was contrary to the national covenant." Rather than toleration, the City demanded that "no person disaffected to the Presbyterian government . . . may be employed in any place of public trust." Besides the establishment of the church the remonstrance to the Commons touched on all areas of state affairs. The City demanded that the peace propositions be expeditiously dispatched to the King, that the union with the Scots be preserved, and that Ireland be reduced. It concluded with a number of specific grievances more properly relating to the City.[53]

Kendricke's presentation produced a lengthy debate. Whitacre recorded that the "House disliked it" and at first it was proposed that no answer be given to the petitioners.[54] Finally after two divisions it was agreed to answer only that the petition would be taken into consideration "when time shall be convenient."[55] Sir Philip

Stapleton and Sir John Clotworthy acted as tellers for the majority but they had not achieved a great victory. With parliamentary affairs again "doubtful" because of the King's flight, privilege was to be sacrificed to necessity. But the petitioners won little more than a demonstration that parliamentary privilege was as variable as the political winds that blew across the Thames. The "convenient time" during which the remonstrance would be considered was never to materialize.

Alderman Foot, the second of the City's sheriffs, led the delegation that simultaneously presented the remonstrance to the House of Lords. In light of the peers' votes on the City militia and their more favorable stance on questions of religion, this remonstrance was more concise and less strident than the one presented to the Commons.[56] Nevertheless, the Earl of Essex had done his work well. Entering the House after prayers, but in time for the arrival of the City delegation, Essex took his place with twenty-six other Lords, the single fullest sitting of the Upper House in the entire year.[57] Essex himself headed the committee appointed to prepare a response to the remonstrance. Over the dissents of nine peers, the committee's resolutions were adopted by the full House.[58] Ironically, the Lords replied that "they are well satisfied . . . with your respect to preserve the rights and privileges of the Parliament," and concluded by stating that they "give you hearty thanks for the real testimonies of duty and good affection which not only by your words, but by your actions, you have constantly manifested upon them."[59]

The May remonstrances marked a new stage in the City's assault on parliamentary politics. By remonstrating for the production of the peace propositions, the union with the Scots, and the reconquest of Ireland, the City again expanded its role in the political process. Although some clauses of the remonstrance to the Commons called for redress of actual grievances, the demands were, in essence, a statement of City policy. It set out London's own platform for a general settlement of the affairs of the nation, and not all its provisions were compatible with decisions already taken by Parliament. Indeed, the call for the elimination of opponents of presbyterianism from office went further than any previous attack on toleration. The independent Army officers were clearly one target of the City presbyterians, but Parliament too contained an assortment of "opponents of presbyterianism." In fact, the Common

Council had provided a model for the elimination of religious opponents when it attempted to oust two of its own councillors who had refused to resubscribe to the covenant.[60] Appearing at the height of political uncertainty, the remonstrances comprised an extraordinary challenge to parliamentary authority. The resolution of the Commons' debate in March, "that no corporation should receive petitions on matters before Parliament," was explicitly breached, and the belief that "parliamentary privilege is inviolable" seriously undermined.[61]

The City's more forceful participation in political decision making was also seen in the methods it adopted to press its demands. By simultaneously presenting separate remonstrances to the two Houses the City hoped to break the back of Parliament's appeals to privilege, which, in one way or another, had effectively forestalled action on the City's desires. Because parliamentary privilege must be necessarily uniform in both Houses, the reception of the initial presentation of a petition was crucial. The City had learned this lesson to its cost in March when it attempted to bypass the uncertainty of a Commons' vote by first presenting its petition to the Lords. This attempt had failed, for the Lords had claimed privilege and had reported the content of the petition to the Commons. By coordinating its activity the City forced each House to arrive at a decision independently.

London's increasing role in the affairs of the kingdom was complemented by an expansion of the function of the Common Council. In its previous petitions to Parliament the Common Council had acted as agent for the desires of its citizens, a neutral though vocal pressure group. Petitions originated outside the Council and were presented to the City government for consideration. The Common Council faithfully committed each document and just as faithfully presented them to Parliament. The remonstrances marked a departure from this procedure. They were initiated in response to religious anarchy in the City. Debates on the remonstrances revealed that the City government had abandoned all pretense of neutrality on political as well as religious matters. No longer was it simply an agent for the interests of its citizens, a fact graphically illustrated when a large contingent of Londoners presented a different type of petition to the Common Council on May 22.[62] On that day the Council had been debating the final form of their second remonstrance, and the citizens, mostly independents and supporters of toleration, had come to request that their paper be simultaneously submitted to Parliament. When they arrived, "the Lord Mayor hearing of it was willing to break up the Court."[63] Although he had eventually agreed to receive their petition, it was neither committed for consideration nor presented to Parliament. As Juxon noted, "it was in general answered that their desires were already granted (without thanks)."[64]

Unable to secure official support from the City government for their petition, these citizens presented it themselves on June 2. Although, much to the surprise of the editors of the London newsbooks, the document did not contain any reference to toleration, it did thank Parliament for all its efforts to preserve the kingdom, including the recent declaration that the religious settlement would have regard for tender consciences.[65] The independent petition was interpreted as a counter to the City remonstrances and thus resulted in controversy among City ideologues. Throughout June charges and countercharges reverberated. The opponents of the remonstrances claimed "that the City remonstrance was an act beyond the sphere of the Common Council."[66] Its adherents parried this contention by questioning the authenticity of the independent petition. One pamphleteer claimed that many who were reputed to have signed the document "never saw it," and Thomason commented that the petition had been subscribed by "Nicholas None and Simon Simple."[67] Indeed, on the day prior to its presentation to Parliament the Common Council entered into the controversy by voting its disapproval of "the clandestine manner" of gaining subscriptions to it as "prejudicial to the City, tending to sedition and to the disturbance of the peace."[68]

The City remonstrances and the Common Council's refusal to present the independent petition spurred more radical action. At the beginning of July there appeared in London "A Remonstrance of Many Thousand Citizens," a bitter denunciation of parliamentary policy.[69] This "Remonstrance" was produced to protest the imprisonment of Lieutenant Colonel John Lilburne by the House of Lords, but it also was written within the context of the City's challenge to parliamentary authority. The proposals of these remonstrants and those of the City government were diametrically opposed: where the City had called for a recomposition with the King, the "many thousand citizens" demanded his deposition; when the City championed presbyterianism, the citizens' desired toleration; and where the City defended its just liberties the citizens called for an end to special privilege. Yet for all of this, the methods of aldermen and radical Londoners were the same – remonstrances superseded petitions. The City's own experience formed part of the radicals' justification for their action: "We can scarcely approach your door with a request or motion, though by way of petition, but you hold long debates, whether we break not your privileges; the King's or the Lords' pretended prerogatives never made a greater noise, nor was made more dreadful than the name of privilege of the House of Commons."[70] The observation of the *Moderate Intelligencer* the previous November had now proven prophetic: "We have seen this by experience, the strange effects of petitions."[71]

The challenge to Parliament posed by the City of London comprised only one part of the spring crisis. In increasing its pressure for a role in political decision making the City adopted an established and orderly procedure. Although the nature of its relationship to Parliament changed during the course of their confrontation, the legitimacy of the Common Council's appeals to Parliament and the legality of petitions were unquestionable. City petitions to Parliament were justified not by London's constancy to the cause, but by ancient privilege and historical precedent. Indeed, the recognition of the City's liberties enabled the Houses to draw the line between custom and abuse, a factor that did much to soften their responses to the Common Council's requests. The City's campaign, however, encouraged other elements among Parliament's supporters to press their own desires in the settlement of the affairs of the nation. Chief among these were the Scots, whose outcries for the establishment of a godly church were even more clamorous than those voiced by the London government. To the Scots, Parliament's delay in establishing true religion was a scandal and their rejection of *jure divino* presbyterianism a national affront.

Yet, unlike the City's representative function, the Scottish role in political affairs derived solely from the exigencies of the war. Their claims to participate in political decision making rested upon their contribution to the war effort, the value of which was bitterly contested. The Scots believed, the accomplishment of their Army notwithstanding, that the terms of the Solemn League and Covenant gave them a voice in the future government of the two nations. But a voice was not a platform; despite their Commissioners in London the Scots lacked a formal role in the political process. Their participation came only through influence among the Committee of Both Kingdoms, the Westminster Assembly, London ministers, and the Common Council. To these bodies the Scots first presented their terms for the establishment of religion and the settlement of the peace. Their exclusion from the preparation of the Newcastle proposals and the failure of the Assembly and the Common Council to attain the Scots' goals led the Commissioners to a desperate appeal to public opinion – an appeal that constituted another assault upon parliamentary politics.

The participation of the Scottish Army in the war necessitated the establishment of formal channels of communication between the two nations. By providing military assistance the Scots gained an acknowledged but unspecified voice in resolving the contentions between the King and his Parliament. The Solemn League and Covenant contained an agreement that the Parliaments of the two nations would "maintain good correspondence" and shortly after the conclusion of the treaty the Estates in Edinburgh appointed a group of Commissioners to reside in London and represent Scottish interests. At Westminster, the English Parliament established the Committee of Both Kingdoms, a quasi-executive council entrusted with the deliberation of military and political affairs, whose members included some of these Scottish Commissioners.[72] But as the Committee of Both Kingdoms was subordinate to the Houses of Parliament, so were the Scottish Commissioners dependent upon the Estates in Edinburgh, a parallel structure of communication that left the Commissioners twice removed from the ultimate source of decision making. To further complicate their function, the Scottish representatives in London funneled a steady stream of information from the continuous sessions of Parliament at Westminster to a body in Edinburgh that met briefly and infrequently.

At the Committee of Both Kingdoms the Scottish Commissioners eagerly supported measures designed to expedite a military victory. Initially they backed the English committeemen who were committed to the war effort, but soon they found these men opposed to the Scottish church platform. During the crisis of the winter of 1644 they had sought an alliance with the Earl of Essex and Sir Philip Stapleton but at that time the Committee was fully occupied with the establishment of the new Army. Military reorganization increased the importance of the Scottish Army and provided an opportunity to bolster Scottish influence. As Robert Baillie wrote in his public letter on April 25, 1645: "None needs talk of any fickleness or ungratitude of the English towards us, of any advancement of the Independent party; for no man here doubts, but if once our Army were in such a condition as easily, if we were diligent, it might be, all these clouds would vanish, and we would regain this people's heart, and do with all sectaries, and all things else, what we would."[73] The failure of the Scottish Army to contribute to the victory at Naseby and the subsequent triumph of the New Model closed even this avenue to power and influence. During the summer of 1645, through the Cranford affair, the Scots had eagerly embraced an alliance with Essex, Holles, and Stapleton, but it was a partnership to which they brought very little. The failures of their army and the rigidity of their church by then had been proved to be political liabilities.

The diminution of Scottish influence at the Committee of Both Kingdoms, indeed the demise of the Committee after the western campaign, was paralleled by the inability of the Scots to affect decisions at the Westminster Assembly. In the Assembly the Scots had taken a leading role in providing the model for church government. Convinced that the presbyterian establishment ordained by Scripture had been achieved by the Kirk, they pressed the Assembly to adopt its structure and doctrine. In many of their specific demands they were opposed by English presbyterians as well as by the few independent ministers known as the "dissenting brethren." After a year of theological debate they finally realized that Scottish presbyterianism would not be accepted without alterations. By the winter of 1644 their main objective had become the prevention of a toleration for sects within an English presbyterian system. In this the Scots were backed by the majority of the Assembly's members, and when Parliament had ordered the establishment of a committee for accommodation a number of Scottish divines, including the intractable Baillie, had been appointed to it. In the winter of 1645 Parliament revived its plans for an accommodation and Baillie and his Scottish colleagues on the committee blocked consideration of a proposal for toleration of tender consciences. Only threats from their parliamentary allies persuaded the Scots to allow the debates to be held, but no amount of political pressure could weaken their opposition.[74] Even when the pragmatic English presbyterians deserted them, the Scots held the line. "Mr. Marshall our chairman," Baillie wrote after one particularly frustrating meeting, "has been their most diligent agent, to draw too many of us to grant them more than my heart can yield to, and which to my power I oppose."[75]

The disintegration of Scottish influence was emphatically evidenced in the debates over the Newcastle proposals. After the victory at Naseby, in July 1645, the Scottish Commissioners formally requested Parliament to resume negotiations with the King.[76] For five months the Houses took no action on this request, and it was not until the King submitted his own plea for the dispatch of propositions that Parliament determined not to negotiate but to send bills to be signed into law. The Scots were curtly informed of this resolve and their objections to it ignored.[77] Parliament advised the Commissioners that "although the Houses have sometimes conferred with your lordships before their resolutions, yet they always had, and have the liberty in business of this nature to make their resolutions within themselves."[78] Although the Commissioners continued to submit papers to Parliament representing Scottish positions on the militia, the church, and the role of their Army in Ireland, none of their suggestions was incorporated into the draft clauses that passed the two Houses. At the end of February the first sections of the completed proposals were sent to the Estates in Edinburgh for approval.[79] The Commissioners' lengthy objections to the severity of Parliament's terms were not considered by the Houses until after the final sections of the proposals were concluded.[80] By then, the King's flight to their Army gave the Scots a surreptitious opportunity to press their own conditions upon Charles. Their failure to gain the King's approval for a presbyterian church settlement was a significant factor in the Commons' decision to dispense with Scottish approval of the completed propositions. At the end of June the Lower House determined that the Scots should have no role in approving terms for the settlement of peace in England.[81]

The exclusion of the Scots from formal participation in parliamentary decision making was not so much a rupture in relations between the nations as it was a reflection of the events of the spring. Even before the rift over the proposals in January, the Scots had begun to exert pressure upon Parliament through their influence in the presbyterian enclaves of London. Without a formal role in the political system the Scots were unconstrained in the avenues they chose to follow in pressing their wishes. While the Common Council warily fenced with Parliament over rights and privileges, the Scots wielded a broadsword in their efforts to establish *jure divino* presbyterianism. In this their lack of a defined position was their chief advantage. The rise of erastianism in the House of Commons effectively diminished Scottish influence upon Parliament's settlement of the church government, "the principal ground of their engagement in this cause."[82] As Baillie wrote in January 1646, echoing a belief he had held since the first debates on ministerial power in April 1645, the House of Commons was composed of three groups of opponents to Scottish interests: the Independents, the lawyers, and "the worldly profane men." "These three kinds making up two parts at least of the Parliament, there is no hope that ever they will settle the government according to our mind if they were left to themselves."[83] Neither Baillie nor his confederates had any intention of leaving Parlament "to themselves" in the critical matter of settling the church.

In their efforts to influence the settlement of religion, then, the Scots proceeded upon two assumptions: that the English could be persuaded to accept the Scottish model for church government, and that Parliament could be pressured into enacting it. Thus the Scots' campaign centered upon converting public opinion and influencing institutions that could, in turn, influence Parliament. To achieve their first objective the Scots exploited the numerous outlets established in the wake of the puritan upheaval. The proliferation of sermons, particularly for fasts and extraordinary occasions like public humiliations and thanksgivings, and the abandonment of the harsh licensing regulations of the Stationers Company, created unprecedented opportunity for doctrinal debate. In London the Scottish Commissioners and the divines appointed to the Assembly used every occasion in pulpit and press to exhort their audiences to embrace the religion of the Kirk. They championed the publication of presbyterian tracts and led an intense doctrinal battle against sectarianism. Their pressure upon the House of Commons, necessarily more covert, came through the London Common Council and the House of Lords. In these bodies the Scots employed varying techniques ranging from official presentations to clandestine meetings in an effort to gain recognition and appproval for their religious proposals.

These interconnected campaigns were led by Robert Baillie, the most active of the Scots in residence in London. Along with Samuel Rutherford, Baillie provided the most sustained Scottish attack upon toleration in the press, and in company with George Gillespie, the most eloquent appeals for *jure divino* presbyterianism from the pulpit. In his intimate relations with the other Scottish Commissioners and his connections with the London ministry he tied together the strands of the Scottish program. Beginning with his arrival in London in November 1643, Baillie had established himself as an implacable opponent of toleration. In July 1645, after Cromwell's appeal for toleration of the opinions of the "honest men" who had served Parliament so well, the debate over toleration reached its peak. For its July fast the House of Commons had appointed the moderate Thomas Coleman to further Cromwell's ecumenical appeal. "The presbyterian way and those that walk therein," Coleman affirmed, "I embrace and love. The congregational way and those that practice it," he added, "I approve and honor."[84] But in the House of Lords on that day it was Baillie who had taken up the cudgels against diversity in religious opinion, and more particularly against toleration for independents. "Independency is a sin which opens the door to all error," he had instructed the peers in a most provocative sermon, "Errors and Induration are the great sin and the great judgment of the Time."[85] The ferocity of Baillie's attack upon toleration was almost unequaled, and among hard-line presbyterians his sermon had been an enormous success. Throughout the autumn, in high spirits over his initial triumph and driven by his obsession to maintain the purity of presbyterianism, Baillie had labored on his magnum opus, *A Dissuasive from the Errors of the Time*.[86]

Baillie's writings and sermons were only a part of his campaign of persuasion. He eagerly promoted publication of works that would have an immediate impact upon the doctrinal disputes in the Westminister Assembly. From London he assessed the potential of the work of the most prominent Scottish theologians: "I wish you might put Forbes to go on with his history, especially of the Anabaptists, libertines and such as presently vex us," he wrote to the Reverend William Spang in January 1646.[87] With Spang coordinating his efforts in Scotland, Baillie directed the work of a group of Scottish disputants. "We are longing for Apollonius against Erastus," he wrote to Spang in April. "It were good to put

Spanheim on the Anabaptists; for that is the predominant sect here. I wrote to you to use means to make Vossius print the treatise against them . . . also that you would speak with Forbes to go on with his book and to use diligence against our perfect sects here."[88] Besides this work, Baillie was busy distributing copies of trenchant English presbyterian tracts where they might do the most good. He reserved special praise for Edward's *Gangraena*, "which must either waken the Parliament and all others to lay to heart the spreading of the evil errors, or I know not what can do it," and made several attempts to have it distributed in Edinburgh.[89] In all these efforts Baillie believed that in the struggle for men's minds he was but one battle away from victory.

Baillie, of course, was not alone in believing in the persuasive power of the Scottish position. Yet the appeal to the example of the "best reformed church" lost much of its vigor with the failure of the Scottish Army to make significant military contributions. Throughout the autumn of 1645 complaints against its soldiers were heard in the House of Commons and repeated in the London newsbooks. "The Scots . . . care not to have the war ended nor are willing to return to water and oatmeal," was one of Thomas Juxon's more bitter observations.[90] Criticisms were also made of the Scots' overzealous attempts to attain the establishment of their model for church government. Such charges not only denigrated Scottish efforts and achievements, they also diminished the effectiveness of their campaign for presbyterianism. In their official capacity the Commissioners in London could not act to counter these accusations except to remind Parliament of the financial needs of their forces and of the moral commitment to establish reformed religion that the English had made. This defense, submitted in private papers, could not dispel public discussion of Scottish activity. Thus a more public defense from a less public figure was necessary. To fill this need emerged David Buchanan, a young, unknown Scotsman who most probably acted as a front through which the Commissioners themselves responded to charges against Scottish conduct.[91]

Buchanan's first defense, *A Short and True Relation*, appeared at the beginning of the agitation against the conduct of the Scottish Army, in September 1645. *The Relation*, belying at least its claim to brevity, chronicled the achievements of the Scottish forces in England and stressed their important contributions at Marston

Moor and Newcastle during the campaign of 1644. Although Buchanan professed to write "without unjust partiality or base siding with any faction," his exoneration of the Scots was achieved by downplaying the contributions of Cromwell and the "Independents."[92] The *Relation* was followed some months later by two other attempts to restore Scottish credibility, *Truth Its Manifest* and *An Explanation of Some Truths*. These were concerned with complaints against Scottish efforts to establish presbyterianism. As Buchanan stated in his introduction to *An Explanation,* he intended to refute charges that "the Scots pursue too rigidly the settling of the church; . . . that they press too much for peace . . . and that they stand so much for royalty."[93] Again the Scots were defended by exposing the "true" intentions of the independents who, Buchanan contended, were opposed to religion and the monarchy.[94] The blame for the conduct of the Scottish Army was also shifted, this time to Parliament, whose failure to provide money and supply was identified as the primary cause of the Scots' inability to conclude the fighting in the north. The danger of these public appeals was quickly perceived at Westminster, where Nathaniel Fiennes began *Vindiciae Veritatis*, a reply to *Truth Its Manifest*. Fiennes condemned Buchanan's publications for "inviting the people to take notice of the proceedings of Parliament, and if they be not such as give them content, to remonstrate against them and enforce that which they approve of, or else let the Parliament know, as they have entrusted them, so they can, when they please, reassume that power which they gave them."[95]

These public appeals were designed to aid the burgeoning relationship between the Scots and the City government. Already the Commissioners had strong ties with London's presbyterian ministry and their campaign for the establishment of "true religion." Indeed the petitions that emanated from the ministers and were presented to Parliament by the Common Council in the winter of 1645 were the single bright prospect in the dim view the Scots took of the settlement of the English church. "The City continues zealous for to press their petition," wrote Baillie in an otherwise glum report at the end of November 1645. "More hope we have from them than ever."[96] As a result of the failures of their Army and their exclusion from official deliberations the Scots had come to depend upon the City's ability to effect change. When the Assembly's opposition to the lay commissioners was set aside by the

House of Commons in March 1646, Baillie frankly discounted the effect of petitions from the Assembly or the Scottish Commissioners. "That which, by God's help, may prove most effectual, is the zeal of the City."[97] The conjunction in their desire for church government was strengthened when London became the direct source of funds for the Scottish Army. But as he had earlier mistaken the role of the Westminster Assembly, Baillie now overestimated the influence of the City's government. Misled by the intensity of the presbyterian ministers and the affluence of London's financiers, the Scots came to assume that the Common Council could achieve parity with Parliament. "No doubt, if they be constant, they will obtain all their desires; for all know the Parliament here cannot subsist without London; so whatsoever they desire in earnest, and constantly, it must be granted."[98]

This fundamental misunderstanding of the nature of English government led the Scots to bolster the City's contest with Parliament over privileges. When the House of Commons had resolved to contract the jurisdiction of the London militia committee the Scottish Commissioners had leaped at the opportunity of creating a *cause célèbre* that might provide the means for securing *jure divino* presbyterianism. "The City is much grieved," Baillie observed, "that what was before granted to them should now be taken away. This controversy makes them more willing to look into the ways of the sectaries."[99] Nor was he alone in this assessment. The Commissioners hastily dispatched a request to Edinburgh that an official proclamation be sent from Scotland to the London government.[100] Their intention was to thank the City for its faithful adherence to religion and to encourage it to continue its efforts. In February 1646 Lord Lauderdale delivered the letter from the Estates to the Common Council with a speech effusive in its admiration for the City's former affections to the Scots and ecstatic in its visions for their future association.[101]

Such overt activity as this letter to the Common Council was uncommon in the Scots' attempts to influence parliamentary decisions. Only their misapprehension of the relationship between City and Parliament and their miscalculation of the significance of the militia controversy had led the Scots openly to flaunt their attempts at political persuasion. With Scottish stock at Westminster nearly worthless, public meddling in parliamentary affairs was a bankrupt strategy. More typically, the Scots attempted to exert private influence behind the scenes, using English allies whose reputations were above suspicion.

These clandestine efforts were exemplified in the documented case of Baillie's maneuvers to prevent the passage of the bill to create lay commissioners. Parliament's decision to establish local commissioners to oversee the coercive power of the ministers was a compromise designed to defuse the controversy over suspension from the sacraments. The Houses were unwilling to allow the presbyteries autonomous powers of suspension, whereas the presbyterian leaders opposed direct parliamentary control. More than any other aspect of the new church, the lay commissioners were anathema to the Scots, who believed that they would effectively prevent the synods and provincial assemblies from establishing doctrinal orthodoxy and would enable independents and sectaries to control individual congregations.

When Baillie learned that the House of Commons intended to approve the compromise that would establish the commissioners he made every effort to block its final passage. If London could be rallied to reject the Commissioners Baillie believed that the compromise would disintegrate. Therefore he sought out his chief associate among the London ministers, Francis Roberts, and warned him of the Commons' impending decision and its consequences. "If your burgesses have allowance, yea, were it but a connivance, from the City to name these commissioners, they will be received in the whole Kingdom."[102] Roberts assured Baillie that the Common Council had no intention of accepting the Commissioners, an assurance that countered information Baillie was receiving from other sources.[103] Nor could Baillie rest easy after the news that the London ministry had the matter well in hand. He again solicited Roberts, this time with a plan to prevent the passage of the compromise in the House of Lords. Informed by the presbyterian M.P.s Francis Rous and Zouch Tate that the peers might reject the Commissioners and give the presbyteries full power of adjudication, Baillie plotted with Roberts to enlist the aid of another London minister, Simeon Ashe. Ashe, chaplain to the Earl of Manchester, would obtain a copy of the ordinance from Manchester before it was debated by the peers so that Baillie, through Roberts and Ashe, could advise the Earl, whose role as Speaker could be turned to advantage, on the precise nature of the amendments the Scots desired. "I am very hopeful that his Lordship will do his uttermost endeavor to make the House of Lords assent, not only to the mentioned amendment, but to others which you might find necessary to move on the sight of the ordinance," Baillie wrote.[104] Needless to say, neither Baillie's frenzied instructions to Roberts – "strike the iron while it is hot!" – nor his elaborate preparations prevented the passage of the ordinance establishing the lay commissioners.

The failure of their campaigns to persuade the people and to influence Parliament clandestinely led the Scots to combine their activities in one final effort. Now that the church had been erected without regard to their opposition, the Scots focused their attention upon the impending votes to establish peace. Excluded from the deliberations and unable to sway more than a handful of M.P.s, the Scots resolved upon a direct appeal to the English people, an appeal that they hoped would spur opposition to the hardening of Parliament's terms. In April 1646 through their agent David Buchanan, the Commissioners arranged for the publication of their many objections to Parliament's peace propositions.[105] This would inform the English nation of Parliament's stiffer conditions and refute accusations that the Scots were delaying the propositions by unnecessary and time-consuming amendments. "The delay of sending the propositions, of late hath busied the fancies and tongues of most men," the Commissioners wrote, "who do make it at this time the ordinary theme of their discourses which everyone frames right or wrong as he is carried by interest."[106] By presenting their own amendments the Scots hoped that their readers would recognize the justness of their position and pressure Parliament to accept it. Consequently, the paper carefully set out each area of disagreement between the two nations, presenting Scottish willingness to compromise against a background of English obduracy. It was organized to demonstrate that Parliament, rather than the Scots, had continually delayed the propositions.

At Westminster the intention of the Scottish publication was clearly perceived. Its preamble, which openly declared the differences between the nations, was judged scandalous and the entire paper was ordered burned by the common hangman.[107] Although Parliament could hardly condemn the Commissioners' papers, their out-of-context publication, ignoring the many conferences between the representatives of the two nations, was unsettling. An official examination of the pamphlet's printing revealed that the Commissioners' clerk, John Chiesley, had been instrumental in delivering both the papers and the preamble to the printer, and that Buchanan's authorship was merely a front. The House of Commons authorized the arrest of both Chiesley and Buchanan, but they had already fled the City and the Commissioners refused to assist in their apprehension.[108] Indeed, the Scots regarded the entire venture as a great success. Baillie recorded that "in two days or three, three or four thousand of these papers were sold. They gave immediately to the people as great satisfaction with our proceedings as was marvellous."[109] Not only had their persuasive purpose been achieved, but the pressure they had hoped to exert upon Parliament was also manifested. "The House of Lords, we hear, have agreed to cause [to] burn the Epistle and the state of the question prefixed to our papers but not the papers themselves," the Commissioners wrote to the Committee of Estates in Edinburgh, adding that the decision to condemn those parts of the publication "was carried by one vote and that was the Lord Saye's proxy."[110]

The Scots' appeals to public opinion and the continued petitions from the City of London finally brought the members of Parliament to a realization that their institution was under attack. By April 1646 the members of the House of Commons awoke to the fact that they too would have to resort to a public explanation of their conduct, both to clear the air of hostility and suspicion and to justify the continuation of parliamentary rule. In "A Declaration of the Commons of England Assembled in Parliament" they set forth "their true intentions concerning the ancient and fundamental government of the Kingdom; the government of the church; the present peace; securing the people against all arbitrary government; and maintaining a right understanding between the two Kingdoms of England and Scotland."[111] In the "Declaration" the Commons affirmed their commitment to the recently erected church government and to the establishment of peace, detailing the progress that had been made on both fronts. They pledged never to alter "the fundamental constitution and government of this Kingdom, by King, Lords, and Commons," and promised to preserve the rights and privileges of the nation by opposing all arbitrary government.[112] The "Declaration" was ordered to be distributed in every county and a copy was to be posted in every parish church by the churchwardens.[113]

The publication of the Commons' "Declaration" was the most cogent expression of the success of the combined assaults on parliamentary politics. The necessity to affirm the unspoken obligations of a Parliament to its people and to defend actions that should not be "prejudged nor precipitated, nor any interpretation placed upon them," clearly portrayed the crisis of authority that Parliament faced. "Our actions and proceedings from time to time, since the beginning of this Parliament and particularly the managing of this great cause are the best demonstrations of our sincerity and faithfulness to the public," the House of Commons asserted.[114]

The efforts of these elements of the parliamentary cause to influence political policy and decision making had wide-ranging effects. Because neither City nor Scots immediately achieved their aims it is easy to overlook the impact of their separate assaults on the parliamentary process. The City's insistence upon expanding its traditional rights and the Scots' willingness to engage in extra-parliamentary activities were the first great breaches in the wall of parliamentary sovereignty. Quickly they were followed by appeals from radical Londoners and eventually they formed a backdrop to the Army's politicization. Moreover, City petitions and Scottish public appeals had succeeded in dividing the two Houses and hardening the parliamentary factions. In the following months, as both Scots and City gained importance, their challenges to parliamentary government were reinterpreted as adherence and faithfulness to the cause. Soon Denzil Holles would consolidate his position in power by coopting the goals of these external pressure groups. But the old was not yet ready to give way to the new. Parliament's need for City finance had not yet became total dependency and the Scots had yet to exploit their last political lever – control of the King. Most significantly, the Houses continued to hope to find agreement with Charles, agreement that would restore the balance of government and alleviate the unbearable institutional pressure they now experienced. Spring had not brought the rebirth of a united English government, but parliamentary politics had withstood the combined assault of City and Scots. Its collapse awaited the darkness of another uncertain winter.

PART II

Parliament Eclipsed

And the soldiers demanded of John saying, and what shall we do? And he said unto them, do violence to no man, neither accuse any falsely; and be content with your wages.

Luke 3:14

Chapter 5

THE COLLAPSE OF
PARLIAMENTARY POLITICS

In all ages those who sought their own greatness have always
sought to diminish the power of Parliament.[1]

———————

The Civil War ended with the failure of the Newcastle propositions. The struggle between the monarch and his subjects, though
inconclusive, had resulted in an unprecedented expansion of the
powers and responsibilities of the Houses of Parliament. Deserted
by the King, proprietor of executive and administrative duties, the
body of legislative consultants had acquired the full scope of civil
power. But neither they nor their supporters yet translated de facto
jurisdiction into de jure authority. Parliament made no claims to
supremacy and had no pretensions to self-sufficiency. For four years
the justification of Parliament's rule had been its single-minded effort to achieve accommodation with the King and to reunite the
institutions of government. "My principles," averred Sir William
Waller in order to demonstrate his steadfast adherence to them,
"were grounded upon the public interest, and had no other ends
than what are laid down in the Declarations of Parliament, and the
national league and covenant; that religion might be reformed and
maintained; the person, dignity, and honor of the King preserved,
and the peace and safety of the Kingdom settled."[2] The formations
of armies, the treaty with the Scots, the imposition of taxation, indeed the entire superstructure of centralized local administration
were expedients to deal with the crisis of war. Even the transfor-
mations of Parliament's time-honored procedures were adaptations
to the peculiar circumstances of legislative government.

   With the end of the war the abuses of parliamentary committees,
the burdens of parliamentary taxation, and the ravages of parliamentary armies were not to be reformed – they were to be abolished. Thus in July 1646 when the House of Commons examined
the conduct of the Committee of Examinations it was concluded
"that because all things now tended toward peace" Parliament's

standing committees could be eliminated.[3] Only the promise of a reunited constitutional government had prevented the complete collapse of parliamentary politics. The preparation of the peace propositions in the spring of 1646 tore at the fabric of the parliamentary process, producing an institutional crisis and a *crise de conscience* for the men at Westminster. Neither could be prolonged without hardening expedients into policy and change into revolution.

By refusing Parliament's terms Charles did more than dash hopes and disappoint dreams. No longer could the parliamentarians pose as caretakers for an ill-advised monarch or as defenders of an unprotected people. If the war had not ended, at least the fighting had. The extralegal arms of wartime administration – Parliament's standing committees, regional associations, and county committees – and the extraordinary exactions of wartime finance – the monthly assessments and the excise – now needed reform or abolition under the scrutiny of the nation. The reins of government must finally be seized; policy to suppress the rebellion in Ireland, to remove the Scottish army from England, and to determine the future of the New Model Army needed formulation. More vexing still, and most symbolic of the constitutional transformation, the fate of the King would have to be determined. Imprisonment, deposition, execution: each option was equally untenable. Although the first would be accepted, the second discussed, and the third would eventually come to pass, none could easily be assimilated by men who had sincerely struggled to preserve the King and the monarchy. The Earl of Essex's dictum that there was "nothing now to be done but to disband the armies and conclude a peace; and that rather than they would consent to make the King a prisoner, they would all die" was less a formulation of policy than a poignant expression of frustration.[4] Shortly, the King would be imprisoned as part of a coordinated program initiated by Essex's parliamentary supporters. Charles's unwillingness to accept Parliament's terms and resume his lawful governance meant that, for the moment, he must be set aside. Thus the first step toward permanent legislative government – the intentional rule of the nation without the monarch – was not taken by those thought to be radicals or revolutionaries, but by others, solicitous of the King's goodwill, whose adherence to traditional political order and whose conduct during the war earned them the opprobrious title "the peace party."

The collapse of parliamentary politics

The failure to achieve a settlement with the King, the near break with the Scots, and the increased and increasing controversy over religion all had profound impact upon Parliament. After six months of deliberations none of the courses adopted by the two Houses had brought the nation any closer to peace. For the first time the possibility was raised that Parliament might not be able to settle the affairs of the kingdom. The struggle to find solutions to these problems strained parliamentary procedure and heightened tensions and frustrations among M.P.s. By the spring of 1646 this was even apparent in Parliament's day-to-day activities. The factions, which had arisen out of personal quarrels and a superficial disagreement over the manner of negotiating with the King, now found themselves separated by the substantive issues of peace and religion. Relations between the two Houses, which had smoothed over since the crisis of self-denial, again showed signs of deteriorating. Within the House of Commons increases in the number of divisions and committees exemplified the lack of executive control and pointed to the emergence of party conflict.

The development of political parties and the manifestation of their struggle resulted from the pressing decisions that appeared simultaneously in the last half of 1646. Both the parties and their policies were in large part responses to the various crises of the moment, the most significant being the King's flight to the Scots' Army. Their contentions and tactics were only the harbingers of party conflict. Without effective executive control Parliament experienced continuous strains upon its procedure and practice. Under the pressure of decision making the emergence of party politics was tolerated and unconsciously encouraged. As long as the parties struggled to find a settlement of the affairs of the nation they appeared, like the standing committees, a natural outgrowth of the crisis of war whose abuses could be checked. As long as they remained configurations of men and issues *within* Parliament, the parties posed little threat to the tasks that faced both Houses.

But the failure to achieve accommodation left government in the hands of those capable of resolving the new crises that arose from the undeclared peace. Foremost among these was the recovery of the King and the withdrawal of the Scottish Army. The urgency of preventing the King from contriving a military alliance that would result in renewed wars was apparent to all. For

once the Scots possessed a bargaining card of value, which they played with skill. Although they sought an agreement with Charles for the establishment of presbyterianism within the two kingdoms, they also negotiated with the English to barter the King for payment of their army's arrears. To the solution of these unrelated problems Holles, Stapleton, and, until his death in September, Essex could contribute most. For over a year, at considerable cost, they had defended Scottish interests against vociferous attacks upon the conduct of their Army. Now that delicate negotiations with the Scots were Parliament's primary concern, this political alliance buoyed their claims for parliamentary leadership. Moreover, their position was further strengthened by ties to the government of the City of London – an alliance cultivated by support for the City's petitions and programs for religious reformation. Thus through their ability to negotiate and finance Scottish withdrawal Holles, Essex, and their supporters gained control of political policy. From this initiative they would soon achieve hegemony in directing the conduct of Irish affairs. But for the first time since the outbreak of war political supremacy within the Houses of Parliament rested upon support from outside political groups.

The power struggle for political ascendency in the Commons centralized party conflict whereas the support given by outside pressure groups consolidated party organization. The cost of both developments was the demise of the unified parliamentary cause. To achieve their immediate goals Holles and Stapleton encouraged further assaults upon parliamentary privilege by their political allies. The religious programs of the City and the monetary demands of the Scots were sanctioned as means to higher political ends. Parliamentary procedure was adapted to facilitate political control of the Lower House. Finally, to finance the Scottish withdrawal and the Irish invasion, the reallocation of wealth, reluctantly initiated during the war, was continued. In the Commons Holles and Stapleton organized the auction of the church's episcopal lands and their programs unwittingly fueled the agitation for the sale of delinquents' estates.

These policies brought the Commons into increasing conflict with the Upper House. There justifications for protracted parliamentary rule were complicated by concern over the usurpations of power by the Commons. Parliamentary government, especially as practiced by local authorities like the county committees, was an attenuation of the individual and collective power of the peers. In the House of Lords there coalesced a group of peers opposed to the extension of political innovations and throughout the autumn of 1646 they directed their efforts against the two institutions that most diminished the traditional powers of the aristocracy: the county committees and the parliamentary armies. Against the former they launched a determined campaign, drafting an ordinance for the suppression of the committees and refusing to sanction the regional associations, which were attenuations of the county committees' powers. Against the armies their action was rearguard, delaying consideration of continuing orders and finance bills and refusing all attempts at compromise.

These differing responses to the prolongation of parliamentary government produced confusion at Westminster. The resolve of the anti-innovatory peers to dam the stream of political decision making created bitter controversy between the Houses and the threat of unicameral government. In the Lower House party conflict was manifested by the disintegration of orderly procedure. Without the King or his armies to unify it, and without the anticipation of the resumption of constitutional government to restrain it, the parliamentary cause was shattered. The first victim of this divisiveness was the political process by which Parliament had governed. Although to the royalists these contentions were but the falling out of thieves, to the parliamentarians it was the honor among them that was most in jeopardy.

Parliament's propositions had been rejected. The bright prospects of peace that appeared with the summer's sun ended in glaring disappointment. On August 13, 1646, the two Houses held a conference to reflect upon the implications of the King's action. Decisions deferred in expectation of Charles's impending restoration now had to be taken and, as the conference made clear, the importance of Parliament's Scottish allies was magnified by their possession of the monarch.[5] To repair relations that had deteriorated during the previous year the representatives of the Houses discussed measures to provide payment for the Scottish Army and prepared a draft of a declaration proclaiming the great affection the Scots had shown the parliamentary cause. The Lords had already moved to suppress printed attacks against the conduct of the Scots' Army and, overcoming intense anger toward Scottish activity in the north, the Commons agreed to these concessions.[6] On August 15 the Lower House voted to provide £100,000 for the Scottish Army if they would relinquish the seven northern garrisons they held and return home.[7] The money and conditions were offered to the Scottish Commissioners, who, recognizing the strength of their position, flatly rejected them as "inconceivable." Instead they submitted their own conditions for the withdrawal of their Army, agreeing to the principle of a lump-sum payment, but setting the figure at £1,800,000, a figure achieved by calculating the full cost of their employment since 1643. They neglected to consider that their Army had never reached full strength and, adding insult to injury, allowed only £50,000 for the years of free quarter taken in the north.[8]

Although the necessity of removing the Scots and retrieving the King was great, the temerity of the Scottish Commissioners' proposal made the task of Holles and Stapleton more difficult. The profuse attestations of harmony between the nations and the suppression of factual accounts of Scottish conduct in the north had already incensed members of the Commons, and the Commissioners' conduct added oil to the fire. When negotiations were resumed and John Crewe reported that the Commissioners might settle for as little as £500,000, the House voted without division to offer only £200,000.[9] By September, however, Holles and Stapleton had persuaded the Commons to vote a total of £400,000.[10] To achieve this concession it was agreed to provide an initial payment of £100,000 and to disburse the remainder over two years. But even these attempts to hold the House together were scotched by the Commissioners, who demanded a down payment of £200,000. "We much resent this," recorded Harington, observing that Holles was extremely "nettled" when the House refused to concede the Scottish demands.[11] When the Commons adhered to their offer and the Scots to their demand, Holles and Stapleton carried another close division, by 10 in a House of 214, to break the deadlock.[12] In exchange for the withdrawal of their Army and the return of the King the Scots would receive £400,000, half as an initial payment. When the Houses of Parliament recessed, Denzil Holles made his way to London to secure a loan.

The £200,000 Parliament sought from the City of London was only part of the extraordinary expenditures authorized during the summer of 1646. The lack of coherent policy making and effective administrative control was particularly noticeable in the area of parliamentary finance. Two months before the Houses had agreed to the Scots' demands, which were truly a King's ransom, they had committed themselves to an even costlier adventure – an invasion of Ireland. This grandiose scheme had begun on a smaller scale with an order for the Committee of Irish Affairs to raise and equip three regiments. To finance this first wave of the assault the Commons had resolved to sell £20,000 worth of estates of delinquents who had been excepted from the general pardon.[13] By this means they hoped to create a new source of revenue to fill their depleted coffers. "The fatal ordinance to sell men's estates," Sir Simonds D'Ewes called it more than once in 1645 when the issue was first raised, and he was not alone in opposition.[14] The consequences of depriving mostly noble families of their patrimonies were acutely discerned in the House of Lords. The peers had refused to consider the measure in 1645 and remained adamant, even in the face of urgent economic necessity. When Robert Reynolds had pleaded for the Lords' assent – "If Ireland be lost, which is to be supplied by this ordinance; if the Armies be not paid their arrears and so not disbanded; if the creditors that have lent monies for the public affairs be not satisfied they [the Commons] did and would hold themselves blameless" – they had protested his immoderate speech, read the ordinance twice, and allowed it to be buried under a mass of other business.[15] Not only was the Committee for Irish Affairs unable to supply the regiments it had been directed to raise, but it soon found itself incapable of repaying its earlier debts. On July 30 the Committee's members and the City M.P.s went bareheaded to Weavers' Hall, seeking an extension for repayment of £40,000 borrowed in September 1645.[16]

Although the charges for the Irish venture and the Scottish withdrawal were extraordinary, they revealed Parliament's precarious fiscal situation. For years the structure of parliamentary finance had tottered and solvency had been maintained through excessive borrowing and the accumulation of arrears. Without a central organ for financial administration Parliament was unable to control its overlapping and contradictory obligations. The chief sources of revenue were the excise, designed for administrative and emergency expenses, and the monthly assessments to fund the armies and regional associations. Additionally, at Goldsmiths' Hall Parliament received the compositions of delinquents, which during the previous two years had amounted to almost £70,000.[17] In theory this division of income and expenditure enabled Parliament to discharge all its financial obligations, but in practice it did not. Neither the excise nor the assessments ever yielded their anticipated revenue. By 1644 the commissioners to whom the excise was farmed had been chosen on the basis of their ability to provide a large down payment – what amounted to an entry fine on the national revenue.[18] The failure of the monthly assessment to maintain the New Model resulted in the borrowing of additional large sums. Although the armies of the Scots and the Associations were never ordinarily important enough to warrant such extraordinary measures, at times of crisis the associations or their individual towns and garrisons were granted the use of their excise collections for military maintenance.

The failure of the monthly assessments to equal the costs of the war left Parliament wholly dependent upon the excise and whatever new schemes it could develop to raise money. Yet the excise was not unencumbered. On July 17 the Commons had ordered £50,000 borrowed against the excise to offset the cost of deploying troops for Ireland. This loan was to be repaid with 8-percent interest compounded semiannually. When on July 23 the Lower House ordered the disbandment of Massey's marauding brigade, a further £15,000 with interest was deducted from excise receipts. Concurrently the Commons determined to continue the Northern and Western Associations, mortgaging half the excise payments from those regions for the maintenance of troops and garrisons. Individual strongholds received similar consideration. Lyme was granted £1,000 from its excise collections and Leicestershire had half its charge rebated for the maintenance of forces.[19]

It was not until Holles returned from his negotiations with the City that the chaotic state of parliamentary finance was exposed. He reported that the City had agreed to lend the £200,000 but that the Common Council had insisted upon two sources for collateral, the excise and the sale of the confiscated bishops' lands. Under the guise of security the London financiers would achieve the abolition of the episcopal church. "By the sale of these lands," Juxon observed, "the bishops will be put out of all hope to be reestablished."[20] Although Holles had negotiated this source of revenue with the City's leaders, Parliament had not even begun consideration of such a complicated and controversial operation.[21] Moreover, as debate on the City's terms revealed, the excise could not provide security for the loan as its revenues for the next two years were already pledged.[22] With parliamentary resources thus straitened, and without the excise to provide security, a new expedient would have to be devised. This was the opportunity to revive the proposal to sell delinquents' estates. Fearing either that this redistribution coincident with the sale of bishops' lands would devalue both or that the Lords would reject the entire package, Holles and Stapleton opposed this measure. But they were defeated in a division, and the security for the City loan became the opportunity for Parliament to attempt to resuscitate its finances.[23]

Although Holles and Stapleton worked to avoid conflict with the Lords over the sale of delinquents' estates they could not be assured that the Upper House would assent to the final dissolution of the church. Even before the end of the fighting in July, the Lords had proved reluctant to continue wartime innovations and intransigent against new expedients. Their refusal to pass the ordinance to sell delinquents' estates was only one part of an effort to restore the normal workings of government. At the end of August the Lords drafted legislation to dissolve the county committees and to restore the Lord-Lieutenants to their primacy in the localities.[24] When the Commons tabled this bill the Upper House refused to pass votes continuing the Northern and Western Associations that implicitly extended the tenure of the county committees.[25] Besides the artificially constructed governments in the localities, the peers balked at maintaining the military establishment. They refused to act on the Commons' request that the treasurers of war be continued beyond the expiration of their present term and pressed for an overall review of military policy.[26]

These efforts to redefine parliamentary government were fully expressed at the end of October. By then the Lower House was busily passing into law many of the clauses of the peace propositions. One of these expelled from the peerage all nobles created by the King since 1642. Nine Lords dissented from the majority of peers who agreed to this legislation, objecting not to the principle of the matter, but to its form. Such an order, as they hardly needed to remind the majority of their House, touched the prerogative of the King and required his consent. In a most telling phrase they demanded that "things that are to be perpetual might be settled in the old way by the three estates."[27] Their minority opinion was the first ray of opposition to continued parliamentary government.

Although disquieted by the prolongation of emergency government, the Lords were no less eager than the Commons to regain control of the King. After brief resistance they assented to the principles negotiated with the City and gave tacit approval to the sale of the bishops' lands.[28] Yet this assent to principle was not matched by practice. For over a month the Lords took no practical steps toward providing the City's security. Finally on October 8 they debated the prelude to confiscation of the church lands: the abolition of episcopacy. Fourteen Lords were equally divided on this essential but irrevocable decision, and the issue was only resolved the following day in a house of thirteen.[29] Although succumbing to economic and political necessity, members of the House of Lords registered deep-seated opposition to continued innovations. For another month they delayed approval of the sale of bishops' lands, debating and amending the most inconsequential details of the plan.[30] From the beginning of negotiations with the City in September to the withdrawal of the Scottish Army in January, four full months went by.

The delay in obtaining funds for the Scottish withdrawal complicated plans for the suppression of the Irish rebellion. At the end of July, when Parliament anticipated either the King's acceptance of the Newcastle propositions or his military resurrection through an alliance with the Scots, a crucial debate was held to determine the composition of the Irish expedition. The House of Commons weighed the alternatives of detaching a brigade from the New Model or of reorganizing and equipping regiments from the Associations and local garrisons. In a vituperative and lengthy session it was resolved, by 1 vote in a division of 181 members, not to divide the New Model.[31] The rationale that swayed the House from the more practical course was fear of the large Scottish Army that remained in possession of the northern garrisons. "Many argue that till the Scots relinquish the garrisons in England and depart into Scotland [they] suspect a plot to weaken our Army in England that after we may be forced to any condition," recorded Harington.[32] Although costly and inefficient, the Irish invasion force would have to be raised in the localities; military considerations were again outweighed by political ones.

The largest of these local units was that of Major General Edward Massey. It was composed of several regiments that had aided the New Model's western campaign and subsequently achieved little more than a deserved reputation for pilfering and debauchery.[33] The disbandment of Massey's brigade would thus solve two problems simultaneously, relieving the countryside of its presence and assigning several regiments for Ireland. For if these troops were judged unfit for continued service in England they were admirably suited to Parliament's notion of the forces necessary to bring order to the Irish. In October, after raising £15,000 on the excise, Parliament ordered six weeks' pay for the disbandment of the brigade.[34] In addition they proposed that each soldier subscribing for Ireland would receive an advance of four weeks' pay. To make the service more attractive and to speed recruitment, Parliament allowed regimental officers to maintain their charges, avoiding reorganization and encouraging soldiers to continue within their troops.[35] This last decision suggested that Parliament anticipated the brigade would subscribe en masse. But this expectation was sorely disappointed when, almost to a man, the officers and soldiers refused to accept Irish service. They found both the conditions of their disbandment – only six weeks' pay – and the prospects for Irish service unattractive.[36] Many held claims for arrears that dated from 1643, and they demanded a fifth of their back pay as well as other considerations before agreeing to the service. "If the Parliament in their wisdom shall be pleased to condescend to these humble requests," Massey's officers declared, "we doubt not but to carry over the brigade very entire; if not we shall submit to their disposal."[37]

Thus the initial progress made by the Presbyterian leadership to resolve the crises of the undeclared peace was slow and uneven. Although they were able to conclude an agreement with the Scots, they were stymied for three months in raising funds for the withdrawal. Their difficulties in organizing a new army for Ireland, as exemplified by their inability to recruit Massey's brigade, also stemmed from the problem of finance. Moreover, their projects had necessitated further concessions to City financiers and the continuation of a wartime economy. Withdrawal of the Scots and invasion of Ireland had exhausted the excise, introduced the sale of episcopal lands, and increased the necessity to dispose of the delinquents' estates. The mortgage on the excise until the winter of 1648 was only one indication that the emergency measures taken by Parliament would outlive the struggle from which they derived.

The pressure to maintain the necessities of government and to finance Parliament's accumulating debts would soon become unbearable. The opposition mounted by Holles and Stapleton to the sale of delinquents' estates turned on a very fine point of principle when juxtaposed to their support of the disposal of the bishops' lands. Once bowed to, financial necessity would reign supreme, even with government in the hands of political and social conservatives.

Even with their programs for the Scots and Irish stalled, the leadership of the House of Commons pressed forward with plans to consolidate wartime institutions and to legislate peacetime innovations. The ambiguity of the political situation was nowhere more evident than in the need to maintain the military establishment. Fear of foreign intervention, whether Scottish or continental, was a check upon immediate disestablishment, and a small group of parliamentary zealots subscribed to the millennial visions of the *Moderate Intelligencer:* "There is an Ireland to reduce, a Prince Elector to restore and an Anti-Christ to destroy."[38] The decision against sending the New Model into Ireland effectively assured its continuation in England, at least until its empowering ordinance expired in November. Besides it largest force, Parliament also supported armies in the north, east, and west. In August, with the ordinances for all three Associations about to lapse, the Commons voted their continuations.[39] At the same time they began to reconsider the monthly assessment used to maintain the New Model. Counties that had passed under Parliament's control since the Army's creation could now contribute to the Army's upkeep, whereas those devastated by the fighting could be relieved from excessive contributions. On October 7, after a lengthy debate, but without division, the Commons directed Robert Scawen to draft an ordinance extending the New Model for another six months.[40] Finally, in November, the House voted to continue the office of army treasurer for ten months, extending the collectors four months beyond the Army in anticipation of arrears.[41]

The perpetuation of the military machinery, especially when coupled with the general desire to end wartime innovations, was bound to rekindle conflict between the Houses. The formalization of military functions and the self-denying ordinance had divested the Lords of their traditional powers. This was one source of their long-standing opposition to the new military arrangements, but eventually they became more concerned with the Commons' arrogation of military control. Like financial matters, but with less justification, military affairs had come within the purview of the Lower House. In July, for example, responding to appeals from the City and the Scots, the Lords ordered the covenant administered throughout the Army and the parliamentary ban on lay preaching enforced. Both demands were extremely controversial; the military situation being uncertain, and the Scots as yet inconsequential, the Commons simply sidestepped these votes.[42] But in August, when the political situation was transformed, the Lords in a conference with the Commons insisted "that such persons may be in command of forces in this Kingdom as shall pursue the end of the covenant."[43] Again the Commons refused to act: Holles and Stapleton were not antipathetic to the motion, but they were carefully guiding the negotiations for Scottish withdrawal through a House hostile to the Scots' political machinations. What was politic to the Commons was to the Lords another example of usurped powers. For the first time they delayed continuance of the Army committee and the treasurers at war.

In October this issue of military jurisdiction between the Houses reached a climax. Consonant with plans for the Irish invasion the Commons ordered the disbandment of Massey's brigade, directing Sir Thomas Fairfax to oversee the disestablishment with two New Model regiments. When the Lords learned of this peremptory action they passed a resolution declaring "that such forces as are raised by Ordinance of both Houses of Parliament cannot be disbanded by any order of either House, without order of both Houses of Parliament," and despatched an unusually curt letter to Fairfax instructing him not to comply with the Commons' order.[44] The Lower House responded by agreeing in principle to the Lords' assertion, but also claimed that Massey's forces had not been raised by both Houses.[45] For his part Fairfax neatly juggled the letters so that Massey's troops were disbanded before the Lords' resolution was officially received at Army headquarters.[46] This fait accompli so infuriated those Lords who were emerging in opposition to continued parliamentary innovations and usurpations that when Fairfax returned to London the following month the Earls of Middlesex, Lincoln, and Suffolk and Lords Hunsdon, Willoughby, and Maynard dissented from a vote that the peers attend his arrival.[47] They and several others who supported them continued to press for an end to military administration. They refused to accept the new monthly assessment and were willing to continue the Army treasurers only until January 1647 for the purpose of collecting arrears upon the original New Model ordinance.[48]

Although the Lords were able to delay the resolution of military administration, they were less successful in postponing a decision on the fate of the King. By accepting the necessity of Scottish withdrawal the Upper House was forced to modify its hostility to the King's imprisonment. When the peers had refused, in May, to accept responsibility for taking control of the monarch, they still had hoped for the success of the peace propositions. Their failure, and Charles's months of captivity in the Scotish Army, softened opposition to such a bold step. Still, the King's flight to the Scots had been voluntary and Parliament had never sanctioned the Scots' decision to confine him. In September, after the preliminary financial arrangements with the Scots had been made, the House of Commons renewed its deliberations on the disposition of the monarch. After opposition was overcome by the defeat of a vote to postpone the debate, the Commons again resolved that the King would be disposed of according to the will of the two Houses.[49] They concurrently decreed that their decision should in no way retard the departure of the Scottish forces.[50] Both these votes were engineered by Holles, who told the majority against delaying the decision and who was appointed to deliver the resolutions to the Lords.[51] In the Upper House the issue remained in doubt. On September 22 eleven Lords favored the resolutions that Holles had presented and eleven others opposed them. Lengthy debate necessitated an afternoon session at which attendance dwindled and a majority of the remaining eighteen Lords accepted the Commons' resolutions. The Earls of Lincoln and Suffolk and Lords Berkeley, Willoughby, Hunsdon, and Maynard entered dissents and again crystalized the opposition to the perpetuation of parliamentary government.[52]

With the King temporarily set aside, the Lower House could continue its plans for the reform of civil administration. Prior to the failure of the propositions Parliament had begun to restructure its regional bodies. The Northern and Eastern Associations, whose tenures were about to expire, were renewed and placed on a firm financial footing by grants of one-half their excise receipts for upkeep. North Wales, recently conquered, was to receive military, civil, and religious leadership as part of its integration into national government.[53] More importantly, with the King's fate resolved Parliament could return its attention to central administration. On September 22 the Lower House appointed a committee of lawyers to redraft the clauses of the peace propositions into parliamentary ordinances.[54] This committee worked quickly: less than two weeks later it reported legislation to confirm the proceedings of Parliament during the period of the war; to settle upon Parliament the control of the militia; and to outline the future government of Ireland.[55] The Commons also determined that the Great Seal, symbol of lawful government, would be removed from the control of parliamentary members and placed in the hands of civil commissioners.[56] Some weeks later the Lower House debated the establishment of a Court of Admiralty, although legal opinion divided on the propriety of such an act, and finally on November 24 it abolished that despised vehicle of personal rule, the Court of Wards.[57] Despite its growing pains, legislative government was succeeding.

The transformation of Parliament's traditional political process had begun in the spring of 1646 and continued throughout the year. By the winter the disintegration of the parliamentary way was apparent as the cracks of personal animosity and factional dispute widened into the chasms of party politics. The crisis of decision making that accompanied the war's end could not be resolved by the slow, evenhanded methods of the past. Unencumbered debate had already been eroded by the work of pressure groups that had made important contributions to the parliamentary cause. Bitter religious dispute and the advocacy of conflicting political alternatives had undermined the quest for unanimity. With the failure to come to terms with the King a new urgency was felt at Westminster. Overwhelmed by the irresolution of their conflict, parliamentary leaders strove for the resolution of their policies. Thus the development of parties and party leaders was a practical and, perhaps, a logical adaptation of parliamentary procedure. Although it was endured, especially by the Lords, as another expedient to be abandoned with the settlement of peace, it developed a form and character of its own.

In the first instance, the operation of the parties necessitated a change in Parliament's methods of decision making. The deliberative process with its practiced speeches and persuasive debates was entirely too cumbersome when confronted by the need for rapid policy formulation and executive control. The very existence of the parties assumed contrariety and opposing opinions, and disputes were to be resolved not by debate but by divisions of the House into majority and minority opinions. This was not of itself an innovation, for the two Houses had always conducted their business by votes on resolutions, but majority rule had never been as important as unanimity. Parliamentary practice had relied upon the deliberative process, through debates and committees, to arrive at resolutions that expressed the sense of the whole House. With the use of divisions the parties inverted this procedure, resolving the issue through the determination of a majority opinion and circumventing the process by which unity was maintained. It was not only that there was more conflict now than in the past, but that the method for resolving it had been transformed. The frequency of divisions in 1646, in contrast to their sporadic occurrence in the years of the war, was indicative of two changes in parliamentary procedure: that debates and committees were no longer able to disperse opposition and that the dynamics of adversary politics were continuously on display. Like the function of debate, the role of committees also altered; where emphasis was formerly placed upon the form of legislation it now centered upon the content. During the spring of 1646 committees were frequently small and composed of members clearly committed to ideological positions; the rule prohibiting an opponent of a bill from sitting as a committeeman had been abandoned.

The growth of party had two immediate effects upon political practice, contributing to the deterioration of relations between the Houses and prompting new changes in the procedures of the House of Commons. In the more conservative House of Lords the innovations that had been acceded to in hope of resolving the conflict with the King were now opposed as unnecessary for the nation and dangerous to the prestige of the peerage. The continuation of Parliament's administrative and military machinery, which had already become a source of contention between the Houses, would soon result in a long and bitter controversy. The Commons' pressure techniques, a by-product of the parties' emergence, would intensify these disputes. Nor was the Lower House unaffected by the changes in its method of decision making. As long as the parties continued to flourish they escalated the use of techniques that contributed to the breakdown of orderly procedure. Although the parties found themselves in general agreement on the major issues of policy throughout the autumn, a new increase in divisions of the House occurred, an indication that party practices had survived the crises of the spring and had come to be used by men who were only peripheral participants in the ideological controversy. The small committees designed for effective and rapid legislating would soon give way to larger bodies, less efficient, but more likely to mirror the divisions of the House. Political maneuvering was exhibited in divisions to delay or continue debates, whereas the acrimony of their sessions was starkly revealed in a motion to introduce a ballot box into the Commons. With controversy between the Houses resulting in frequent legislative impasses and with the escalation of conflicts in the Lower House that could only be resolved divisively, Parliament witnessed the collapse of traditional decision making.

The changes in political practice initiated in the House of Commons had their greatest impact in the House of Lords. The encroachments upon the peers' civil and military authority, no less than the domination of their institution by the Commons, created anxiety for both the present and the future. Unlike the members of the Commons, the peers would continue in their places after the reunification of the Kings' government and that handful who had supported Parliament would be overwhelmed by the return of the royalist nobility. Indeed their sparsity was one explanation for their conservatism. In 1646 attendance in the Upper House never exceeded twenty-nine, once sank to eleven, and normally averaged twenty.[58] A sense of being beleaguered was perhaps inescapable, the more so because the House's strictly defined order of precedence had left the parliamentarian Lords with few of their natural leaders – the King's ministers. Consumed by their own customs and precedents they accepted their actions only as temporary ones, going so far as to appoint a "temporary" speaker every three months.[59] Thus the thinness of their numbers and the uncertainty of their role made the Lords jealous of their privileges and suspicious of innovation.

This was particularly true when they became targets of social reformers who called in question the fundamental rights of the nobility. The fear, expressed most poignantly by Lord Willoughby, "that the nobilty and gentry are going down apace," was ever present, manifest in Manchester's accusation against Cromwell and in the Upper House's opposition to self-denial.[60] As the war progressed and as social considerations were replaced by political ones, the House of Lords found itself increasingly under attack. Such assaults never constituted a greater threat nor were they made more vociferously than by John Lilburne. In June 1646 the Lords had committed Lilburne to prison for his denunciation of the Earl of Manchester in the long-festering dispute over the Earl's military conduct in 1644.[61] There was nothing unusual in this, for the practice of punishing citizens for writing or speaking against members of Parliament was endorsed by both Houses, and Lilburne's case was no different than those of a number of others. It was Lilburne's self-advertisement that elevated his case into a *cause célèbre* and his calculated defiance that frightened the Lords. In July Lilburne was brought to the Upper House for examination and there disputed the Lords' judicial privileges.[62] He contended with the peers on two separate points: that they should not judge a case involving one of their own members; and that they had no right to examine a commoner, who was guaranteed a trial by a jury of his peers. To illustrate his belief that only the House of Commons could hear his case, and with the theatrical flair that enhanced his reputation, Lilburne refused to kneel at the bar of the Lords' House and placed his fingers in his ears so that he could not hear the charges that were being read against him.[63] To both his attack upon Manchester and his conduct in their chamber the Lords responded with a savage sentence, ordering an exorbitant fine and long prison term and barring Lilburne from all civil and military office.[64]

The Lords imposed their stiff penalty against Lilburne as a deterrent against further encroachments. The day before his appearance at the bar, Lilburne's offending pamphlet, "The Sum of the Charge Given In by Lieutenant-General Cromwell," was ordered burned by the common hangman, and at that time it was necessary for the Upper House to order the London sheriffs to protect the hangman "that there be no affronts offered him."[65] But neither this public desecration of Lilburne's work nor his continued imprisonment fulfilled the Lords' purpose. In August Richard Overton published an attack on the Lords' actions in the Lilburne case, "An Alarm to the House of Lords."[66] His pamphlet was also ordered to be destroyed by the hangman and Overton was called to be examined in the Upper House. In a repeat of Lilburne's performance Overton disputed the peers' right to try him and refused to answer any questions put to him.[67] He was committed to Newgate and there he escalated the dispute by penning an even more provocative pamphlet, "A Defiance Against All Arbitrary Usurpations or Encroachments Either of the House of Lords or Any Others upon the Sovereignty of the Supreme House of Commons."[68] These assaults upon the Lords, especially their appeals to the supremacy of the Commons, did little to soothe the institutional insecurities of the Upper House and naturally made the peers even more adamant in the defense of their rights and privileges.

Yet the House of Lords was not a monolith; among its members could be found the same broad spectrum of political and religious viewpoints that bedeviled the parliamentary cause. In fact the social and institutional emphasis upon individuality in the Upper House made for an independence that defied political organization. But, like the City of London, the House of Lords could be counted upon to react, in unison, against threats to its institutional rights. The transition from the undeclared war to the unresolved peace was made far more smoothly in the Lower House than among the peers. Administrative innovation such as the county committees and the military machinery were personal irritants to the nobles. Support or opposition to their continuation by individual peers was a result of inclination rather than religious or political persuasion. There was no party whip in the Upper House and opposition among supposed "Presbyterian Lords" to policies presented by Holles and Stapleton antedated the Earl of Essex's death. It is most revealing that this "Presbyterian party" relied upon Say, Warwick, and Northumberland to pass the bill for the sale of bishops' lands and to approve advances from the excise to finance the Irish expedition.

More importantly, by the autumn of 1646 it is possible to discern a division in the Upper House – one that would grow in importance in the coming year – between Lords committed on either side to the ideological contentions now dominant in the Commons and those opposed to all innovation in government. These "anti-innovatory" peers included the Earls of Lincoln, Rutland, Middlesex, and Suffolk, the newly created Earl of Mulgrave, and Lords Robartes, Willoughby, Hunsdon, and Maynard. They were a loose group, characterized by their very lack of ideology, and they were joined on specific issues by the Earls of Stamford and Salisbury and Lords North and Berkeley. Among the reasons they came to exist as a group were the growth of opposition in the country to the abuses of government and hostility to the growth of faction and interest in the House of Commons. Their constant attendance made them a formidable presence in the Upper House, where they occasionally held a majority. But with the single exception of the ordinance to suppress the county committees, they acted to obstruct rather than to propose legislation.

Throughout the winter of 1646 and the spring of 1647 the anti-innovatory peers acted as a counterweight to the policies presented from the Commons. When the ideologically committed Lords opposed each other on specific issues the result was certain to favor the status quo. Thus, what appears to be a "Presbyterian" majority in the Upper House on issues such as relations with the Scots and the City was really a combination of a group of the ideological Lords and those who opposed further innovation. The anti-innovatory peers' opposition to continued military taxation was coupled with the hostility of other Lords to the New Model Army, which resulted in the blockage of military legislation. Only because the policies of committed political moderates and radicals coincided during the fall of 1646 was progress made in resolving the Scottish disengagement and the Irish venture. Although Presbyterian Lords, in the political and religious sense, outnumbered Independents, they would have been hard pressed to push through a program that was opposed by both the Independents and the anti-innovatory peers, a fact manifested in March 1647 when a showdown occurred on the composition of the Derby House Committee.[69]

The influence of the anti-innovatory peers and the general malaise the Upper House felt at continuing to govern without the King was exhibited even before the failure of the Newcastle propositions. After concluding the proposals the Lords were strongly disinclined to proceed with any new business until the negotiations had been completed. On the contrary, they had set about to dismantle much of the nation's war-making machinery. On July 1 they sent the House of Commons an ordinance to abolish the county committees and a week later they entered into a long debate on the disbanding of all the nation's forces.[70] Moreover, the peers refused continuation of the Northern Association, dividing evenly when the ordinance was reported on July 24 and rejecting it outright the following week.[71] The Lords also provided an icy reception to the Commons' order for the sale of the estates of delinquents who had been excepted from the general pardon.[72]

In further demonstration of their attention to the individual and institutional rights of the nobility, in August the Lords appointed a committee to examine the "great fines which the Peers of the realm are set at for their compositions at Goldsmiths' Hall, being far greater than their estates are able to bear."[73] This action came in response to the complaints of a number of royalist peers that the fines set by the committee were so exorbitant that they threatened some nobles with fiscal extinction. Although the committee made little headway on this issue (social discontent was hard to disentangle from antiroyalism), their examination of the practices of the Goldsmiths' Hall committee revealed that money was being distributed by the committee's treasurers without the order of the Upper House. More than the assault upon individual royalist peers, this practice threatened time-honored institutional rights and the peers moved quickly to prohibit it, reminding the treasurers that funds could not be disbursed without the express order of both Houses.[74]

This usurpation by the Commons, for the treasurers had been acting upon their orders, soon became entangled in a controversy over the power to disband troops. It was the clear understanding of the Lords that troops could be employed or disbanded only by order of the two Houses together, a principle they had enunciated to Sir Thomas Fairfax when they attempted to delay the disbanding of Massey's brigade.[75] This procedure was tested in mid-July when the Commons decided to disband the reformado regiment commanded by Colonel Sanderson. They did not report this order to the House of Lords, and a month later, after preparations for the disbanding had been completed, the Commons ordered that Sanderson's troops be paid out of money at Goldsmiths' Hall.[76] Disregarding the order they had received from the Lords that they were to make no disbursements without orders from both Houses, the committee's treasurers complied with the Commons' order. When these events were disclosed in the Upper House the treasurers were called to the bar to explain their actions. There, in justification, they produced a provocatively worded resolution from the House of Commons directing them to pay Sanderson's regiment "notwithstanding any order or orders of the House of Lords to the contrary."[77] The Commons had further assured them, the treasurers related, that in issuing this money or in making any future disbursements contrary to the Lords' orders, they would be "saved harmless and kept indemnified" by the Lower House.[78] To this affront the Lords could respond only by reiterating their order to the treasurers and by appointing a committee to prepare for a conference with the Commons upon the issue. Although unable to punish the insubordination of the treasurers without further dividing the two Houses, the Lords ordered an audit of all the accounts of the Goldsmiths' Hall Committee.[79]

This overt controversy over the Lords' participation in control of parliamentary standing committees and in the disbanding of parliamentary armies made plain the hostility engulfing the two Houses. Beneath these interrelated battles a sniping war was also being waged across the field of orders and appointments. In July, for example, the Lords had refused to act on the ordinance for the sale of delinquents' estates on a declaration that the nation no longer had need for the Scottish Army, and on the order to pay for the disbanding of Massey's brigade.[80] In the Commons the orders to suppress the county committees, to release Sir William Murray, and to appoint Lord Bruce to a Lord-Lieutenancy, and the Lords' vote to enforce the covenant in the New Model all languished.[81] When the declaration that the Scottish Army was no longer necessary in England stalled in the Upper House, the Commons attempted to reapply the pressure techniques that had been successful in the spring. First, Sir Peter Wentworth was appointed to carry a message concerning the Scottish Army to the Lords, "and nothing else to go with it."[82] Then, two weeks later, when the Lords had continued to postpone action, Sir Henry Mildmay and John Gurdon were ordered, in a breach of etiquette, to peruse the Lords' Journals and determine what orders the peers had made concerning the Scots.[83]

By mid-September the Houses were also clashing over questions of appointments. When the Lord-Lieutenancy of Yorkshire fell vacant on Essex's death, the Lords nominated the Earl of Northumberland, the greatest North Country peer, to fill it. In the Lower House the nomination was given to Ferdinando Lord Fairfax, the general's father and a powerful Yorkshire M.P.[84] This difference resulted in immediate stalemate and the office remained vacant. Then in October the Lords decided to continue the Earl of Warwick in his post as governor of the island of Jersey. To this the Commons refused assent, alleging that Warwick held sufficient power in his almost total control of the American territories.[85] On the following day when Lord Fairfax proposed to the Commons that the maintenance grant voted to his deceased kinsman the Earl of Mulgrave be settled upon the Earl's widow, the Commons spitefully voted that it be paid to the widows of parliamentary soldiers.[86] The height of this backlash against the peerage was reached when the Commons refused to agree with the Lords in granting permission for the Earl of Essex's brother-in-law, the royalist Marquis of Hertford, to mourn at Essex's funeral.[87]

Legislative functioning was severely impaired by conflict between the Houses. The procedures developed for parliamentary interaction had been designed to achieve the consent of the two estates to the desires of the King. As accord was expected for the King's business, discord between the Houses was rare and few techniques had developed to settle disputes. The single outlet was the conference, a meeting of a small number of Lords and Commoners to hear the arguments for and against stalemated legislation. The conference held no adjudicative powers; for its success it relied upon the assumption that reasoned debate would persuade men of goodwill. The normal course of affairs was for one House to accept the reasons offered to it and defer to the legislation, a procedure easily maintained when parliamentary sessions were brief and disagreement between the Houses rare. The crisis between the Houses, perhaps the result of the decline of reasoned debate and men of goodwill, had predictably turned the conference into an arena for confrontation. With increasing regularity both Houses prepared the heads of the conference, those topics that alone would be discussed and the arguments to be offered under each head. In this their explicit intention was to make their representatives mouthpieces of their Houses rather than debaters of issues, and on occasion, as in the conference over the Goldsmiths' Hall controversy, one House would present not arguments but a prepared set of grievances.[88] These developments coincided with a rapid increase in the number of conferences. By the winter several conferences a week would not be unusual. As an extraordinary measure the conference had served the legislative body well, but with its increased frequency and formal presentation of prescribed arguments, it soon lost its ability to resolve crises, developing into one more of Parliament's interminable committees.

Without the conference as an effective means of breaking deadlocks and with both Houses willing to table rather than compose legislative differences, Parliament found it necessary to seek other methods to overcome stalemate between the Houses. This became imperative when the bills that the Lords refused to act upon dealt with issues vital in the Commons' perception of the nation's security. In September the Lords had refused to aid in the removal of the Scottish Army, to continue the regional associations, or to extend the tenure of the Army committee and the treasurers at war. By this inaction they threatened to leave Parliament incapable of defending itself against the Scots or a royalist resurgence. Thus when Holles reported the results of his negotiations with the City for the £200,000 loan, the Commons debated whether it was necessary to obtain the Lords' concurrence in borrowing the money.[89] This attempt to exclude the Lords from participation in a matter of primary concern to both Houses, and to the nation, indicated that a fundamental change in the relationship between the Houses was underway. By a majority of only 18 in a House of 146 the Commons defeated this first proposal for unicameral government.[90]

The reasons that persuaded this slender majority not to exclude the Lords from the deliberative process did not persuade them to allow the peers a small amendment in the language of the order. To ensure compliance the Commons fixed upon a device only one step less extreme than dispensing with the consent of the Upper House. On September 11 they adhered to their original bill over the Lords' objections and returned it to the Upper House with neither the reasons for their action or a call for a conference.[91] This tactic of adhering to votes in the face of amendments sidetracked, for the moment, thoughts of eliminating the Lords from the legislative process. Twice more in the next week the Commons employed this strategy: when the peers, still insistent upon the abolition of the county committees, amended the continuance order for the Northern and Western Associations; and when the Lords granted only a two-week extension to the treasurers of war.[92] Although the Lords immediately gave way on the bill to borrow the £200,000 from the City, and eventually backed off from their refusal to continue the regional associations, the two

Houses had not resolved their procedural controversy.[93] When dispute erupted over the appointment of a commissioner to hold the Great Seal, Henry Marten, not the Commons' most respected jurist, postulated that "when we have sought concurrence of the Lords and they will not we have lawful power to do it ourselves."[94]

On this occasion unicameral action was again delayed, although the reasons for not adopting Marten's position did not result from the principle of the matter. The political leaders in the Commons were divided on the question of excluding M.P.s from holding the Seal, and this opposition made a break with the Lords unnecessary. Their refusal to accept the Commons' nominations played into the hands of Haselrig and Evelyn of Wiltshire, who opposed farming the Seal to civil Commissioners. Holles and Stapleton, who supported the measure, could not press it without also sponsoring a vote to dispense with the Lords' approval; a cruel dilemma, and another illustration of the independence of the Upper House. It was not long, however, before an issue emerged in which politics and procedure came together.

In September the Scottish Commissioners again appealed to public opinion to vindicate their conduct by publishing their account of the Newcastle negotiations. They blamed their failure upon the Independents and their supporters in Parliament, inflaming those members of the Lower House who were already enraged at being forced to accept unreasonable Scottish monetary demands in order to achieve the withdrawal of their Army.[95] When, in the following month, the Scottish Commissioners protested the vote by the two Houses that they dispose of the King without consulting the Scots, the Commons found an opoprtunity to vent its anger.[96] A committee was formed to respond to the Commissioners' contentions and their report was drafted into a letter to be sent to the Scots. Then the Commons debated whether the letter should be sent to the Lords, where it almost certainly would be rejected. By a majority of 20 in a House of 210 Haselrig and Evelyn of Wiltshire secured the elimination of the words "Lords and" from the preamble that began "The Lords and Commons Assembled."[97] Holles and Stapleton achieved a pyrrhic victory when, after this vote, they staved off another to put the question of the necessity of the Lords' concurrence.[98] It was left for the Scots to maintain the dignity of the peerage by returning the Commons' missive unopened because it did not come from both Houses of Parliament.

Although government did not collapse under these controversies, orderly procedure did. In the House of Lords there remained a slender majority of peers who were willing to suffer the encroachments of the Commons on procedural questions in order to move forward on policy decisions. Significantly, they were the same Lords who held to the divergent ideological positions so inadequately described as "Presbyterian" and "Independent." In the winter of 1646 major policy decisions did not divide these two viewpoints. Withdrawal of the Scots had been the established policy of parliamentarians who opposed both their religious objectives and their political meddling. Now this policy coincided with that pursued by the English Presbyterian leaders, who planned a new round of peace negotiations with the King. Suppression of the Irish rebellion was also embraced by both sides as a crusade to establish reformed religion in the last British stronghold of popery. The necessity of controlling the King, either to separate him from the dangerous influence of Scottish proselytizing or to gain his ear for new terms of settlement, again made for a coincidence of policy between the political parties.

In the Lower House the corrosive effect of constant decision making upon parliamentary practice had been first indicated in the spring by the increase in the number of divisions. Procedurally the division was an official count of votes that enabled the Speaker to identify the majority position. It was effected by physically dividing the adherents and appointing tellers to count their numbers. Although the division was a practical procedural device, the course of parliamentary practice ascribed political significance to it. Traditional procedure had worked to inhibit division. When an issue engendered opposition in the full House the Commons turned further debate over to a committee, where the force of argument could reshape the issue to eliminate opposition. If contention continued when the committee reported its findings, the issue could be recommitted or sent to a new committee. Most frequently, however, consideration of matters that continued to attract vocal opposition was postponed, buried under the mass of new business that awaited parliamentary consideration, from which it might never emerge. When Parliament was unable to resolve conflicting opinions in any other manner divisions occurred; their infrequency was a tribute to parliamentary success in achieving unity. Only in the crises of 1641–2, when royalists and parliamentarians sat together, had divisions been used to decide large numbers of issues.

Although the early months of 1645 had seen controversy over the creation of the New Model and votes for appointments of individuals to military and civil commands, only forty-one divisions occurred between January 1, 1645, and January 31, 1646.[99] In the following six months the increase in divisions exhibited the effects of the weight of decision making and the lack of executive control on Parliament. From the beginning of February 1646 until the submission of the peace propositions to the King at the end of July, forty-eight divisions took place, thirty of them between April 1 and June 30. Significantly, the increase in the number of divisions was accompanied by a shift in the nature of the issues they sought to resolve. Whereas a large number of the divisions in the previous year had concerned local affairs or were decisions relating to specific persons, the divisions of the first half of 1646 were almost always over substantive matters. For example, of the twenty-two divisions in April and May only three were tangential to settling the peace of the kingdom.[100]

The increase in divisions also provided opportunity for parliamentary leadership. The role of teller gave the emerging party leaders a visible manifestation of their positions. Minimally, an analysis of the teller appointments reveals a hardening of factional opposition and the emergence of Sir Arthur Haselrig and Sir John Evelyn of Wiltshire as consistent opponents of Holles and Stapleton. In the forty-eight divisions between February and July 1646, Holles appeared as teller thirty-three times and Stapleton on twenty-two occasions. The two were paired on eighteen divisions in this period. Haselrig matched Holles's frequency, also being appointed thirty-three times, and Evelyn was named to twenty-four of the counts. These two appeared together sixteen times. Although this is strong evidence of consistent leadership and opposition, there remain glaring anomalies. On March 9 Haselrig and Evelyn were on opposite sides of the House in a division over compositions; on the following day Holles was paired with Haselrig against Evelyn and Stapleton on a second vote over exceptions to the general pardon. In the first vote on that day, Haselrig and Evelyn again took opposite sides.[101] In April a division over Irish affairs was another occasion for Haselrig and Evelyn to be pitted against each other, and in June Holles and Haselrig were again paired, this time against Oliver St. John and Sir Richard Onslow.[102]

A second indication of the effect the events of the early months of 1646 had on parliamentary practice was in the proliferation of committees. Committees were appointed to provide careful consideration to specific issues. During committee debates, members could speak as frequently as they desired, a privilege denied them in the full House. By its full and open discussion the committee provided an effective buffer between the opposition that might appear at the initial consideration of an issue and its final resolution. The increased frequency of committee appointments provided another channel for parliamentary leadership. From January to July 1646 the number of committees appointed by the House of Commons increased steadily from six to nineteen per month.[103] Although their business was not concentrated on the peace settlement, many were involved in considering letters from the King and papers from the Scots.

Thirteen members of Parliament appeared on at least one-third of the ninety committees selected in these months. The list included the old factional leaders, Vane and St. John, and the emerging party leaders, Evelyn, Haselrig, Holles, and Stapleton. It was headed by two members who had been reinstated in the House of Commons after enforced absences: Nathaniel Fiennes and Henry Marten. The City of London was represented by its recorder, John Glyn, and the one-time alderman and common councillor, Francis Allen. Two leading jurists, Samuel Browne and Bulstrode Whitelocke, provided legal skill. Edmund Prideaux, a powerful West Country gentleman, completed the list.[104] These men consistently dominated the small committees that were appointed to debate crucial decisions. Indeed, the increased frequency of small committees numbering less than fifteen or twenty can be taken to indicate one attempt to impose executive control. In January 1646, for example, five of the ten members chosen to consider the Scots' plea to treat with the King were from the thirteen. In a thirteen-man committee appointed to prepare the bill for the peace propositions, seven were from this group.[105] Although this might be coincidental, the trend by which these men constituted a bare majority on small committees is marked throughout the spring. In February ten of eighteen were appointed to prepare an answer to the King and five of ten to preserve parliamentary privileges on the revenue; in March, eight of sixteen to examine the French ambassador, ten of nineteen to consider a paper from the Scots, six of ten to invite the Prince of Wales to London, and five of seven to answer another letter from the King were all from this group of the most active committee-men. In the two small committees appointed in April, the thirteen continued to hold majorities: six of eleven were appointed to communicate a breach of privilege to the Assembly of Divines and four of six to examine a letter from the Army.[106]

As these leading committeemen included members from both emerging parties, the traditional practice of embracing men of different persuasions on issues seems to have continued. But there do appear to be cracks in this foundation of unity. Holles and Stapleton are conspicuous by their absence from several committees dealing with the Scots and their various papers. They were also not among the eleven members chosen to inform the Assembly of Divines that their petition for increased ministerial powers in the church was a breach of privilege.[107] In July neither appeared on the forty-nine-man committee selected to prepare the ordinance for the sale of delinquents' estates, a bill continuously opposed by their allies in the Lords, but supported by the Scots. In the same month they failed to appear on the equally large committee that prepared an answer against the City's petition to the King.[108] Vane, St. John, Haselrig, and Evelyn did not sit on the committee appointed to enumerate scandalous sins or on the large committee chosen to examine John Lilburne.[109] Absence from committees can be attributed to numerous factors that go beyond the issues, and too much weight should not be placed on these instances. The traditional practice of incorporating all important parliamentary leaders on committees deciding key issues was too well entrenched to be easily discarded. Indeed, as committees were generally chosen by the shouting of names from the floor of the House, a new method of appointment would have had to have been developed to exclude members who wanted to participate. Nevertheless, on some important issues the beginning of what may have been a boycott of committees can be discerned.

The increase of divisions and the proliferation of committees provide indications that Parliament was finding its task of settling the peace of the kingdom difficult. Moreover, as both the ambiguous results of the divisions and the continued participation of all parliamentary leaders on committees attest, the House was not yet dominated by party politics. But tensions and frustrations were heightening. In January contentions gave rise to a physical confrontation between Walter Long and Francis Allen.[110] Indeed, Long's temper might be considered a weathervane of tensions in the House; during self-denial and the debates over the New Model he had assaulted William Cawley.[111] The vivid expression of Long's frustration could also be seen in the development of questionable parliamentary practices. On January 31 the Commons found it necessary to revive the order that no new bill could be brought in after twelve o'clock, when most members left the House to attend committees.[112] On the same day the House voted that the Speaker be required to inform the Commons when messengers from the Lords appeared at their doors so that they could be admitted into the House immediately.[113]

The problem of new business being introduced in the absence of members was complemented by the absence of members when unpopular business was debated. As occasions in which divisions on whether to put the question preceded actual votes indicated, more members would reveal their opinions on the procedural question than on the substantive one. On April 11, for example, the House debated the petition presented by the Assembly of Divines. Because the petition concerned votes already made by the House many M.P.s considered it a breach of privilege. A division ensued on whether to put this question and 191 members voted, the majority for putting the question. On the issue, however, only 164 members expressed opinions.[114] Accordingly, when the crucial vote on removing the King from Scottish custody was taken, Holles and Stapleton attempted to force the hand of those who refused to commit themselves to any course of action. In an extraordinary motion they requested that the doors of the House of Commons be locked before any votes on the issue were taken. On this motion they were defeated by 5 votes in a total of 241. Their fears proved justified, as only 218 members voted on the first issue of substance and only 186 on the second.[115] Characteristically, on an intervening bid to put a question 236 members voted. For the time being the leaders of the Commons could not force uncommitted members to choose.

The sharp conflicts of the spring abated considerably after the failure of the peace propositions. Although parliamentary practice continued to alter, the party leaders were less certain of their courses. During the autumn few issues found them in constant opposition to each other. Perhaps the growth of parties made it unnecessary for Holles, Stapleton, Haselrig, and Evelyn to appear in tandem against each other, but the fact remains that in the forty-six divisions between September and December 1646 the two pairs of party leaders appeared in opposition to each other only five times.[116] Additionally, in these same forty-six divisions Holles and Stapleton were paired together only nine times and Haselrig and Evelyn appeared together on just twelve occasions.[117]

Although the party leaders continued preeminent as tellers in divisions (Haselrig and Holles both appeared in twenty-two), the relative infrequency of their appearances in tandem and in opposition to each other is one indication that the division was not strictly the preserve of the parties. This is also suggested by the fact that 20 percent of the divisions held in the autumn did not contain any of the four party leaders as tellers.[118] The continued proliferation of divisions over their startling increase in the spring, occurring while the parties were in agreement on major issues of policy, reflects the transformation of the political process. In July and August political decision making was in abeyance as Parliament awaited the King's response to the peace propositions. During August only five divisions were recorded, of which three occurred in the last week of the month. In September decision making heated up in unprecedented fashion. Twelve divisions were recorded in only sixteen parliamentary sessions. This was followed by thirteen divisions in October, only seven in November, but fourteen in December.

The remarkable increase in divisions in the autumn was accompanied by increasing acrimony and tension within and between the Houses of Parliament. Proceedings during the month of September serve as a weathervane for these winds of change. On September 1 Holles and Stapleton forced three divisions through the House over efforts to postpone consideration of the question of the Scottish withdrawal. "Many of us would have put off the paper until tomorrow," Harington recorded, "but it was carried against us."[119] On the 2nd came the acrimonious debate on the Scottish demand for a £200,000 down payment, and on the 3rd John Gurdon and Henry Marten "inveighed" against the Lords for their delays on the ordinance for the Great Seal.[120] On the 4th and 5th the House held divisions and then adjourned until the 10th, when two more divisions occurred. The controversy with the Lords over the ordinance for the City's loan and their amendments to the bills for the Northern and Western Associations came on the 11th.[121] The following session on September 15 was cut short by the death of the Earl of Essex, but on the 17th controversy between the Houses continued over the appointment of the new Lord-Lieutenant of Yorkshire.[122] On the 18th there was another division and, after an adjournment until the 22nd, new contentions with the Lords over the continuation of the treasurers of war.[123] The House avoided divisions on September 23 by spending the entire day in grand committee debating the explosive issue of the growth of heresy. But two divisions occurred on both the 24th and 25th.[124] After another four-day respite from meeting, the House found it necessary on the 29th to order the halls and stairways of their building cleared of all unauthorized persons who were apparently interfering with Parliament's business.[125] Fittingly, the month ended with a day of public humiliation.

Beyond the divisions in the Commons, which reflected the growing hostility among the membership, and the controversies with the Lords, several other changes in parliamentary routine provide evidence of the ongoing transformation of the political process. On September 18 the Commons attempted to order its business by appointing times for the consideration of eight separate matters.[126] Although the House frequently appointed times for the consideration of business that could not immediately be resolved, the votes on September 18 represented a clear attempt to establish an agenda. On October 1 four additional items, of particular local interest to North Country M.P.s, were placed on the agenda. On the 9th five items of national import, including the assessment for the New Model, were given places on the parliamentary docket.[127] The necessity for more orderly consideration of bills and resolutions resulted from the disintegration of procedure in the face of party controversy.

The appearance of votes on the future determination of issues was a clear outgrowth of the need either by the parties or the full House to impose order upon its procedure. A more striking indication of the same need came on October 10. The turmoil of sessions in September had been repeated the following month. Three divisions in the first week of October were followed by the Commons' rejection of several appointments made by the Lords.[128]

On October 9 a heated debate on the Army was held and on the following day the House debated a grant for Sir William Brereton, the parliamentary major-general who had commanded the Cheshire forces with great success throughout the war. The consideration of Brereton's grant degenerated into conflict and in the heat of the debate Sir John Clotworthy rose and moved that a ballot box be brought into the House to resolve all questions of offices and money secretly. Clotworthy's suggestion was defeated by only 2 votes in a House of 110.[129]

The attempt to introduce the ballot box reflected the inability of parliamentary procedure to regulate the affairs of the House. It indicated disenchantment with the process of division, which had doubtless created hostility among uncommitted members who were forced to choose sides, as well as among party members who came to look upon each other as adversaries. By the autumn even the most trivial matters could be resolved only by tallying votes. In August the House divided on whether to adjourn for a four-day weekend. This same question was the occasion for three more divisions in September and October.[130] On September 24 the House divided on whether to allow certain horses to be taken out of the kingdom.[131] In October, as suggested by the attempt to introduce the ballot box, three divisions centered on questions of individuals.[132] Atlhough there was a sharp decrease in divisions in November, two of the seven concerned additions to local county committees.[133]

A symbolic measure of the deterioration of reasoned debate among men of goodwill occurred in December. Only seven of the fourteen divisions focused on issues of policy and two concerned whether debates should be prolonged by bringing candles into the House.[134] On December 12 the House spent the entire day discussing matters of religion until the early afternoon darkness reminded the members of the length of their deliberation. A motion was made to bring candles into the House to continue debate, but this was opposed with enough vigor that a division was necessary. By that time, however, it was too dark for the tellers to produce an accurate count of the division and it was suggested that candles be brought in for the purpose of the division. This precipitated the question of whether candles could be brought in before the House had called for them. To resolve this issue it was ordered that the candles brought in to tell the division would not be set on the tables until the results of the vote were known.[135] In this way the men at Westminster groped toward a settlement of the future of the nation.

The strain of decision making in the face of an uncertain future took its toll upon the parliamentary cause. The clamor of outside pressure groups had already eroded the ability of Parliament men to debate and determine policies without regard for special interests. The necessity of first agreeing upon a set of proposals that it was hoped the King would accept, and then of settling the peace of the kingdom without Charles, further eroded parliamentary practice. The rise of parties and the development of techniques designed to achieve rapid decisions transformed the methods by which Parliament had maintained its cohesiveness despite religious and political differences. The uncertainty created by the irresolution of the war spurred the growth of an obstructive group of anti-innovatory peers and fed conflicts between the Houses that worsened throughout the autumn. The general insecurity of the peers was exacerbated by the pressure tactics generated from both of the Commons' ideological camps, culminating in efforts to dispense with the Lords on vital policy decisions. In the Commons as well, dispute and distrust informed a changing political process as heated debate and frequent divisions replaced reason and unanimity. As its traditional political methods disappeared, the parliamentary cause was shattered.

Moreover, government without the King had not successfully resolved the major issues that confronted Parliament. Although Scottish withdrawal had been accomplished, neither the rebellion in Ireland nor the disestablishment of Parliament's bloated military forces had been settled. Despite the rise of party techniques, political decision making was still not sufficiently centralized to allow the coordination of a single, concerted policy. If legislative government was to continue, an executive mechanism and a political leader would have to emerge. Symbolically, both awaited the return of the King into English custody.

Chapter 6

THE REIGN OF PARTIES

The Presbyterians now carry all things with a high hand.[1]

By the close of 1646 the transformation of the political process was completed. For four years the ties that bound together the diverse supporters of the parliamentary cause had remained tangled and knotted. Throughout the war conflicting partisan alternatives had been either encompassed or circumvented as Parliament refused to choose between war and peace in 1643–4 or to decide the establishment of the church in 1645. Whether, in the absence of the monarch, parliamentarians consciously refrained from innovations that might impede a settlement, or, in the confusion of rebellion, they were simply incapable of policy making, parliamentary unity had endured. Through the tensions heightened by the creation of the New Model Army, through the establishment of permanent poiltical factions, and through the machinations of the Scots and the City, political power had remained diffused.

Yet the political practice that had been so well suited to waging war quickly became an obstacle in settling peace. During the fighting political indecision had been relieved by the appointment of executive committees and military councils, but once the war had ended Parliament again assumed the burden of decision making. Almost immediately the political process convulsed. Pressure groups emerged from among those who had provided the cause with its money and manpower. Their claims to a voice in guiding the nation to peace were accepted by leaders of the parliamentary factions who had vied for the adoption of their own visions of the future. To factional dispute was added ideological commitment, religious and political, and the resultant admixture marked the first appearance of parties. Although their concept of politics still abhorred faction and interest, the practice of the men at Westminster gave way before it. Parliamentary procedure was adapted to permit efficient and orderly resolution of policy, and policy became the focus of debate and decision making. Uncommitted members

139

of the Lower House, still a numerical majority, could no longer avoid partisan alternatives as the party leaders used committees and divisions to accomplish their aims. The acrimony of debate and the political bludgeoning of the small Upper House were apt examples of the emergence of adversary relations.[2]

Although the political process had been transformed, the implications of party rule were not immediately experienced. During the autumn of 1646 the continued presence of the Scots' Army and their negotiations with the King left both parties reluctant to dissolve Parliament's military might or to press forward with the divisive church settlement. Renewed fighting would mean the resuscitation of the coalition of groups and factions that the parties had replaced. Therefore, the policy devised by Holles and Stapleton – the removal of the Scots and the preparations for an invasion of Ireland – was contested only on points of detail. On the central questions of the Scots, the Irish, and the King, agreement existed between the parties. In concert with Holles's attempt to secure a peace, Haselrig and Evelyn maintained their watchful belligerency, preparing the nation against a new war. For both parties the hinge of policy remained the Scots, who, contrary to their protestations, expressed their dissatisfaction with the progress of the church settlement by negotiating with the King for the establishment of presbyterianism. Until the completion of Parliament's own negotiations with the Scots, or at least until Scottish intentions were clear, neither party could be assured of the support of the uncommitted members or of the direction that their own policies should take.

It was not until the winter that Holles and Stapleton emerged as leaders of an incontestable majority in the House of Commons. The successful negotiation of Scottish withdrawal and English custody of the King resolved the fear of royal alliances and renewed fighting. Political policy was now shaped by efforts to ameliorate the economic hardships of the war, to disband or reconstitute the military, and to lighten the burden of taxation. If successful, important differences between King and Parliament would be eliminated. With religion settled, the military forces carefully stationed in scattered garrisons, and the Irish rebellion suppressed, the King could be brought to London. If Charles remained recalcitrant, the onus of undoing the parliamentary settlement would clearly be on him. Many of the recruited members who entered Parliament throughout 1646 shared these principles and came to support the programs that Holles had developed. This is not to say that the recruiters joined Holles's party in greater numbers than they did Haselrig's.[3] Whereas some had stood for Parliament on ideological grounds, the majority were simply representatives of the parliamentary country gentry, buoyed to places of prominence by the elimination of their royalist counterparts. The parties had developed from internal controversy as much as from principled commitment, and the recruited members were free from the bitterness of the past. They were also unconstrained by the time-honored methods of decision making, having had little parliamentary experience and having taken their seats amidst the developing party controversy. Thus they were a curious hybrid: with their perception of policy akin to that of the Lords who opposed continued governmental innovation and their understanding of procedure adopted from the party leaders.

Holles's majority was constituted from support he received from those outside his party. Godly Presbyterians, anti-innovatory peers, uncommitted country M.P.s, whether recruiters or perdurable backbenchers, swelled the small core of his party supporters. However much confrontation dominated daily routine, the House of Commons was not divided only into two political parties. Holles was the beneficiary but not the initiator of the revival of agitation for religious reformation. The weekly debates on lay preaching and the growth of heresy were conducted by a group of orthodox Presbyterians. Holles shrewdly threw in his lot with their program for church establishment, although their political support was easily exchangeable for his own opposition to proposals for religious toleration. Similarly, the resurgence of the House of Lords' political initiative was not of Holles's making; indeed the Lords' unwillingness to provide financial support for the Army obstructed Holles's program of military reconstruction. Not until he coopted the anti-innovatory peers onto the Derby House Committee was his majority secure.

Policy and circumstance thus produced the single most powerful leader of the Long Parliament. Since the conclusion of fighting in June, Holles had proposed plans to dissolve the military establishment, reform parliamentary finances, and suppress the Irish rebellion. As his opponents had chosen to prepare for further war and continued taxation, once the tide turned toward peace the political initiative fully passed into Holles's hands. Unrestrained by the procedural safeguards that had enmeshed Pym and no longer controlled by the need to maintain unity, he was free to pursue a single-minded and coordinated political policy. The strength of his majority enabled Holles to attain total political control. By securing Scottish withdrawal and preparing Irish invasion, he controlled important standing committees; by introducing legislation across a wide range of issues he came to report and manage much of the Commons' business with the Lords; by recasting the Derby House Committee into an executive body, Holles ruled over both the Irish invasion and the military disestablishment. In all of this he replaced not only his political opponents but also those administrative experts who had overseen Scottish and military affairs and had partaken in the diffusion of political power. Haselrig, Evelyn, and their supporters were also effectively eliminated from political participation. With control of an insuperable majority, Holles worked not only to achieve his policies, but to crush his political opposition. During the first half of 1647 Parliament witnessed the brief but tumultuous reign of "King Party."

Before Holles could secure his majority he had to face the repercussions that party conflict had created in relations between the two Houses. During the autumn of 1646, as tensions rose and attitudes hardened, the House of Commons had ordered troops disbanded and funds disbursed without the consent of the peers. They had pressured the Lords to accept legislation by constant bullying, by adhering to their own votes, by threatening unicameral action, and finally, in the dispatch of an important communication to the Scots, by circumventing the Upper House entirely. Nor did the ascendancy of Holles and his party arrest this development. Initially, as the parties in the Commons struggled for power, the group of anti-innovatory peers supported those of Holles's programs that coincided with their own aspirations. But the intricate procedures for inter-House communication and decision making could not withstand the transformation of the political process in one House alone. Cooperation between the party-controlled Commons and the institutionally unsophisticated Lords would soon lead to Lower House dominance. Whether or not they were conscious of the process of political change, the Lords, especially the anti-innovatory ones, were acutely aware of their loss of power and initiative. By the beginning of 1647 they began to combat the Commons on their own grounds, using the same pressure tactics to achieve legislation and to confront the Lower House in defense of the rights of the peerage. Not surprisingly, their foray into adversary politics gave the Lords a taste for the other techniques developed to aid the workings of the parties. Soon divisions replaced dissents and sharp parliamentary tactics appeared as the Upper House underwent changes in political practice similar to those that had occurred in the Commons.

Contentions between the Houses continued to focus upon delays in considering legislation and refusals to pass ordinances. Many issues remained unresolved since the autumn and provided the soil for the regeneration of political initiative in the Upper House. Chief among these was the controversy over the Goldsmiths' Hall Committee. In October the Commons had preemptively ordered the Goldsmiths' Hall treasurers to disburse funds without the Lords' approval. As they had also indemnified the treasurers against punishment by the Lords, the Upper House could retaliate only by ordering an audit of the treasurers' accounts. This began on January 4 and by then the Lords had completed an ordinance to define the powers of the Committee, prohibit its activities without orders from both Houses, and expand to fifteen the number of peers who would be commissioners to the Committee.[4] Two days later the Lords presented their bill to the Commons and requested that it be considered expeditiously. The Commons thereupon appointed a committee to examine the ordinance and required it to meet in daily session until its report was ready.[5] So far the legislative process was running smoothly. On January 14, according to their charge, the Commons' committee reported the Lords' ordinance and a number of amendments they had made to it. In the course of its ensuing debate the full House determined that the intent of the Lords' action could as easily be accomplished by fresh instructions to the old commissioners as by a new ordinance. They therefore returned the matter to their committee, which was to prepare instructions to eliminate the abuses of which the Lords complained.[6]

As the Lords' chief concern was the ability of the Commons to enforce its own orders upon the Goldsmiths' Hall Committee, a set of new instructions from the Commons, rather than rectifying the abuse, compounded it. Moreover, in abandoning the Lords' bill in favor of instructions the Commons had suspended the parliamentary procedure that established that all bills must either be approved or amended. Finally, the Lower House did not find it necessary to inform the peers that their bill had been discarded.

But the Lords were now determined that the Goldsmiths' Hall Committee be reformed by legislation and appeared willing to devise pressure tactics of their own to secure the passage of their bill. Almost two weeks after they had first requested expedition of their ordinance, on January 18, the Lords found a means to express their resolution. On that day the Commons proposed a conference to discuss the Lords' refusal to approve the ordinance for the Army assessment and the bills to continue the Army Committee and the treasurers at war. The Lords flatly refused the conference. This was a dramatic and radical action, for the conference was the single safety valve preventing parliamentary deadlock. Aware of the consequences of their decision, the Lords then voted a second time on whether to meet with the Commons. Again the conference was refused, and subsequent debate revealed that the majority of Lords were using it as a lever to reopen the consideration of the Goldsmiths' Hall ordinance. Only after agreement was reached that the conference would also discuss that legislation did a majority of peers accede to the Commons' request.[7] In their afternoon session prior to the conference, the Lords prepared instructions for the debate on Goldsmiths' Hall. They advised their speaker to inform the Lower House that "their Lordships conceive that the not giving expedition to that ordinance gives an obstruction to all their affairs there."[8] For their part, the Commons prepared instructions for the debate on the Army.

The Lords' determination to empower the Committee at Goldsmiths' Hall with an ordinance of their own making, thereby ensuring their participation in the Committee's activities, was not achieved through this conference. Although they had forced the topic on the agenda, the Houses worked at cross-purposes, with two different topics to be discussed. The threat not to confer until their ordinance was considered did not accomplish its intended effect, but this failure did not weaken their resolve. Further pressure was necessary and the Lords were ready to provide it. After waiting another two weeks for the Commons to act upon their ordinance, the peers decided upon unilateral action. They prepared a public declaration stating that the activities of the Goldsmiths' Hall Committee were without parliamentary authority. On February 1 the peers debated the final draft of this declaration along with a proposal that it be presented to the Commons at a conference before its publication. This compromise suggestion was rejected by a majority in the Upper House, who now felt that only by decisive action could the Commons be made to respond to the Lords' legislative initiative. The declaration was ordered to be printed and distributed to all the county sequestration committees. They were instructed that compositions at Goldsmiths' Hall were suspended "until such time as a committee or commissioners to that purpose be settled by ordinance of Parliament."[9]

This peremptory action finally awakened the Commons to the firm intention of the Upper House to have their ordinance passed. On February 2 the Commons was informed of the Lords' action and of the document they had ordered printed, "which declaration the House did resent very much."[10] They attempted to halt its publication, arguing in a communication to the peers that the declaration "takes away the reputation of Parliament" and "calls their justice into question."[11] They did not need to add that the compositions at Goldsmiths' Hall were a vital source of ready cash. Now it was the Lords who turned a deaf ear; the declaration would be rescinded only after the Commons had passed a new empowering ordinance. The next day the Lower House examined all former ordinances, orders, and de facto actions that constituted the mandate of the Goldsmiths' Hall Committee.[12] If this dredging of precedents was prelude to a challenge of the Lords' contention that the Committee was acting without authority, it was soon abandoned in preference to a reexamination of the amendments to the Lords' original bill.

With uncharacteristic haste the Commons made minor changes in the ordinance and returned it to the Upper House. At this point the prime movers of the ordinance revealed themselves and their motives. In one of their amendments, the Commons had reworded the bill to signify that the members of the Goldsmiths' Hall Committee were committeemen rather than commissioners. This was no quibble, for the principle of proportional representation decreed that committees were to be composed of two commoners for every Lord, whereas the Houses could appoint equal numbers of commissioners. On the basis of their amendment, therefore, the Commons had added sufficient M.P.s to achieve its two-to-one ratio. But in the Upper House a group of peers insisted that the members of the Committee were commissioners to a committee that sat outside Parliament; they therefore demanded that the number of Lords and commons be equal. Insistence upon this safeguard suggests that some Lords believed that the two Houses had come to represent competing interests. But with the war won, the majority of peers saw no need for further battle. They reamended the ordinance to establish that the members of the Goldsmiths' Hall Committee were commissioners, but they did not insist upon equal representation. This vote drew dissents from five peers: the Earls of Lincoln, Suffolk, and Middlesex and Lords Hereford and Willoughby.[13] The Lords had recaptured their ability to initiate and accomplish legislation in the face of opposition from the Lower House; at the forefront of their militancy were the leaders of the group of anti-innovatory peers.

The protracted controversy over the committee of commissioners who sat at Goldsmiths' Hall was only one indication that the rule of Holles' party did not extend to the Upper House. Another was the Lords' refusal to accede to the Commons' ordinance, twice brought to their House by Holles himself, on keepers for the Great Seal. When Holles presented the Commons' request that the seal be held by three civil Commissioners to the Lords on January 16, it crossed a bill sent by the Lords to the Commons desiring that the Seal be held by their speaker, the Earl of Manchester. After the Commons refused to consider this ordinance and again pressed the Lords to accept the bill for civil Commissioners, the Upper House refused a request for a conference, and in their next session rejected the Commons' proposal.[14] Nor did the Lords knuckle under to pressure from the Lower House to accept the bills for the maintenance for the Army and the establishment of a new monthly assessment. On January 11 Richard Knightly, a leading member of the Army Committee, was sent to the Upper House to urge the Lords to act on these matters, "and to acquaint them with the important great necessity of the speedy passing them."[15] Despite this appeal, and the Commons' arguments that the money raised would be used to pay arrears and reimburse free quarter, the Lords refused to assent to a continuation of wartime taxes.[16] Although the

Commons would continue to press, it was not until March 4 that the Lords finally acted upon the proposals for continued military assessments. On that day it rejected them.[17]

The Lords' resurgence as a partner in the legislative process was linked to the emergence of the group of peers opposed to continued governmental innovations by the Lower House. Throughout the winter their philosophy was made clear both in pronouncements during conferences with the Commons and in the initiation of a program of legislation. In January the Lords had accepted the final official correspondence of the Scottish Commissioners with the asseveration that their letters "show faithfulness and fidelity."[18] Concurring with the Scots' requests, the Lords avowed that no harm would come to the King once he was placed in the custody of the parliamentary commissioners and "that there will be no change of government other than has been these three years past."[19] This same note of conservatism was sounded in February, when the Lords, insisting on their ordinance to suppress the county committees, attended a conference with the Commons. The dissolution of the county committees, their spokesmen told the Lower House, "is expected from both Houses according to the several declarations of Parliament to bring things into the old course and way of government."[20] Pointing to the chaotic Somerset Committee and to the absence of committees in Yorkshire and Lincolnshire, the Lords importuned the Commons to eliminate all the committees and to return local government to the traditional county officials. "They hold themselves obliged as well by the great sense they have of the Kingdom's desires herein, as making good to the world, that these extraordinary ways of proceeding shall not be continued."[21]

The "great sense" the Lords had of the kingdom's desires emanated from the coincidence of their programs with the wishes expressed to them from citizens of the nation. In December 1646 the City of London had presented yet another petition to Parliament. As in the previous May, the Common Council had prepared separate addresses to the two Houses. In their representation to the Lords they requested that the Army be disbanded and its assessments abolished, that debts incurred during the war be repaid by the sale of delinquents' estates, that illegal lay preaching be suppressed, that the covenant become a test of loyalty to Parliament, and that the abuses of parliamentary committees be rectified. Almost every point of the City's petition appealed to the Lords' own concerns, and the complaints against abusive committees and excessive taxes gave support to their disputes with the Commons. To stress the urgency of this new entreaty, and to remind the Parliament that the City's remonstrances remained unanswered, the Common Council devised a sophisticated lobbying campaign. In a geographical progression that began in the City's easternmost wards, two common councillors were to attend the doors of the Houses of Parliament daily and to beseech the members to grant the City's requests.[22]

Nor was the Londoners' appeal the only expression of "the desires of the nation" to which the Lords responded. On February 16 a delegation from Suffolk presented a petition to them. They praised the efforts of the City and repeated the solicitations for the establishment of a reformed church, the suppression of heresy, relief from excessive taxation, and the disbanding of the Army. Echoing the Lords' own promulgations they also advocated "that special care may be had for the preservation of his Majesty's person and authority in the maintenance of true religion, privileges of the Parliament, and liberties of the Kingdom."[23] One month later Essex added its collective voice to these pleas for military disestablishment and financial relief.[24] To all these the Lords responded not only with the thanks of their House for the concern of the citizenry, but with a program of legislation designed to restore normality to church and state. Indeed their enthusiastic reception of the City's petition prompted Thomas Juxon to reflect that "it was certainly to carry on their own designs."[25]

With a philosophy and a constituency, the majority in the House of Lords was now shaping its own political policy. The willingness of the conservative peers to confront the Lower House on legislation such as the Goldsmiths' Hall ordinance and to resist the pressure for the strengthening of the Army demonstrated the revival of the Lords' initiative. Yet this resurgence was not without cost. The anti-innovatory peers could command a majority but their single-minded pursuit of policy was achieved only by sweeping aside the objections of their colleagues. As it had in the Lower House, forceful decision making was transforming the political process, this time with the added irony that it was accomplished in a cause that sought to reassert traditional political arrangements.

The signs of transformation were unmistakable. In January, by refusing to grant a conference with the Commons until their own legislation was considered, the conservative peers displayed their readiness to manipulate the most basic elements of the deliberative process for political advantage. In February, imitating the Commons, they took their first unilateral action, publishing the declaration suspending the activities of the Goldsmiths' Hall Committee. These courses bitterly divided the Upper House, for both occurred after the rejection of more moderate alternatives. Soon the consequences of these divisions came clear. On March 1 the Lords found it necessary to establish that no bill could achieve three readings and passage in one session.[26] Like the order that no new business could be debated after noon, this was designed to inhibit manipulation by temporary majorities. Indeed, with attendance in the Upper House sometimes as low as eleven or thirteen, a majority could comprise only six or seven. With the House polarized, majorities were as much a matter of daily attendance as ideological commitment. But it was fear of manipulation rather than sparsity of attendance that spurred this tightening of procedure.

In the following week a far more significant procedural innovation occurred in the Upper House. After hearing amendments to a bill authorizing payments owed to two arms merchants, Pennoyer and Hill, the House voted on its committee's report. Seventeen Lords were in attendance, but rather than computing the majority and recording its decision, the peers instead held their first formal division with the Lords De La Warr and North appointed tellers to tabulate the ayes and noes.[27] On the same day two further divisions were recorded, with tellers appointed to count the votes of fourteen and fifteen members who were then in attendance. Obviously, these divisions did not result from the Speaker's inability to determine a majority, nor were they simply a manner by which the minority could express its opposition to a motion. In their practice of entering dissents, the Lords traditionally maintained the right of individual peers to dissociate themselves from the actions of their House. In two critical ways did the division differ from the dissent: it diminished the importance of the individual peer and it institutionalized opposition. The dissent was a moral rather than a political act. It emphasized the individual importance of each peer above the cumulation of opinion and was not used to express ordinary contrariety. The division was, by now, an explicitly political device used to effectuate leadership by the tellers and to identify support and opposition. Its appearance was ample proof that a tyrannical majority had abandoned the quest for unity in the House of Lords.[28]

The assumption of party techniques by the peers was another indication of the predominance adversary politics had achieved at Westminster. With the Lords now as capable of unified and decisive action as the Commons, an alliance between Holles and his party and the anti-innovatory peers would transform both Houses into a single efficient decision-making body. This was the setting for Holles's rise in the Lower House. As autumn turned to winter and Parliament occupied itself with preparations for the reception of the King and hopes for the settlement of peace, Holles began the solidification of his political power base.

The disengagement he had negotiated with the Scots was effected smoothly and efficiently. The fears of the King's flight abroad and of the intentions of the Scottish Army were finally laid to rest and the two Houses were fully assured that the war was over. The dominant role played by Holles and Stapleton in securing the City loan and achieving the Scottish withdrawal was soon translated into a position of primacy in the House of Commons. The major political issues that faced the nation now were the resolution of the Irish rebellion and the dismantling of the military machinery. Holles and his followers had proposed to resolve both problems with a single solution in July: the deployment of the New Model Army. Although this recommendation had been then rejected in favor of recruiting forces out of the local and reigonal establishments, the rationale for keeping the New Model in service was removed with the last of the Scottish infantry. Already in December the London Common Council had petitioned that the Army be disbanded, and the pressure the Commons placed upon the Lords to continue the New Model assessment stemmed, in part, from a desire to have funds available for the settlement of their arrears.

That the suppression of the Irish rebellion and the dissolution of the military establishment appeared as interconnected problems brought the fate of the New Model into the hands of many who had opposed its creation. The paramount position Holles achieved in the Lower House resulted partly from the successful accomplishment of his policy for Scottish withdrawal and partly because

he and his followers had always appeared as leaders in the movement for peace. The desire of parliamentarians for an end to the
burdens brought about by the war and of the godly for a final
establishment of religion that would halt the dizzying proliferation
of profane practice made support for Holles's policies inevitable.
Holles's rise as a parliamentary leader is thus indisputable. Besides
his control of the Derby House Committee, from which he personally reported important calculations on troops and finances,
Holles was the prime mover of the ordinance for the Great Seal,
twice carrying votes to the Lords and once, with Stapleton and
Browne, managing a conference.[29] On January 9 he delivered votes
to the Upper House on the regulation of the admiralty and the
Cinque Ports, replacing the usual naval administrative experts Sir
Henry Vane, Jr., and Giles Green.[30] When the Scots sent in their
final requests prior to surrendering the King it was Holles who
reported the conference with the Lords and who, some days later,
sent a letter of thanks to the Earl of Leven.[31] At the beginning of
February he and Stapleton were added to the Goldsmiths' Hall
Committee and became Commissioners when the Committee was
expanded.[32] In seven divisions in which he acted as teller during
the first quarter of the year, only one was carried against him, and
that was on the relatively unimportant question of an appointment
of a circuit judge.[33] By the end of March Holles stood atop a
process of decision making that enabled him and his followers to
pursue and coordinate political policy.

The program that Holles undertook at the height of his power
was designed to facilitate an accord with the King by eliminating
issues that could not be compromised. Suppressing the rebellion in
Ireland and dissolving much of the nation's future militia were
important first steps. Although Holles is generally conceived to
have been an opponent to the Army, until the end of March the
measures he developed had sound military and monetary bases.
Beginning in November 1646, when the Commons first passed a
new assessment bill for the Army, Holles became intent upon
furnishing the New Model with money to alleviate the burdens it
placed upon the countryside. In a conference with the Lords on
January 18 the Commons summarized their arguments for the continuation of the assessment. A part of the Army was currently
employed at Newcastle attending the King and would be needed
there or at Holmby House, the Army's arrears would have to be

discharged, and the communities in which the Army had quartered would have to be reimbursed.[34] These were the same reasons presented by a minority of peers when the assessment bill finally reached its third reading in the House of Lords on March 4: "their Lordships being sensible of the great services done by the Army and holding it just and honorable that the officers and soldiers there should receive satisfaction before their disbanding, and being very desirous the country should have allowance for the free quarter which the Army was necessitated to take for want of pay." Claiming they knew of no "other or better means of raising money speedily for the said purpose," a group of peers led by the Earls of Northumberland and Kent entered dissents to the refusal of the majority in their House to pass the assessment ordinance.[35]

The other or better means for redeeming the Army's arrears was also a topic of concern in the Commons. On January 16 the House turned to military affairs and, despite the Lords' refusal, empowered the Army Committee to continue its operations.[36] On that day, as the Commons sat in grand committee to resolve a course for auditing and paying the Army's accounts, Colonel John Birch delivered in an ordinance for the sale of delinquents' estates to pay "the soldiery of the whole Kingdom."[37] During the next two weeks the House continued to debate this proposal and nearly succeeded in establishing a deadline for compositions after which time estates might be sold.[38] These inconclusive deliberations were given impetus on February 4 when 700 soldiers from Edward Massey's disbanded brigade arrived en masse in London to deliver a petition for their arrears. Their complaints of penury prompted the House to vote them £1,000, about a month's pay for an infantryman.[39] Their behavior also prompted the House to order Massey to disperse them to their homes "that they may not come to solicit or further trouble the Parliament."[40] Although no means were found to repay arrears, a committee was appointed to prepare an order to prevent disbanded soldiers from imitating this unruly conduct.

The problem of maintaining the Army was directly related to the general financial difficulties faced by Parliament at the war's end. Although they proffered no solution for settling the kingdom's debts, the Lords' refusal to pass the Army assessment demonstrated their opposition to the perpetuation of the heavy wartime levies. Indeed, their fiscal conservatism bordered on impracticality.

As the Commons prepared to seek another massive loan from the City, the Lords were considering a bill that would lower interest rates from 8 to 6 percent.[41] Since the autumn Parliament's most pressing debts as well as its payments to high-ranking military commanders and insolvent Lords and Commons' members were satisfied by the compositions received at Goldsmiths' Hall. In January Sir Robert Pye, Hardress Waller, Sir Samuel Luke, and Major General Richard Browne, among others, had been given orders allowing them to nominate delinquents' compositions that would settle their accounts.[42] The Earl of Northumberland was granted £10,000 for the losses he incurred during the war.[43] On March 9 a majority in a sparsely attended Commons' session set a precedent with staggering implications when it granted Sir William Constable the portion of his pay that had been held back on the public faith.[44] Even the maintenance of the King was a costly business, the revenue committee estimated twenty days' entertainment of the monarch and his entourage at £3,000.[45]

The compositions being received at Goldsmiths' Hall could not bear the full burden of these extraordinary charges and the social consequences of allowing prominent military officers to search for compositions may have outweighed the extra revenue that was obtained in this manner. Although the Lords had proved unwilling to continue the Army assessments, the other cornerstone of wartime finance, the excise, had been guaranteed perpetuation by huge deficit spending. On January 20 Miles Corbett reported that over £400,000 had been charged against the future receipts of the excise, and this sum did not include the 8-percent interest that had been granted to raise the most recent advances.[46] In addition, Corbett related the difficulties collectors were now experiencing in obtaining the excise taxes. Entire communities were proving recalcitrant, even important market centers like Norwich. Butchers and brewers were hardened excise evaders, Corbett stated in February when he suggested improvements in tax-collecting procedures.[47] The Commons ordered not only the reformation of the abuses of the subcommissioners, who were proving the equal of the tax dodgers, but also the publication of a justification for the continuation of excise collection. But rather than making it more lucrative or more palatable, the streamlining of the excise collection only led to a riot in Smithfield the following week. A tumultuous crowd led "by a great mutiny of butchers" burned the

Smithfield custom house after first assuring themselves of the destruction of the excise records.[48]

The inability of Parliament to improve its financial condition in the face of a taxpayers' revolt and the unwillingness of the Lords to continue the Army assessments made both the Irish venture and the military reorganization more difficult. Although unable to resolve upon a course for paying the forces, Holles moved forward with his plan to dismantle the obsolescent military machinery. On February 17 the Commons held the first of three long debates on the fate of all of Parliament's forces. Without the certainty of paying its arrears, Haselrig and Evelyn attempted to forestall votes on the New Model's disbandment until after the dissolution of the forces in the localities was accomplished. This vote was carried against them by Holles and Stapleton.[49] Their slender majority of 2 in a House of 292 did not reveal the strength of either party, for the consideration of local forces attracted support for various reasons, whereas the absence of an arrangement to pay the New Model's arrears was a further cause for delay. But once their priorities were established, the House resolved on the following day to maintain in England a force of 5,400 horse and 1,000 dragoons exclusive of those in local garrisons.[50] Holles and Stapleton carried another close division on the 19th to disband all infantry that were not to be placed in the garrisons.[51] With the fate of the New Model determined, the Commons then turned to the question of local disestablishment. For the remainder of the month the majority of the nation's strongholds were ordered demolished or made "untenable."[52]

It was not until the beginning of March that the Commons returned to the issue of the forces that were to remain as a standing Army. On the 5th, by 12 votes in a House of 306, it was decided to organize the troops remaining in England into an Army to be placed under the command of Sir Thomas Fairfax.[53] Although this vote was carried by a narrow majority, it was more an administrative than a party issue. Neither Holles nor Stapleton acted as teller, and the alternative to a single Army was dispersed local regiments. Many who voted against Fairfax's command did so in hope that he would then lead the Army in Ireland. Moreover, on March 8 the Lower House debated and resolved far more volatile issues without divisions. On that day it was established that no other officer in the English Army would hold a rank above colonel, that no M.P. would hold command, and that none would continue in service without taking the covenant.[54] This revival of the principles of self-denial was, doubtless, the source of renewed bitterness. "There wants not in all places men who have so much malice against the Army as besots them," Cromwell wrote to Fairfax some days after these votes.[55] Nevertheless merely noting the conflict between adherents and opponents to the New Model does not provide a full explanation of these resolutions. Cromwell was not the sole officer who held a rank above colonel, and if this order was a parting shot at him it is curious that Major General Philip Skippon should have been caught in the crossfire. Nor was Cromwell the unique victim of the renewal of self-denial. Skippon, Harley, Pye, and Rossiter, as well as Rainsborough, Ireton, Harrison, and Fleetwood, were all M.P.'s. In addition, by now the covenant was as much a test of political as religious allegiance; it had been wholly ineffective in sifting religious radicals out of either the New Model or the Parliament, and its revival was accompanied by an order prohibiting any who had served the King from future military employment.[56]

The vote to reapply the covenant was also a reaction by the large group of members who demanded the continuation of godly reformation. Throughout January and February the House sat in weekly Grand Committees to discuss the problem of lay preaching that, despite its prohibition by an ordinance of 1645, continued unabated. Doubtless the regiments of the New Model that were dominated by adherents to radical religion were a source of abuse, and the House head numerous complaints about preaching by soldiers. But the New Model was not the only place where lay preaching flourished, and dramatic examples of other profane practice, like the minister who despite Parliament's prohibition continued to observe Christmas Day, reminded the Commons that reform of the Army was a small beginning.[57] Nor was the problem of lay preaching one with an easy solution. The distinction between the usurpation of the professional prerogatives of ordained ministers and the saints' duty to expound the Scriptures was one that trod the fine line between orthodoxy and heresy. The spread of heresy, undeniable in the face of four years of religious confusion, lack of trained ministers; and the implications of puritan theology were the deeper issues that occupied the godly M.P.s and colored at least some of their political decisions. An extraordinary fast to seek guidance in suppressing the spread of heretical doctrine was appointed for March 10.[58] On March 8 the Commons had voted that all who were to be governors of garrisons would have to conform to the established church.[59] Although this vote was resolved in a division in which all four party leaders acted as tellers, it was intimately connected to the movement for religious stability, and was followed by an order "that no profane curser, swearer, drunkard, or whoremaster" be employed in the public trust, traits from which the radical sects, at this time, were particularly immune.[60]

It is important to distinguish between this current of religious reformation and the political program pursued by Holles for military disestablishment. Holles was supported by the elements in the House – men like Yelverton, Tate, Whitacre, and Yonge – that were appalled by the spread of heretical practices, as well as by those faceless M.P.s who craved a return to normality. Conformity to the church remained a keystone to settling the affairs of the nation and did not necessarily represent doctrinaire presbyterianism, for the dimensions of the accommodation for tender consciences were yet to be measured. Indeed this point may have been the one that allowed Haselrig and Evelyn to carry 108 votes against the motion linking military employment to conformity to the church. These decisions, which appeared provocative to some members of the Army and which have always been interpreted to represent Holles's blind opposition to the New Model, stemmed from other sources. Actually, Holles's posture toward the New Model has been wildly misconstrued.

It is of considerable importance that Holles's majority supported the new Army assessment, which had been drawn up by the Army Committee during the previous autumn. Throughout January and February the Commons, under Holles's leadership, pressed the House of Lords to accept the ordinance that would keep the Army solvent regardless of the service it would be called upon to perform. In January a committee had been appointed to investigate the prosecutions of soldiers for acts committed during the war and, in response to numerous petitions from aggrieved officers and soldiers, was revived the following month.[61] In March circuit judges were instructed not to try wartime acts as criminal cases. In addition to reprieving those who were imprisoned, Parliament acted to relieve those who were destitute. At the end of February the Committee that paid the accounts of widows of parliamentary officers and soldiers was furnished with £50 a week in addition to the £10,000 that had been borrowed in the autumn.[62]

Besides the concern for the Army's material well-being, the House of Commons also supported Fairfax's autonomy in stationing and quartering his forces. In early March the Lords had attempted to diminish this power by ordering that none of the New Model forces be quartered in the Eastern Association.[63] This order resulted from a complaint from the Eastern Counties that the Army's recent stationing there was an insupportable burden. Fairfax communicated the Lords' orders to the Lower House along with the details of how the Midlands and the counties of the Thames Valley were depleted of supplies from the many months they had suffered the Army's presence.[64]

Fairfax's letter arrived on March 11, the same day that the Commons received a petition from Essex. The Essex petition not only requested relief from burdens imposed by the Army's presence, but accused the Army of disaffecting the people from true religion by its preaching of false doctrine. Impugning the Army's intentions, the petitioners claimed that the New Model's decision to quarter so near London "makes us fear there is some design to have an awing influence upon the proceedings of Parliament."[65] In response to the Essex petition the Commons forthrightly expressed its sense of the Army and its conduct. "This House has no cause of jealousy of the Army: but as they have been constantly faithful, so they cannot doubt but they will continue faithful."[66] The Commons directed Fairfax to quarter the Army at his own discretion in spite of the Lords' votes that he should clear his regiments from the Eastern Association. The difference in attitude between the Houses was clearly evinced when Fairfax reported the Commons' votes to the Lords on March 19. The peers divided evenly on whether Fairfax's letters were an adequate response to their orders.[67] By then Parliament had received another petition from the City of London requesting the removal of the Army from its environs as well as its disbanding. To this petition the Commons affirmed only that the Army should quarter twenty-five miles from the City, a line that Fairfax had established well within the borders of the Eastern Counties.[68]

That Holles was not directing a campaign to ruin the New Model is clearly demonstrated by these actions. The Army was still linked to his plan to invade Ireland. When the Committee for

Irish Affairs had reported that suppression of the rebellion could best be accomplished with the immediate dispatch of an army of 3,000 horse and 8,400 infantry, it was made clear that the invasion force could not be raised in the localities.[69] Therefore, without division, the Commons reversed its vote of the previous July and ordered seven infantry and four cavalry regiments detached from the New Model.[70] The Derby House Committee was also instructed to raise 1,200 dragoons, a number larger than the whole of Okey's New Model regiment.[71] On March 17 the Committee began consultation with Fairfax to determine a course for sending these New Model regiments into Ireland.[72] At the same time, an ordinance was brought in for a new military assessment, a monthly charge of £60,000 for all the forces that were to be continued in England and Ireland.[73] Thus Holles's plan for suppressing the Irish rebellion and thinning out the forces in England was complete. An Army equivalent in size to the New Model would remain deployed, although it would be divided into a standing Army, an Irish invasion force, and troops to man the nation's garrisons. Its pay would be provided by a new monthly assessment. Short of maintaining the entire military establishment, an obvious impossibility, Holles's plan for reorganization was the least painful one possible, and within Parliament it aroused little opposition.

By linking the disbanding of the extraneous soldiery to the plans for the Irish invasion, Holles had effectively gained control over all military matters. This was seen on March 23 when the Lords requested a conference to discuss the future of the Army. For the first time the Commons did not appoint any of the leading members of the Army Committee among its reporters. Instead, Holles, Stapleton, Pierrepont, Glyn, Wheeler, and Lewes were now in control of military affairs.[74] In this conference the Lords bitterly protested the Commons' refusal to remove the Army from the Eastern Association. They argued that the New Model's presence so near to London would place an insupportable burden upon the City's food supply. They also hinted that its proximity to the capital was an encouragement to disaffected citizens who looked to the Army for support. For these reasons the Lords demanded that the New Model be disbanded.[75] In response, Holles was able to report his own plans for resolving the military situation. A delegation had already been sent to meet with Sir Thomas Fairfax and his officers to arrange the details for the dispatch of eleven regiments to Ireland. Once these arrangements were completed, the Lords' concerns would be mollified by the discharge of the remaining soldiers.

On March 27 this parliamentary delegation returned from the Army. Sir William Waller and Sir John Clotworthy reported that they had informed the Army officers of Parliament's votes and had received a series of questions from them relating to the terms of the Irish service and the satisfaction of their material grievances.[76] They also presented a statement from twenty-eight officers who were willing to subscribe for Ireland "resting confident of the Parliament's care to give satisfaction concerning their arrears, and to provide a competent maintenance for the subsistence of that Army in their service and also for making provision for their indemnity for past services."[77] Finally Waller and Clotworthy informed the House that a petition was being circulated among the soldiery that might prove detrimental to the venture. Although disquieting, this news did not impede Holles's plans. Fairfax was directed to halt the circulation of the petition and the House appointed a day to debate the command of the Irish expedition, one of the questions put by the Army officers. To prevent any misunderstanding, the Commons passed a resolution declaring "that notwithstanding any information this day given to the House they have a good opinion of the Army."[78]

In their next session, on March 29, the House turned its attention to the creation of the new standing Army. Although it had been decided that the administrative structure of this force would be centralized, the regiments themselves were to be locally based. The Northern Army, the largest of all of Parliament's supernumerary forces, was ordered disbanded with the exception of the three regiments under Colonels Poyntz, Bethell, and Copley.[79] In the midst of the debate over recruiting men to fill these regiments, Colonels Edward Harley and Edward Rossiter rose in the House to report dramatic new developments within the New Model. That morning they had each received communications from trusted members of their regiments informing them of the continuation of the soldiers' petition. The letters spoke of a widespread and successful subscription campaign led by high-ranking Army officers, including Commissary General Ireton. Harley's own major, Thomas Pride, was accused of threatening to cashier any soldier who refused to put his name to the petition.[80] A copy of the illicit document was then read out in the Commons. It made manifest that subscribers to it would not engage for the Irish service until Parliament redressed their grievances.

The report of the petition threw the House into turmoil and Holles's plans into disarray. Without volunteers for the Irish service neither the creation of the standing Army nor the disbanding could proceed. The challenge to Holles's hegemony that could not be mounted in Parliament was now being launched in the Army. Thus his reaction to the news of the petition was immediate and uncompromising. As the grievances listed in the petition were already under review, a conciliatory response was possible. But Holles was determined to cut off the agitation at its head. All officers named as participants in the campaign were ordered to appear before the bar of the House of Commons. Major General Skippon was directed to repair to Army headquarters and personally to put an end to the petitioning campaign. The Derby House Committee was instructed to draw out all officers and soldiers willing to subscribe for Ireland and to disband the rest immediately. A committee of four, headed by Holles, was appointed to prepare an appropriate response to the petition, to be considered as the first order of business the next morning.[81]

But Holles was unwilling to allow the passions of the House to cool. Rather than leave the House, which was now thinning after the votes against the petition, he reportedly "scribbled on his knee" to draft the declaration.[82] At nine o'clock that night he presented it for consideration.[83] Beginning with a statement of Parliament's "high dislike of that petition," it ordered the Army to forebear from proceeding with it and warned "that all those who shall continue in their distempered condition, and go on in advancing and promoting that petition shall be looked upon and proceeded against as enemies to the state and disturbers of the public peace."[84] The declaration and all the extraordinary Commons' votes were sent to the Upper House, which passed them the following morning without dissent.[85] Holles's determination to settle the Irish rebellion and to disband the remainder of the New Model was now clear; within Parliament his ability to do so was now incontestable.

Throughout the spring of 1647 Holles and his majority reigned supreme at Westminster. By coupling the invasion of Ireland with the military reorganization his policies appealed to a broad range of parliamentary members and created an insuperable majority in the Lower House. "All the Independent party are exceedingly sunk in spirit," wrote Clarendon's London correspondent in April, a judgment substantiated by the lack of political initiative Haselrig and Evelyn displayed throughout the opening months of the year.[86] Holles's coordination of policy was accompanied by a consolidation of the mechanisms of decision making. The Derby House Committee, called into existence with the cessation of hostilities in Ireland, soon became his base of operation. By a vast extension of power and a thorough alteration of membership the Derby House Committee was transformed into an executive body. In the House of Commons it replaced the Committee of Both Kingdoms as the locus of policy formulation and implementation. In the House of Lords, once the group of anti-innovatory peers was added in April, it became the vehicle by which contentions between the Houses were finally eradicated. In this manner Holles was able to secure a vital element of his majority as well as an institutionalized channel for his power.

In attaining this predominance, Holles left his political opponents desperate. No longer could they expect their proposals to be considered by the full House, where an unsympathetic majority could and would stifle debate and carry divisions. Nor could they hope to influence the implementation of policy by appointment to the House's customary working committees. The accumulation of power by the Derby House Committee attenuated the power of all other "ordinary" units of administration, and the few committees now called into being were either unmanageably large or carefully composed. The traditional inclusion of spokesmen of differing persuasions had given way to the rule of a tyrannical majority. "The authority of Parliament," wrote William White, M.P. for Pontefract, to Sir Thomas Fairfax, is "that which is passed by a majority of votes however contrary to particular opinions."[87] The transformation of the political process was as evident in White's need to define Parliament's authority as in the definition itself.

Although his power was institutionalized through the Derby House Committee and his programs were supported by a majority in both Houses of Parliament and by vocal pressure groups within the City, Holles ruled almost alone. He personally directed each aspect of his political program: reporting the votes for the creation of the Irish invasion force; carefully organizing the military dissolution; negotiating a loan from the City; and coordinating a new appeal for peace to the King. The frustrations experienced by Haselrig and Evelyn were complete. From January to the end of May Sir Arthur was a teller in fifteen parliamentary divisions, of which he was able to carry just one.[88] Evelyn achieved only slightly better results, telling the majority in four of the fourteen contests that he counted, although two of these came when he appeared with members of Holles's party, Sir William Lewes and Sir Philip Stapleton.[89] Moreover, their inability to carry even the most insignificant political decisions was aggravated by Holles's willingness to turn parliamentary procedure to his advantage. Not only were temporary working committees replaced by permanent standing ones, but apolitical administrative committees were jettisoned in favor of the burgeoning Derby House Committee. Even undeniable privileges of the House of Commons were set aside to further political programs, as when the Lords were permitted to initiate a finance bill, or the City allowed to dictate the terms of its loan. Soon the consequences of the political transformation were apparent to all. By dividing the parliamentary cause into contending parties and providing the mechanisms for majority rule, Holles's brief reign was the origin of England's political revolution.

Because his program hinged upon raising an Irish invasion force and disbanding the New Model, the Army's petition was doubly dangerous. The success of both efforts depended on the cooperation of military commanders and the forces at their disposal. Thus Holles had assiduously cultivated moderate Presbyterian colonels like Edward Harley, Sir Robert Pye, and Edward Rossiter who now sat in the House of Commons and could lend support to his military strategy. He gained the nomination of Philip Skippon to lead the expedition and prevailed upon him, over pleas of age and infirmity, to accept the command. The choice was fortunate for both of Holles's projects, for Skippon was a revered military leader who had taken the leading part in the peaceable discharge of the Earl of Essex's Army in 1645.

Holles's design was carefully drawn. By the end of March he had probably conceived of the scheme to separate politically unreliable regiments of horse from those who would be recruited for the Irish service.[90] The five horse regiments he appointed to remain in England were those of Fairfax, Cromwell, Whalley, Graves, and

Rossiter.[91] The first three were reputed the most radical in the New Model, Fairfax's and Whalley's being Cromwell's old double regiment raised in the Eastern Association. In place of two of these Holles might have selected those of Sir Robert Pye and John Butler, both moderate presbyterian commanders favorable to his plans. But by stationing radical regiments in England, Holles revealed his plan to recruit the invasion force from among loyal ones. He, at least, did not view the New Model monolithically. With trustworthy military leaders in the House and reliable commanders in the field, his grand strategy would be realized.

The news that soldiers and high-ranking officers were obstructing the service threatened the foundations of Holles's edifice. It was especially disturbing that the agitation had taken hold in two of the regiments upon which he had pinned his hopes. In fact, the letter Harley and Rossiter received on March 29 suggested that absentee colonels were losing control of their regiments. "For my part," wrote one of Rossiter's officers, "I and the rest of *my* officers are resolved not to act without you," a clear indication that other companies were not equally steadfast. Harley's informant melodramatically asserted that subscriptions to the petition totaled 1,100, more than the regiment's entire membership.[92] If the Army petition could dissuade these soldiers from accepting Irish service, then all of Holles's plans were in jeopardy.

While Holles attempted to quell the Army's discontent, he also pressed forward with arrangements of the final details for the Irish expedition. On April 1, as a prelude to appointing a general for the service, the House of Commons voted to divide the military and civil commands in Ireland. Sir William Waller was nominated for the military post, but debate revealed that he was as unwilling to accept the position as the House was to grant it to him.[93] The next day Waller recommended Philip Skippon for the overall command and Major General Edward Massey to lead the cavalry; both nominations were approved without division.[94] With the commanders chosen, Holles next moved to define the pool from which officers and soldiers would be drawn. On April 8 the Commons assigned the cavalry regiments that would be stationed in England, replacing Cromwell and Rossiter, who were excluded by the new self-denying ordinance, with their majors, Robert Huntingdon and Philip Twisleton.[95] To encourage enlistments, the House also voted to provide higher wages to commanders who enlisted in the Irish service, and to secure the part of their pay respited on the public faith by grants of Irish lands. On April 13 the pay scale for the soldiery was settled, those going to Ireland given a larger allowance than those who were to constitute the standing Army.[96]

The proposals that resulted in these votes had been made by the Committee for Irish Affairs at Derby House. Under Holles's control this body had assumed de facto power over Irish affairs and the military matters related to them. Its genesis was in early October when the Marquess of Ormonde communicated the decline of the parliamentary interest in Ireland that had resulted from the cessation of fighting negotiated by the King.[97] "In respect to the secrecy and expedition thereunto necessary," the Commons elected to appoint a new group rather than to work through the Committee of Lords and Commons for Irish Affairs that sat in Star Chamber.[98] Thus the Derby House Committee was devised to consider policy rather than to handle administrative detail. It was to be composed of the members of both Houses who had sat on the Committee of Both Kingdoms with the addition of Holles, Lord Lisle, Sir John Clotworthy, Sir John Temple, Nathaniel Fiennes, Sir William Lewes, and Robert Goodwin.[99] It is unclear, however, that in forming the Derby House Committee Parliament intended to create another standing committee. But the first report from Derby House, which favored the immediate dispatch of an invasion force into Ireland, had that effect. At once it was permanently distinguished from the committee that sat in the Star Chamber and its power to formulate policy for the Star Chamber Committee to implement was sanctioned.[100]

As the basis of the group at Derby House was the membership of the Committee of Both Kingdoms, it contained leaders of both parties. The additions to that membership in October, however, heavily weighted its composition in Holles's favor. Besides those like Lord Lisle and Sir John Temple whose long-standing Irish interests were likely to lead them to elevate the invasion above political considerations, the appointments of Clotworthy, Lewes, Goodwin, and Holles himself tipped the scales in the Committee of Both Kingdoms. Indeed, during the spring of 1647 Holles's political opponents abandoned all pretense of participation and boycotted the Committee's sessions.[101] But one political grouping was not represented on either the old Committee of Both Kingdoms or the new Derby House Committee. This was the anti-innovatory peers, who could claim only Lord Robartes as a transient inhabitant of their ideological dwelling. In addition, the death of the Earl of Essex and the addition of seven commoners to the Committee of Both Kingdoms disturbed the original proportion of Lords and Commons at the very moment when the conservative peers were straining to reassert their power. A confrontation was not long in coming. At the end of February 1647 the Commons voted to add still another member of Holles's party, Robert Reynolds, to the Derby House Committee. To this the Lords refused their assent.[102] At the same time, the peers delved into Irish affairs, requesting their members who sat on the Star Chamber Committee to bring in a report on the disbursement of funds for the Irish service.[103] In March, when Holles decided to coordinate the military disestablishment from the Derby House Committee, the conservative peers rebelled. Although they acceded to all the extraordinary votes brought from the Commons on March 30, they also ordered that all business concerning the Kingdom of Ireland would henceforth be directed from the Star Chamber Committee and not from Derby House.[104]

More than any other action taken by the conservative peers, this vote demonstrated the divergence between their campaign to reassert the rights of the House of Lords and the programs followed by Holles. The threat to strip Holles's majority at Derby House of power did not signify disapproval of his policies, but rather insistence that committees be properly constituted and the Lords be adequately represented. This principle had been clearly enunciated on March 18, when in another context the Lords resolved that all committees of the two Houses would be composed of one Lord to every two commoners.[105] By continuing to operate from a body in which the Commons held a vast numerical majority, Holles violated this principle and found himself opposed by the new militancy of the Upper House.

Yet the Lords' vote did not pose a serious stumbling block to Holles's plans. He was not averse to incorporating the conservative peers into the Derby House Committee, for their addition would be accompanied by further nominations from the House of Commons that would increase his preponderance still further. Indeed, the inclusion of these peers might finally assure their support for his policies. On April 7, therefore, Sir Philip Stapleton proposed to the Commons that the Derby House Committee be composed of the former members of the Committee of Both

Kingdoms, the seven commoners who had already been added in October, and Robert Reynolds, Major General Edward Massey, Zouch Tate, William Jephson, and Richard Salway.[106] In agreeing to this composition from the Lower House, the Lords could add their own new members in proportion. Not surprisingly their appointments were the core of the anti-innovatory peers, the Earls of Lincoln, Suffolk, and Middlesex, and the Lords Dacres, Willoughby, and Maynard. As a further indication that their objections to Holles's rule from Derby House had been purely procedural, on the same day they voted to abolish the now superfluous Star Chamber Committee.[107]

Along with the recomposition of the Derby House Committee came vast extensions of its powers. Originally the Committee had been created to deal with extraordinary problems relating to the affairs of Ireland, but it soon arrogated to itself complete control of Irish policy. Its permanent status was recognized by the House of Commons in November 1646 when it was formally named the Committee for Irish Affairs at Derby House, and in April 1647 it assumed the demeanor of an executive council, replacing the Committee of Both Kingdoms from which it had grown. Beginning on April 6 the Committee met almost daily after each parliamentary session and on the 16th it was ordered to meet during recesses.[108] Its regulatory powers were also expanded. On April 7 it was empowered to transport forces from England into Ireland, an initiative that soon encompassed the commissioning of officers and the composition of companies and regiments.[109] On April 15 the Derby House Committee absorbed the administrative functions of the Star Chamber Committee, including full fiscal authority to disburse the funds ordered for the Irish service.[110] As a corollary to its activities in preparing the Irish invasion, the Derby House Committee was given charge of the military reorganization. At Derby House the regiments to be maintained in England were appointed, and on May 18 the Committee was authorized to plan the details of the disbandment of the New Model.[111]

The growth of the Derby House Committee into an executive body that formulated and implemented Irish and military policy was another indication that party politics was reconstituting the parliamentary process. Besides sharing in the diffusion of power, Parliament's standing committees had originated as administrative bodies to implement long-term policies or programs. Their composition reflected their charge, members being expert through long-standing interests and experience or generally capable adminis-trators. The Derby House Committee usurped the function of two of these committees, the Committee for Irish Affairs at Star Chamber and Scawen's Army Committee. It also overwhelmed its own administrators. Sir William Armine, William Pierrepont, and Sir John Temple, who attended meetings regularly between November 1646 and February 1647, only occasionally appeared after the Committee's politicization. Pierrepont, who had missed only two sessions between November 17, 1646, and March 22, 1647, did not attend at all after May 27.[112] Moreover, the composition of the Derby House Committee was irregular, and its function included policy initiation.

Although the Committee of Both Kingdoms had occasionally formulated policy without the direction of the full House, its operations were closely regulated by an unpolarized House of Commons as likely to reject its proposals as to accept them.[113] More frequently, the formulation of specific policy was left to ad hoc committees. As we have seen, these committees could not easily be dominated by political parties, for they were rarely limited in size and were chosen by open nomination. Party leaders could boycott particular committees but they could not exclude their political opponents. For this reason, once Holles secured his majority in the Lower House he preferred to work through select committees, whose small membership his party followers could dominate, rather than through the amorphous bodies traditionally nominated by the full House. Indeed, in February, Holles may even have experimented with bypassing the nominated committees entirely, for he sat on only one of the thirteen committees selected that month.[114] This attempt (if that is what it was) to eliminate the role of the nominated committees does not seem to have succeeded, for in March, April, and May, at the height of his power, Holles resumed his participation on ad hoc committees.

But if the ad hoc committees could not be bypassed, their organization and function could be transformed. During the spring of 1647 such committees were infrequently appointed, their memberships were neglectfully enlarged, and the significance of the business that they performed declined. During March the House of Commons appointed only seven committees, in April, eight, and in May, ten. The use of the small committee to effect policy, which appeared so prominently in the spring of the previous year when the Commons was groping for a method of executive control, was now replaced by the nomination of inordinately large ones. In these months, of the twenty-five committees appointed only two had fewer than fifteen members: the nine-man committee chosen to prepare the heads of a conference with the Lords on the regulation of Oxford University, and the committee of twelve directed to draft a letter to be sent to Holmby.[115] Interestingly, none of the four party leaders sat on either committee. At the upper ends of the scale, more than 106 members were named to consider the City militia ordinance, and 79 members and all the lawyers of the House were chosen to prepare an ordinance to restrain malignant ministers from preaching.[116] Even the important committee appointed on March 27 to examine the first charges against the Army petition contained sixty-five members. Its unmanageable size notwithstanding, it was unique in being chosen to consider an issue of political importance. During the first four months of 1647 not a single committee was created to consider the reports or votes of the Derby House Committee, and no other committee was independently chosen to deal with Irish affairs or the military disestablishment. The symbolic eruptions in parliamentary procedure during these months, Ireton's famed challenge of a duel to Holles, and Holles's and Stapleton's inglorious flight from the floor of the Commons to avoid appearing on opposite sides of a division, were hardly as revealing as the fact that in each of these months the House held more divisions than it appointed committees.[117]

Holles's uninhibited rule from Derby House was strengthened by the backing he could expect from the City's financiers. At first, the Irish invasion was to be funded from the receipts of the Goldsmiths' Hall Committee. But as the compositions of delinquents now provided Parliament with its only source of ready cash, plans to drain this income indefinitely were unrealistic. The impracticality of depending upon the Goldsmiths' Hall revenue must have become apparent to Holles once he became a Commissioner to the Committee. To pay, equip, and transport eleven regiments required still another extraordinary loan. On April 2 Holles was selected to lead a delegation from Parliament to the London Common Council. Its mission was to obtain another £200,000 from London citizens through the auspices of the City government.[118] To emphasize the gratitude with which they would receive the City's favorable response, Parliament appointed Skippon and Massey, two of the City's favored military commanders, to lead the expedition to Ireland. In addition, the City's request to appoint its own militia committee was ostentatiously committed for study.[119]

On April 6 the parliamentary delegation arrived at the Guildhall. Holles and the Earl of Northumberland presented the brief for the exigency of the loan. They reminded the Council of the clauses in its December petition that urged the relief of Ireland and the disbanding of the Army. The City's own wishes could be met only if it was willing to lend the money needed to pay for such costly projects. The Parliament, they affirmed, was ready to offer the same collateral given for the Scottish loan, namely, the value of the bishops' lands and the revenue from the excise.[120] As was customary, after the parliamentary delegation withdrew, the Common Council appointed a committee to evaluate Parliament's request and the security that had been offered for the loan.[121]

While the Common Council's committee studied the parliamentary proposal, the two Houses continued to show their affection for the City. On April 9 the Lords took up their demand that the covenant be given to all men in places of public trust, appointing a committee to draft an order. Four days later they prodded the Commons to conclude its study of the City's militia ordinance. This was achieved on April 15, when the Lower House accepted the City's plan and defeated a motion to delay its implementation until December.[122] On the following day the Common Council was empowered to nominate thirty-one members to serve for one year as its Militia Committee. Later that afternoon the Lords agreed to all these provisions, ending the year-long controversy over the City's militia.[123]

Not coincidentally, the Common Council met the following day to consider the report of its committee concerning the £200,000 loan. The similarity between this request and the loan made for the same amount in November to finance the Scottish withdrawal suggested that the same methods be used to appropriate the funds. In particular, the Committee urged the continuation of doubling – allowing citizens to advance an amount equal to an interest-free loan they had earlier made in return for securing interest on both halves. Loans that would qualify to be doubled were now extended to the earliest outlays made in 1641–2 and the rate of interest to be retroactively accrued was fixed at 8 percent. The few imperfections of the earlier doubling scheme were now repaired. Parliamentary creditors unable to double their previous advances could sell their loan debentures to new investors who, by doubling the sum themselves, would receive the accumulated interest on the original loan. In further consideration of citizens who had provided Parliament's earliest financial support, the Committee also requested that an additional £30,000 be raised to repay advances made by Londoners who were now impoverished. To secure this £230,000 the Committee suggested four sources of parliamentary income: the fines and compositions received at Goldsmiths' Hall; the bishops' lands; the excise; and the estates of papists and delinquents excepted from pardon, either by sale or composition, or by the confiscation of their rents. To assure that this income would actually provide security for the loan, the Common Council, acting on the report of its committee, desired Parliament to agree to make no further charges on either the monies received at Goldsmiths' Hall or on the excise. Finally, the City government proposed the appointment of a committee of original subscribers to the Irish venture who would oversee the disbursement of the £200,000.[124]

The audacity of these conditions again reveals the independence of the groups that are generally thought to have composed Holles's party. The City government was willing to grant Holles's request for a loan, but it would not let slip the opportunity to strengthen its own position. The demand that the committee of Londoners monitor the disbursement of the loan was tantamount to an oversight committee regulating the activities of Derby House. The request for £30,000 to be given to indigent citizens, later raised to £50,000 by a demand for a £20,000 grant to the Militia Committee, amounted to a 25-percent surcharge on the loan.[125] Moreever, the City's claims for security, especially from the compositions at Goldsmiths' Hall against which no further charges could be made, would effectively pauperize Parliament and increase its dependence upon London's finance.

Even with his majority, Holles could not secure the acceptance of such restrictions, nor is it clear that he approved of the City's temerity. When Holles reported the terms proposed by the Common Council to Parliament on April 20 the Lower House immediately rejected the three most controversial points: that compositions be accepted on the estates of papists or delinquents excepted from pardon, or that the rents of their estates be used for security;

that the Goldsmiths' Hall revenue be pledged and that no further charges be made upon it or upon the excise; and that the Irish Adventurers' Committee would oversee Derby House. In addition, the Commons laid aside, but did not reject, the request for repayment of £30,000 of previous loans. The House did agree to the sale of papists' estates and of the estates of delinquents excepted from pardon and even accepted that the City might appoint a committee to confer with the Derby House Committee on Irish affairs.[126]

The unacceptability of the City's proposals in the House of Commons was further complicated by the long-standing differences between the Houses over the sale of delinquents' estates. The Lords were willing to add the £30,000 for the City's impoverished lenders, but refused outright to make charges on delinquents' estates. To provide sufficient security the peers instead agreed, after a division, to grant all the revenues received at Goldsmiths' Hall.[127] These votes were unacceptable to the Commons, where members insisted upon the sale of papists' and delinquents' estates "that those that have been fomenters of the war should be [an] advantage to the Parliament and pay the public debts."[128] They rejected the Lords' inclusion of the revenues at Goldsmiths' Hall "because it is the only power and means of raising money if there should be any extraordinary occasion."[129] But the resurgent peers were no longer moved by cries of wolf. On April 30 the Lords concurred only to the sale of papists' estates, adhering to their refusal to confiscate delinquents' lands, and offering the Goldsmiths' Hall revenue as a sufficient substitute. In the House of Commons a majority of 12 in a slender House of 104 again refused to mortgage their only certain source of revenue, a decision that the Lords were finally persuaded to accept.[130] The end product of resolving these disputes was that now neither House could offer sufficient security for the loan, and the parliamentary Commissioners returned to the City with an emaciated version of the Council's terms.

When Parliament's decisions were read to the Common Council on May 3 the City government frankly expressed the impossibility of raising such a large loan on such thin collateral. They argued that the security of the revenue at Goldsmiths' Hall was essential for securing subscriptions, for the plight of the excise was well known and the choice bishops' lands had already been sold. The need to provide £30,000 for "poor and decayed" citizens was as much a test of Parliament's credit as it was a gesture of goodwill. If loans made in the early years of the war could not be repaid, in a time of great necessity to those impoverished citizens, the ardor of affluent citizens to part with their capital might cool; the ravages of war had shown the vagaries of fortune.[131]

Again the Commissioners returned to Parliament to report the result of the negotiations. As Harington recorded, the City's reasserted terms were "contrary to both Houses' " previous vote.[132] Their proposals had already been considered and it was not for the City to set conditions upon Parliament. Sir John Evelyn led a motion for the Commons to adhere to all their original decisions, and thus to resist the demands of the Common Council. But in the face of the necessity of obtaining the loan, more moderate counsel prevailed. The House resolved to offer the City half the revenue from Goldsmiths' Hall and the whole of the excise, both unencumbered by further charges. This, they hoped, would leave Parliament sufficient funds to meet a crisis and provide enough security to satisfy the City. They also directed their Commissioners to assure the Common Council that a program to aid indigent citizens would be established.[133] These compromises were accepted by both the House of Lords and the City government. The loan was raised in less than a week, with generous subscriptions given by the Earl of Northumberland, Lord Grey of Warke, a number of M.P.s including Holles and Stapleton, and the bulk of the City's aldermen.[134]

The settlement of the City loan revealed the distinction between Holles's majority and his party in the House of Commons. The concessions made to the City financiers and the House of Lords enabled Holles to secure the money necessary for his political programs. But the terms of the loan drew Parliament even deeper into debt, depriving it of half its single constant source of cash, and leaving Holles with little maneuverability in financing the military disestablishment. The Lords still refused to pass the ordinance to maintain the forces that Holles was now able to recruit and equip. This reluctance to continue the wartime assessments in the counties, and their rejection of the sale of the estates of delinquents excepted from pardon, manifested their commitment to restore political normality and to preserve the rights of the peerage, whatever its political composition. The City, too, had flexed its muscle, securing not only advantageous terms for its loan but sovereignty for its militia committee. The power of appointment granted to the Common Council allowed for the purgation of members whose religious and political loyalty was suspected by the majority in the City government.[135] Holles was clearly not in control of all elements of his majority, and the political behavior of both the City and the House of Lords remained unpredictable. The concessions he made to accommodate them were in exchange for the continued rule of his party in the House of Commons.

With the loan secured, Holles was able to put in motion his plans for the Irish invasion and the military disestablishment. The broad administrative details for the Irish venture having already been settled, it remained only to attract subscribers from the regiments in the Army. Since the beginning of April parliamentary Commissioners had attended the Army's headquarters at Saffron Walden, communicating to the Army the decisions concerning the Irish service and soliciting volunteers. On April 19 the Commissioners reported their suggestions to complete the subscriptions. They urged that money be sent to the Army to pay the advance to be given to soldiers enlisting for Ireland. They also recommended that the proportion of arrears that was to be paid upon the Army's disbandment be established. They thought that a declaration in favor of the Irish venture pronounced by Sir Thomas Fairfax would ensure the rapid conclusion of their task, and they advised Parliament that they had already prepared such a statement. Their strongest appeal, however, was that the Army be disbanded, "whereas when a relation to the Army is at an end, there will be greater incapacity, both in ill-affected officers and soldiers, to do mischief . . . as also a liberty and necessity of accepting other employment when they shall stand discharged to this."[136] The commissioners assured the two Houses that the officers who were disaffected were "but few in number" and that their influence would be easily eliminated by the decomposition of the regiments.[137]

Despite the "ill-affected officers and soldiers" and the petitions of grievances presented by the Council of Officers to the parliamentary Commissioners, the Irish service seemed to be progressing well. At the end of March, twenty-eight senior New Model officers, including four colonels – Fortescue, Harley, Sheffield, and Pye – volunteered for Ireland.[138] On April 13 Sheffield offered his entire regiment for the venture, an offer accepted with gratitude by both Houses. A week later the Derby House Committee implored Fairfax to remain at headquarters despite his ill health because "they doubt not in a very few days to complete the numbers designed." At the end of the month the Commissioners presented an optimistic report of their progress. At least half of four foot regiments had already been subscribed, those of the general, and Colonels Hammond, Waller, and Fortescue. In addition "a considerable part" of Colonel Edward Harley's regiment and all of Colonel William Herbert's had also enlisted, which was more than half the foot soldiers necessary for the service.[139] In light of the facts that Skippon had yet to accept the command (on April 8 he had requested to be passed over because "of my own exceeding indisposedness of mind, inability of body, distractedness of estate and family") and that no money had been provided for the soldiers, the response was remarkable.[140] In the cavalry the proportion of enlistments was almost as great. The establishment called for four horse regiments to be drawn from the five New Model regiments that would not be kept up in England. From these five, Sheffield's regiment was fully subscribed, and Colonel John Butler had engaged his service along with two of his officers. Colonel Robert Pye had also enlisted, although his regiment had not yet been canvassed by the parliamentary Commissioners.[141] In Nathaniel Rich's regiment Major John Alford and Captain Jonas Neville, the regiment's senior captain, were both committed to the venture. Additionally, one of Graves's captains, William Lord Caulfield, whose family's baronetage was acquired through service in Ireland, volunteered himself and the company he had raised.[142] Added to these New Model regiments, Colonel John Birch, who had served with Skippon at Bristol and Newcastle, had enlisted his regiment, and Major General Edward Massey, who was to command the cavalry forces, had also undertaken to recruit a full regiment.[143] Holles and his party could hardly have been better pleased. The recommendation of the parliamentary Commissioners that the dissolution of the Army would further the service seemed to assure the completion of subscriptions by the end of May.

The progress of the Irish venture and the suggestion that the breakup of the Army would facilitate its completion coincided with a general desire to disband the Army. Although the declaration that Holles had drafted in March expressed Parliament's "extreme dislike" of the soldiers' petition, the economic and judicial grievances of which it complained were seen as legitimate. "All agree," wrote Harington, "that the Army is to receive justice, full pay and what part deferred to be secured to their content, also to grant them all their other reasonable desires."[144] On April 27 when the parliamentary Commissioners reported the progress they had made in enlisting troops for Ireland they reiterated the need to disband the Army to prevent the spread of discontent over the Irish service. This prompted the House of Lords to vote six weeks' pay to be provided for the disestablishment, the same allowance as had been given to Massey's brigade the previous autumn.[145] When their vote was communicated to the Commons, a debate ensued over the Lords' right to introduce a money bill into the Lower House.[146] Although the Lords had clearly breached parliamentary privilege by their order, the untrammeled success of Holles's plans made him less jealous of rights and privileges than he had been in March. A motion to examine the Lords' conduct was brushed aside when Stapleton and John Glyn led a majority in agreement with the Lords' vote.[147] Some weeks later the two Houses determined to sweeten the pot for the soldiers, adding two weeks' pay both to the arrears to be paid those being disbanded and to the bonus for those subscribing for Ireland.[148] In sum, a soldier subscribing for Ireland would receive fourteen weeks' pay, cash in hand.

Parliament responded just as forthrightly to the remainder of the material grievances expressed in the Army's March petition. The continuing failure of parliamentary orders to circuit judges prohibiting prosecution of soldiers for crimes committed during the war necessitated action on the soldiers' claims for indemnity. On May 1 the Lower House debated a comprehensive indemnity ordinance. The tangled legal problems in distinguishing civil and military crimes and just and abusive acts necessarily delayed its completion. Not until the 14th was the Commons' bill prepared and sent up to the Lords. Another week was to pass before it received the peers' assent, one of a flurry of votes taken that week to satisfy the Army's desires.[149] On May 27 the Commons also established a course to satisfy the claims of widows and of soldiers maimed in Parliament's service. This bill, too, raised complicated issues of documentation and authenticity, problems the Commons had been working to resolve since the previous autumn.[150] The final resolution of the projects for indemnity and relief for widows and maimed soldiers revealed the tortuously slow pace of parliamentary business as well as the legitimacy of the soldiers' grievances.

The actual votes on disbanding the Army awaited the completion of subscriptions to the £200,000 loan. For the entire day on May 18 the House debated the question of disbandment. A motion to settle the business in a grand committee failed when the House resolved by thirty-nine votes that the issue should be sent to a committee.[151] Predictably, it was to Derby House that the Commons committed these deliberations. On the same day the House was informed, by the military members it had sent to Army headquarters, of increasing distemper among the soldiery. "We must acknowledge," Skippon, Ireton, Cromwell, and Fleetwood concurred, "we found the Army under a deep sense of some sufferings, and the common soldier much unsettled."[152] This report and the completion of the City loan hastened the process of disbandment. On May 21 Cromwell returned to London to report on those of the Army's grievances yet to be resolved by Parliament. First, however, he assured the Commons that the soldiers were calmer than they had been three days earlier, and that he was certain they would peaceably disband.[153] Upon this statement, the Lower House moved to rectify the remaining grievances of the soldiery. The auditing of accounts would proceed without delay; apprentices who had served during the war would be given their freedom; soldiers who had volunteered for the Army would not be subject to impressment in any foreign wars; and the ordinance for widows and maimed soldiers would be completed.[154] Once these votes were established, the Derby House Committee presented its plan for disbandment.

They had determined that Fairfax's infantry would be mustered out at Chelmsford on May 28, a date the full House set back to June 1. Parliamentary treasurers would pay the established arrears and take subscriptions for Ireland.[155] The Derby House Committee settled upon disbanding Fairfax's regiment first, both for the good example it would set and because, as Holles had reported three days earlier, the bulk of the regiment had enlisted for Irish service. Along with the majority of its senior officers, Lieutenant Colonel Nicholas Kempson would lead the Irish volunteers. Once Fairfax's regiment had been discharged, the Derby House Committee appointed the time and place for the release of the rest of the cavalry.[156] For the unpaid portion of their arrears, junior officers and common soldiers would have the security of the excise. The senior officers with outstanding claims were given the security of the estates of delinquents excepted from pardon.[157] With the passage of the ordinance for widows and maimed soldiers on May 28 the program was completed.[158] As the Lords officiously declared, "The Parliament . . . have taken it into their special care to give all just satisfaction to those who have served them."[159] After two months the Army's petition, never delivered, was answered. After two years, the New Model had come to an end.

For six months Holles and his majority directed political activity. His plans to restore an outward calm to the nation had progressed smoothly. Through the newly created Derby House Committee he had coordinated the two most essential aspects of his program, the Irish invasion and the military disestablishment. Loyal commanders, had been chosen to lead the expedition and attractive terms had been provided for the soldiery. The politically and religiously diverse New Model had proven a fertile recruiting ground for the large Army that would be expected to end Irish resistance swiftly. Despite some unrest in the Army, chiefly from the supporters of his political opponents, the plans for the Army's dissolution had been implemented. Each element of Holles's majority had aided in these successes. His political party in the House carefully controlled procedure to ensure the completion of the details for the Irish service and the satisfaction of the legitimate grievances of the Army. The group of conservative peers, now members of the Derby House Committee, had accepted the necessity of Holles's program and had guided it through their own House.[160] The City government had again provided the money necessary to effect Holles's plans. Even the King seemed willing to aid this success, sending, at the end of May, the most conciliatory answer yet given to parliamentary propositions.

Holles's success was made possible by political hegemony. Though his plans were well drawn it was not simply efficiency that underlay their implementation. Through his majority Holles had assumed complete control of political decision making. This came not only from the support he received from nonparty M.P.s who longed for peace, but through the techniques of adversary politics. At every turn the party opposed to Holles's plans and to his unassailable power was excluded from political participation, totally unable to influence debate or decision. Their few allies in the nation now faced the same ostracism.[161] Through its loan the City government had purchased the right to purge its militia committee of religious and political dissidents. Conformity to the still imperfectly established church had finally become a test of civil and military employment. The plan to take subscriptions for Ireland rather than to detach a brigade of the New Model also succeeded in sifting out opposition. This entire process had strengthened Holles's support at the expense of those who opposed him. The obstacles to leading a diverse and divided cause had finally been overcome. Adversary politics had provided a course for unity – a course that Holles and his majority pursued headlong.

Holles's brief reign created not one unified parliamentary cause, but two homogeneous ones. His coalition, a combination of self-interested but ideologically compatible groups, spawned a broader-based opposition than the small party that existed in the House of Commons. The practice of the past would not have erased religious dispute or political difference, but the desire to maintain unity would have ensured the representation of all elements of the cause. Adversary politics neatly compartmentalized the distinction between political position and political participation. Opposition to Holles's policies, whether from Haselrig and Evelyn in the Commons or from petitioners in the Army, could be treated in the same high-handed manner. The legitimate privileges of the Commons and the legitimate grievances of the Army could both be viewed as the policies of opposition parties. As parliamentary government came to be identified with Holles's overwhelming majority, his opponents, as he so succinctly reminded them, became "enemies to the state."

Chapter 7

THE RISE OF THE
NEW MODEL ARMY

Who would have thought that so modest an address as the late
petition drawn up to be subscribed by the Army, to be presented
to the general, would have raised so much dust?[1]

Not until the spring of 1647 did the New Model Army become a
political participant. During the first two years of its existence the
Army acted only in a military capacity, both as a fighting force
and as a deterrent to renewed war. To its officers and soldiers the
Army's success was plainly the manifestation of God's will. "God
is never more seen in his Glory then when He does the greatest
works by the most contemptible means; therefore let that new
moulded Army be honored."[2] Military victory vindicated the parliamentary cause and confirmed the special sense Army members
had of submerging particular interests in the welfare of the whole.
The harmony of heterogeneous political and religious beliefs was
exemplified by the New Model. "Presbyterians, Independents, all
have here the spirit of faith and prayer, the same presence and
answer; they agree here, have no names of difference. Pity it is it
should be otherwise anywhere."[3] By the war's end the soldiery possessed a deep self-esteem derived from their valor, their unity, and
their triumph. It was this confidence in their righteousness that encouraged the Army politicization.

The political transformation at Westminster, particularly the
emergence of Holles's party and the pursuit of policy to the detri-
ment of unity, did not go unwitnessed by the Army. The development of pressure techniques by the City and the Scots had as their
aim the purgation of religious dissidents from positions of influence.
Quickly the target of both became the Army. The revival of the
movement for religious reformation in Parliament also struck at
those who would not conform to the presbyterian establishment,
explicitly denying them civil or military employment. Religious
radicals within the Army were directly threatened by these de-

velopments, but as the charges were leveled indiscriminately and their emphasis was on undermining the Army's unity, they did not succeed in dividing the New Model. Rather, continued assaults from London brought the Army into opposition to elements of Holles's majority. Adversary relations had a precise meaning to soldiers who had fought against an unequivocal enemy, and once their petition was rejected the Army had this experience to call upon.

In this setting the New Model Army rose. Its entry into politics and its subsequent radicalization were the inevitable consequences not of its supposedly radical composition, but of the uneven and unpredictable emergence of political consciousness. This was not the "Cadmean Brood" that Holles claimed "turned their swords against their fellow subjects, and their masters the Parliament."[4] More than anyone, it was Holles who had sown the teeth from which the Army's political action grew. Still less was the emergence of radicalism within the Army the product of the agitation of John Lilburne or the influence of his ideas. Those who claimed that "Lilburne's books are quoted by them as statute law" and that the Army was "one Lilburne throughout," sought a scapegoat rather than an explanation.[5] To the ascendant party that Holles led, the Army appeared only as the manifestation of their political opponents: the tool of Cromwell and the Independents. To the dominant majority of social and political conservatives that Holles controlled, the New Model symbolized the rising of the masses to destroy the foundations of ordered society. Unhappily, both judgments have survived; both are wrong.

Instead, the Army's politicization derived from two interrelated sources: the soldiers' material grievances and Parliament's peremptory rejection of their right to petition. In the Army, the settlement of arrears, indemnity, and consideration for those who had been the victims of the war (widows and maimed soldiers) were universally accepted as preconditions for foreign service or discharge. All these material grievances were expressed in the petition the soldiers intended to present to Sir Thomas Fairfax. Despite its elevation to a *cause célèbre* and the savage declaration against it, the petition was a further indication of the Army's unity. The March 30 declaration against the petitioners cast doubt not only upon the redress of grievances, but raised the most basic issue of the soldiers' rights as citizens. Followed by accusations that the

Army intended to overawe the nation and compromise the parliamentary cause, the declaration incensed the soldiery. Their material grievances, which were shared by men of every viewpoint, soon gave way to demands for a vindication of the Army's honor. The threat of judicial retribution that had spurred the desire for an act of indemnity was refocused. The enemies whom the soldiers feared would become their judges did not reside only in the localities.

Thus relations between Parliament and its Army became supercharged with misunderstanding and mutual distrust. To the soldiery, the Irish venture came to be seen as "a design to ruin and break this Army in pieces" rather than as a legitimate and necessary military operation; plans for disbandment were soon interpreted as attempts to divide infantry and cavalry, officer and soldier.[6] Unable to secure redress of its grievances in a parliamentary way, the Army developed its own representative institutions: the Council of War and the agitators. Throughout April a reexamination of the Army's condition and its relations with Parliament was undertaken. By May each regiment had drawn a new statement of grievances, no longer centered upon material issues but focused upon retrieving the Army's reputation and the soldiers' rights. These were the motivations for the Army's subsequent actions.

Yet despite its rapidity, the Army's radicalization was not premeditated. At almost every step the escalation of methods and demands was forced upon the soldiers. The ban on petitioning led to desultory attempts at expressing material complaints and finally to an appeal for protection to their field commanders who sat in Parliament. This was drafted by elected regimental representatives, who became known as the "agitators." Their election resulted not from an effort to organize the soldiery or propel them into action, but from the failure of Parliament to recognize the soldiers' material grievances. The consolidation of the role of the agitators and the election of officer agitators who acted as a conduit to the Council of War occurred when Parliament appointed commissioners to examine the Army's distempers. This investigation resulted in the composition of the regimental statements of grievances, a process that required the soldiers to consider their discontents. Finally the precipitous order for disbandment forced the Army into positive action. The mutiny of Fairfax's regiment at Chelmsford and the seizure of the King at Holmby were desperate gambles, with unanticipated consequences. Throughout the summer, the restraints on the Army's radicalization were self-imposed, motivated by the belief that commanders, officers, and soldiers shared the same fate.

As the reaction to the March petition was the most significant factor in awakening political consciousness among a soldiery concerned with material grievances, so the Irish venture became the means by which the heterogeneous political and religious character of the New Model was finally changed. Holles's insistence upon pushing forward with subscriptions for Ireland before the resolution of the Army's complaints made the venture a test of allegiance. Promotion of the petition of grievances was equated with obstruction of the service for Ireland. When senior officers were charged, by unnamed informants, with placing redress before reconquest, they were called before the House of Commons for examination. When ensigns and lieutenants volunteered for service in Ireland they were promoted to captains and majors in regiments created at Derby House. Those who resisted the proposed service in Ireland saw their struggle not only in terms of arrears and indemnity, commands and employment, but as a trial of the Army's integrity. Those who accepted it defined their choice as loyalty to the lawful commands of Parliament. "The Army look at their pay for their service and at their honor. . . . The Parliament have a watchful eye on their honor and think it should be supported by obedience from the Army to their just commands."[7] With right on both sides the Irish venture pruned from the Army the bulk of its moderate and presbyterian officers, eliminating their counsel at a critical moment and placing the solidified Army in an adversary relationship to Holles's party at Westminster.

In June 1646 the royalist capital of Oxford surrendered and for the next six months the New Model lay idle. Few Cavalier garrisons still remained intact, and with the fall of his capital the King acceded to Parliament's request that his remaining strongholds be given up. Yet the existence of the Army did not end with the combat. Charles's flight to the Scots outweighed the submission of his garrisons and clouded both the miliary and political situation. Although the visible enemy had been vanquished the state of war continued. Throughout the following autumn fear of French intervention and Scottish invasion gripped a majority of members in both Houses of Parliament. These presentiments, periodically invigorated by the capture of correspondence or the confessions of spies, resulted in the maintenance of Parliament's full military might. Thus as the negotiations for possession of the King and removal of the Scottish Army progressed, the dormant New Model quartered freely in the counties of the nation. By September the Army regiments were dispersed in a circle radiating from Oxford. The mobile companies of cavalry were scattered as far as Sussex in the south and Wiltshire in the west; the foot concentrated in Oxfordshire, Worcestershire, and Staffordshire.[8] Without employ and without money they awaited developments to which they would respond: war and renewed service or peace and disbandment.

In these months of waiting, the political process at Westminster underwent its transformation and godly reformation its revival. Army members, whether presbyterians or sectaries, could not remain unaware of the implications of these changes, but their practical effects did not take shape until the spring. In the ever-shifting sands of Parliament's religious settlement, the declaration of April 1646 had promised the establishment of presbyterianism and that a future resolution would be taken that "tender consciences, which differ not in fundamentals of religion, may be so provided for, as may stand with the word of God and the peace of the Kingdom."[9] The revival of the debates on heresy and schism in the House of Commons and the reinvigorated campaign in London for orthodox presbyterianism on the Scottish model were out of step with the continuing need to preserve political and military unity. When, for example, some M.P.s attempted to prevent the Earl of Chesterfield from using the Book of Common Prayer, Bulstrode Whitelocke, the weathervane of moderate opinion, spoke against it "as contrary to the liberty of conscience we ourselves claimed formerly, and fit to be allowed."[10] Nor had party politics hardened sufficiently to threaten the commands of senior New Model officers. Until the conclusion of negotiations with the Scots no alterations could be made which might jeopardize military efficiency. Even the practical attempts to send several of the Army's regiments to Ireland had been opposed on these grounds. Not until the spring, when Holles's party triumphed and his majority coalesced, would the New Model face disestablishment.

Although the political upheaval at Westminster would soon have its effect upon the Army, for the moment the scattered regiments faced a more potent danger from the collapse of the monthly assessment scheme. Until June, the regular pay that had characterized the Army's early history continued. New Model members could anticipate disbursements sufficient to satisfy their needs and to prevent their becoming an excessive burden upon the communities in which they quartered. But the fall of Oxford was a fiscal watershed: the breakdown of military finance thereafter was swift and complete. During July the twelve foot regiments went unpaid for the first full month since September 1645. Not until the third week in August did the infantry again receive their wages, twenty-eight days plus an additional two weeks' pay to compensate for the previous month's neglect.[11] This forty-nine-day hiatus in pay was the longest since the Army's creation. The compensatory pay that the soldiers received in August almost certainly went to repay the debts they had accumulated over the previous two months. The process by which the soldiery borrowed and lived on credit is unclear, but in March 1647 the parliamentary Commissioners who attended the Army commented upon one of its dimensions: "Three weeks' pay is lately sent down to the Army (which amounting to fourteen shillings for each foot soldier, is by the settled rules of the Army to be paid half to the soldier and the other half to discharge his quarters)."[12] Indeed, even the most frugal soldier had little comfort from the extra two weeks' pay, for immediately after the August disbursement wages again fell into arrears. From August until the final week in November the infantry received nothing.[13] The effects of these eighty-six unpaid days may only have been mitigated by their coincidence with the harvest. Although the foot received six weeks' wages in both November and December, the irregularity of their pay was now a critical factor in the soldiers' perception of their material condition. Large sums of money at irregular intervals left them exposed to their creditors both on paydays and in the long intervals between them.

Excepting that they ordinarily received a larger daily allowance, the regiments of cavalry fared no better than their counterparts in the infantry. Their higher wages were seized upon by the Army treasurers, who were hard pressed to spread insufficient funds throughout the regiments, and although their pay was no more regular than the infantry's they did not receive extra money in compensation. In June the regiments commanded by Fairfax, Rich, Fleetwood, and Graves received no pay.[14] In July, when they were given three weeks' wages, five of the other six cavalry regiments went unpaid.[15] Only Colonel Edward Whalley's regiment obtained its pay in both June and July, and not coincidentally it was the only cavalry regiment to receive no money in August. The treasurers, in a period of financial stringency, were maintaining parity among all regiments. Between June and August, then, each regiment of horse went one month without pay.[16] This interval was extended during the autumn, when the cavalry collected salary in either September or October.[17] In addition, the regiments of Colonels Rich, Butler, and Fleetwood continued without pay in November.[18] The remaining seven regiments lost another month's wages in either December or January.[19] In sum, like the foot, most cavalry regiments were without money for three consecutive months. In the most extreme case, Colonel John Butler's regiment collected its pay in only two of the last six months of 1646.

The New Model's monetary crisis reached its climax in the fall of 1646. Beginning in August, the Lords continually refused to renew the New Model ordinances, but this had little effect upon the Army's financial condition.[20] The treasurers were simply ordered to collect the sums still due on the assessments levied prior to November 1646 and, when the ordinances lapsed, these arrears were sufficient to provide for the Army's needs. During the first half of 1647 the New Model again received regular pay.[21] Thus the enunciation of their material grievances, which began in March, did not occur in an atmosphere charged by the penury that had been experienced during the previous autumn. The Army's radicalization did not simply derive from their "gut" demands; their entry into political action was not a rising of the unpaid and underfed.

The irregularity of their pay was the most pressing problem the Army faced during its enforced idleness, but it was not the only one. When they returned to their communities, officers and soldiers were called to account for acts they had committed during the war and for the bills they had left unpaid. Captive military officers soon flooded the House of Lords with petitions for release from imprisonment for debt. Inasmuch as the New Model remained intact, it was the local military commanders who were first singled out for retribution. Their experience was a sufficient guide to the fate that awaited members of the New Model, but in an extreme case, Colonel William Herbert was arrested and imprisoned in July 1646. Although the Upper House ordered Herbert's immediate release, and summoned his captors for examination, less spectacular incidents were not as easily resolved.[22] In general, if the petitioners could establish that the debts for which they were imprisoned were smaller than the arrears to which they were entitled, the Lords would order their release.

But the petitions that reached the Lords in increasing volume during the autumn and winter were a small part of the cases that were rumored to exist in the Army. Recounting one such incident in March 1647 the *Perfect Diurnal* warned that thousands would suffer imprisonment unless Parliament took preventative action.[23] Nor were Army members the only ones affected by this problem. The County Committee of Suffolk reported that "many well-affected to Parliament" are called to account for their actions, adding, dramatically, that the crimes of which they were accused ranged from commandeering horses to collecting the monthly assessment.[24] Conviction for horse stealing caused the greatest concern among the soldiers; it was both a regular occurrence and a capital offense. When Colonel William Kenwricke was arrested in Kent for horse theft, the news spread quickly throughout the Army.[25] Despite Parliament's attempts to prohibit such prosecutions, each case created a new panic. A soldier in Edward Rossiter's regiment was convicted of manslaughter and burned on the hand in a humiliating punishment that neither Fairfax, Twisleton (the regiment's major), nor the House of Parliament could prevent.[26] In June 1647 a surgeon in the Northern Army stirred his comrades to mutiny by advising them that "if they had not an act of indemnity they should be most of them hanged when they were reduced: and for an example, told them the judges had hanged fourteen soldiers already which took horses by order from their officers."[27]

Despite some exaggeration, the soldiers' fears were well founded, for the House of Lords heard petitions only from senior officers who, at least, held the rank of captain and were capable of channeling their complaints to the Upper House. No instances survive of common soldiers petitioning the Lords for release from imprisonment, and it is unlikely that they could obtain reprieve for their war-related actions in this fashion. More importantly, the Lords appear to have adjudicated only cases of imprisonment for debt, leaving the broad range of crimes against persons and property unresolved. Without an act of indemnity, the New Model soldiers would be at the mercy of sheriffs and courts who frequently had their own sources to settle with the victorious parliamentarians: grievances that were complicated by the conduct of the old parliamentary armies and the local levies.[28]

The recovery of their arrears and the security of their persons became crucial issues once the clamor for disbandment began. With the loan for the Scottish withdrawal raised, and the negotiations for the possession of the King completed, in December of 1646 the City of London made the first public appeal for the discharge of the New Model. They provided both economic and political justification for their request. First, the City contended that the Army's continued maintenance placed an insupportable burden upon the nation, and their call for disestablishment was accompanied by a proposal to repeal the taxes that financed the Army. Second, the City argued that some officers and soldiers had refused to take the covenant and thus were disaffected to the newly established church. "The pulpits of divers Godly ministers are often usurped by preaching soldiers and others who infect their flocks and all places where they come, with strange and dangerous errors," they contended. "We humbly submit to your lordships," the City's petition to the Upper House suggested, "what security or settlement can be expected while they are masters of such a power."[29] The City's appeal was soon echoed by one from Essex. When the resources of the counties around Oxford were depleted by the Army's prolonged encampment, Fairfax had moved several of his regiments, for the first time, into the Eastern Association. It was not long before the Army's presence there sparked a petition for disbandment. Although the Essex petitioners claimed that "they did not mean to cast aspersions on the Army, but only on persons in it," they concluded their request, which repeated the City's economic arguments, with the provocative claim that the Army's change of quarters "is some design to have an aweing influence upon the proceedings of Parliament."[30]

Simultaneous with these petitions for discharge, the New Model was confronted by the first formal request for subscriptions for service in Ireland.[31] On March 20 a parliamentary delegation composed of Sir John Clotworthy, Sir William Waller, and Richard Salway appeared at Army headquarters. They had come to consult with Sir Thomas Fairfax on the fittest means of recruiting eleven New Model regiments for the Irish service. In response to their request, Fairfax convened an assembly of Army officers the following day to hear the Commissioners' report. The officers were informed that Parliament would offer six weeks' pay to those who would subscribe for Ireland. Unwilling to make an immediate commitment, spokesmen for the officers replied that whatever course they individually pursued, they would all act to further the service among their soldiers. They then countered by "answering propositions with propositions" and propounded four questions to the Commissioners: what troops would be kept up in England; what commanders would lead the expedition to Ireland; what assurances would be given for their pay while in service; and what satisfaction would be granted for their arrears and indemnity?[32] Although the propriety of the first two questions was not unanimously accepted among the officers, all agreed that the establishment of regular pay in Ireland and satisfaction of their material grievances in England should precede enlistments for the Irish venture.[33] Until answers were returned to all their questions, the majority of officers resolved to delay their own subscriptions. The subsequent report, that the House of Commons had voted to establish a new monthly assessment of £60,000 for all of the forces to be kept up in England and Ireland, thus had little effect.[34]

The officers' determination not to subscribe for the Irish service until essential preconditions had been met was equaled by their soldiers. While the Commissioners were using their personal influence to gain support for the venture, they were informed that a petition against the service was being circulated amongst the soldiery. Sir William Waller thought this activity of such "dangerous consequence" that he sought out Sir Thomas Fairfax with news of it.[35] Fairfax assured the Commissioners that any petition that might be afoot in the army would first be cleared through him, "and that it should be his care to suppress whatsoever might give offense."[36] It was not until March 27, when the Commissioners returned to London and informed the House of Commons both of the officers' conduct and the soldiers' petition, that the first confrontation between the Army and Parliament began. On that day, with the reports of the petition by Waller and Clotworthy unsubstantiated, the Lower House appointed a large committee to investigate the Army's conduct and directed Sir Thomas Fairfax to prevent the spread of the petitioning campaign. At the same time the Commons passed a resolution "that not withstanding any information this day given to the House they have a good opinion of the Army."[37]

While Essex petitioners were complaining of the Army's contraction and the parliamentary Commissioners of its conduct, readers of the London newsbook were given a glimpse of the Army's agitation. In mid-March the *Perfect Diurnal* printed an anonymous letter from a correspondent in the Army stating that the soldiers in Colonel Nathaniel Rich's regiment were circulating a petition opposing the Irish service unless they were assured that their own officers would accompany them.[38] This confused report also related that the regiment's officers had prevailed upon the soldiers to petition General Fairfax rather than directly to Parliament. Coming on the heels of the Army's movement into the Eastern Association, the news of the petitioning campaign among the soldiers was unsettling. Moreover, uncertainty over the Army's intentions and actions was exacerbated by the simultaneous appearance of a petition from a group of London citizens, the so-called Large Petition "To the Right Honorable and Supreme Authority of This Nation the Commons in Parliament Assembled."[39]

Both London citizens and Army soldiers believed their affairs had reached a crisis by the middle of March, but there was little similarity in their appeals. The two petitions were linked only by the opposition that they aroused. As soon as the Londoners began circulating the Large Petition for subscriptions, the leaders of the City government initiated a counter-petition. In it they denounced the desires of the citizen petitioners, reiterated the demands the City had made in its remonstrances, and insisted upon a reform of their militia committee. To strengthen their appeal for increased power and security, the City fathers drew the connection between the London and Army petitions. "The Army (which they hoped ere this should have been disbanded) is now drawn so suddenly and quartered so near the Parliament and this City; besides that in the same juncture of time, a most dangerous and seditious petition (as they conceive) is set on foot." "What effect," the City governors asked rhetorically, "the unexpected approach of such an army and the concurrence of such a petition may work in the people?"[40] Although the two petitions were thus set in tandem, they actually revealed opposite ends in the political spectrum: the disparity between demands for social reform and desires for material satisfaction.

The Large Petition, which Gardiner shrewdly judged a program "for three centuries rather than for a single Parliament," implored an end to arbitrary punishments; protection from self-incrimination; a Christian codification of the law translated into English; the elimination of monopolies; and full religious toleration.[41] In the single clause that spoke to the problems affecting the Army, the petitioners desired "that you will not exclude any of approved fidelity, from bearing offices of trust in the commonwealth for nonconformity."[42] Among its goals were "that this nation no longer be a shame to Christianity" and that "the true ends of Parliament" be fulfilled.[43] In contrast to this program of total political reorganization, the Army's petition was both simple and direct. It requested indemnity for acts committed during the war; the auditing of accounts and security for arrears; freedom from impressment for those who volunteered for service in Parliament's armies; and care for widows and maimed soldiers. Cast in submissive rather than strident tones, the Army's petition sought only to redeem Parliament's "manifold promises and declarations to defend and protect those that appeared and acted in their service."[44]

Although categorically different from the appeals made by the London citizens, the major points of the March Petition were substantially the same as those expressed at the general meeting of officers on March 22. There, too, concern was voiced over indemnity and security for arrears, and there, too, the unanimity that was reportedly being given to the March Petition was found. The dissent among the officers centered only on the organization of the Irish forces – the appointment of commanders and the designation of the regiments to be kept up in England – and the appearance of the March Petition belied the claims of the parliamentary Commissioners that the officers who had gathered at Saffron Walden were unrepresentative both of their colleagues and of the soldiers in their regiments. It was this conspicuous unity between officers and soldiers over material issues that gave rise to claims that the officers themselves had engineered the March Petition. Waller argued that the petition was "pretended to come from the soldiers, but framed and minted by some of the principal officers," and the first reports reaching the Houses of Parliament accused several high-ranking New Model officers, including Commissary General Ireton and Colonels Hammond and Lilburne, of being its chief organizers.[45] Whatever the role of these officers, the significant distinction between the March Petition and the four questions propounded by the officers was that they embraced two separate constituencies; together, they expressed the universality of the Army's material concerns. It was into the face of this unanimity that the draconian response of Parliament flew.

Proclaimed as obstructors of the relief of Ireland and threatened with the brand of enemies to the state, the soldiers retreated from their proposed petition. Both they and Sir Thomas Fairfax were quick to express dismay at the misunderstanding that had occurred. "They did generally express a very deep sense of their unhappiness of being misunderstood in their clear intentions, which were no other, than by way of petition to represent unto me those inconveniencies, which would necessarily befall most of the Army after disbanding," Fairfax wrote to Speaker Lenthall even before news of the parliamentary declaration had reached Saffron Walden.[46] The publication of the declaration brought immediate disclaimers from within the Army itself. In "amazement and astonishment" an anonymous correspondent wrote to John Rushworth in London and denied in each particular the charges asserted in the parliamentary document. Especially important were the soldiers' attitudes toward the Irish service. "The Parliament will find those men, who were most forward in this petition, more ready to go for Ireland, than any of the *septem dicem viri* who only to curry favor and ingratiate, have tendered their service."[47]

If this was a true statement of the Army's initial intentions – and there is little reason to doubt that it was, for the Irish service had already proven unattractive to the entirety of Massey brigade – the climate soon changed. At the same time that the parliamentary Commissioners reported the response of the officers and the existence of the soldiers' petition, they also presented the Lower House with a declaration signed by twenty-nine Army officers who, without condition, but with expectation that the Army's material grievances would be requited, engaged "to advance that service by all good means and to improve our interest with the officers and soldiers under our respective commands, to go and engage in the same."[48] Only seven of these twenty-nine had been present at the convention of officers and the appearance of the remainder gave hope to Holles and the Derby House Committee that a sufficient number of officers and soldiers might subscribe without delay. To the remainder of the Army, however, the emergence of these undertakers posed a serious threat to their belief that redress of grievances should precede foreign service or discharge. The leading figures among the group, Colonels Harley, Sheffield, Fortescue, and Pye, were singled out for special abuse. "All our friends here do think these seventeen undertakers will prove very knaves and therefore that we do let them go on quietly."[49]

This cautious strategy of watching and waiting was abandoned once Parliament again decided to take the initiative. In the middle of April a second group of Commissioners was sent to the Army and directed to prevent obstructions and enlist subscriptions for the Irish service. On April 15, these Commissioners – the Earl of Warwick, Lord Dacres, Sir William Waller, Sir John Clotworthy, and Edward Massey, the newly appointed commander of the cavalry forces for the Irish venture – met privately with Sir Thomas Fairfax. "Hearing daily of more and more aspersions cast upon the Irish service," the Commissioners attempted to persuade the general to issue a declaration, which they had drafted, against such malefactions.[50] Fairfax refused this request, claiming that the impact of the declaration was "to adjudge his Army guilty before any proof made that there were any that did retard the service."[51] Instead, Sir Thomas offered to hear what evidence the Commissioners could produce against individual officers or soldiers and promised appropriate punishment for those found guilty.[52] The general's insistence upon orderly judicial procedure was particularly significant, for many Army officers had been incensed when anonymous accusations made against Lieutenant Colonel Thomas Pride and Colonel Robert Hammond resulted in their examinations before the House of Commons at the beginning of the month. Although unwilling to accept the Commissioners' declaration, Fairfax asserted his own intention to make a public pronouncement in favor of the service when the convention of officers met that afternoon.

Fairfax's refusal to issue the stern declaration against obstructions to the Irish service – he had reminded the Commissioners "that the Army was already in some heat upon occasion of a late declaration" – was only one of the setbacks suffered by the Commissioners in their second attempt to recruit the eleven regiments for service in Ireland.[53] While they were meeting with Fairfax, some two hundred New Model officers were holding their own assembly in anticipation of again being requested to subscribe for the venture. After agreeing upon the points to be presented in response, the officers chose Lieutenant General Thomas Hammond and Colonels John

Lambert, Nathaniel Rich, Robert Lilburne, and John Hewson as spokesmen for their group. When the convention assembled, Fairfax addressed the officers, "expressing how necessary the work was, and that who ever did not intend it in their own persons should lay their hands to it [recruiting volunteers]."[54] Then the Commissioners reviewed all the parliamentary votes for the Irish service, which now included the appointments of Sir Philip Skippon and Massey as commanders of the expedition and the assignment of the several regiments that were to remain in England. In response, the officers' spokesmen reiterated their commitment to further the service among the soldiery, but inquired whether the Commissioners had brought explicit answers to the two questions that concerned their material grievances, and urged the appointment of their own field commanders, rather than Skippon and Massey, as leaders of the expedition to Ireland. This, they suggested, would do much to encourage both themselves and their soldiers to enlist for the venture.[55]

The pressure for subscriptions to the Irish service, which was intensified by the Commissioners' second appeal, was driving a deep wedge within the Army. The attempts to gain satisfaction for material grievances had made little headway, whereas the appearance of the undertakers and the positive reports listing large numbers of volunteers sent to Derby House by the parliamentary Commissioners was a direct challenge to the unanimity that had been expressed at the two conventions of officers. Nor were these the only divisive factors to appear. Letters from anonymous Army correspondents to their London communicants spoke of dissimulation and chicanery in the process of gathering subscribers. Whereas the Commissioners reported that more than half the necessary eleven regiments had already volunteered, sources in the Army claimed "that of all the horse officers in the Army from captains upwards not above six captains, majors, or colonels have subscribed to go in person. . . . For the foot . . . Colonel Herbert and Lieutenant Colonel Kempson are the only two field officers; the rest are captains and they but a few."[56]

This dispute over numbers was a crucial one to those who hoped to secure the redress of their grievances. If the Commissioners succeeded in raising eleven regiments, those who were to be disbanded had little hope of securing their back pay or of protecting themselves from judicial retribution. Thus the conduct of the undertakers in eliciting new subscriptions became another divisive issue within the Army. On Aprl 18 the troopers from Colonel Robert Lilburne's regiment protested the conduct of their Lieutenant Colonel, Nicholas Kempson. Kempson had appointed a muster for pay, not at the regiment's headquarters but at Chester, the regular embarkation point for Ireland. The soldiers feared that in order to receive their wages they would have to subscribe for the service and complained to Fairfax of Kempson's machinations.[57] This led the General to seek the least disruptive method for recruiting the Irish regiments. He reached an agreement with the Commissioners that each regiment would be assembled to hear the parliamentary decisions and those soldiers willing to enlist for the venture would immediately be drawn from those who elected to remain. Yet the sobriety of this arrangement did not prevent Kempson from carrying out his own plan. As Colonel Robert Lilburne prepared to read the parliamentary votes at the regimental rendezvous, Kempson, in possession of the regiment's colors and treasure, led four companies towards Chester.[58]

The inducement of pay was not the only incentive provided to soldiers by those officers willing to subscribe for Ireland. Captain Charles O'Hara was accused of weakening the resolve of his men with large quantities of intoxicating drink and then procuring their signatures for the service.[59] Those who opposed the venture were perhaps equally ingenious in making its terms appear unattractive. Lieutenant Colonel Thomas Pride, it was attested by Captains Edward Wogan and John Farmer, had threatened that those of his soldiers who refused to sign the March Petition "should be blotted out of the rolls," thus making it doubly difficult for them to procure their arrears.[60] After Kempson and Colonel William Herbert had drawn their regiments together, they alleged that a party of soldiers had "endeavored to seduce, corrupt, and draw away" those who had volunteered for Ireland. They petitioned Fairfax "to give command that no interception be made or interruption given to any person or persons employed to London or to our affairs by any of your Excellencies' Army."[61] By the middle of April feelings were running high and the vaunted peace and harmony of the Army was dissipating. Indeed, Captain Lewis Audley, the only man against whom accusations of obstructing the service were made to Fairfax, was reputed to have said, "that those who were now so forward for the service of Ireland were not worthy to come near his horse's tail."[62]

The passions generated by supporters and opponents of the Irish venture marked the first tangible division within the New Model. Both obstructions and enlistments to the service reflected the strains upon Army members. Loyalty to officers and camaraderie with mates were now bound up by political and religious pressures. During the controversy over Kempson's conduct in leading four of his regiment's companies toward Chester, the issue of religion was first explicitly raised in the Army. One of Kempson's cohorts in this affair, and one of the undertakers, Captain Francis Dormer was accused of informing his company "that the intention of their drawing out was not to promote the Irish service but to go against an Independent army that was gathering together in the Kingdom."[63] Even those who were most unsympathetic to the Army, and were most likely to view it as a sectarian monolith, could now observe the New Model's religious diversity. "Though the Army differ in judgment about religion, yet they all agree in their discontented speeches against the Parliament," wrote a Suffolk man in April.[64] Edward Wogan, a captain of dragoons, would claim that before this time the "presbyterians had much the stronger part in the Army."[65] Religious and political divisions, though increasing at Westminster, were uncommon in the Army. They were now being created by the Irish venture.

The most apparent breach in the New Model's unity was seen at the convention of officers of April 15. Those commanders who had already subscribed or had expressed their inclination for the Irish service were conspicuous by their absence. The unanimity voiced by the more than two hundred officers who had assembled at the church in Saffron Walden was the concurrence of like-minded men, and the absence of the undertakers and their supporters was duly noted by the parliamentary Commissioners. Even after the discourse by the officers' spokesmen was seconded by cries of "All, All!" the Commissioners requested that those willing to subscribe for the service should come forth to identify themselves.[66]

Mindful that the weight of numbers would make some reluctant to proclaim publicly their allegiance, Waller and his colleagues worked behind the scenes, privately persuading and cajoling.[67] They never doubted that the eleven regiments would be recruited and their confidence was highest on April 17 when they offered a powerful new inducement to those willing to subscribe: an audit of their arrears.[68] This appeal was the most alluring yet made to the soldiery, for the taking of accounts was de facto assurance that arrears would be paid and that the individual soldier's family would be protected in the event of his death. More than the threat of retribution in the communities, the soldiers feared long attendance on the Army treasurers in London, which would be more costly than the arrears to which they were entitled.

The willingness of the Commissioners to provide further financial concessions to volunteers for the venture revealed the progress which they believed was being made. Although the officers had interjected a new issue on April 15 when they requested that Cromwell and Fairfax be given command of the Irish forces, ground was rapidly being gained by the parliamentary decisions establishing the terms of the service. Three of the four questions propounded by the officers in March were now resolved; commanders for the venture had been chosen; the regiments to be maintained in England selected; and the regular payment for the service established, although this last condition had been met only by the House of Commons.[69] The entire weight of the officers' stated objections now rested upon the satisfaction of material grievances. Here, too, Parliament had made progress, granting six weeks' arrears for subscribers to the Irish service, initiating inquiries into an ordinance for indemnity, and continuing to make reparations to widows and maimed soldiers whose accounts had cleared examination.[70] But at the very moment when the tangible grievances of the Army were being removed, the Irish service was beginning to assume the shape of a symbolic confrontation involving the integrity of the Army.

While the New Model directed its attention to the immediate impact of the Irish venture, the simultaneous appearance of several other areas of conflict between Parliament and Army served to generalize the soldiers' discontents. When the Army petition was first investigated in the House of Commons, Lieutenant General Thomas Hammond, Colonels Robert Hammond and Robert Lilburne, and Lieutenant Colonel Thomas Pride had been called to London to answer charges presented by unnamed informants. Although they were questioned sharply concerning their activity in promoting the petition, each in turn denied the contentions and insisted that the source of the accusations be revealed.[71] Their release from subsequent examination resulted as much from the disinclination of the full House to provoke a confrontation on the eve of the Army's disestablishment as from the credibility of their story. Holles, for one, believed that the officers' responses had been "mere collusion and equivocation (as by name Lieutenant Colonel Pride's who being charged with causing the petition to be read at the head of his regiment, denied it stoutly, because, it seems, it was but at the head of every company)."[72] The examination of the officers and the publication of the declaration against the Army's petition raised for the first time the issue of the soldiers' rights as subjects. The refusal of Parliament to confront Pride, the Hammonds, and Lilburne with their accusers, no less than the denial of the Army's right to petition, aroused the gravest concern over Parliament's attitude toward its soldiers.

The declaration against the Army's petition came only two weeks after both Houses of Parliament had graciously received a petition for the New Model's disbandment from the citizens of Essex, and only four days before a second petition from that county was circulated. This new petition was the result of a carefully orchestrated campaign to gain the widest possible support for the disbandment of the Army. The brief document complained only of the excessive burden of the Army's quartering, the depletion of the nation's resources, and the need for the relief of Ireland. In vague but foreboding phrases it requested "the speedy disbandment of the Army as a plenary expedient against the worst that in general may be feared by you and us." On Saturday, April 4, the petition along with two blank sheets of paper was distributed to the county's parish churches. The parishioners subscriptions were taken on the Sabbath, in many cases following sermons supporting the campaign.[73]

Occuring in the midst of the Army's quarters, the vitality of the Essex campaign contrasted sharply with the suppression of the March Petition. The several regiments of horse that were quartered in the county seized upon the contradiction "that they may be petitioned against but not petition," and resolved to prepare a defense of their conduct.[74] The contentious author of "A New Found Strategem Framed in the Old Forge of Machivilism and Put upon the Inhabitants of the County of Essex to Destroy the Army" denounced the petition and "the proud covetous priests" who led the campaign.[75] But others understood the complexity of the problem that now confronted the Army. "Who can blame the county of Essex?" wrote Rushworth's Army correspondent, "or any county in this kingdom else to desire a present disbanding since the work is done? It is as much irksome to us, when there is not need of soldiers, to quarter upon the country as it can be to the country to quarter us."[76]

Whether justified and well intentioned or insufferable and factious, the Essex petition constituted a further assault upon the New Model. Denied the right to express its own grievances, the Army was now the focus of the complaints of others. Along with the heavy-handed conduct of the supporters of the Irish venture, these attacks led Army members to compare the treatment they felt they were receiving with the merit they believed they had earned. Their self-justification, more than the accompanying self-righteousness, transformed the nature of the Army's grievances. In March material well-being had been the soldiers' sole concern; by April they demanded a defense of their honor and a vindication of their liberty. The campaign to obtain what was rightfully theirs had become a movement to secure their rights.

During March and April the New Model Army faced two separate challenges: the denial of their petition of grievances and the attempt to elicit volunteers for the Irish venture. The soldiers' initial response to both was an insistence upon their material well-being. Those officers and soldiers who stood ready to accept the Irish service were no less concerned over the payment of their arrears and the provisions for indemnity than were those who placed redress before enlistment. But Parliament's refusal to accept the soldiers' expression of their grievances raised issues that were to become more central than the material concerns that initiated the conflict. In the context of the demands for the vindication of the Army's honor the Irish service was doubly significant. The parliamentary Commissioners were not only raising a new army, but testing the unity of an old one. The enlistment of the eleven regiments meant the division of the New Model; the appointments of Skippon and Massey equaled the rejection of Fairfax and Cromwell. It was this atmosphere that generated new conflicts over subscriptions and further opposition to the Irish venture.

The elevation of questions of honor and rights to the center of the developing controversy between Parliament and its Army was of critical importance. The material grievances of which the soldiery complained were issues unrelated to the changes in parliamentary politics. The propriety of their satisfaction was universally accepted, and the process to secure the soldiers' arrears and indemnity was already underway. On the other hand, the vindication of the Army was a matter inextricably connected with the emergence of party politics. Although misunderstood, the transformation of the parliamentary process was observable in the Army, where soldiers would soon claim that the Irish venture was "a mere cloak for some who have lately tasted of sovereignty and being lifted beyond the ordinary sphere of servants seek to become masters and degenerate into tyrants."[77] By the end of April the conflict between Parliament and Army hung suspended between resolution and escalation.

By resisting the Irish service and insisting upon the satisfaction of its material complaints, the New Model Army had revealed an emerging political awareness. Its officers and soldiers had come to perceive that their contentions with the two Houses at Westminster involved more than the Army's petition and the Parliament's privileges. That political awareness became clearer during April when Army grievances were decisively transformed as the concern for individual rights was superseded by the assertion of collective liberties. Material considerations remained primary, the expression of the lowest common denominator among the heterogeneous beliefs and motivations that predominated in the ranks. But alongside arrears and indemnity were now placed honor and justice: the affirmation of good service and integrity. "In the Army . . . some content themselves with present enjoyments, others with the Commonwealth, at more certainty in the foundations of freedom," wrote William Walwyn, who claimed to have witnessed the Army's radicalization.[78] This interplay of material and political considerations soon reshaped the nature of each. Against the royalist reaction now taking hold in the nation, the payment of arrears would be the symbol of the honorable cause; against the parliamentary declaration that branded them enemies assurance of indemnity would vindicate the Army's character.

The events that had elevated political concerns above material ones, the rejection of the soldiers' right to petition and the petitions and accusations against the Army and several of its officers, promoted justifications and apologies that aided the Army in defining its role in the struggle with the King. The process of the Army's politicization, therefore, was a responsive one; a series of reactions to both real and imagined threats posed by Parliament's actions. Its manifestations were necessarily diverse, ranging from the tightly reasoned "Vindication" of the Army officers to the pipe dreams of London extremists. Being responsive, it was also uncontrollable and undirected, arising from the distinct actions of the officers and soldiery, a fact the Parliament was to learn when it attempted to suppress the nascent political organization among the soldiery by appealing to the traditional military chain of command.

Acting upon the hierarchical assumptions of military organization, the parliamentary Commissioners concentrated their recruitment efforts among the New Model officer corps. It was not optimism, but their experience in raising armies, that led the Commissioners to credit to the Irish venture the addition of a regiment on the subscription of a colonel, the accession of a company by the enlistment of a captain. In recruitment, as in battle, officers led and soldiers followed. It was through the initiative of the Commissioners that the convention of officers had first assembled, and through the officers that the Commissioners, and hence Parliament, were officially informed of the Army's grievances. It was to a second officers' convention that the parliamentary palliatives were reported, and from that convention that the Army demands were escalated.[79] Whether the officers had assumed a paternalistic relationship between themselves and their men as they would later claim, "we engaged but in the second place to regulate the soldiers' proceedings and remove as near we could all occasion of distaste," or whether a commonality of interest between superior and subordinate existed, it was the Army officers who presented a coordinated expression of desires and demands.[80]

Despite the officers' cogent presentation of the Army's grievances and their steadfast adherence to their redress, the movement to formalize these desires had emanated from the soldiery. Unlike their officers, who were able to submit petitions for arrears to the House of Commons and requests for release from imprisonment to the House of Lords, the common soldiers had no channel for the satisfaction of their complaints. The model provided by Massey's troopers, whose recent riotous conduct in London resulted in the payment of a portion of their arrears, had little to recommend it from a procedural point of view. The urgency of an audit of the soldiers' accounts and a general act of indemnity prior to disbandment thus initiated the petitioning campaign.

In the middle of March, perhaps in Rich's regiment, the first formal expression of grievances took shape.[81] The soldiers' intentions, though far from clear, were to express their material concerns and their desires for the settlement of the kingdom in a petition to the two Houses at Westminster. Beyond the points of arrears and indemnity and their corollaries of aid for widows and maimed soldiers, there may also have been complaints against malignants who had ensconced themselves into positions of power, and, perhaps even an unspecified plea for equity and justice at law. These latter issues grew directly from the fear of judicial retribution, and were unlikely to have been seen as matters of principle. Certainly their absence from the final petition indicates that they were not primary goals. Indeed, issues of principle were still submerged under the expectation of an impending settlement with the King. This anticipation of Charles's imminent restoration was seen in the Army's desire that the royal assent be obtained for the parliamentary act of indemnity.[82] More importantly, within the regiments, political awareness, as distinct from concern for material welfare, was still inchoate. As late as the middle of May Captain William Rainsborough could claim, "to speak seriously many of them did not know what they did, for many of them cried out 'Indemnity,' 'Indemnity,' and afterwards asked me what it was."[83]

As their followers groped for an understanding of the issues, the organizers of the March Petition sought a method for their presentation. It was at this point that the Army officers joined the campaign, providing the natural channel of command and the necessary link between the regiments. Besides exerting a controlling influence by removing "all occasion for distaste," the officers aided in presenting a concise statement of material complaints and an assertion of the loyalty of the Army. Their participation in the campaign also coincided with the decision to channel the grievances through the Army chain of command to General Fairfax instead of presenting the petition directly to Parliament.[84] Whether these modifications represented tactical decisions or were simply by-products of the agitation – a process in which officers and soldiers shared – is impossible to determine. The crucial contribution made by junior officers, and then by several regimental commanders, was the circulation of the petition for subscription among the soldiery. Although contemporaries underestimated the role of the rank and file in the process of the Army's politicization, and historians have exaggerated it, the common soldiers had no organization capable of directing a petitionary campaign; that development would mark an important step in the Army's entrance into politics.

The Army petition united officers and soldiers not only in goals, but in methods. The campaign to gain the signature of every soldier and officer was intended to demonstrate the universality of the Army's desires while assuring equal treatment for those enlisting for Ireland, remaining in England, or accepting disbandment. By petitioning through their officers to their general, the soldiers accomplished their primary goal, "to represent the inconveniencies which must necessarily befall the Army after disbanding," without developing their own organization for political action.[85] This was immediately apparent when their petition was outlawed by the parliamentary declaration. Although the majority of officers were able to express their grievances in another way, making them preconditions for enlistment to the Irish service, the unity of interest represented by the Army petition was shattered. Once more soldiers were expected to follow the lead of their officers, officers who now were divided over service in Ireland.

With the dissolution of the union between officers and soldiers came the first sporadic attempts of the soldiery to express their own opposition to the Irish service. In mid-April, after the apparent success of the Commissioners in recruiting officers to staff the eleven regiments, attention turned to filling the ranks. Although many officers had promised the engagement of their men to the service (Colonels Thomas Sheffield and William Herbert had committed their entire regiments), a concentrated enlistment campaign among the soldiers was still necessary. On April 18 Fairfax ordered each regiment to a rendezvous where the parliamentary votes for the Irish service would be read and those willing to subscribe drawn off, paid their bonus, and regrouped into new companies.[86]

Isolated and disorganized, troopers who opposed the Irish service seized on extraordinary means to express their discontent. In Robert Lilburne's regiment, several soldiers who discovered that they were to be marched against their will to an embarkation point for the Irish service appealed directly to Fairfax, arriving unexpectedly at his quarters. There they related not only the disingenuous conduct of their officers, "who had not well used them," but also their personal disinclination towards the venture: "They had served the Parliament some three, some four years, and now desired to return to their trades."[87] The men of Captain Arthur Evelyn's company, troops volunteered for the service by their colonel, Thomas Sheffield, issued a manifesto. "Though we are persuaded that that Kingdom stands in need of help, yet we conceive that we are not so to help them as wholly to deprive ourselves of our just rights and freedoms," they wrote, demanding the payment of their arrears and satisfaction to the four questions propounded by the officers.[88] A trooper from Cromwell's regiment met with an ensign of foot in a tavern at Bury St. Edmunds. He "asked the said ensign how the foot stood affected to the horse and whether they would join with them and stand for their arrears. ... That the country had paid it and there was no reason but they should have it before they were disbanded."[89]

Yet such desultory activity could hardly succeed against the combined ministrations of the Commissioners, the general, and the undertakers. Despite the chicanery of men like Kempson and O'Hara, the prospect of ready money had its own allure. Four whole companies had followed Kempson when he secured the regiment's treasure, and commanders like Graves, whose troops were stationed at Holmby, believed a disbursement of cash would outweigh the clamor for all other grievances.[90] If the Army was not to succumb piecemeal to Irish service, an actuality that would leave those who were disbanded at the mercy of overworked treasurers and overzealous local officials, a new method of unification would have to be developed. Not surprisingly, this was first sought by attempts to revive the March Petition. In East Anglia, where the troops of Ireton and Cromwell were quartered, "some troopers in the four regiments in Norfolk had a meeting about asserting their former petition."[91] This agitation was abbreviated by Major Robert Huntingdon, Cromwell's second-in-command, who prescribed instead an assemblage of representatives of officers and soldiers where the latter might express their desires.[92] In Lilburne's regiment, where the political differences of colonel and lieutenant colonel had already manifested themselves, Ensign Francis Nichols began his own agitation for the revival of the March Petition. As his constituency he chose the five companies that had already been drawn off from Army headquarters and were to be transported to Ireland. Nichols pleaded with those who had engaged, falsely suggesting that Lilburne's regiment would be kept up in England, but perceptively reminding his fellow soldiers "that those who went with him should fare no worse than the General fared."[93] For his efforts, Nichols was promptly arrested and brought to London by the parliamentary Commissioners who, before the Derby House Committee, charged him with obstructing the Irish service contrary to the parliamentary declaration.[94]

These efforts to resurrect the March Petition had little hope of success. None of the New Model field commanders had favored the initial campaign, although Ireton had been charged with complicity and Cromwell had spoken in favor of the grievances, but not the methods employed in their expression.[95] Moreover, the Damoclean sword of the parliamentary declaration had finally fallen, severing Ensign Nichols from his regiment and threatening to cut a swath between those who opposed the service and others willing to comply with Parliament's terms. The unity of the soldiery could not yet be expressed through petitions; a new device was imperative.

Unwittingly, the opportunity for concerted action was provided by the meetings in Norfolk and the regimental rendezvous for the Irish recruitment. At the end of April, the eight cavalry regiments centered around Army headquarters at Saffron Walden each selected two troopers to prepare a letter to the New Model field commanders.[96] These men, and those who followed them in the office, came to be known as agitators, and the document they presented was the first cogent representation of the fears of the soldiery at the prospect of disbandment or service in Ireland. In the estimation of the agitators, an active conspiracy was under way, orchestrated from Westminster where "some who have lately tasted of sovereignty, and, being lifted beyond the ordinary sphere of servants, seek to become masters and degenerate into tyrants." The seemingly random events of the previous months, the persecution of soldiers at assizes; the reemergence of royalists to positions of power in the counties; the removal of New Model officers from commands in Ireland, when linked to the development of party leaders and adversary politics, all revealed the contours of "a design to break this Army in pieces." No longer could the soldiery accept the expectations of parliamentary justice or the promises of parliamentary Commissioners. Only those officers who were M.P.s and could observe the conspiracy from within were capable of protecting the New Model from the "mercilessness of our malicious enemies."[97]

The selection of agitators as agents to represent the grievances of the cavalry troopers was an important breakthrough in politicizing the Army. Until then, despite occasional unrest, extramilitary activity was purely conventional. The petition of grievances had been channeled through the chain of command, and the insistence upon the Army's right to petition was based upon recent and clearly established parliamentary precedent. The New Model officers in their "Vindication" cited the declaration of November 2, 1642 ("it is the liberty and privilege of the people to petition unto us for the ease and redress of their grievances and oppressions, and we are bound in duty to receive their petitions"), and reminded the House of Commons that it had "well received" petitions from officers in the armies of Essex and Waller "even whilst they were in arms."[98] Only the rejection of the legitimate method of expressing discontent had led the Army to develop a new one.

Yet it was the appearance of the agitators rather than their initial actions that broke with precedent. Besides some intemperate language, which was, in any case, obscure, the agitators had only requested protection by their own commanders. Although the subsequent careers of Edward Sexby and William Allen might seem to imply a radical breakthrough, their appointment to journey to London in the company of Samuel Sheppard and to deliver the letter merely followed the logic of the military hierarchy: each represented a cavalry regiment whose colonel also held a field command.

The appearance of the agitators was innovative, not radical. There is no evidence to suggest that the agitators or the regiments they represented were the authors of the polemical "Second Apologie of All the Private Soldiers . . . to Their Commissioned Officers" that called for "an end to all tyranny and oppressions so that justice and equity, according to the law of the land, should be done to the people and that the meanest subject should fully enjoy his right, liberty and properties in all things."[99] It is not "probable that the first movement to elect agitators was itself a result of the infiltration of Leveller principles."[100] The impetus for the agitators' selection and the desires they most clearly expressed in the letter to their commanders derived from the attempt to assert the Army's material complaints; the more ambitious plans for organization and action, and the "Lilburnian" principles voiced in the "Second Apologie," emanated from London. Nor were the agitators the "spirits of [Cromwell's] . . . and his son Ireton's conjuring up," the tool of radical officers pressing their own designs upon the nation.[101] They were not even, as Waller claimed, "things never known before in any army in the world, and now set up, in confutation of Ecclesiastes, to show, there might be a novelty under the sun."[102] It was not radical puritanism that fed the development of similar "spirits and dominations" in the Spanish Army of Alva.[103] Instead, if a model for the agitators existed, it was much closer to the traditional one suggested by Clarendon: "The common soldiers made choice of three or four of each regiment . . . who were called agitators and were to be as a House of Commons to the Council of Officers."[104]

The unrest and discontent of the soldiery, displayed by the election of agitators and the presentation of the letter from the cavalry regiments to Cromwell, Skippon, and Ireton coincided with the effort of the Army officers to present a defense of their conduct. Since the declaration against the March Petition and the recrudescence of the Essex petitioning campaign, many felt the need to respond to the charges made against the New Model's conduct: to vindicate the honor of the Army. As in the case of the soldiers, it was the industry of the Commissioners that provided the opportunity for the officers' concerted action. Twice they had been summoned to conventions to hear the parliamentary votes for service in Ireland. Twice the officers, over two hundred in number, selected spokesmen to respond to the request for enlistments, and on both occasions the parliamentary Commissioners had challenged the right and ability of these spokesmen to represent the body of officers. With the appearance of the undertakers and the progress made by the Commissioners in filling the Irish regiments, the bulk of the New Model officers decided upon a show of unity more palpable than cries of "All!, All!" From these conventions emanated "The Vindication of the Officers of the Army," at the end of April.[105]

Unlike the anonymous March Petition, the officers' "Vindica-

206

tion" was prepared and presented in full view of the nation. It defended the Army against both the charges contained in the parliamentary declaration and the current crop of rumors that grew in London. Temperately, the officers sought recognition for the Army's right to petition, requesting that Parliament "be pleased to allow us our liberty of petitioning in what may concern us now as soldiers, and afterwards as members of the Commonwealth."[106] Two regimental commanders led a group of officers to the House of Commons, where the "Vindication" was presented on April 27.[107] Three days later, when the Lower House began its consideration of the officers' moderate appeal, Major General Philip Skippon, sitting in the Commons for only the second time, produced the agitators' letter, which had been presented to him on the previous day.[108] The officers' "Vindication" was promptly laid aside in preference to an examination of the three troopers who had delivered the letter.

Appearing as representatives, and doubtless aware that their safety lay in the collectivity of their actions, Allen, Sheppard, and Sexby refused to interpret the more offensive passages in the document upon which their interrogators had seized. As this list of unanswered queries grew, the agitators suggested that they might bring the examiners' questions back to the regiments for a response.[109] This, however, was precisely what was most galling about the situation: the organization and united action of the regiments. On this point the agitators were closely examined. Had there been a secret rendezvous appointed by the officers for the drafting of the letter? Their election, the troopers replied, came at the rendezvous ordered by the Commissioners, the document had been drawn at several meetings of the representatives, and as to their officers, "they thought very few of them know or took notice of it."[110] Unable to find conspiracy within the Army, some M.P.s sought it from without. Were these agitators malignants, royalist agents stirring mutiny and sedition within the ranks of a loyal Army? To this accusation each man catalogued his lengthy service in the parliamentary cause, one narrating his capture and escape from a royalist prison, another his dangerous wounds and Skippon's touching generosity.[111] These were Parliament's faithful soldiers acting in their own cause with neither the instigation nor the collusion of their officers.

In Parliament the letter presented by the agitators to their commanders aroused anxiety for the maintenance of military discipline. To Holles and his majority the obedience of officers and soldiers was a critical necessity in the program of military reorganization. Already, in mid-April, the Commissioners had reported opposition to the Irish service that, contrary to Parliament's orders, continued unabated. When they returned to London with Ensign Nichols in their custody, the Commissioners complained of the renewed petitioning campaign. As troublesome as the activities of the officers had been, it was not nearly as threatening as the unexpected emergence of dissent from the rank and file. When the examination of the agitators revealed the spontaneity of their actions, the House of Commons moved to reassert military order. The senior New Model commanders who sat in Parliament, Skippon, Cromwell, Ireton, and Fleetwood, were dispatched to headquarters "for the better preventing of any disorder in the Army."[112] On May 1, Sir Thomas Fairfax, under the direction of the Lower House, ordered all New Model officers to repair to their regiments "under pain of such severe punishment as shall be inflicted upon them for the neglect therein."[113]

Beyond the question of discipline, the activities of the soldiery nurtured fears of a military uprising; the agitators were not the only ones who believed in conspiracy. Throughout the spring proponents of an immediate military disestablishment were consumed by paranoiac speculation over the Army's intentions. Petitions from the City of London and the county of Essex hinted at dark contrivances to overthrow the very structure of parliamentary government. Some volunteers for the Irish service believed that they were recruiting a loyalist force to oppose "an Independent Army."[114] Indeed, their activity prompted a reciprocal belief that the volunteers for Ireland would be used to spearhead an attack upon the New Model. On May 3 it was rumored at Army headquarters that orders had been given for the opening of such an assault. That night soldiers stationed in Saffron Walden were issued powder and ball, and "kept guards with their swords drawn at the street corners."[115] But the most potent rumor of all asserted an alliance between the New Model and the monarch. During the first week of May letters circulated throughout the Eastern Counties revealing secret negotiations between Army and King. They asserted that a petition had been sent to the King inviting him to

Army headquarters where the soldiers "would set the crown upon his head."[116]

It was this association between the soldiers' agitation and royalist designs that struck a responsive chord among members of Parliament. "The rumor of the Army's holding intelligence with the King spreads apace in the Kingdom. . . . It's talked of in the City further, that now your Army begin to keep strict guards and fortify their headquarters, nay some say further Major General Skippon will be detained until the Army be satisfied in their demands."[117] Although the greater part of these rumors were "London stories," fear of a revival of the King's cause was still prevalent at Westminster. When the agitators were examined in the House of Commons they had been accused of acting as royalist agents and their record of service was investigated to determine whether they were actually spies. Although Allen, Sexby, and Sheppard successfully repudiated these charges, they continued to be indiscriminately applied to the Army. The group of Parliament men who pressed for disbandment of the New Model was now swelled by those who feared either a military putsch or a royalist resurgence. On May 3, parliamentary Commissioners renewed their efforts to secure from the City of London a loan for the reorganization of the Army. To underscore the urgency of the City's compliance with Parliament's terms, the Earl of Pembroke repeated the rumors of the Army's overtures to the King, and informed the City fathers that the New Model now contained over 4,000 former royalist troopers. "All the hopes (he told them) of the King and the malignant party depended upon that Army. . . . He conceived it were high time they were disbanded."[118] To a City still menaced by apprehensions of a siege, Pembroke's insinuations were clear.

While these plans for the disestablishment of the New Model were being made at Westminster, an inquiry into the conduct of the soldiery was launched at Saffron Walden. On May 7, Skippon, Cromwell, and Ireton convened another meeting of officers to discover the "distempers" that gave rise to the actions of the cavalry troops "and some other proceedings which they (the House of Commons) conceived illegal."[119] Acting as Commissioners, the three commanders requested that the regimental colonels prepare an account of the dissatisfactions among their troops. Clearly, the military M.P.s had yet to grasp the meaning of the events that caused the election of the agitators and the presentation of the letter from the cavalry regiments. The Army officers who had remained in the field understood that they could no longer speak for their troopers. A statement of grievances by the officers, they informed their commanders, "might perhaps be taken as an unadvised and forward act in them, to declare the sense of the Army before they know the general resolution of the soldiery."[120] They would not repeat the error of the undertakers, who "subscribed their names, whereby the Parliament was inclined to believe they could engage their whole regiments."[121] Instead, they requested a week for consultation with the soldiers and for preparation of a written statement of "distempers."

By opening an inquiry into the soldiers' conduct, Parliament unknowingly provided a channel for the expression of the Army's complaints. "They found no distemper in the Army, but grievances many which the soldiers complained of," the officers would report, and from the first, Parliament's efforts to quell the Army's extramilitary activity became the Army's opportunity to press its demands.[122] This was the avenue that the soldiery had sought since the suppression of the March petition: a means to represent their material necessities and to press for a confirmation of their rights. Thus the gathering of regimental statements furthered the process of the Army's politicization. Organization within the ranks coalesced as the role of the regimental agents was reinforced by the compilation of the lists of grievances. Imitating the example of the eight cavalry regiments, the infantry elected its own agitators. Most importantly, like the March Petition, the preparation of the regimental statements unified officers and soldiers in a single effort to seek redress. Unexpectedly the quest to reunite the Army was fulfilled.

The preparation of regimental statements of grievances revealed the diversity of the Army's organization and the unity of its concerns. Three-fifths of the New Model regiments presented written reports to the new parliamentary Commissioners: eight cavalry and six foot.[123] Only two of the horse regiments, those of Graves and Sheffield, reported no grievances beyond arrears and indemnity, and these statements were challenged at the full meeting of officers and representatives on the grounds that they were drafted by the commanders.[124] The remaining regiments, which provided more lengthy enumerations, employed a variety of means to sound the opinions of their troops. In the horse regiments that had been most tightly organized, those of Fairfax, Cromwell, and Ireton, a core of grievances common to all three was agreed upon, to which was appended additional individual material separate to each.[125] In the infantry, the regiments of Fairfax and Hewson also collaborated on a single statement, although different from that produced by the cavalry.[126] These documents emanated from the elected representatives of the rank and file, as did those of the regiments of Colonels Butler and Harley. In other regiments officers took the leading part in both drafting the statements and in serving as spokesmen for the regiment's grievances. It was this process that led, to the election, for the first time, of officer agitators.[127] Indeed, in Colonel Harley's regiment these two procedures merged as the officer corps subscribed to the document prepared by the soldiery and framed it as a petition, requesting Skippon, Cromwell, and Ireton "to become suitors to the Parliament on our behalf that we may have a reasonable and effectual redress."[128]

Although Harley's regiment presented a "petition" to the Commissioners and Rich's troopers produced a lengthy apologia to Parliament reminiscent of the early City petitions, the gathering of regimental statements was not a petitionary campaign.[129] Rather than a prearticulated account of grievances to which the mass of soldiers could subscribe, the process of compiling regimental statements encouraged the individual soldiers to examine their own conditions and express their own beliefs. Thus, unlike the March Petition, which presented a small number of general desires, the statements of grievances in May expressed the Army's specific complaints. Among the issues raised by the cavalry troops was the cost to the individual troopers of providing horses "when the state's horse miscarried," as well as their concern for the collection of that part of their pay which was deducted on the public faith.[130] The less prosperous infantry men were more unsettled about the prospect of impressment: "we are under many fears and jealousies," wrote Harley's soldiers, "that . . . we shall after our disbanding be forced against our will to serve as soldiers out of this Kingdom."[131]

Individual regiments also voiced distinctive complaints. Hardress Waller's men singled out the conduct of one of their own captains, Daniel Thomas, who, in recruiting for the Irish service, castigated the soldiers as "seditious, rebellious disturbers of the peace of this Kingdom," adding "that those who refused to go to Ireland shall be forced to follow like dogs."[132] In a veiled reference to their own colonel, Harley's regiment also voiced a unique objection, relating to the "incendiaries" who had given information against the March Petition. "This is the great grievance to us by how much the more we have cause to believe that one of those incendiaries hath so near relation to us that we should rather have expected that he should have spoken on our behalf than presented false information against us."[133]

The disparate complaints of the regiments and the diversity of the production of the statements are further evidence of the gestation of the Army's political consciousness and organization. Neither radical politics nor political radicals were yet dominant within the New Model. The program for religious, social, and legal reform that had attracted support in London was scarcely recognized within the Army regiments. Fears of religious persecution were expressed by only two regiments: Waller's, whose troops complained, "we are denied the liberty which Christ has purchased for us . . . to serve God according to our proportion of faith," and Harley's, who suspected they would be "pressed beyond the light they have received." Both these clauses came near the end of lengthy lists of grievances.[134] Opposition to the establishment of the covenant as a prerequisite to holding public office was the current rallying cry of London radicals, but only Cromwell's regiment voiced concern over this precursor to the Act of Uniformity and the Tests.[135] Significantly, this was not one of the eleven common points of the three regiments. Lilburnian rhetoric and Lilburne's cause, so much in the air in the capital, were also absent from the Army's statements. Only in the lists of the general's two regiments could oblique references to the Large Petition and Lilburne's imprisonment be found. Yet these, the cavalry's protest of Parliament's rejection of petitions from the "free denizens of England," and the infantry's concern that freemen were imprisoned without charges, had more than passing connection to the Army's own plight.[136]

At its core, the New Model's agitation centered upon its explicit grievances: material necessity, the rights of the soldiery, and the Army's honor. Every regiment listed the payment of arrears and the passage of a parliamentary act indemnity as its first material complaints. Even the reports of Colonels Sheffield and Graves, which emphasized the lack of grievances, cited arrears and indemnity as major issues.[137] The general's lifeguard asked for a "considerable proportion" of their arrears; Graves's regiment requested an additional grant of two weeks' severance pay, equal to that received by the Earl of Essex's army; and the companies under Colonel Lilburne's command desired that there be a "visible care taken for the payment of their whole arrears."[138] The considerable proportion of arrears that would satisfy most of the regiments had a corollary in the demand for an audit of accounts, "for the attainment of the remainder of our arrears without the great expense, trouble, loss of time, which others have undergone in waiting for their arrears in so much that the benefit hath not counter-valued their great expense occasioned by their tedious waiting."[139] Invariably, the regiments stressed a connection between the satisfaction of arrears – a proportionate payment and an audit of accounts – and "the sudden intention to disband the Army."[140] The continued appeal for an act of indemnity was best summarized by the statement from Rich's troops: "After our disbanding we have no security to free us from the inveterate malice not of private but of public enemies who gladly would have sheathed their swords in our bowels."[141]

Wedded to material grievances, and in number and emphasis surpassing them, were the issues touching the Army's honor. The declaration against the March Petition had aroused the deepest suspicions of parliamentary injustice, and in conjunction with the continued affronts to the Army – the arrest of Ensign Nichols and the Earl of Pembroke's speech – had effloresced into the very symbol of the Army's cause. "If we not have full reparation," the officers and soldiers of Harley's regiment claimed in advocating the recall of the declaration, "we conceive it impossible for the Parliament ever to give us the due reward of our faithful service, for that we account our honor and reputation more dear unto us than anything in the world besides."[142] The joint statement of the regiments of Fairfax, Cromwell, and Ireton concluded that the declaration "remains upon the file as an everlasting brand of infamy upon this Army to posterity," a sentiment echoed by Waller's regiment, who believed that it "must needs render us infamous to succeeding ages."[143] The reparation they and most others advocated was "that that erroneous and contemptible Declaration against this

Army be forthwith called in and razed out of the books and burned by the hands of the hangman and the occasioners thereof be brought to condign punishment."[144]

Resentment toward the declaration was reinforced by successive assaults upon the Army's character. The examination of the New Model officers in April, based upon unsubstantiated information, and the subsequent investigation of the role of Colonel Lilburne and two captains in printing the pamphlet "A New Found Strategem," gave great offense. "We cannot but sadly take notice of it, that the Parliament can spare time from the affairs of the Kingdom to trouble, if not imprison, our officers about such a trifle as a pamphlet which is common in the Kingdom," the men of Lambert's regiment complained.[145] The arrest of Ensign Nichols was assailed both for the treatment he received ("imprisoned and barbarously used") and for the manner in which Fairfax's autonomy had been abridged ("in affront to his honor's power and dignity").[146] But the loudest protests were reserved for the most recent transgression, the speech of the Earl of Pembroke before the London Common Council. Only Harley's regiment named the Earl and repeated the content of his remarks, although all the troops were sensitive to accusations of treachery. "False and calumnious aspersions are cast upon this faithful Army," wrote Hardress Waller's soldiers. Their authors, it was intimated, "were men who have been employed agents to scatter such to render us ignominious to the Kingdom."[147] The Earl's exalted position necessitated such veiled references and moderated the Army's response. "That we should be scandalized by the spreading of a petition pretended to go from the Army to the King . . . we detest," Lambert's regiment proclaimed, but desired only "that the author of it may receive the punishment which the Parliament shall please to inflict upon him."[148]

It was the Army's honor, not its material condition, that was uppermost in the minds of the soldiery. Regiment after regiment recalled the hardships and sacrifices of the war: "Many of us lost the affection of our nearest friends and the benefit of our trade whilst we have exposed ourselves to the extremest difficulties and constantly hazarded our lives."[149] Although such self-justification bred romanticism, the fidelity of the troops was seen in stark contrast to the vindictive parliamentary declaration and the charges being leveled against the Army. "This Army which . . . brought peace and safety to this Parliament and Kingdom with their lives and estates is now undervalued, dishonored and despised and those which have been the breaknecks of the Kingdom's enemies are now voted as enemies themselves."[150]

Only a vindication of the Army's conduct, the recall of the declaration, and punishment for those responsible for the Army's derogation would now satisfy the troops. Votes to supply arrears and ensure indemnity were in themselves insufficient. The events generated by the March Petition superseded the desires that had initiated it. More than the need for redress it was the right to petition that became crucial. "We who have adventured our estates and lives, yea all that was near and dear unto us, not only for our freedoms, but for the privileges of Parliament and the safety of the Kingdom, should now at length be denied to step over the very threshold of liberty (to wit) petitioning."[151] It was the future, not the past, that troubled the Army. The fear of men "who having lately tasted of sovereignty . . . degenerate into tyrants" remained omnipresent; little by little the Army came to recognize the changes that had taken place in the political process. The strident words of the agitators' letter to their commanders now gave way to the doleful phrases of Lambert's infantry. "In the sadness of our spirit, we profess we can find little joy either disbanded or in arms, for whereas after so great expense of blood, treasure and time we look for the execution of justice but behold tyranny and oppression and that from those who we had hoped under God had been the deliverers of our Israel, so that for anything, as we conceive we can expect none other but to be under as great slavery and bondage as we were before."[152]

The despondency that permeated Lambert's regiment derived not only from disappointment with Parliament's performance. The Army was becoming a model in miniature of the political process, replete with factionalism and divisiveness. The regimental statements had provided an opportunity for the reunification of officers and soldiers in seeking the redress of grievances. Representatives were sent to the convention on May 15 with instructions to integrate the clauses of their statements with those of others, "that whatsoever might relate to any one particular regiment might be left out and the general grievances of the whole Army represented."[153] This process was undertaken by Colonels Lambert and Whalley, who attempted to draft a single statement of the grievances of the Army that could be presented to the Commissioners.[154]

But the unity sought by these organizers was the solidarity of like-minded men. Those who had stated their preference for Irish service were now excluded from the process that would represent the desires of the whole Army. "I know nothing of it," protested Colonel Thomas Sheffield after hearing of the collation, "and I conceive I, being Colonel of a regiment may know of it, as well as a trooper or inferior officer."[155] Lambert justified his selectivity by asserting that the material deprivations in which all shared were no longer the center of the Army's complaints. "We found the greatest grievance of the Army is the rejecting the late petition and representation that himself [Sheffield] and many of the rest of the worthy gentlemen did declare no grievance at all," Lambert informed the Commissioners.[156]

In truth, the officers and soldiers who pressed forward with the statement of grievances did not see the contradiction between their emphasis upon the Army's unity and their exclusion of those who had volunteered for the Irish service. "You will please to satisfy the Commissioners that there is not so much dissenting as they speak of, for seven or eight men do not make a dissent in the Army," claimed Mark Grimes, Lambert's lieutenant colonel.[157] Yet despite this commonly held conviction that the Army remained unified, the conventions of May 15 and 16 revealed deep discord. First, several regiments returned conflicting accounts of their desires, which led to acrimonious exchanges and accusations of prevarication and treachery. This might be expected from the infantry regiments of the general and Colonel Lilburne, where contests over recruitment for the Irish venture had already inflicted deep wounds. But other regiments also evinced divisions. Several separate companies of dragoons reported no discontent within their ranks, a flat contradiction to the support Colonel Okey had given to the preparation of the general statement. Colonel Graves had reported that his regiment was satisfied by the parliamentary decisions. This was challenged by Graves's major, Adrian Scroope, who contended that the regiment had not been assembled to have the decisions read.[158] Divisions in Sheffield's companies, which might have been anticipated, were matched by disharmony in Hardress Waller's, where Captain Daniel Thomas defended his conduct in recruiting for Ireland, and Major Thomas Smith his conduct in advising the soldiers to "stand for your liberties and privileges now and ever."[159]

The strains of the previous months had taken their toll and the famed unity of the Army was stretched taut and brittle. "Betwixt them and us is something past of heat and animosity, especially betwixt Colonels Sheffield and Whalley, but I hope it will go no further," Lambert reported to Sir Thomas Fairfax.[160] The task of moderating and adjudicating these dissensions fell, as it had so often in the past, to Major General Philip Skippon, whose valor and honor were as revered in the Army as his moderate religious and political views were acceptable to Parliament. From the first, Skippon demanded that the officers "so represent and so adjutate things as may become your Christian profession and as may become sober-minded men, as may become servants to the public."[161] But the heavy-handed policy of Lambert in excluding the undertakers from the collation of grievances and the exasperation of Sheffield in being treated with less respect than the common soldiers were irreconcilable. When minority opinion was quashed by the weight of the majority, Sheffield interceded. "I do not think but that any man hath a liberty to speak; 'tis true there are more of the one side than of the other."[162] Sheffield's persistent interruptions finally provoked Colonel Edward Whalley. At the end of the meeting, to prevent the Parliament from being misinformed and the Army from being slandered, the officers voted to send representatives to report the proceedings of the conference. When Sheffield, who had long lain under a cloud for his role in reporting the organization of the March Petition, objected to this superfluous procedure (communication with Parliament, after all, was the role of the Commissioners), Whalley snapped, "Does your conscience accuse you?," a retort to which the disconcerted Skippon replied, "Speak with moderation or be silent."[163]

Recruitment for the Irish venture began the process of dividing the Army; the order for disbandment completed it. The caustic exchange between Sheffield and Whalley was but one indication of the depth of feeling on both sides among men who together had fought for the preservation of the kingdom and had now to choose between conflicting loyalties. Those who, throughout the months of the subscription campaign, had avoided a commitment were soon brought to the test. Without waiting for the result of their inquiry into the Army's distempers, Parliament completed its financial arrangements with the City of London and ordered the Derby House Committee to disband the Army. On May 21, after the Commissioners submitted their report, votes were passed for the disestablishment, regiment by regiment, beginning on the first of June. Not surprisingly, the first to be discharged was one that had suffered most from the rancor of Irish recruitment, Fairfax's regiment of foot. In a parody of their lengthy delays during the previous months, Parliament accompanied these orders for disbandment with the passage of successive votes for the satisfaction of the soldiers' material grievances. Although only eight weeks' arrears were offered, all the other central desires of the abortive March Petition were satisfied.[164]

The order for the disbandment ended the existence of the New Model Army. Although the soldiers successfully resisted Holles's plan for disestablishment – on May 31 the general's regiment mutinied at Chelmsford – the Army that survived to dissolve Parliaments and draft visionary constitutional platforms had, like the parliamentary process, been itself transformed. In reaction to the threats posed by the Irish venture, political logic replaced its military counterpart. The strict standards of martial order, the chain of command and the regularity of promotion, were loosened to respond to and reflect political considerations. Sheffield's sneer that a colonel was at least equal to a trooper or inferior officer had military as well as social content. By the end of May, fueled by the grievances Parliament had not redressed – the vindication of the Army's honor – the efficient fighting force had become a tumultuous political forum, another of the nation's pressure groups. Beyond efficiency and order, beyond martial spirit and triumph, the New Model Army possessed one other unique trait: the harmonious coexistence of diverse religious and political opinions. This, too, was sacrificed to political uniformity, and the extensive changes in the Army's composition reflected the profound transformation of its character.

The changes in the New Model officer corps were completed shortly after the mutiny at Chelmsford. Although some of the original undertakers had been replaced as early as April, it was not until June that the wholesale reorganization of the Army's personnel occurred.[165] On June 14, the second anniversary of the battle of Naseby, William Clarke, the Army's secretary, recorded a number of withdrawals, promotions, and transfers within the regiments. Clarke's record is highly reliable – it was undertaken to update salaries – but some of the promotions he recorded were changes that had occurred prior to the spring and may have been unrelated to the Army's agitation, whereas others, which undoubtedly took place, went unnoted.[166] Despite the survival of Clarke's account, then, difficulties remain in assessing in detail the reconstruction of the Army's senior officer corps. Fortunately, however, these problems are weighted toward underestimation rather than exaggeration, for withdrawals from the Army can, with few exceptions, be independently linked to the agitation surrounding the Irish service. This corroboration all but eliminates the possibility that many of the departures were esoterically inspired; the changes in the Army officer corps were directly related to the Army's conflict with Parliament.[167] On the other hand, whereas the evidence allows for a complete account of the changes in the cavalry, it is not as revealing in the case of the infantry. Therefore, it is likely that more infantry officers, especially captains, left the service than were recorded.[168]

Twenty-nine percent of the Army's senior officer corps are known to have left service by June 1647.[169] Infantry and cavalry experienced equal loss: the foot regiments replaced twenty-nine of their one hundred officers and the horse, twenty-two of their seventy-six. The dozen cavalry regiments lost a higher proportion of their most senior officers than did the ten of the infantry. Five colonels – Butler, Graves, Pye, Rossiter, and Sheffield – and four majors – Alford, Fincher, Moore, and Sedascue – retired from the cavalry, necessitating the replacement of one of the two ranking officers in eight of the twelve regiments. In the foot, three colonels, Fortescue, Harley and Herbert; two lieutenant colonels, Jackson and Kempson; and three majors, Duckett, Gooday, and Masters, left the infantry, affecting six separate regiments. Thus nearly a third (32 percent) of the highest-ranking New Model officers supported Parliament in the agitation of the spring and withdrew from the Army at the beginning of June. At the next lower echelon, a slightly smaller percentage of captains departed from their companies: in the horse thirteen (25 percent) and in the foot, twenty-one (30 percent).[170]

These statistics reveal a change in the Army's officer corps larger than has been generally assumed. Almost a third of all senior officers were replaced in the early summer of 1647 at a time when departure from the ranks was equated with disloyalty to the Army. As numerous as these replacements were in the whole of the corps, they were still greater when seen in the regiments in which they took place. For varying reasons the commands of three cavalry and four infantry regiments remained intact.[171] In the remaining nine horse and six foot regiments, 43 percent of all officers withdrew from service. Eight of the nine horse regiments lost one of their two highest officers as 55 percent of the colonels and 44 percent of the majors departed from the ranks. All six of the infantry regiments replaced either a colonel (50 percent), lieutenant colonel (33 percent), or major (50 percent). Half the foot captains and almost a third of those in the cavalry left their companies.

The process by which these officers withdrew from their commands remains obscure. Some soldiers later declared that they had ousted those of their superiors who supported the Irish venture and disbandment, "hooted diverse officers out of the field, unhorsed some and rent their clothes," but this probably only occurred at Chelmsford, where Fairfax's bitterly divided infantry regiment mutinied.[172] More likely, the officers abandoned their commands following the mutiny and the King's abduction, which occurred two days later. The protestation that many of them sent to Fairfax indicated that they continued to perceive themselves to be loyal members of the Army whose first duty had been to Parliament.[173]

Within the Army, however, volunteers for Ireland and supporters of the order for disbandment were quickly replaced by their pro-Army subordinates and by other newly commissioned officers. The two commanders whom Cromwell had recommended to Fairfax in March, John Barkstead and Robert Overton, both received colonelcies in reorganized regiments.[174] Overton, like Lilburne and Lambert, came from Fairfax's northern forces, whereas Barkstead, a London goldsmith, had served as governor of Reading. In the two infantry regiments most divided by the Irish service, Fairfax's and Lilburne's, new men from outside the companies were brought in: Major William Cowell was transferred from Harley's regiment to be Fairfax's lieutenant colonel, and Henry Lilburne (the Colonel's brother) and Paul Hobson were commissioned to be lieutenant colonel and major in Robert Lilburne's regiment.[175] In the cavalry, Sheffield's companies lost both their colonel and major, and command of these troops passed to Thomas Harrison, who was transferred from Fleetwood's regiment and promoted to colonel.[176]

All these appointments, promotions, and transfers were irregular in the Army's traditional seniority system. They were undertaken to produce solidarity for the Army's demands and were coupled with a larger number of more customary advancements. Five of the eight colonels who left service were succeeded by their majors: Adrian Scroope (Graves); Thomas Horton (Butler); Matthew Tomlinson (Pye); Philip Twisleton (Rossiter); and Thomas Pride (Harley). These direct promotions suggest that some colonels and majors of different political and religious outlooks may have been deliberately balanced upon the Army's creation. This supposition cannot be carried too far, for the Army's creation was a military rather than a political event, and its radicalization was sudden and unpredictable. Nevertheless, the number of regiments in which only one of the two highest commanders withdrew is more than coincidental. In the cavalry, seven of the nine affected regiments lost either colonel or major, but not both; Colonel Thomas Sheffield and Major Richard Fincher resigned from the same regiment.[177] In the infantry, five of the six reconstituted regiments lost either their colonel or lieutenant colonel, no regiment lost both, and the sixth regiment lost its major.[178] Whatever the explanation for such a well-patterned reorganization, the New Model Army had been transformed.

With the transformation of its leadership, the rise of the New Model Army was completed. The threats posed by the Irish venture and the order for disbandment had been met by a reorganization that brought political unity to a formerly heterogeneous military body. In a series of unorganized and conflicting responses aroused by pressures that emanated from Westminster, the Army acquired political awareness. The Irish service and plans for military disestablishment first generated the expression of the soldiers' material concerns. The need for security of their arrears and indemnity for their actions prompted the March Petition. Parliament's rejection of the soldiers' right to express their desires confused and embittered the Army. The parliamentary declaration coupled with continued recruitment for the Irish service led the soldiery to subordinate their material grievances to considerations of rights and liberties. Thus was born a cause to which political rhetoric and organization was a natural outgrowth. The election of agitators and the preparation of the regimental statements led to the coordination of the Army's political activity and reemphasized the need

PARLIAMENT ECLIPSED

for unity. Concurrently, those officers who supported the Irish venture were ostracized for their opposition to the Army's politicization. When the crisis reached its climax and the Army refused to disband, a thorough reorganization of the Army's officer corps resulted. Singular political purpose and concerted political action were now possible in the remodeled Army.

The Army's entrance onto the political stage also signaled the demise of parliamentary politics. The torpid, convoluted political process, even when transformed by the parties and their leaders, was as alien to the course of military decision making as the decisive and irretrievable actions of the Army were to the parliamentary way. Parliament's dealings with its Army called into question not only its judgment, but also its legitimacy. Unrestrained by tradition and unused to compromise, the diet of the Army's ensuing activity would be the staple of "politics by other means" – physical force. Its confrontation with Parliament was not a struggle between political personalities but a contest between political methods. It was the City of London, where the techniques of power politics first originated, and not the Parliament, that understood this new mode of political expression and that attempted, for a brief moment, to meet the Army on its own terms. Thus the rise of the New Model Army was the harbinger of the emergence of radical politics that transformed civil war into revolution.

Chapter 8

THE EMERGENCE OF
RADICAL POLITICS

And always men may see it, that Parliament privileges, as well as
Royal prerogative, may be perverted and abused, or extended to
the destruction of those greater ends for whose protection or
preservation they were admitted or intended.[1]

"To speak a sad truth," Sir William Waller reflected when he
reconstructed the events that led the Army to march on London in
August 1647, "the destruction of the Parliament was from itself."[2]
Like Holles and Whitelocke, Waller attributed the decline of parliamentary authority to its failure to suppress the Army's incipient
mutiny in March, when they might have "crushed the cockatrice
in the egg." Their concessions had served only to increase the
Army's appetite for power and to encourage its supporters at Westminster. "The Parliament fell neither bound nor fettered," Waller
concluded, "but betrayed by the insidious practices of its own
members."[3] Neither in 1647 nor in later years when these men
penned their apologetic memoirs did they understand the change
they had wrought in political practice or the consequences that
change had for the system of government they had fought to defend. To them the explanation for the Army's actions in the
summer of 1647 was remarkably clear: the Army and its party in
the Commons had betrayed their trust and their nation. As Holles
sardonically stated: "These are they who fight for privilege of Parliament, – who have made a covenant with God and man so to do;
and well they perform it; those they mislike must be thrust out by
head and shoulders; and such as remain, if they be not obedient to
them shall be served with the same sauce: and this is to make a free
Parliament."[4]

"A free Parliament" was the summer's theme. Each of the groups
that took part in those frenetic events expressed fervent and *sincere*
concern for the freedom and privileges of the two Houses. While
the Army disregarded direct orders and showed its strength to the

City, it repeatedly declared its adherence to the ideals of parliamentary freedom. "We took up arms to assert and vindicate the just power and rights of this Kingdom in Parliament," the Declaration of June 14 averred.[5] Nor were the Army's public pronouncements mere cant for popular consumption. "The Parliament is not free," Rushworth wrote privately to Ferdinando Lord Fairfax, "nothing will set it free . . . but the Army."[6] The Army's concern for parliamentary freedom stemmed from the throng of reformadoes – soldiers reduced from disbanded parliamentary armies – who crowded the doors and hallways of the Parliament building. For their part, the reformadoes desired to serve the Parliament "in regard their [the Parliament's] privileges together with their own liberties were in danger by the Army."[7] At the end of July, they and many other young Londoners engaged to defend "the privileges of Parliament and the liberties of the subject in their full and constant freedom."[8] The frequent appeals from the City of London for expanding the jurisdiction of its militia committee had the self-same ends. In demanding the revocation of Parliament's order reinstating the old London Militia Committee, the Common Council contended that its new committee had been created by the "authority of a free Parliament."[9] Finally, when the Houses of Parliament were stormed by those who had pledged to preserve and protect parliamentary freedom, the Army marched to London so that "those members of either House . . . may with freedom and security sit there, and again discharge their trust as a free and legal Parliament."[10]

First in June and then at the end of July the Army and the City, to defend the same ends, stood poised on the precipice of armed confrontation. For them, as well as for the apprentices and reformadoes, the "honest" and the "well-affected" citizens, the necessity of maintaining parliamentary freedom meant different things. For the Army, Parliament must be kept free from the influence of those who had neglected its material grievances and declared against its petition. To the City, parliamentary freedom meant its ability to resist the demands of the Army and to reassert the City's rights to regulate its own militia. Parliament, free from the influence of the Army, would pay the arrears of the reformadoes, debts more long-standing than those owed to the New Model. For each, a free Parliament would satisfy its own just desires and oppose the abusive conduct of its opponents.

Unpressured and unimpeded debate could no longer prevail over the weighty matters of state. The process of sacrificing means to ends that had begun as long ago as the spring of 1645 had reached its culmination. "We wish the name of privileges may not lie in balance with the safety of the Kingdom," the Army wrote at the end of June when submitting charges against the eleven members.[11] Their impeachment was matched a month later by the apprentices' invasion of the two Houses and the flight of some seventy-odd Lords and commoners. In these turbulent months, the resolution of issues, and not debate, held center stage. "Vote!, Vote!," screamed the apprentices when they turned the House of Commons into a virtual prison on July 26. Though heard from a distance, the Army's demands for votes to satisfy its proliferating grievances were no less resounding.

Although the ways to achieve parliamentary freedom and privilege were contested and the actions of the contenders plainly diminished Parliament's authority, the ideal of parliamentary freedom remained unaltered. Those like Holles who saw only hypocrisy and disingenuousness in the conduct of their opponents could not perceive how the meaning of Parliament and its authority had been transformed; those like the Army who were willing to bring force into the political process could not foresee that in their effort to preserve Parliament they might destroy it. Just as the parliamentarians had engaged in war against the King for his own protection, so the Army and City assaulted Parliament in its defense. "All authority is fundamentally seated in the office," the Army declared, "and but ministerially in the persons."[12] The authority of Parliament, therefore, had been corrupted by parliamentarians and the contaminating influence was manifest to all in the growth of party and interest. Party was antipathetic to the welfare of the nation, it was the advancement of the particular against the whole – the supersession of the public good. In the Houses of Parliament, parties, whether of malignants who served the ends of the King, recruiters who followed the whip of Walter Long and Anthony Nicholl, supporters of the Army, or Holles's clique at Derby House, now predominated.

Constantly the Army repeated its opposition to party and interest. "We do not seek anything of advantage to ourselves, or any particular party whatever, to the prejudice of the whole," they declared in June. "We have nothing to bargain for or to ask, either from His Majesty or the Parliament for advantage to ourselves or any particular party or interest of our own," they reiterated in July.[13] As the chain of events that began with the order for piecemeal disbandment moved to its inexorable conclusion, the Army justified its extraordinary actions by its opposition to party politics: "Those worthies who have formerly acted, and carried on things for public good, right and freedom, are now awed or overborne by a prevailing party of men, of other private interests, crept in, and that neither we, nor any other can expect right, freedom, or safety (as private men) or to have things acted in Parliament for public good while the same parties continue there in the same power, to abuse the name and authority of Parliaments, to serve and prosecute their private interests and passions."[14]

Nor was the Army alone in identifying party as a corrosive development in political practice. Holles claimed that the Independents discredited themselves in Parliament by being "a known, engaged faction." Prynne argued, in defense of the eleven members, that the Army's charge of impeachment was "only to weaken the Presbyterian party so the Independents might overvote them," whereas Waller thought the charges made reflected more upon Parliament than upon the impeached members of whom he was one: "It resembled an arraignment of the House of Commons, supposing them so weak and corrupt as to be acted by particular interests."[15] Even the vituperative Clement Walker, the bane of religious independents, could diagnose the disease, publishing his remarkable backbencher's manifesto *The Mystery of the Two Juntoes* in June. The war, Walker reasoned, "working upon the human frailty of the *speaking* and *leading* members of the Houses, caused them first to interweave their particular interests, and ambitions with the public welfare, and lastly, to prefer them before the public welfare." He identified these usurpers as Grandees, the leaders of the "two factions of Juntoes or Presbyterians and Independents."[16]

There was an element of utopianism in the Army's appeal to public good and liberty, to their desire "that such men and such men only might be preferred to the great power and trust of the Commonwealth as are approved, at least, for moral righteousness."[17] But the growth of parties and interests was more than the violation of a political ideal. The Army's potent fear, antedating its political activism, was that its enemies would come to be its judges and that the service it had performed would furnish the grounds for judicial retribution. There was more than a casual connection between its demands for indemnity and vindication of its honor. Initially, those the Army feared most were former royalists and neutrals who had opposed the war and were unsympathetic to the logic of military necessity. Soon, however, those who came to judge the Army were the leaders of a party at Westminster, the incendiaries who had impugned the Army's conduct. While these men remained in power the soldiers could neither disband nor accept the service in Ireland. Thus each action the Army took was as much motivated by fear as by principle: fear of piecemeal disbandment; of the raising of new armies; of foreign intervention and renewed fighting; fear even, as ever, of a royalist resurgence. "Doubts and fears are all of the sharpest passions, and are still turning distempers to diseases."[18]

In the City, too, the spread of party was expressed by fear. There the Army's power and its willingness to use it to achieve its desires was seen as the work of a particular interest. Although the government was sympathetic to the Army's material grievances it had been taught to view the New Model as a haven for religious dissidents who were prone to riot and mutiny. "O know and foresee that if the Parliament and City's just rights and privileges be battered down by the blustering winds of distractions and roaring storms of an Army . . . you shall reap no other fruits but the height of slavery," wrote one feverishly imaginative citizen in July.[19] When the Army marched toward London in June the City's omnipresent fear of being sacked revived. Despite the Army's disavowal, "although you may suppose that a rich City may seem enticing bait to poor hungry soldiers," the image of plunder was much too vivid.[20] For the first time the City called out its militia and listed men from the crowds of reformadoes who flocked unwelcomely within the walls. After the apprentices rioted in July, the City again raised forces in a brief and unheroic attempt to meet the advancing Army. Again the specter of a City in flames haunted London's leaders and was an important element in their decision to "invite" the Army to return the members to Parliament. But, like the Army, their actions were defended by claims of preserving Parliament from the overawing influence of one party or interest.

"I attended less in the House when these matters were in agitation," the dissembling Whitelocke recalled, "being unsatisfied that the Army and City should thus seem to impose upon Parliament."[21] Throughout June and July political power resided not in the Houses in Westminster, but in bodies spawned by the tacit encouragement of parliamentary members. The similarities between the City's use of political pressure and that adopted by the Army are striking. The Army's unanswered petition was superseded by a remonstrance urging political reform. The City's lobbying campaign in which aldermen and common councilors importuned conspicuously at Parliament's doors was imitated by the Army's threatened occupation of London – its studied advances and retreats in response to parliamentary concessions. "Did not the City Remonstrance hang like a petard upon the Parliament door week after week, and every ward in course, to attend and fire it?" Hugh Peter asked rhetorically as he defended the Army's conduct.[22] When the City turned to listing soldiers and the Army to demanding the reconstitution of the militia committee, armed conflict was the all but inevitable result.

It was fitting, then, that the struggle to preserve parliamentary privilege should be conducted by the Army and the City through threats of force and violence. For Parliament, either in 1646 when it surrendered to City divines and financiers, or in 1647 when it collapsed in the face of a militant Army, had proved unable to preserve its institutional prerogatives. It was not coincidental that this confrontation should center upon opposition to parties and interests, upon the repudiation of the transformation that had occurred at Westminster. Although the apprentices could restore the eleven members, and the Army those who fled the mob's violence, neither could revive parliamentary unity. The decline of parliamentary authority – so much the result of the growth of adversary politics – also meant the eclipse of parliamentary legitimacy. The emergence of radical politics, in opposition to the parliamentary way, was never better expressed than by Sir Thomas Fairfax. When asked by the King "by what authority he durst thus resist him and his Parliament," Fairfax forthrightly replied, "There was necessity."[23]

When they came, the New Model's political actions were swift and decisive. News of the parliamentary order for disbandment reached the Army on May 27. Even at Westminster few anticipated compliance: "I do not think that it is expected by any," Sir William

Constable wrote to Ferdinando Fairfax, "that obedience will be yielded by the soldiers, the provocations being so resented and grown to such heights."[24] In the Army Sir Thomas Fairfax immediately sought the advice of his Council of War. It met at Bury St. Edmunds on the 29th and debated the order to disband and the hastily taken votes to satisfy the Army's grievances. Without dissent the officers agreed that their material demands had not been fulfilled, and suggested that the Army's quarters be contracted to prevent disorder.[25] Acting as swiftly as the general, the agitators had already prepared a petition expressing their opposition to the disbandment. They protested the suddenness of Parliament's resolve, and more particularly the methods to be used to effect it: "The strange, unheard of and unusual way of disbanding us apart, one regiment from another contrary to the example of other Armies disbanded in this Kingdom."[26] They presented their petition to the Council of War, demanding that the general order the contraction of the Army's quarters and appoint a rendezvous for the full Army. Indeed, the agitators conceived a general gathering so important that they declared themselves ready to order it without Fairfax's approval.[27]

Although the Council of War, reconvening to hear the agitators' demands, agreed to recommend the contraction and rendezvous, the agitators had already acted to ensure that the disbandment would be stymied.[28] At Chelmsford Fairfax's infantrymen conducted a small insurrection on May 31, the day before they were to be mustered out. Led by Captain William White, they seized the regiment's drums and colors and marched toward Newmarket in anticipation of the rendezvous. When confronted by their officers the men justified their actions as having been ordered by the agitators and attacked their lieutenant colonel and major, Jackson and Gooday, as enemies to the regiment.[29] While this mutiny was taking place at Chelmsford, Rainsborough's troops, stationed near Oxford, were similarly distempered. They feared that their projected service in the island of Jersey would violate the soldiers' principle of redress before disbandment or acceptance of foreign service. Tempers ran so high that officers and soldiers drew swords against each other, at the cost of several lives and maiming injuries.[30] When the pay intended for the disbandment of Colonel Richard Ingoldsby's troops passed through Rainsborough's quarters at Culham it was seized by the soldiery.[31] In the face of these seemingly spontaneous disorders, Fairfax could only inform Parliament that he could not carry out their instructions for disbandment, saying frankly to Speaker Lenthall: "I shall do my endeavors though I am forced to yield to something out of order to prevent disorder."[32]

Although given the protective coloration of the Council of War, the Army's refusal to disband was the work of the soldiery. As Fairfax admitted to Lenthall, he was no longer in control of the Army he commanded. The agitators had already shown their willingness to assume leadership during a crisis, and there was much anticipation that the mutiny at Chelmsford might lead to more dangerous acts. William White, M.P. for Pontefract, one of Sir Thomas's parliamentary correspondents, had advised the general to abandon the Army in the event that it rejected Parliament's commands. "I cannot see that your stay in the Army in any unquiet distemper (upon this occasion) can be for your safety," he wrote at the end of May, adding, "nay I am sure it must be to your apparent danger."[33] Another observer within the Army, reporting that the soldiers had begun to purge the dissenting officers from the ranks, concluded, "I pray God the soldiers get not too much head; the officers must instantly close with them or else there will be disorder."[34]

As expectations of mutiny and violence filled the air, both at Bury St. Edmunds and in London, the agitators pursued a more calculated plan. With a party of horse drawn from several regiments, Cornet George Joyce rode to Oxford to secure the train of artillery and its store of powder and balls, and then continued on to Holmby House to prevent the King's removal by Colonel Robert Graves and the parliamentary Commissioners who attended him. Joyce arrived at Holmby on the night of June 2 and his presence in the courtyard, coupled with the unwillingness of those guarding the monarch to fight with their comrades-in-arms, forced Graves, with a handful of loyal officers, to flee from the manor. The next night Joyce presented himself to the King. He acquainted Charles with his intention to remove him from Holmby to the Army's headquarters, and the following morning produced a file of musketeers as his commission. Although the parliamentary Commissioners objected vehemently to Joyce's proposal (at one time they even contemplated making a stand that would undoubtedly have led to the issuance of four new writs to Parliament to fill seats of deceased members), under the circumstances neither they nor the King could resist.[35]

The seizure of the King – Joyce had almost certainly overstepped the agitators' intention to reinforce his guards with loyal troops – climaxed the soldiers' efforts to prevent their disbandment.[36] The fears of renewed war and of a counterplot to remove Charles from Holmby were doubtless sincere – Rushworth wrote privately to Lord Fairfax, "if they had the King, I mean Holles, Stapleton, etc., the Scots had come in to have crushed this Army" – but actuated by misperceptions and deep-seated suspicions.[37] One communication from the Army even spoke of the City's annual request for £20,000 "to be employed about the line of the communication in order to make war against us as we apprehend."[38] Skippon himself was suspected of being "not right," and Joyce's removal of the King was followed by the withdrawal of the officers known to have favored the Irish service.[39] Rumors fed fears both in the Army and in London: "Our chief news here is of your Army," one frustrated correspondent wrote to headquarters from the City, "and I can assure you we have twenty stories a day and scarce ever a true one."[40] Truth and fiction had become intertwined. Joyce claimed he acted "to prevent a second war by . . . some men privately to take away the King."[41] His removal of the King, however, revived accusations that the Army intended only to erect its own religious and political establishment. Preconceptions dominated the interpretation of unanticipated events. "Provocation and exasperation makes men think of that they never intended," Ireton had written.[42] In actuality, Holles and his party could not have reacted to the Army's refusal to disband before Joyce arrived at Holmby; and the Army's officers had not directed Joyce's actions.

As Joyce began his march from Holmby the soldiers held their rendezvous near Newmarket. When Fairfax was apprised of the King's removal he dispatched Whalley's regiment to intercept the party and return the monarch to Holmby. But Charles, no stranger to fortune, declined Whalley's offer and insisted upon being led to Army headquarters.[43] At the rendezvous, Fairfax viewed the troops and attempted to soothe their discontent with assurances that Parliament would satisfy their desires.[44] He accepted a lengthy account of their grievances, "An Humble Representation of the Dissatisfactions of the Army," and advised the soldiers "not to fall into any distempers or mutinous expressions against the Parliament."[45] The "Representation" reiterated the Army's familiar material complaints. The soldiers continued to protest the inconsequential sum to be paid at disbandment and added new objections to the specific plan Parliament had devised for the payment and security of their arrears. The large sums to be deducted to discharge free quarter were especially resented, for some soldiers had paid much of their quartering costs, and the sum fixed, three shillings a week for an infantryman, was nearly twice the actual expense for food and shelter. In numerous clauses the soldiery recounted Parliament's denial of their right to petition and the affronts given to the Army's honor. As they had in the regimental petitions, the soldiers demanded "the discovery and censure of those who have wronged the Army and abused the Parliament," again calling for the expunging of the March 30 declaration.[46]

"We are still tender of the Parliament's privileges," they assured the two Houses, "but we shall yet hope and desire that the wisdom of Parliament would find how to disengage the honor of Parliament from the desperate practices of such incendiaries."[47] After agreeing to the clauses of the "Representation," the soldiers then subscribed to an engagement not to disband until all their material demands had been satisfied and their honor vindicated. Again they recounted the series of events that began with the March petition, defending the election of the agitators and the preparation of the regimental statements, and concluding with an explanation of their refusal to disband. They disavowed any intention "to the overthrow of magistracy, the suppression or hindering of Presbytery," or "the establishment of Independent government."[48] Their Solemn Engagement concluded, as would so many of the Army's subsequent documents, with a denunciation of parties and interests: "Neither would we (if we might and could) advance or set up any other particular party or interest in the Kingdom (though imagined never so much our own) but shall much rather . . . study to promote such an establishment of common and equal right and freedom to the whole, as all might equally partake of."[49]

At Westminster news of the Army's actions confounded the Houses of Parliament. On June 1 the two Speakers received letters from Fairfax informing them that in view of the unredressed grievances that continued to oppress the Army, the Council of War had voted against disbandment. Then came a report from the parliamentary Commissioners sent to Chelmsford recounting the mutiny there and the soldiers' march to Army headquarters.[50] The House of Commons, which had been peaceably debating delinquents' compositions and relief for London's indigent citizens, immediately set aside their scheduled business to consider this startling information. Reflexively the money dispatched for disbandment was recalled. Then the Commons' doors were locked "and none permitted to go out without leave."[51] For the remainder of the morning, through the afternoon, and well into the night the debate raged. To Holles and his followers the Army's refusal to disband constituted a mutiny that, they contended, must be suppressed either by loyal New Model troops or by forces raised in London. "It was proposed in the House," one of Clarendon's correspondents reported, "to declare those in the Army traitors who have been so refractory to the commands of Parliament."[52] Others insisted that the most expedient way to secure the Army's obedience was to satisfy their desires. Although neither side could convince the other, Holles's majority, united for peace, disintegrated over the prospect of renewed war. "When it came to the pull, so much sadness, fear and deadness was over their party, that they were ready to sink with thoughts of it," wrote an Army supporter from London, adding, "I never saw men's looks so changed."[53] After long and passionate consideration the House resolved to delay decision until Philip Skippon could return from the Army and provide fuller information.

The Lower House resumed its debate on Thursday, June 3. Again Holles pressed for decisive military action, but Skippon, who was now present, took the lead in persuading Parliament to make every effort to propitiate the soldiers.[54] Meeting that afternoon, the Commons resolved that upon disbandment or enlistment for the Irish service the soldiers would be paid their full arrears, and the commissioned officers would receive an additional month's pay.[55] Even this debate was heated, for, as Harington recorded, using party labels for the first time, "the Presbyterians would pay all arrears to the common soldiers, the Independents oppose it for that might set divisions between officers and soldiers."[56] It was no longer clear, either from Fairfax's letter or the Commissioners' report, that the officers and soldiers remained united, and Parliament could not hope to raise sufficient cash to discharge the officers' arrears. It was thus agreed, by 154 votes to 123, to satisfy the soldiers' accounts immediately.[57] Most of the evening was consumed by this debate and candles were brought into the House before the Commons could consider a more critical matter, the recall of the declaration of March 30. It was nearly 2 A.M. when the vote to expunge the declaration was taken, and it was adopted by only 17 votes in a House of 175. In full view of the membership the clerk obliterated Holles's handiwork.[58] Although Whitelocke would later think that "here the Parliament began to surrender themselves and their power into the hands of their own Army," these decisions were taken in expectation of gaining the soldiers' compliance.[59] Before this extraordinary session was adjourned the Commons resolved to entreat the Lords to follow their example, and to send a letter to the Army detailing their actions.[60]

On Friday the Commons' bleary-eyed members learned of the seizure of the King. Unconfirmed reports of military activity near Holmby had reached the House of Lords on the 3rd, but it was not until Captain Titus appeared at Westminster the next day that Joyce's arrival and Graves's departure were established.[61] Despite this news the Commons continued on the course it had set the previous day, sending its votes to the Lords, appointing one committee to draft a letter to the Army, and another to prepare a new ordinance for military indemnity. On the 5th this bill received two readings in the morning and a third, of amendments, in the afternoon.[62] By then the House had prepared an explanation for expunging the March 30 declaration, emphasizing its understanding "that the petitioners intended not thereby, to give any offense to Parliament or in any way to reflect upon or lessen their authority."[63] In its eagerness to remove all obstacles to a settlement it even appointed a session for Sunday June 6 following morning sermons. By the middle of the following week the indemnity ordinance and a revised statement explaining the revocation of the March 30th declaration had been passed into law. A new group of parliamentary Commissioners was appointed to report these votes to the Army and to reside at headquarters for the maintenance of good correspondence.[64]

The Lords, though their activity was no less frantic, were not as willing to collapse in the face of the Army's disobedience. The anti-innovatory peers were not a majority in the Upper House, but they were powerful enough to delay portions of the Commons' stampede legislation and to attempt to repair their own

fences. It was not until the 5th that they considered the Commons'
vote expunging the March 30 declaration. They agreed to this
decision, over six dissents, but they would not accept the public
explanation drafted by the Lower House.[65] Provocatively, the
Lords spent most of Saturday considering the parliamentary peace
propositions that had been submitted at Newcastle and the King's
most recent response to them.[66] The conservative peers, at least,
preferred compromise with Charles to concessions to the Army.
After long debate the decision to accept the King's May 12 reply
was deferred, but in their Sunday session they reminded the Commons of their previous vote to bring the King to Oatlands; nearer
to London and, perhaps, to accord.[67]

As the two Houses worked in their separate ways to redress the
Army's material grievances, they were confronted by another of
their unresolved military obligations. Since the end of winter, reduced officers and soldiers from the old parliamentary armies had
been gathering in London. The decision to disband the New Model
and repay its arrears encouraged these reformadoes to hope that
their accounts would also be cleared. Each day they flocked to
Westminster, pressing individual members of Parliament, like Sir
Philip Stapleton, Sir William Waller, and Edward Massey, for
restitution of their back pay. Their swelled ranks filled the Parliament building and resulted in an order for the guards to keep the
Commons' stairs and outer chamber clear.[68] On June 3 John Birch
reported the cause of the reduced officers and soldiers. He made a
special plea for those officers who were imprisoned for debt and
the House responded by providing £10,000 to settle their accounts.[69] This opened the floodgates for the reformadoes' claims.
On June 4 a throng of reduced soldiers appeared at Westminster
to present formal petitions for their arrears. They crowded around
the Commons' doors and accosted the Speaker and other M.P.s
with claims that "they had always obeyed them and when were
commanded did disband; yet were not their arrears voted."[70] In
answer to this petition "of all private soldiers in general" the House
ordered another £10,000 to be distributed by the Committee of
Accounts.[71]

Again the vote to pay some whetted the appetites of others. An
even larger contingent appeared to petition the Commons' members on Monday June 7.[72] Ordered according to the armies in
which they had served, this group was better organized than the

first, but equally distempered. Their unabated clamor interrupted the House's pressing business. Members of the Accounts Committee were sent to inform the crowd that £10,000 had already been provided for them.[73] Whereas the Lower House sought to appease the reformadoes, the Lords essayed to subdue them. They demanded that the City militia bring troops to protect Parliament and suppress these tumultuous gatherings.[74] The Commons agreed to their plan, but the presence of the troops, many of whom awaited the settlement of their own arrears, did little to disperse the petitioning soldiers. Parliamentarians were no longer solicited at their doors or in their halls, but the crowds of reformadoes, enlarged daily, continued to appear at Westminster. Revealing that neither their conciliatory approach nor the Lord's belligerent one was having much effect, on June 10 the Commons ordered the immediate payment of £5,000 to the reformadoes and requested an entire regiment of City militia troops be stationed at their doors.[75]

While the City teemed with reformadoes whose petitions for money had turned into ugly demonstrations outside the Parliament doors, the military population of London was enlarged by the arrival of officers and soldiers leaving the ranks of the New Model. The refusal to disband and the seizure of the King drew the line between hypothetical and actual revolt; no longer could the soldiers afford the luxury of differing points of view. Those who had supported Parliament's commands, especially those willing to accept the Irish service, were enemies to the Army, and their desertion from the ranks was encouraged not only by the soldiery but by the Houses of Parliament.[76] Although Holles could not persuade the Commons to suppress the Army's mutiny forcibly he did gain approval to continue to recruit forces for Ireland. On June 2 the Lower House reaffirmed its readiness to provide a month's pay to all who seceded from the Army and enlisted for Ireland.[77] The first of these men, Sir Robert Pye's troops of horse, arrived at Westminster on June 5. They were immediately provided with £200 and were soon joined in London by parts of Fairfax's infantry regiment and a company of Graves's horse from Holmby.[78] All three units were quartered in the environs of Westminster. Two days after their arrival they were regrouped into a new regiment and directed, on June 8, to advance to Worcester for embarkation to Ireland. Ten thousand pounds was ordered from the accounts at Weavers' Hall to pay and equip these and all other forces willing to serve in Ireland.[79] In contrast to the Army's unexpected actions, this operation proceeded precisely as Parliament had planned it.

Parliament was now entrapped between the demands of its former and present soldiers. Few had come in to accept the Irish service, and the money borrowed from the City for that purpose was instead being used to satisfy the reformadoes' persistent claims. Their arrears petitions contrasted faithful service and obedience to parliamentary commands with the Army's mutiny, infuriating the soldiers in Cambridgeshire, where news of the reformadoes' meetings and offers to defend Parliament against the Army's demands spread quickly. The Army had not been paid since April and the £20,000 provided for the reduced officers and soldiers might as easily have made two weeks' pay for the New Model. But the reformadoes represented more than another competitor for parliamentary funds. From the moment they refused to disband, the soldiers expected Parliament to raise forces to compel their dissolution. This fear motivated Joyce to remove the King to Army headquarters, and others, like Rushworth, to anticipate Scottish intervention. Thus the reformadoes, most of whom had served under members of Holles's party, were a palpable danger. Together with the City's militia and the troops that had withdrawn from the Army for the Irish service, they were a force of almost equal size to the New Model.[80]

The news received from London at headquarters, when compounded by suspicion and fear, pointed to the formation of such an Army. On June 8 the reformadoes again repaired to Westminster, where they "blocked up the House of Commons' door about two hours, refusing to let any member pass until the House had granted them their arrears."[81] In the wake of this disturbance the City's sheriffs presented a petition from the Common Council that desired that their reconstituted militia committee be given power to raise cavalry troops, make searches, and suppress disorderly meetings.[82] These requests were accepted with little debate, for Parliament was now literally at the mercy of the City militia for protection from the reformadoes. "The House understands very well that the committee of the militia is very sensible of the tumultuous and distempered humors that are now stirred," the Speaker told the City's delegation, promising prompt action on their petition.[83] On the same day, £10,000 was voted to pay and equip the forces that had withdrawn from the Army and were now directed to Worcester.[84] In reaction to tumults in London and to a rebellion in Ireland, Parliament had raised the core of another Army. With Holles and his party urging defiance, and the Lords considering an immediate settlement with the King, Parliament's acts of conciliation, which were being reported to the Army, had little hope of placating the soldiery.

In the Army political activity continued its lightning pace. At the news of Joyce's action Fairfax and the Council of War determined to move Army headquarters from the royal residence at New-market. Before leaving, the general and his senior officers met with the King at Childersly on June 7. They assured Charles that they had not ordered his removal, and convinced even the parliamentary Commissioners of their innocence. Unable to induce the King to return to Holmby, Fairfax sent Whalley's regiment to accompany him to Newmarket.[85] The rendezvous to hear the latest parliamentary votes from the new Commissioners was scheduled for the following day, but the King's arrival forced its postponement until June 10 at Triploe Heath near Royston. There the regiments were arrayed for the second time in less than a week, and on this occasion it was Skippon who exhorted the troops to obey Parliament's commands and seriously to consider accepting the offer of arrears and the revocation of the declaration of March 30.[86] When these votes were presented to Fairfax's cavalry regiment, however, they requested that they be considered by the newly created Council of the Army, a body of officers and agitators.[87] By then the Army was extremely apprehensive about events in London.

Sometime during that day, probably after the official rendezvous ended, the decision was made to march toward London. Rumors of an invasion from Scotland and enlistments of forces in London persuaded the senior officers that assuming an aggressive attitude, within striking distance of the capital, was necessary. The designs of Holles and his party could succeed only by aid from the City, and it was upon the City that the Army determined to apply its pressure. That evening the Council of War drafted a letter to the London government advising them of their intention to move southward. They accused a "wicked party that would embroil us and the Kingdom" of attempting "to interest their design in the

City of London, as if that City ought to make good their miscarriages and should prefer a few self-seeking men before the welfare of the public."[88] To prevent this the Army was marching toward London, but they sought only "a settlement of the peace of the Kingdom and of the liberties of the subject according to the votes and declarations of Parliament." They disclaimed any intention to harm the City or its inhabitants but concluded with a dire warning: "If after all this you, or a considerable part of you, be seduced to take up arms in opposition to, or hinderance of, these our just undertakings," the Army would not be responsible for "all that ruin which may befall your great and populous City."[89]

News of the Army's march outran its letter to the City. When the House of Commons met on June 11 all its energies were directed to its own defense. If the Army did not actually invade London, its approach might be sufficient to ignite riots among the reformadoes or malignants. Handbills like the one Thomason found – "Gentlemen Apprentices: To uphold the King now is the time to fight for peace" – appeared everywhere.[90] First the Commons passed the ordinance empowering the City militia to raise cavalry. The bill received three readings and passed into law at once, the only stipulation being that these powers would terminate in a month.[91] Then the Army was ordered to approach no nearer than forty miles from the City. To prevent disorderly demonstrations of any kind, the two Houses appointed a number of their members to meet with the London Militia Committee. They were directed to recall all former New Model troops into the City, and the Houses reemphasized the material benefits, including full arrears, that awaited all who voluntarily deserted the Army.[92] By the time the Common Council reported the receipt of the Army's letter, in the small hours of the following morning, Parliament had only to revive the Committee of Safety in order to complete its protective measures.[93]

As the Commons held another marathon meeting – this one lasted almost the entire night – the institutions of London's government were also working to prevent an invasion of their City.[94] Upon receiving the Army's letter, and news of their movements, the Common Council held two lengthy sessions on June 11. Discussion centered almost entirely upon resistance, and it was not until early evening that a committee was appointed to prepare a response to the Army's missive.[95] The chief work of the day was done at the meeting of the London Militia Committee. There reports from three of the militia's colonels suggested that the Army's disclaimers were a cloak for their actual intention to advance upon the City and obtain all their arrears by force.[96] These rumors spread throughout the City and at seven o'clock that evening "many reformadoes came down to Guildhall" where the Militia Committee and the members of Parliament chosen to meet with them to suppress tumultuous gatherings were sitting.[97] The reformadoes volunteered to serve the City against the Army, and three regiments, led by Colonels Dalbier, Sanderson, and Essex, were quickly organized.[98] The Militia Committee, also sitting long into the night, ordered that the blockhouses around the City walls be secured and that a general alarm be raised throughout London. The next morning the Lord Mayor ordered out the trained bands with proclamations that those who refused to muster would be executed. All the City's shops were ordered closed in expectation of the Army's arrival.[99]

In all these actions the Militia Committee acted without the consent of the Common Council.[100] Even before the trained bands refused the summons to muster and the shopkeepers the order to suspend their business, the committee appointed by the Common Council to reply to the Army's letter had decided to attempt an accommodation. They would send a delegation with their letter, "to prevent all misunderstanding betwixt your so well deserving Army and this City." [101] They requested that the Army advance no nearer than thirty miles to London for fear of the disorders that might result from steeply rising food prices. The Common Council assured the soldiers that they would raise no forces and would not be a partner to any designs to engage the kingdom in a new war. The City had always supported the Army's just grievances, they reminded them, and their most recent petition had requested the auditing of soldiers' accounts. But they had one reservation to the Army's demands, perhaps to prove that they had not simply been overawed: they suggested "that you be careful when you descend into particulars to desire no more than what shall be just and reasonable; and in such a way as may consist with the honor, power and privilege of Parliament, the liberty of the subject and the safety of the City and Kingdom."[102]

The turmoil that its march created at Westminster and in London was not apparent in the Army. The decision to encamp nearer to the City had calmed the soldiery almost as if it had been preparatory to battle. "The Army have resigned themselves in all business to the hands of their superior officers," the general's chaplain wrote to Lord Fairfax.[103] By June 12 the Army had established its new headquarters at St. Albans, one day's ride from London. There the general was presented with two petitions, from inhabitants of Norfolk and Suffolk, requesting that the Army not disband until after the peace of the kingdom was settled. They related how their appeals to Parliament had been ignored, and the Norfolk petitioners, echoing the Army's own complaint, feared "a most abhorred design to ruin the native liberties and privileges of the subjects, whereby discontents are fomented in the hearts of the people and the kingdom like to be divided into factions."[104] These petitions, along with one from inhabitants in Essex, delivered to the general at Triploe Heath, were given over to the parliamentary Commissioners residing with the Army. Fairfax wrote directly to the two Speakers that the Army's encampment at St. Albans would allow them to keep better correspondence with Parliament (the vote of the two Houses for the Army to withdraw forty miles from London had not reached headquarters before their removal) and, of greater consequence, their presence there would "prevent the raising of any new war."[105] His letters also requested that a month's pay be sent to the Army to prevent the taking of free quarter, or as the Commissioners related, the levying of a tax by the Army. On this matter Fairfax advised Lenthall rather sharply: "The private soldier is not ignorant that you have money by you; and certainly the knowledge of that, and the sense of their own wants, doth not a little heighten them in their discontents."[106]

It was only after settling in at St. Albans that news reached the Army of the efforts to raise forces in London. The refusal of the trained bands to assemble and the decision of the Common Council not to support its Militia Committee were heartening, but the confluence of reformadoes, New Model deserters, and the City's forces was precisely what the Army had feared. Moreover, by creating a committee with power to recruit soldiers and call in troops intended for Ireland, and by offering deserters from the New Model their full arrears, Parliament had willingly aided this movement. On the evening of June 14 Fairfax met with the parliamentary Commissioners to inform them that the vote encouraging desertion from the Army "doth draw the soldiers into a very great suspicion and jealousy."[107] At a meeting earlier that day with the City Commissioners the general had also expressed the soldiers' discontent at the raising of forces in London: "The soldiers here do apprehend themselves betrayed by their officers that they should thus lie still, whilst such preparations are making against them."[108] These anxieties were heightened by news of another gathering of reformadoes in Westminster. Early that morning over a thousand reduced soldiers surrounded the House of Commons, assaulting members as they entered: "(by name Sir Henry Vane jr.) threatened to be cut in pieces and many others of these insufferably abused: and demanding their arrears."[109] In light of the weekend's events, Parliament's request for a larger and better armed contingent of City troops could be interpreted at St. Albans as "a handsome foundation to raise another Army upon."[110] Reports of the enlistment campaign were so inflammatory that the parliamentary Commissioners wrote to the House of Lords: "Unless we receive from you, by tomorrow night something that may give satisfaction, therein, we fear they may speedily march nearer to London.[111]

In the midst of these developments, which added to the soldiers' grievances and discontents – the listing of forces, after all, was a more tangible danger than the March 30 declaration, especially when sanctioned not by Parliament "but by some committee in a private way" – the Army published its first political manifesto, the Declaration of June 14. Since the rendezvous at Triploe, perhaps even as early as Newmarket, a general statement of the Army's desires was in preparation. The use of forces intended for Ireland to create a new Army in London, however, tied together what the Army saw as a calculated design "by the same persons who have all along appeared most active and violent in the late proceedings against the Army."[112] The enemies who they feared would become their judges were no longer country magistrates, but members of Parliament, who had denied the Army's right to petition, harangued their officers at the bar of the House of Commons, and now plotted a new war to overthrow the kingdom's liberties and to establish their own power. Without presenting specific indictments the Army demanded that these men "may be some way speedily disabled from doing the like or worse to us."[113]

Although its prologue again recounted the events that began with the March Petition, the Declaration of June 14 was not simply another statement of the injustices the Army had suffered at the hands of their parliamentary opponents. The usurpation of power that had brought about the war in which the soldiers had fought was now imitated by a party of men at Westminster. The future not only of the Army but of the nation must be secured against "some men ruling merely according to will and power": Parliament must be reformed so "that however unjust or corrupt the persons of Parliament men, in present or future, may prove ... they shall not have the temptation or advantage of unlimited power fixed in them at their own pleasure." This the soldiery recommended a purge of members illegally elected and a fixed period for parliamentary sessions, thus guarding against premature dissolution by the monarch and unlimited extension by the members.[114] A reformed Parliament would then firmly establish the citizens' right to petition Parliament for redress of their grievances and end all other interference in the affairs of the citizenry, either by courts or arbitrary committees. All this must be done, the Army asserted, to prevent "injustice or oppression upon any without end or remedy, or to uphold any particular party, faction or interest whatsoever to the oppression or prejudice of the community." These desires were presented for the benefit of the nation, for the citizenry that the disbanded soldiers would join. The declaration concluded by denying charges that the Army had acted only from self-interest, appealing "to all men, whether we seek anything of advantage to ourselves or any particular party whatever, to the prejudice of the whole."[115]

For the Army's program of political reform to succeed it was first necessary that the real leaders of party and interest be removed from Parliament and the forces they had generated to oppose the Army be dispersed. To these purposes Fairfax presented two additional papers to the parliamentary commissioners on June 15. The first was "The Heads of a Charge," the Army's impeachment of eleven parliamentary members, including Denzil Holles and Sir Philip Stapleton. The general charges against these members were that they had corrupted justice by attempting "to overthrow the rights and liberties of the subjects of this nation," and that they had abused the Parliament and the Army by false accusations and the advancement of "their own ends, faction and design."[116] More specifically, although no particular instances could be provided without an open breach of parliamentary privilege, it was charged that these members had enlisted forces, including those designed to serve in Ireland, to create a new war, and that they had "invited,

243

encouraged, abetted or countenanced" the reformadoes' riots at Westminster in order to "awe and enforce the Parliament."[117] The Army's second paper dealt with these recent events in London. During the time that Parliament investigated the charges made by the Army, they demanded that the eleven members be suspended so they could not inhibit "the Army's satisfaction and the peace of the Kingdom." Then they turned to consideration of their purses and their persons. Their desire for a month's pay was now enlarged to the sum received by those who had withdrawn from the Army, and they insisted that these "deserters" should not receive their arrears until after the rest of the soldiery. Finally, they cautioned Parliament to halt the enlistment of forces in London and to suspend consideration of inviting foreign armies into the kingdom.[118]

Even more than the refusal to disband, the Army's march to St. Albans was a demonstration of the pressures it was willing to exert for the satisfaction of its demands. Parliament and City were thrown into turmoil by reports of the Army's approach, and much soul searching and face saving ensued. Yet, although the Army professed tender concern for the privileges of Parliament, its actions generated reactions by agents outside parliamentary control. The initiative to raise forces among the reformadoes and the New Model deserters came from the revived Committee of Safety and the mobilization of the militia from the London Militia Committee. News of the Army's encampment at St. Albans was followed by Parliament's and the Common Council's dissociation of themselves from these activities. The Commons nullified the Committee of Safety's authorization of enlistments on June 16 and the following day the Common Council ordered the disbandment of all troops raised by its Militia Committee, requesting that the two Houses expel from the City any who had volunteered to oppose the Army. Upon prodding from the Army the City soon petitioned that all reformadoes be directed to withdraw from London.[119] Although their counsels were divided, and the panic on the night of June 11 had led to ill-considered judgments, both Parliament and City could truthfully inform the soldiers that no forces were being raised by their orders.

But, although keeping the Army at bay, Parliament could not ignore the demands of the reformadoes. Enlistments to protect the City from siege could be halted, especially when the threat of force failed to materialize, but subscriptions to arrears petitions could not.[120] Reformadoes continued to troop to London – "they came from all parts of the Kingdom," Juxon observed as he, doubtless, elbowed his way among them – hoping to attach their names to a petition that would reach the consideration of the Committee of Accounts.[121] By mid-June perhaps ten thousand officers and soldiers had joined the campaign, for when the funds available to them reached £33,000 the editor of *Perfect Occurrences* believed the sum barely constituted one month's pay.[122] Fearful of the repercussions of dismissing these soldiers with so little reward, Parliament rejected the City's recommendation that they be removed from London. Although Juxon believed that the decision to provide so much cash to the reduced soldiers "was indeed to oblige them and have them ready in London when occasion should offer," like the Army, the reformadoes were not a force that anyone in London could control.[123]

The votes to propitiate the reformadoes were made from necessity. Parliamentary refusal to pay them their due or to order them out of the City before a program for their arrears had been established would only have resulted in new riots, and perhaps the necessity of calling upon the Army for protection. But the continuation of recruitment for Ireland, consideration for New Model deserters, and a political counterattack against the Army were decisions of choice. Momentarily parliamentary resolve stiffened, either as a result of the Army's march toward London or its unexpected halt at St. Albans. On June 15 after long debate in the Lower House, and much pressure from the Lords, the Commons resolved to order the removal of the King to Richmond.[124] The royal residence there was little more than ten miles from Westminster and the City, sufficiently far from London's disorders but sufficiently close for an immediate restoration. Fairfax was directed to return Charles to the parliamentary Commissioners, Whalley's troops were discharged from their service, and Colonel Edward Rossiter's regiment was appointed as the monarch's guard.[125] The next day a vote to provide a month's pay for the New Model passed through the Commons only after a compromise that would have made a twenty-mile retreat by the Army a precondition for its pay was narrowly defeated.[126] At the same time the Lords had prepared an indemnity bill for those soldiers who had withdrawn from the New Model, and the Commons continued to recruit forces for Ireland – a new regiment under Colonel Ponsonby and the remainder of Graves's troops were ordered dispatched, and another £40,000 at Weavers' Hall was set aside for the service.[127]

These proceedings were all the more provocative to the Army because they were taken under the leadership of the impeached members. For an entire week after Parliament's reception of "The Heads of a Charge" no consideration was given to the Army's demand for the suspension of the eleven. Henry Elsynge, the parliamentary clerk, was instructed to prepare a list of precedents for such action from the cases of the five members, Sir John Eliot, and Sir Dudley Diggs, but these were hardly comparisons designed to flatter the Army and were in fact precedents likely to assert the inviolability of the parliamentary members.[128] While Elsynge was searching the records, Holles and Stapleton were acting as tellers in a division against providing a month's pay for the Army and in another favoring Fairfax's return of the King to the parliamentary Commissioners.[129] In fact, other than the bitterly contested wages and the assurances that Parliament had ordered no forces enlisted against them, none of the Army's desires, presented in the Declaration of June 14 or in the paper to the Commissioners that accompanied "The Heads of a Charge," had been met. A half-hearted debate on June 21 had finally resulted in a vote that men who had fought for the King would be barred from serving in Parliament, but a more heated discussion on June 23 concerning the termination of the present parliamentary session was inconclusive.[130] Moreover, the lack of any positive response was compounded by two challenges to the Army's bargaining power: the vote to remove the King from the Army's control by sending him to Richmond and the order for the Army to withdraw forty miles from the City.

Neither of Parliament's votes had much impact upon the Army. The Council of War believed that their desires had been plainly presented to Parliament and they impatiently awaited its response. The direct order to surrender the King to the parliamentary Commissioners who were to escort him to Richmond was contravened by a deft bit of stonewalling. Between June 15 when the order was first received and the 21st when it was reissued, correspondence between the Commissioners and the general was conducted through Edward Whalley, doubling the time necessary for queries and responses.[131] When Parliament renewed the order for the King to be placed in the hands of its Commissioners, Fairfax continued the charade, replying directly to the Houses that "the Commissioners have attended the person of the King ever since his coming from Holdenby [Holmby] and have been desired, by me, to continue the discharge of the trust which was committed to them by the Parliament."[132] No mention was made of Charles' transfer to Richmond despite the fact that Parliament had communicated this decision to Fairfax, Whalley, and the King. But to Parliament's directive that the Army retreat forty miles from London there was no equivocation: "as to our removal a further distance from London, we entreat we may receive an answer to the desires of the Army in the papers we last sent you."[133]

For a full week neither Army nor Parliament acted upon each other's desires. Headquarters remained at St. Albans, where Rushworth reported on June 19, "There's no talk of drawing to a rendezvous nearer London, as some would have it; all is very peaceable in the Army, and the unanimity betwixt officers and soldiers to be admired," and the eleven members continued their parliamentary functions.[134] If this was a stalemate it was broken by the Army in dramatic fashion. On June 23, adopting the City's strident form of appeal, the Army presented "An Humble Remonstrance . . . Concerning the Present State of Affairs." To all of the papers submitted to Parliament since the Declaration of June 14, "we have yet received no answer. or resolution, nor can find any consideration at all had for them," the soldiers complained, detailing the continuation of enlistments among the reformadoes and the troops that had deserted the New Model. The eleven members impeached by the Army "continue in such power and prevalency, both in the House and all Committees of the highest trust, as leaves little hope of right or satisfaction to the Army or the Kingdom." Indeed, their influence had gained the votes to remove the Army further from London and the King nearer to it, to "strengthen themselves in their mischievous designs, the better to uphold and establish their faction and intended domination."[135] No longer could the Council of War advise the general to remain passive while party and interest prevailed against the Army at Westminster. They demanded the end to enlistments in London by expulsion of the reformadoes and those who had deserted the Army; the rescission of the King's transfer to Richmond; and the suspension of the eleven members. Parliament was given twenty-four hours to comply with these demands or the Army would "endeavor in some extraordinary way, the vindicating of Parliament's freedom from tumultuous violence, the breeding of those designs and preparations that otherwise threaten a present embroilment of the Kingdom in more blood and war, and a future perpetual enslaving of it under faction and tyranny."[136]

The confrontation between Parliament and Army had now reached its first climax. Debate in Parliament on June 24 revealed a willingness to risk the wrath of reformadoes rather than face the swords of the Army, but the legalistically minded House of Commons could not sanction the suspension of the eleven members.[137] On Friday, June 25, the day after the deadline for their response, the House of Commons declared: "that by the laws of the land no judgment can be given to suspend these members, or any of them from sitting in the House upon the papers presented by the Army before particulars and proofs made."[138] At the same moment the Army was again on the march toward London.

———

The events of June demonstrated that threat of force had become a mode of political expression. Army and reformadoes quickly discovered that whereas petitions, declarations, and remonstrances might set the terms of parliamentary decision making, force or threat of force, undisguised and unabashed, activated it. The stormy gatherings of reduced officers and soldiers who accosted members of Parliament yielded far better results than the tedious auditing of accounts by the paymasters at Christ's Church. Prompt and conciliatory responses were also elicited from Parliament after the Army's seizure of the King and its march toward London. The gale winds generated by such decisive participants mocked Parliament's careful attempts to navigate a course between them. Efforts to satisfy the just desires of the reformadoes increased the Army's hostility toward them just as concessions to the New Model enlarged the appetites of the reduced officers and soldiers. As the reformadoes prepared to resist an invasion of London the Army took precautions against efforts to begin a new war through the recapture of the King. With anxiety and antagonism thus heightened, the danger of armed confrontation mounted.

This was particularly true after the Army's impeachment of the eleven members. For the soldiery, a peaceful settlement of the kingdom's affairs necessitated the removal of those who followed party and interest in the House of Commons. The Army's actions, as they continually professed, were motivated by a desire to free Parliament from these corrupting influences. But, by demanding the members' suspension from Parliament they removed the arena of conflict to outside the two Houses and by taking their stand against Holles's party they aroused the suspicion, if not the wrath, of Holles's majority. If Holles's parliamentary followers were helpless, those of his constituents who flourished outside Westminster were not, and they too faced the loss of their own influence. Many of the reformadoes had served under impeached members or their undoubted allies like the Earl of Essex. They had counted upon their former commanders to obtain the payment of their arrears and made no attempt to hide their sympathies on the night of June 11. The City, too, lost the patronage of its staunchest allies and had little hope of defending the composition of its Militia Committee once the Army leveled charges against it. By introducing the dimension of force and by dividing parliamentary members into opponents and supporters these extraparliamentary bodies had made a showdown imminent. It is only remarkable that Parliament, shorn of so much of its authority, could avert it for so long.

The Army's second march toward London produced spectacular concessions. Although Parliament would not suspend the eleven members without particular charges, when the Army contracted its quarters to Uxbridge the Commons accepted its impeached colleagues' request for a temporary leave of absence.[139] The voluntary withdrawal of the eleven members – Holles characterized their action in images of martyrdom, "rather than that a breach should be made upon their occasion, and that through their sides, the Parliament should be struck through the very heart and die forever" – headed off an immediate confrontation between Army and Parliament.[140] Relieved of a task it could not accomplish the House of Commons turned to one it could: the Army's demand for the dispersal of the forces in London. On June 28 the Lower House rescinded the invitation for New Model soldiers to come to London to receive their arrears, resolving that no officer or soldier could henceforth leave the Army without the general's consent. Those who had already entered the City were to be immediately dispatched for Ireland or else disbanded.[141] On July 1 a bill ordering all soldiers, reformadoes and New Model deserters alike, to depart

from the environs of Westminster, was read for the second time
and after declaring "that they do own this Army as their Army and
will make provision for their maintenance," preparations were
made to furnish another month's pay for the soldiery.[142] Finally,
to ensure that the King would come no nearer to London than the
Army's headquarters, the House of Commons ordered Charles back
to Holmby House.[143]

The City government was no less conscious of the Army's
march, having received news of it in a letter to its Commissioners
on June 25 that described the soldiers' continued discontent.[144] This
provided London's leaders with an opportunity to test the new
parliamentary waters, and on the following day the Common
Council began consideration of a lengthy petition that was finally
presented to the two Houses on July 2.[145] The Army's recent
demands and the City's long-standing desires now intermingled.
The City seconded the soldiers' call for the removal of the reformadoes, malignants, and those who had come from the New Model,
but attributed their "late discontents and disorders . . . unto the
want of such monies, as if duly collected and faithfully managed
might have in good part, if not fully, satisfied the soldiery."[146] A
consistent and conscientious management of revenue was necessary
to exonerate Parliament from charges of fiscal corruption, and this
included the return of public funds from private hands. To counter
claims of political corruption the City desired that Parliament investigate those of its members whose elections may have been unlawful, and disqualify all who had taken up arms for the King.[147]
But the commonality of interest between Army and City was not
universal. The council's familiar demands for the settlement of the
church, the suppression of the Irish rebellion, and the continuation
of correspondence with the Scots were all included in this petition,
and four days later it sought the renewal of the ordinance that
empowered the Militia Committee to raise cavalry troops and make
searches, along with another £20,000 for maintenance.[148] Concerning the most critical issue of all, the impeachment of the eleven
members, the City was silent.

The withdrawal of the eleven members from Parliament was accompanied by assurances that they would be provided an opportunity to exonerate themselves. The Army's charges were irrefra-
gable simply because they were so general. As the members took
their leave they demanded that the accusations against them be

submitted swiftly. In the Army, however, two impediments delayed the presentation of specific indictments. The first was the fact that charges against individual members constituted breach of privilege and could not be tendered without Parliament's sanction, "though if way were given and opened without breach of privilege, for us to charge them with, and for others to be examined freely to testify unto such things, we should not doubt to make such proceedings and practices of theirs in the House to appear, for which, according to former precedents, they justly might and ought to be suspended."[149] More importantly, the soldiery at Uxbridge was not certain that an indictment and trial of the eleven members should precede the settlement of the kingdom's more pressing affairs. "It will protract the great business of the Kingdom which will admit of no delay," Rushworth wrote to Lord Fairfax, indicating that a settlement between the King and Parliament was of greater concern to the Army.[150] Indeed, the Army declared itself content with the withdrawal of the members, arguing ominously that the precedent for their suspension lay not with the five members and Bacon, but with Strafford and Laud. As long as the members refrained from interfering in the settlement "of the perplexed affairs of the Kingdom," the Army was willing to maintain its distance from London.[151] Four days after arriving at Uxbridge, Army headquarters removed to Wycombe, and three days later the troops were withdrawn as far as Reading.[152]

The soldiers' first constraint to submitting their charge was overcome on June 29 when Parliament directed that the specific indictments against the eleven members be presented.[153] But the removal of the procedural reservations did not eradicate mental ones. Sometime between the arrival at Uxbridge and the retreat to Reading, probably on July 2 or 3, a debate was held to decide whether the charges against the eleven members should be pressed.[154] Five questions were propounded and answered to determine the Army's course of action. Each pointedly dealt with the Army's right to act on behalf of the nation, particularly if opposed to the will of Parliament. Two questioned the Army's own motivations: the first characterized its charge as self-interested, pursuing "the injury which they conceive those persons have done to the Army," and not "the interest and safety of the public," and the second questioned its integrity, claiming that officers were forced to acquiesce to the soldiers' demands or "they will cashier their officers and choose them others or act their disorderly confusion by their agitators."[155] Another two queries defended Parliament's conduct, asking "what hath the Army to do in settling the peace of the Kingdom which belongs wholly to the Parliament into whose seat they intrude themselves when they meddle with anything of that nature," and challenging them to state what more could be done by the Parliament to settle the peace of the kingdom or satisfy the Army "in the point of their arrears and indemnity and also in point of honor in recalling the declaration against them." Finally, it was suggested that by acting "as party, accuser and in effect judge" against the eleven members the Army was creating a dangerous legal precedent.[156]

The arguments supporting the indictment of the eleven members all centered on the corruption of Parliament through the growth of party. "By their undue practice with a Court party in the City, the Scots Commissioners and otherwise, and by bringing and keeping in the House of Commons corrupt and delinquent members [they] have so enthralled and made themselves masters of the Houses' resolutions that for private persons to bring any accusation against them were to run apparently to their own ruin." Although like Samson, the Army had entered the political arena in a private matter, its proposed remedies were for the preservation of the nation as a whole.[157] It justified its intervention by Parliament's inability to free itself from the design and deceptions of a ruling clique: "When all politic constitutions fail either through disability or corruption those that have the power and means in their hands to save the commonwealth ought not to doubt of their care and warrant to undertake it."[158] The supporters of the indictment now believed that the injuries Holles and his party had inflicted upon the Army were not as dangerous as their intention to conclude a peace with the King upon any terms – to enslave the nation by restoring the monarch with undiminished power. This explained their frenzied attempt to disband the Army and to set their own commanders over the Irish forces; their opposition to Fairfax's command of the new national forces; and the Lords' refusal to supply funds for the maintenance of the military establishment. Here was the connection between their correspondence with the King and Queen and their support for recruited members from Cornwall and Wales whose loyalty to the parliamentary cause was, at best, dubious. Thus the leaders of faction and interest were ready to sacrifice the blood and treasure of the nation for their own reward and profit. As the indictment's proponents concluded, "Surely the Kingdom would be in a very sad condition if it should depend wholly for its safety upon a Parliament so constituted, so circumstantiated and that at present are so little masters of their own resolutions, and it is not the desire of the Army to make themselves masters of the Parliament, but to make the Parliament masters of themselves."[159]

The Army's charge against the eleven members was submitted on July 6.[160] Its comparison between the suspension of these members and those of Strafford and Laud was apt, for like the indictments of the King's advisors, the impeachment brought against the eleven was clearly insufficient to obtain a legal conviction. Although he had already been acquitted by the House, Holles was again accused of having held correspondence with the King at Oxford and Uxbridge. All of Savile's charges were reiterated, causing a terrified Bulstrode Whitelocke to flee Westminster for fear that his own part in the business might be reopened.[161] The remaining members were impeached for allegedly communicating with the Queen during the summer of 1647, although the scanty evidence for this claim was, like Savile's, tainted at the source.[162] Allegations that in June the members participated in raising forces against the Army, invited the Scots to reenter the kingdom, and encouraged the demonstrations of the reformadoes were also made, followed by the long list of affronts given the Army that included the Irish venture, for which Clotworthy was particularly named, and Holles's authorship of the Declaration of March 30.[163]

More to the point of the Army's contention that the members "by many undue practices have made themselves in a manner masters of the Houses' resolutions" were the specific accusations against Anthony Nicoll and Walter Long. They were singled out as the organizers and enforcers of party politics. It was charged that Nicoll, whose own election for Bodmin had been disputed, "by his power and threats in the west countries, and by his solicitations and indirect practices, hath . . . procured to be brought in, about 28 members more out of Cornwall, on purpose to carry on the designs and practices before mentioned, and to make a faction in the said House."[164] If Nicoll had acted as the party's electioneer, Walter Long had served as its whip. "He hath used such tamperings and violence to such of his party as would go out of the House, and hath persuaded them to continue there for their votes," the Army contended. Indeed, these practices of his were so frequent that they had earned him the name of "the Parliament-driver; whereby the freedom of the members was taken from them, the manner of the Parliament's proceedings much scandalized, and many times evil and dangerous designs drove on in a faction by votes to the great prejudice of the commonwealth."[165] Although its charges remained vague, its evidence tainted, and many of the most important accusations insupportable, the Army demonstrated that it understood the transformation that had occurred in the political process.

Even before Parliament could consider the Army's charge, the indictment produced a public debate focusing upon its central issue: the authority of Parliament. Only two days after the delivery of the charge to the Commons, the first defense of the eleven members was printed. Almost predictably, it was the disputatious Prynne, later to be appointed counsel for the members, who launched the first volley, entitling his denunciation of the Army's action "A declaration of the officers' and Army's illegal, injurious proceeding and practice against the eleven impeached members (not to be paralleled in any age) and tending to the utter submission of free Parliaments." Belittling the obvious legal deficiencies of the indictment, its generalities and ambiguities, Prynne, not without irony, cited the execution of Thomas Cromwell on vague and general charges and cautioned the namesake of Henry VIII's great minister to beware of continuing such precedents. He praised the integrity of the eleven members and explained their impeachment in political rather than legal terms: "these eleven must all be impeached only to weaken the Presbyterian party, that so the Independents might overvote them."[166] Thus, Prynne concluded, as would Waller, that the Army's charge was more an affront to the institution of Parliament than to the indicted members. Although "not to be paralleled in any age," the Army's intervention into parliamentary affairs was akin to the usurpations of the King that resulted in civil war. A free Parliament could not endure such assaults upon its loyal members, and "most men now conclude that the Army's flourishes against arbitrary power and unjust proceedings in the Houses, and for the advancement of public justice are but mere hypocritical pretenses."[167]

The reactions to Prynne's "Declaration" and his subsequent "A Brief Justification of the Accused Members" also focused upon the rights and responsibilities of Parliament rather than upon the legal or factual issues raised in the impeachment. To Prynne's contention that the affair was strictly a party controversy one pamphleteer replied: "O! but to take so many out of the House at once he sayeth will weaken the Presbyterian party. A fine business to have parties to carry on designs in the House."[168] Another author addressed himself to the fundamental nature of representation, arguing that the object of civil government was the safety and prosperity of the people and that when the highest magistrates failed in their duty to pursue that end the people were absolved from complying with their orders. Even the normal process of law could be suspended in extraordinary situations like the impeachment of corrupt parliamentary members. "Princes have no prerogatives nor Parliament's any privileges but such as are consistent with and in no way prejudicial to the common good of men."[169] On this theme a third disputant propounded that the members of Parliament were fully responsible to the people who chose them and must be removed from office when they had betrayed their trust. He advocated not only the expulsion of corrupt members but a reform of parliamentary procedure that would make the institution responsive to those that it represented. Debates and committee reports should be made public and a register of how each M.P. voted, complied and published. To ensure that the people were fully represented in parliamentary decisions, no votes should be taken with less than three-quarters of the members of the Commons present.[170] Such suggestions grew from the Army's own demand that members of the Commons, like the Lords, be allowed to enter individual protests against the resolutions of the majority.[171] Thus, although appeals to popular sovereignty and individual conscience were still muted by attempts at parliamentary reform, the debate over the Army's charges uncovered the fragility of Parliament's authority at the same moment that powerful agencies outside it were challenging Parliament's power.

Although the Army's impeachment of the eleven members immediately engaged public attention, it was tabled in the House of Commons. The demand that the members be incapacitated from preventing an amicable composition of the soldiers' grievances had been satisfied by their voluntary withdrawal. The settlement of the kingdom's affairs was of greater consequence to both soldiers and members than the protracted legal battle over the conduct of individuals, despite the invective of firebrands like Lilburne and the impatience of the eleven to return to power.[172] Immediately following their departure, Parliament empowered its Commissioners residing in the Army "to treat and debate with the General and such in the Army as he shall appoint" in an effort to appease the soldiers' most pressing discontents.[173] The first fruits of this resolution were Parliament's votes for the expulsion of the various forces that remained in London and the Army's retreat from Uxbridge. At Wycombe, on June 30, the parliamentary Commissioners presented Fairfax with a formal request that Army representatives be appointed for the negotiation of the soldiers' demands. Ten senior officers, to whom, after agreement between the officers and parliamentary Commissioners, were added two agitators, were selected to begin consultations on July 2.[174]

The necessity of preparing the particular indictment upon which the eleven members had insisted delayed the proceedings between the military and parliamentary Commissioners. In this interim came several developments that were to have profound impact upon the negotiations. The debates to determine whether the Army would press charges against the eleven members had also resolved that in its function as broker between people and Parliament the Army should insist upon an overall settlement of the kingdom's affairs.[175] The petitions that Fairfax had received in early June were the first of many that appealed to the Army to delay its disbandment until after the establishment of a "safe and well-grounded peace."[176] The soldiers, too, were weary of paper guarantees – "then may every honest man be hanged with his ordinance of indemnity around his neck" – and began to insist upon a settlement that would be sanctioned by the King.[177] Thus, while Parliament endeavored to remove material obstructions, the Army again focused upon larger considerations. In addition, the Houses had now proved unsuccessful in removing the throngs of soldiers from the City.[178] Implementation of the order sending those who had withdrawn from the New Model into Ireland was delayed, partly because the exclusion of the eleven members denuded the Derby House Committee of its active participants.[179] Nor could the reformadoes be expelled until their accounts had been audited according to previous parliamentary votes. To examine their accounts, the treasurers at Christ's Church relied upon lists of reduced officers and soldiers, and this

continued listing of reformadoes increased the anger of the Army.[180]
In this, however, there was more than mere posturing. Many reformadoes had, after all, volunteered to combat the New Model troops when the Army first marched toward London. Despite numerous direct appeals from the City they remained in London and their numbers had actually increased. In the first week of July, Sir Francis Pile informed Lieutenant Colonel Henry Bowen that some sixteen thousand reformadoes had already been enlisted in London, intimating that they would soon be sent to Kent to await a landing of the Scottish Army.[181] Subscriptions for the Irish service also continued to be gathered among these soldiers in spite of the fact that most of the troops recently subscribed for Ireland were yet to be dispatched.[182] Even more alarming were reports that the London Militia Committee had begun to purge its ranks of supporters of the Army and independency. On July 5 and 6 depositions were presented at Army headquarters detailing changes made among junior militia officers in various City wards. They provided evidence that removals were prompted by political rather than military considerations: "Upon these grounds that he differed in judgment from them" was William Shambrooke's explanation for the loss of his command, whereas Lieutenant Curtin of Walbrooke ward was cashiered "for being an independent."[183] Together with the continuation of forces of all description in the City, the purgation of independent militiamen, following the reconstitution of the Militia Committee, incensed the soldiers. On July 6 the agitators prepared a petition, which was subsequently presented to the Council of War, demanding that the London Militia Committee be returned into the hands of its previous members. They declared that the change in the Committee's composition in May "did savor of nothing but evil intendments and factions as since hath appeared by the said committee's actions in putting out men of known integrity."[184] By interjecting these new issues, the Army again demanded that Parliament choose among it, the City government, and the reformadoes.

The reiteration of the Army's demand for the removal of the reformadoes complicated Parliament's efforts to find an equitable procedure for settling their accounts. The complexity of distinguishing legitimate from spurious claims slowed the work of the treasurers while the continued influx of new claimants lengthened it. Both Parliament and City agreed on the necessity of limiting this concourse of reduced officers and soldiers, and under pressure from the Army, Parliament finally took positive steps to relieve the situation. On July 6 the Lower House proclaimed that it would audit the accounts only of soldiers who had served in Parliament's general armies, leaving the localities the burden of providing for their own forces.[185] This directive incensed those soldiers who had journeyed from home on the promise that London would settle their accounts, and when Parliament next met on July 8 it was greeted by a tempestuous crowd of reformadoes. One member, Thomas Pury, was assaulted as he made his way into the House, prompting Parliament to increase the power of its guards in apprehending perpetrators of these continued outrages.[186] On the following day a parliamentary committee was directed to prepare an ordinance expelling the reformadoes from the City for at least the next two months. More concretely, all papists and delinquents were ordered outside the walls by July 14, and no new soldiers were to receive any payment from the funds being distributed at Christ's Church. Thus the House hoped to end "all tumultuous meetings and assemblings together of people upon any pretense of listing."[187]

These efforts had the twin aim of easing the Army's apprehension and lowering the political temperature in London. The City was now swelled to overflowing by soldiers of all descriptions and the attempt to stem the tide of reformadoes was only partially successful. One petition from a new group of reduced officers was presented to the Commons on July 13 and another was given in to the Lords three days later. On July 20 the worst disorders that had yet occurred inside the Parliament building necessitated the stationing of 100 halberds in the halls and on the stairways.[188] Moreover, the endeavor to eliminate the large gatherings and tumultuous meetings that kept the political situation constantly at the boil was dealt another setback with the appearance of two groups of apprentices, who used the opportunity of the first day of public recreation, July 13, to perfect petitions to the Houses of Parliament.

The first group's petition "of many thousands of young men and apprentices" was presented to the House of Commons that afternoon. It demanded the restoration of the faithful militiamen who had been removed from their commands by the recomposed London Militia Committee and the speedy trial of "those prisoners who have appealed to this honorable court for justice," namely John Lilburne and Richard Overton, who remained imprisoned for their breach of privilege in the House of Lords. Desiring a "composure of differences on all sides so far as may be congruent to the rules of piety and equity," the petitioners suggested that Parliament publicly denounce the "invectives of the clergy, or others tending to the aggravation of differences amongst peaceable spirits."[189] Following the Army, they blamed "the late abuse of the authority of this House by the too great influence of some arbitrary spirits," but it is by no means clear that this petition, a sequel to the "Humble Petition of Divers Young Men and Apprentices" of March 1, was inspired or encouraged at headquarters.[190] Nor, as Gardiner reasons, is it likely that the document presented to the Lords the following day by a second group of apprentices was directed either by Holles or his parliamentary supporters or the City government. Claiming the signatures of over "10,000 well-affected young men and apprentices," these petitioners called for the preservation of the King, the vindication of the rights and privileges of Parliament, the settlement of the church, the suppression of independent conventicles, and the disbandment of the Army.[191] Their explanation for the great distractions of the commonwealth, though directed against the Army and religious dissidents in London, found expression in common political terms. It was "incendiaries, malignants and evil instruments which hinder the reformation of religion, dividing the King from his people, or one of his Kingdoms from another, or making any factions or parties among the people, contrary to the Solemn League and Covenant."[192]

The emergence of the apprentice petitioners was a further indication of the deterioration of the political situation in London. The fragmentation of political opinion and the Common Council's own loss of influence at Westminster could be seen in the fact that neither group first presented its appeal to the City government. A petition from those who supported Lilburne and Overton and demanded some action against London's clergymen had earlier been rejected by the Common Council. These petitioners appealed instead to the Army and were most probably responsible for the submission of the depositions against the London Militia Committee. Their address to Parliament was both an expression of solidarity with the Army and an attempt to hasten action at headquarters, where their charges and the agitators' petition were already a week old. The petition of the second group of apprentices repeated many of the desires expressed by the Common Council before it had struck its conciliatory pose toward the Army. If these petitioners received any official encouragement it was from those aldermen and common councillors who had argued the hard line against the Army and had supported the votes of the Militia Committee on June 11. These men now were willing to sacrifice the Common Council's right to represent the desires of London citizens to Parliament for the expression of individual opinion.

The apprentices' competing visions of the settlement of the nation's affairs were far outdistanced by the preparation of the Army's own blueprint for the restoration of civil government. Whereas religious and political contention in the capital revolved around the conduct of individuals, the invectives of the clergy, and the designs of factious spirits, the Council of War, led by its parliamentary members, attempted to provide an institutional remedy to reunite monarch and Parliament. Since their inception on July 2 the negotiations between the parliamentary and military Commissioners had made no progress. When the Army was accused of delay on July 7 its representatives countered by reminding both the Parliament and the City that the dispersal of the reformadoes and the cessation of enlistments by the London Militia Committee were preconditions to the negotiations.[193] Nevertheless when Parliament removed these obstacles as best it could, the Army continued to stall. Its resolution to work for a settlement of the kingdom's affairs was broader than a simple treaty with Parliament. Despite the accuracy of Fairfax's insistence, on July 9, that the Army had undertaken no secret agreements with the King, Charles had been informed of the June 14 Declaration and the Remonstrance of June 23.[194] In the second week of July, as the Council of War began to draft its formal set of propositions, its leading members secured the cooperation of Sir John Berkley in sounding the King's own position on a number of critical issues.[195] As they revealed in discussions with this royalist go-between, a treaty satisfactory to Army and monarch would find favor in London.

Consultation with the King was a first step in preparing the Army's proposals. Although a group of officers was involved in the

preliminary discussions, the task of composition had fallen to
Ireton. He readied his first elucidation, "The Heads of the Proposals," for a full Council of War scheduled for July 16. When
the Council met, however, it was not Ireton's proposals but an
agitators' petition that was the topic of debate. Three officer-
agitators presented the Council with a list of five demands that
they submitted on behalf of the soldiery. They called for the suspension and permanent exclusion of the eleven members from the
House of Commons, the restoration of the old London Militia
Committee, a parliamentary declaration against bringing foreign
troops into England, the release of political prisoners like Lilburne
and Overton, and payment to the Army equal to that provided for
its deserters. To secure Parliament's immediate compliance with
these demands the agitators desired that the Army march on
London. They believed that Parliament's long delay in responding
to the Army's requests stemmed from no other cause than the
removal of headquarters from London's environs: "upon the
Army's drawing back from the City, the Parliament's proceedings
for the good of the people and Army hath been slacked."[196]

Though prepared well in advance, the agitators' petition took
the Army high command by surprise. Ireton clearly expected to
present the proposals he had drafted, and neither he nor Cromwell
anticipated the demand for a march on London at the moment that
their efforts to settle a peace had the greatest prospects for success.
The Council of War was adjourned until late afternoon so that
Fairfax and the senior officers could consider the agitators' paper.[197]
When it reconvened it was more properly a Council of the Army
than a Council of War, for both soldier and officer agitators were
now present.

The agitators argued that necessity of a march on London. The
voluntary withdrawal of the eleven members had not put an end
to their design to instigate a new war. They reasoned that the
threat of force would succeed where compromise had failed. "We
seem to be startled at the expression of forcing things – Do we
force or do we desire by forcing [anything] but that with [once]
forcing there should be no more forcing? That by the sword we
may take the sword out of those hands that are enemies to justice,
to equity?" asked Adjutant General Tulidah, who was personally
involved in the cause of Lilburne and Overton.[198] Parliament had
not acted to satisfy the Army's just grievances and would not do

so as long as it continued under the influence of the eleven members and their supporters. The declaration that proclaimed the Army "Parliament's Army" "was upon this ground," Sexby averred, "that they did [it] rather out of fear than love."[199] Nor could they expect a voluntary change in Parliament's attitude. Those parliamentarians who supported the Army's cause "are a losing party, and losers rather than gainers," William Allen responded to Cromwell's contrary assertion.[200] Their impatient arguments revealed that the soldiers they represented were ready for action.

Cromwell and Ireton carried the weight of the opposition to a march on the capital. As Ireton made clear, they needed time to produce their proposals and to gain the acceptance of the King and Parliament.[201] This was a business of greater importance than the particular grievances, however justified, presented by the agitators. But it was Cromwell's arguments that were most persuasive. As he had defended the Army in Parliament, now he defended Parliament in the Army. He praised the service of the many faithful members who, at considerable risk, had supported the Army's desires and cautioned the agitators not to disaffect "the middle party" who were now being persuaded to that point of view.[202] He reminded them that the Army's goal had always been the preservation of Parliament: "It hath been in most of our thoughts that this Parliament might be a reformed and purged Parliament, that we might see there men looking at public and common interests only. This was the great principle we had gone upon, and certainly this is the principle we did march upon, when we were at Uxbridge and when we were at St. Albans."[203] The treaty upon which the officers had labored was the surest way to preserve the ideals of their cause and protect the rights of the citizens of the nation. "Whatsoever we get by a treaty ... it will be firm and durable, it will be conveyed to posterity, as that that will be the greatest honor to us."[204] As Cromwell passionately concluded at the end of the debate: "Really, really, have what you will have, that you have by force I look upon it as nothing. I do not know that force is to be used, except we cannot get what is for the good of the Kingdom without force."[205]

Cromwell's passion and persuasiveness were not alone sufficient to satisfy the agitators. It was Desborough's practical suggestion that the four days necessary for a march to London be given to Parliament to respond to the agitators' demands that formed the basis of compromise.[206] With a few politic changes in wording, the petition was officially submitted to the parliamentary Commissioners in the name of the Council of the Army and the four-day limit was unofficially communicated to them.[207] Rushworth reported to Ferdinando Fairfax: "The agitators were higher in proposals than the officers, who were more expert in state affairs. I only mention this, that you may be assured the inferior, upon good reasons, submitted to the superior so that it is not will but reason that guides the proceedings of the Army."[208] Yet it was an uneasy calm that pervaded headquarters. The compromise had been made for the sake of unity – "if you be in the right and I in the wrong, if we be divided I doubt we shall all be in the wrong," was Cromwell's poignant aphorism – but the officers believed that the agitators' intervention was untimely and the agitators feared that the officers were dilatory.[209] Neither anticipated that the demand for the restoration of the original London Militia Committee would make their debate superfluous.

The agitators' petition was sent to Parliament on July 19. Although the clause requesting the permanent exclusion of the eleven members had been eliminated – their conviction would accomplish that – the remainder of the document was left intact.[210] Simultaneously the Council of War dispatched a letter to the City government informing them that they had asked Parliament to recompose their Militia Committee "unto those hands out of which it was taken; of whose care and fidelity to the public there hath been so long and so large experience."[211] The reluctance of the officers to press this demand was apparent in the wording of their letter, and they hastened to remind the City, whose Commissioners had constantly attended the Army since mid-June, that their proposals for the settlement of the nation's peace were nearly completed. The second day's session of the Council of War was spent considering Ireton's draft, and a committee of officers and agitators was appointed by Fairfax to make a full study of the proposals. A copy was taken to the parliamentary Commissioners to reaffirm the officers' sincerity in working for a treaty and to demonstrate the actual progress that had been made.[212] Although the proposals remained mere heads, outlines to be completed, in view of the agitators' ultimatum the officers were now pressed to finish their work.

At Westminster the Army's new demands sapped the last bit of parliamentary independence. Perhaps reveling in the division between officers and soldiers and doubtless infuriated at the constant proliferation of the Army's desires, members moved in the Commons that this new petition not be considered until all the Army's proposals had been delivered. This defiance failed by only 12 votes in a House of 148, and was the final indication that a narrow majority was willing to accede to all the Army's requests.[213] On July 22 the Lower House issued its declaration that no foreign forces were to be brought into the kingdom and that afternoon agreed to restore the former committeemen to the London Militia.[214] Provisions for the Army's pay and the disbandment of the New Model deserters had already been voted. Nor was any fight left in the House of Lords, where only eight peers appeared on July 23 to pass the ordinance reinstating the former London Militia Committee.[215]

If spirit was lacking at Westminster, it was overabundant in the City. Even before the Common Council could organize its own protest at this unexpected encroachment on its hard-earned privileges, crowds of apprentices and reformadoes plunged into action. Whether their deeds resulted directly from the Army's new demands or were the outgrowth of the movement that began with the petition of July 14 is unclear; and it is equally uncertain what the role of the eleven members may have been.[216] Juxon stated unequivocally that the young men's petition emanated from Holles and his followers, and by July 23 they knew that they would be suspended indefinitely from sitting in the House.[217] But the precedents for enlistments and engagements were manifold and both reformadoes and apprentices had experience in organizing petitions. However adumbrated, the citizens' covenant campaign had every appearance of a spontaneous event. On Friday, July 23, a petition in the form of a covenant was presented to Parliament subscribed by members of all the diverse groups that had appeared in various political roles against the Army. "Taking into serious consideration how religion, his Majesty's honor and safety, the privilege of Parliament and liberties of the subject are at present greatly endangered, and likely to be destroyed," the petitioners demanded that the King be called to London, where his May 12 answer to the Newcastle propositions be accepted as the terms for the settlement of peace.[218] In imitation of the Army, they entitled their covenant "A Solemn Engagement" and pledged to obtain the signature of every City freeman to it, warning that they would not "admit, suffer or endure any kind of neutrality in this common cause of God, the King, and Kingdoms."[219] Without hesitation the Commons condemned the Solemn Engagement. Echoing Holles's words of March 30, Henry Marten drafted the Commons' response, which declared all who proceeded in the campaign guilty of high treason.[220]

Parliament's declaration had no effect upon the petitioners. On Saturday the Solemn Engagement was proffered to the full Common Council, where it was demanded that the City's governors, all freemen, subscribe to the covenant.[221] No record of the Council's response survives, but the only other business conducted that day was to set aside the following Wednesday for fast and humiliation and to make a precise list of the quarters of the Army's regiments.[222] In the City the subscription campaign continued unabated. Apprentices and reformadoes streamed into Skinners' Hall to put their hands to the engagement, and others were solicited in the streets despite the public pronouncement, to the beat of a drum, of Parliament's prohibition against it.[223] When the restored Militia Committee met at Guildhall to seek means to end these disorders and to prepare to dispatch an even stronger battery of guards for Monday morning's parliamentary session, a boisterous throng of "young men" broke up their meeting and turned the Committee out of the Hall, "telling them if they caught them there again they would hang their guts about their ears."[224] Meanwhile the Common Council, stirred to action by the arbitrary removal of their new Militia Committeemen, prepared their own petition to Parliament.

On Monday, July 26 the sheriffs and a delegation of common councillors appeared at the House of Commons with this petition. They were accompanied on their journey to Westminster, perhaps not of their own choice, by a group of substantial citizens and a multitude of apprentices and reformadoes. Leaving this large convoy outside, Sheriff Edmunds presented the Common Council's petition, which desired that Parliament nullify its July 23 order.[225] Unable to claim the right to nominate its own Militia Committee, the Common Council insisted upon its privilege of prior consultation. The sudden change in the City's military organization had come without the Council's foreknowledge and its deleterious effects were already apparent, for the City was now unable to provide protection either for itself or for Parliament.[226] Moreover, Parliament's vote had created considerable unrest among the citizenry. Two petitions demanding the restoration of the new Militia Committee had already been presented to the Common Council, Edmunds informed them, as he submitted the documents to the Speaker.

It was in support of these that the crowd had gathered outside Westminster Palace. The first, "The Humble Petition of Divers Well-Affected Citizens," simply asked the reinstatement of the ousted militia committeemen, but the second, "The Petition of Young Men, Citizens and Other Apprentices," insisted upon a response to the July 14 petition, which had called for the preservation of the King, the settlement of the Church, and the disbandment of the Army. Doubtless it was a representative of this group who demanded to be heard in the Commons and was rebuffed.[227] The House took notice only of the City's official delegation and replied that it would take their representation into consideration.[228] The Lords were more forthright. They assured the sheriff that their interests would be preserved by Parliament, but added, "they do expect in the meantime compliance with the late ordinance of the 23rd, that the safety of the Parliament and City may not be neglected."[229]

The nine peers in the Lords' chamber were well to be concerned with the safety of Parliament. The contingent of City troops that had been stationed within and around the palace had not appeared that morning, and the contention over the rights of the Militia Committee suggested that they would not return without the consent of the City government. Outside the Houses the group of citizens and apprentices that had submitted the petition of July 14 awaited a more positive parliamentary response, unwilling to accept again the assurance, given two weeks earlier, that their desires would speedily be considered. To them were added the regular concourse of reduced officers and soldiers, and sometime in the early afternoon this mass was swelled by the arrival of the covenanters whose Solemn Engagement had been declared traitorous. They, too, had a petition to present to Parliament and the news that the Commons had refused to hear a representative of the apprentices' group and that the Lords had reconfirmed the change in the Militia Committee's composition cannot have assuaged their own ire at the reception their engagement had received. Into the hall they stormed, gathering in front of the doors to the House of

Lords, where their presence and threats forced the frightened peers to recall the ordinance of July 23 and the declaration against their engagement.[230]

As the Lords hastily adjourned until the following Friday, fleeing the palace down the backstairs, the mob carried their votes to the Commons.[231] Although some compromise was attempted with the leaders of the engagement campaign, the House now faced not a political movement but a frenzied mob.[232] "Follow on, follow on," cried Captain Musgrave as he stood at the top of the Commons' lobby. Then the doors were forced open and the apprentices streamed onto the Commons' floor. They crowded in the aisles and at the bar calling out to Lenthall that the House would not be permitted to rise until their demands had been met. When the first question to recall the vote on the Militia Committee was posed, "the prentices voted with them," and an heroic attempt was made at a division to settle the issue.[233] This punctilious adherence to procedure further exasperated the invaders, who screamed "Vote, Vote!," until the Speaker reluctantly determined that the question had carried. Until nine o'clock that night the proceedings of Parliament were controlled by the mob, and all during that time many members actually feared for their lives.

There can be no doubt but that aldermen like Bunce and common councillors like Bellamy, as well as officers of the trained bands, were deeply involved in these events.[234] Juxon recorded that Bunce directed the entire scene: "All the while there was in the palace yard Alderman Bunce with some Common Council man and others as a committee for to give direction for the management of this business; to whom there came continually some from the Commons' door to give them account of what was done and to receive directions what to do."[235] While the mob did its work the Common Council was also meeting, relishing Parliament's discomfiture and refusing to dispatch its forces until late that night.[236]

Yet if individual officials connived at the mob's actions, and the government itself winked at it, it does not follow that this day's dizzying events were engineered as part of a larger scheme to build an army in opposition to the New Model. It was Parliament's loss of authority in the eyes of the citizens, its perceived partiality, working the will of whichever group was powerful enough to dominate it, that allowed for the apprentices' invasion. Even the belief that they acted to preserve "a free Parliament" could not have justified to the eleven members this violation of their institution any more than the agitators' identical justification could persuade Cromwell to authorize a march on London. The parliamentarians' own assault upon the authority of Parliament had been inadvertent: the logic of destroying things to save them had not yet become part of political theory. Rather, the apprentice riot was a tide taken at the flood, by the eleven members, by the City, by the Army too, in fact – a tide of anxiety, righteousness, and exuberance that had swept the City for two long months and could not be dammed; a flood in which some would drown and others would learn that they could swim.

The mob riot in London jettisoned the treaty between the Army and the parliamentary Commissioners. The votes taken to satisfy the agitators' demands had succeeded in alleviating their pressure for a march to London. Army headquarters removed from Reading northeasterly to Aylesbury and finally to Bedford, some fifty miles from the capital.[237] The reports of the engagement campaign temporarily inflamed the soldiers, but Parliament's declaration against it soothed this irritation.[238] On Sunday, July 25, several officers met with the parliamentary Commissioners to agree upon a timetable for concluding the treaty. Debate on general points, particularly the suppression of the Irish rebellion, would begin the following morning and the final draft of the specific proposals was to be presented by midweek at the latest. All thoughts at headquarters had turned to peace, concluded the Earl of Nottingham in his first optimistic report to the House of Lords.[239] On the 26th, debate on the relief of Ireland began. Sir Hardress Waller, who had briefly served in Ireland under Lord Lisle and had long-standing interests there, presented the Army's proposals. Only the final details remained to be settled when the initial news of the tumults in the City reached Bedford. Immediately, negotiations were broken off and a Council of War convened.[240]

The first reports that reached headquarters were confused and incomplete. Mabbot's account, written as he stood in the crowd outside the palace, was penned at the end of the riot but neglected to relate the Commons' votes, and with the Army more than a day's ride from Westminster, there was considerable delay before the full story was pieced together.[241] By Wednesday night the Council of War had resolved to march on London and the following morning Fairfax paused to inform both Parliament and City that the Army would soon arrive "to be an effectual saving of the great and just authority of the Kingdom in Parliament."[242] Fairfax's letter to the City was uncompromising and heartfelt. The City government was sworn to protect Parliament and had given its assurance to the Army that it would do so. But eyewitness accounts incriminated aldermen and common councillors in the mob's violence and bemoaned the City's failure to provide troops to suppress the riot. "I cannot but look upon you, who are in authority," Fairfax decried, "as accountable to the Kingdom for your present interruption of that hopeful way of peace and settlement things were in for this nation."[243]

Before these letters could reach London, late on the night of the 29th, the Common Council, now dominated by the restored new Militia Committee members, had determined to make the best of Monday's events. At the Common Council on July 27 the Militia Committee drafted a declaration inviting the King to London and justifying the apprentices' actions as taken "to establish religion and preserve the rights of the Kingdom."[244] The Army was to be officially notified of what had taken place, specifically that the City's freely nominated Militia Committee had been restored, and if they were inclined to accept this result, the City would guarantee the payment of its arrears and the settlement of its indemnity.[245] After prayers on the following day, which the Common Council had set aside for a fast, the City government again met, this time to prepare a petition to Parliament giving thanks for the restoration of their Militia Committee and assurance that the passions of the citizens had been eased.[246] At eleven o'clock that night Fairfax's letter arrived, confirming rumors of the Army's advance and placing the onus for the interruption of the negotiations upon the City's government. Quickly the Common Council drafted its reply, attesting that it had acted faithfully to suppress the riot, for the entire council had repaired to Parliament at news of it. It was not the quelling of the disturbance but its cause that interested the City, and it laid the blame for that upon the Army for meddling with London's institutions of government.[247] To the end the Common Council believed that the apprentices' actions related only to the controversy over the militia.

When Parliament met on Friday, the 30th, this illusion was quickly dispelled. Neither Speaker appeared to take his chair and some seventy-odd commoners and five Lords who had suffered Monday's indignities were also absent.[248] A search for them and the Commons' mace revealed that Lenthall and Manchester had taken flight.[249] The alternatives before the handful of remaining members were to back the City and invite the King to London or to suspend the session indefinitely. The decision was soon made. New speakers were chosen in both Houses; the eleven members were recalled to the Commons; the Committee of Safety was revived; and the London Militia Committee's powers were expanded.[250] The following day the King was invited to London and the City placed in an attitude of defense.[251] Letters from both speakers to the Army protested its continued advance, claiming that Parliament was well protected by the City and that "the undue liberty" taken by the apprentices would not recur.[252]

What was deemed "undue liberty" by the speakers was viewed in the Army as "prodigious and horrid force."[253] Their march to London was swift and direct. Arriving at Hounslow Heath on Friday they met with the parliamentary members who had fled Westminster the day before upon rumors that an even larger mob would assemble for their next session.[254] As the Army came to London to restore order, its purpose was now doubly endowed, for with order could also be restored the speakers of Parliament and many of its faithful members. For a brief moment the City government authorized a desperate stand, raising money and forces to combat the Army.[255] But by August 2 calmer heads had prevailed. Siege, plunder, and occupation involved a far greater loss of liberty than a handful of Militia Committeemen.

By then the Army had erased any doubt concerning the outcome of confrontation. Desborough had scattered the New Model deserters who camped in Kent, Tilbury blockhouse had been seized, and the trained bands of the surrounding counties called to arms.[256] On August 6 the Army escorted the speakers and members to Parliament.[257] Their march through London the following day was impressive and well ordered: " 'Twas not heard of so much as an apple taken by any of them to the great admiration of all that beheld them."[258] Although the eleven members were again forced to flee the House, the Army's claim to support "a free and lawful

Parliament" was now demonstrated by its restoration of other parliamentary members.

———

" 'Tis remarkable that it never was in the minds of the Army to carry it so far; but were brought to it, one thing after another, and that by the designs of their enemies."[259] So Thomas Juxon assessed as he watched the great parade of soldiers troop through the City. The Army's march on London ended the long chapter of Civil War and was the prologue to the revolution that followed. Since the Army's refusal to disband in May Parliament had been tossed among the demands of soldiers, the desires of citizens, and the necessities of government. The changes in its political practice, which in large part occasioned these assaults, assured that parliamentary privilege could not be maintained above political necessity. As it was, two long months of threats and provocations ensued before Army and City were brought to massive demonstrations of force. Both occurred in the name of parliamentary authority and freedom, but by then the extraparliamentary bodies identified the institution only as the group of members that supported its particular cause. The events that ended in the apprentice invasion and the Army's march were all motivated by the same single desire: to enable Parliament to act in the interest of the nation. Neither Army nor reformadoes, apprentices nor levellers, Presbyterians nor Independents could yet realize that the interest of the whole might be smaller than the desires of its parts – that an organic cause had become a pluralistic one.

"I see, methinks, a contention between the long robe and the short; the one upon the interests of the state's trust, the other for the price of blood, the honor of his arms and the indemnity of his person," Colonel Robert Overton wrote as the struggle between Army and Parliament unfolded. "I trust piety and public respect will on both parts prevent and persuade; I wish the variety of opinions and capricious parties multiply not old diseases beyond state remedies."[260] In this hope, Overton and all who believed with him that piety and public respect were the guiding lights of political action were to be disappointed. As the events of the summer had shown, parliamentary politics had been replaced by force. Votes superseded debate; confrontation replaced conciliation; action had overcome reason; radical politics had emerged. New participants, unimagined when the struggle began, now crowded the political scene. "We are most of us young statesmen," agitator Allen reminded Ireton and Cromwell, unaware that the experience of the past was no longer a guide to the future.[261]

Tightly leashed by the Army, Parliament strained for a settlement with the King for another year while the fragmentation of its cause continued. "The Heads of the Proposals," which the Army officers allowed to be published on August 1, was the first of a number of constitutional experiments that would engage public debate in the succeeding months. Each would attempt to find a means of delimiting the authority of King and Parliament while maintaining order within the nation: each would fail. Major Francis White's theorem, "that there is now no power left in the state but the sword," would be demonstrated time and again – at Burford, Westminster, and Whitehall; at Worcester, Dunbar, and Drogheda. Although radical politics would spawn political radicals of multitudinous varieties, those that brought about the fall of parliamentary politics had not aimed at the mark they hit. At the juncture of Civil War and Revolution they now stood, and if the impulse of the future was to turn the world upside down, the wisdom of the past had been to make it whole.

CONCLUSION

The mobs' violence and the Army's march on London completed the transformation of the political process. With soldiers and citizens competing for the preservation of Parliament, political development reached a new level. Parliamentary authority had been superseded by force and the sanctity of the institution and its privileges debased. In victory, the institution whose power and prestige had reached its apex during the struggle with the King found itself bereft of all ability to rule the nation. The parliamentary way had succumbed to radical politics as the members of Parliament were bypassed by a host of new political participants. Although variously composed Parliaments would be a part of each new constitutional experiment, by 1647 political power had passed from the hands of the men at Westminster to those who held the sword.

It is traditional to explain the ascendancy of the New Model Army as a mere usurpation of power and to pass off the mobs' violence as mass hysteria accompanying the breakdown of institutional restraint. The origins of both is thought to be puritan extremism. The story narrated here has had a different emphasis. It suggests that the erosion of parliamentary legitimacy resulted from a change in parliamentary practice. The commonly held concept of a unified and organic political order had been violated by the rise of party and interest at Westminster, prompting forces outside Parliament to enter the political process and attempt its amelioration. Thus the emergence of radical politics in the nation was preceded by the emergence of adversary politics in Parliament.

During the early years of war Parliament had maintained its traditional process of decision making. Reasoned debate and unanimous resolution had characterized the proceedings of an institution designed to do the King's business and these methods survived the stresses and strains of internecine struggle. Lacking executive and administrative capacities, and antipathetic to innovation, for three years Parliament waged a cautious and conciliatory war. Consensus decision making was not an effective method of resolving unprece-

273

dented political and military problems, but it had the virtue of perserving parliamentary unity and authority. Although the desultory pursuit of the war and the efforts to achieve a religious *via media* resulted in stalemate on both fronts, this only mirrored the confusion in Parliament and the nation. The institution drifted from one crisis to another: it was not guided by competing ideological parties pursuing coordinated and contradictory policies. The methods of consensus ensured that where opposition could not be overcome it would be encompassed. Proponents of a negotiated settlement and of a full-scale war worked together both in drafting peace propositions and in erecting armies.

The first real challenge to parliamentary unity occurred in the winter of 1644–5. The military campaign of that summer had begun with great expectation of success and had ended in despair. The inefficiency of Parliament's forces and the lack of fervor displayed by some of its commanders combined to produce a disaster at Lostwithiel and a debacle at Newbury. In the frustration of defeat the constant quarrels and bickerings that resulted from imprecisely drawn lines of command boiled over into formal charges and countercharges among members of the senior officer corps. As these accusations were heard at Westminster the members of Parliament sought their own explanation for the failure of the armies and the fissures in their cause.

This they found not only in the errors of man, but in the judgment of God. Defeat in battle was a sign of heavenly wrath that could not be overlooked – an edict to reform the sins of men. In Parliament thoughts turned to church building and to reuniting and reinvigorating the parliamentary cause. The military setbacks posed two interrelated problems: the reconciliation of the commanders and the reconstruction of their decimated armies. In this atmosphere of introspection with its emphasis upon reformation, the self-denying ordinance was proposed. By eliminating all M.P.s from civil and military office, the men at Westminster could demonstrate their own willingness to sacrifice while simultaneously overcoming the military disputes. Instead of the divisive process of resolving individual accusations, self-denial would remove their source. Despite the bitterness of the commanders' contentions, the principles of consensus were still at work.

Although Parliament pursued a radical resolution of its internal problems, military reform proceeded along familiar lines. The

Conclusion

Committee of Both Kingdoms, which had overseen the establishment and deployment of Parliament's military might, was chosen to initiate the reorganization and it resolved to conduct two separate theaters of war: a northeastern front controlled by the Scottish Army and a southern campaign by a single English force. It was on this second body, the New Model Army, that attention was focused. The Associated Armies commanded by Sir William Waller and the Earl of Manchester would be combined with the national force that the Earl of Essex had led. Manchester's horse and Essex's foot, both recently recruited and reequipped, would be the core of a 21,000-man force. All officers would be drawn from the three armies and the entire establishment would be financed through the monthly assessment schemes that had funded the old armies. As economy measures, the New Model would be smaller than the combined strength of the older forces, would eliminate the overlapping general staffs, and would have no lieutenant colonels in the horse regiments. But in its essential features the New Model departed little from the armies it replaced, providing as much continuity and as little disruption as possible.

Despite these moderate procedures, the hostility provoked by the contentions over self-denial were renewed over the officer list approved by the Commons and the de facto abolition of the peers' military role. A constitutional crisis was narrowly averted when the officer list passed the Upper House by a single proxy vote. This bitterness that surrounded the creation of the New Model Army outlasted the issues over which the two Houses contended. The replacement of the Earls of Essex and Manchester and the subsequent exemption from self-denial for Oliver Cromwell perpetuated the personal animosities that the ordinance had attempted to compose. As the campaigning season began those who had opposed the replacement of the commanders now feared that the New Model would be incapable of holding off the advancing royalist troops. At the Committee of Both Kingdoms a plan was devised to gain the most benefit from the untried Army with the least amount of risk. While the Scots and a detachment of cavalry would protect the Eastern Association, the New Model would besiege the royalist capital at Oxford. The strategy of the Oxford siege remedied the Army's growing pains but it also demonstrated that the new modeling had not resolved the fundamental conflict between those advocating active and passive prosecution of the war. The plan also

Conclusion

depended upon cooperation between the Scottish Army and Cromwell's Eastern Association regiment, forces that had become the bitterest of enemies during the campaign of the previous year. Thus in the first action of the new season Parliament's forces were plagued by the recurrence of military dispute and disunity. Unopposed, royalist forces stormed and sacked the city of Leicester.

To opponents of the military reorganization the loss of Leicester revealed the folly of creating the new Army. While the New Model encamped around Oxford, the war had been brought to the Eastern Association. To Army supporters, Scottish obduracy and the continued influence of men uncommitted to the war had undermined the military effort. The animosities among individual parliamentarians now overflowed, resulting in the formation of factional rivalries. Advocates of the competing military philosophies sought to lay blame for the loss of Leicester upon their opponents. The Earl of Essex and his supporters, now fearful of military defeat, accepted an alliance with the Scots as protection against the failure of the New Model. An accusation by James Cranford against the leaders of the war faction was followed by a formal investigation of the conduct of Denzil Holles and Bulstrode Whitelocke at the negotiations at Uxbridge. Personal rivalry had given way to political dispute while the faltering war effort heightened tension at Westminster.

As all sought to evade responsibility for the discredited Oxford siege, the New Model was ordered into action. The new parliamentary Army met the King and the largest part of his forces in mid-June at Naseby. There the evenly matched armies struggled indecisively until a parliamentary cavalry charge turned the tide of battle and shattered the royalist forces. In rapid succession the New Model recovered Leicester and relieved parliamentary garrisons in the west. In the following year they cleared, one by one, all the royalist strongholds, bringing to Parliament an irreversible and unexpected military triumph.

The universally successful New Model remained an amalgam of men who held diverse religious and political principles. The ranks were filled by impressment and the Army was constantly under strength. The officer corps remained remarkably stable; the few officers killed in action or who voluntarily withdrew from service were replaced exclusively on the basis of seniority. The New Model experienced no institutional development through the

Conclusion

Council of War, for after the victory at Naseby separate detachments with distinct military objectives were organized. Nor did the troops experience the kind of financial deprivation that might have turned their thoughts toward collective action. During the first fifteen months of its existence the Army received regular but not full pay, disbursements sufficient to discharge quartering and maintenance costs and frequent enough to leave little impression of hardship. Rumors that the Army exerted political influence upon the recruiter elections came from London rather than the localities and little evidence survives to suggest interference on the part of the New Model. In short, for fifteen months the Army acted as an efficient and uniformly successful fighting force that brought Parliament and nation the hope of peace.

The New Model's triumph brought into focus the institutional shortcomings of Parliament and the diverse outlooks of the constituents of the parliamentary cause. During 1646 critical policy decisions to define the settlement of the kingdom had to be made. Parliament's lack of established channels of leadership and executive skills made it prey to the factions that had developed during the previous year. Their personal contentions were exacerbated by the interjection of the religious issue foisted by the Scots upon Essex, Holles, and their followers. The *jure divino* presbyterianism that only a minority of parliamentarians supported would soon become a major concern, aiding the escalation of factional rivalry into party conflict. The cracks in consensus decision making widened throughout the early months of 1646 as Parliament adapted new procedural techniques and as the constituents of the cause became more adamant in urging their competing visions of the nation's future.

Pressures from outside Parliament were exerted by the government of the City of London and the Scottish Commissioners residing in England. Both believed that the contributions made to the cause by the groups they represented earned them a place in Parliament's counsels. The City government pressed its desires in a series of petitions, developing techniques to pressure Parliament into accepting their wishes. Parliament's privileges and traditions of unencumbered and unpressured debate were put to their severest test as the City sought to divide the two Houses over the question of what constituted breach of privilege. Their insistence upon an uncompromising religious settlement and the expansion of the

Conclusion

powers of the London Militia Committee found Parliament indecisive in protecting its institutional prerogatives. London petitions
were alternately presented first to the Commons and then first to
the Lords and finally simultaneously to both Houses. Their remonstrances in May were accompanied by the constant presence of
aldermen and common councillors, who daily importuned their
acceptance at the doors of the House of Commons. Scottish appeals
were made directly to the nation in provocative pamphlets that
attempted to divide the religiously and politically diverse parliamentarians. They laid blame for the failure of the Uxbridge
proposals and for the religious anarchy in London upon the independents. Their influence upon City divines led to an association
between independency and sectarianism that initiated a campaign
to suppress all religious nonconformity and to establish the *jure
divino* presbyterian settlement.

The pressures of both Scots and City succeeded in widening the
breach between the factions. Both groups lent support to Essex's
followers in the Lords and Holles's in the Lower House. Anti-
Scottish sentiment buoyed the faction led by Haselrig and Evelyn,
but these constituencies had serious implications for Parliament's
institutional privileges. When City petitions and Scottish pamphlets
violated the secrecy of parliamentary proceedings and the ability
of the Houses to conduct unencumbered debates, votes of privilege
came to be political rather than procedural decisions. Combined
with the ministrations of outside pressure groups, factional strife
began the transformation of the political process.

Yet despite factional struggle and religious controversy, Parliament continued to search for middle ground. Factional dispute
could not obscure the large areas of agreement that existed in the
House of Commons. Charles's captured correspondence established
beyond the most charitable doubt that he intended to bring foreign
forces into the nation and that he had not negotiated in good faith
with Parliament. The propositions to be sent to him were thus
made uncompromising, bills to be signed into law rather than
clauses to be negotiated into a treaty. But the Commons' resolve,
shared by both factions, was not held by either the Lords or the
Scots. New contentions between the Houses and long delays characterized the establishment of the terms for peace. Scottish obstruction of the propositions made the conduct of their Army in the
north a source of bitter dispute, forcing Holles and Stapleton to

Conclusion

defend the indefensible and driving another wedge between the factions. While the two Houses contended over the specific details of the terms for peace, and the Commons searched for a device to circumvent the Scots' delays, the King fled his garrison at Oxford and threw himself upon the mercy of the Scots. Ensconced in their Army, and fully apprised of the differences between them and Parliament, in August Charles summarily rejected the Newcastle propositions.

The failure to secure a settlement with the King presented Parliament with an entirely new set of problems. Throughout the long years of war the legitimacy of parliamentary rule had rested upon its intention of separating the King from his evil advisors and restoring him to his rightful constitutional role. Wartime innovations, like the changes in county government and the new and burdensome taxation, were seen to be expedients that would be abandoned at war's end. But the conclusion of the fighting had not been accompanied by peace; and although it could no longer be justified, continued wartime rule remained necessary. Decisions that had been deferred in anticipation of an accord with the King now presented themselves for resolution. Parliament had to secure the return of Charles to England, the withdrawal of the Scottish forces, and the creation of an army to suppress the Irish rebellion. These three interrelated problems presented the Commons' faction led by Denzil Holles and Sir Philip Stapleton with an opportunity to achieve political hegemony. Their alliance with both Scots and City in the tumultuous months following the New Model's triumph gave them the ability to raise the funds to pay Scottish arrears and to convince the Scots to return Charles to parliamentary control. Although both factions agreed upon these central issues of policy, only Holles and Stapleton had the confidence of the extra-parliamentary bodies whose support was not essential.

The coordination of policy achieved by Holles and Stapleton came at the cost of a fundamental change in political practice. Parliamentary privilege could no longer be defended against outside pressure groups, to whom it was necessary to grant important political concessions. The urgent pursuit of policy making finally shattered parliamentary unity. In the Lower House sharp adversary techniques replaced unencumbered debate and the quest for unanimity. Majority rule, the pursuit of numerical superiority, rather than the process of encompassing opposition, became primary and divisions on political issues of first importance alarmingly frequent. Personal factions were gradually transformed into political parties, especially as the religious issues and the support of outside pressure groups solidified their differences. Adversary practice provided the opportunity for political leadership and uncommitted members were driven into the ranks of the parties as issues were presented without the possibility of compromise.

Adversary politics also was apparent in relations between the Houses. The end of the fighting presented the Lords with their opportunity to recoup attenuated powers. They had been willing to suffer wartime expedients but proved adamant against their continuation once the fighting had ceased. A group of anti-innovatory peers emerged in the Upper House who were principally concerned with abolishing the administrative changes necessitated by the civil war. They passed an ordinance to suppress the county committees and refused to continue the wartime taxation necessary to maintain the New Model. They protested the extended authority of the House of Commons over parliamentary standing committees and military forces, demanding the equality of power that had been a principle of wartime government. These stands taken by the anti-innovatory peers led to deadlock between the Houses and the suggestion in the Commons that the Lords be excluded from the process of decision making.

Initially the ascendancy of adversary politics was mitigated by the common concerns of the two parties. For different reasons the return of the King, the withdrawal of the Scots, and the invasion of Ireland were supported by both of the Commons' ideological groupings. The obstructions of the anti-innovatory peers frustrated the policies of Holles and Stapleton as much as they infuriated political radicals like Haselrig and Marten. It was not until 1647, after the return of the King and Scottish withdrawal had been accomplished by Holles and Stapleton, that party rule came to dominate the proceedings of the two Houses. With the threat of the King's foreign intrigues eliminated, attention could be turned to dismantling superfluous military forces and to preparing the Irish invasion. Holles's success with the Scots, his support from the City, and the coincidence of his policies with the aims of godly presbyterians and anti-innovatory peers gave him an incontestable majority at Westminster. Rather than direct his new programs from the floor of the House of Commons, Holles used the Derby

House Committee as a new executive council. He packed the Committee with his party followers and the core of the anti-innovatory peers. From Derby House all policy concerning Irish and military affairs was devised and implemented, bypassing the Commons' traditional administrative committees and debates of the full membership. Thus Haselrig and his followers were effectively eliminated from political decision making.

Holles's program was designed to reorganize the nation's forces into three groups: an Army to invade Ireland; troops for the garrisons that were to be maintained in England; and a small contingent of standing cavalry. The remainder of the men at arms, some 10,000 New Model soldiers and the bulk of the local forces, would be disbanded. Seven regiments in England were to be taken from the New Model for Irish service, and Holles carefully chose politically reliable New Model officers to command the Irish invasion. Both the invasion of Ireland and the demobilization of the superfluous forces were to be financed by £200,000 borrowed from the City of London. Six weeks' severance pay would be granted to those soldiers who were to be discharged, with additional benefits for those volunteering for Irish service.

By the end of March recruitment for the venture had begun with every expectation that the ranks would quickly be filled. When Parliament was informed that a petition was circulating in the Army pressing the redress of grievances before enlistment for foreign service, Holles prepared a savage declaration against any who continued in the petition and summoned senior officers implicated in the agitation to be examined at the bar of the House of Commons. The ferocity of this response was calculated to suppress the campaign, which had spread among the troops commanded by supporters of his program. In this he was at first successful. Subscriptions for Ireland continued throughout April and by the beginning of May Holles began coordinating the disbandment of the remainder of the New Model, hoping to quell the continued discontent among the soldiery and to encourage those who desired to remain in service to subscribe for Ireland. Although little could be done to increase the proportion of the soldiers' arrears that would be paid out at disbandment, their other material grievances were carefully considered. An act of indemnity and provisions for widows and maimed soldiers were hastily passed at the end of May just before the order for disbandment was issued. It was not so

Conclusion

much Holles's policy as his high-handed method of pursuing it that opened the breach between Parliament and Army.

Holles's plan for military disestablishment proceeded without any understanding of the Army's material or psychological condition. Although politically and religiously diverse, the officer corps and soldiery were unified in concern for financial and personal security and in pride over their military achievement. In the nine months since the fighting had ended the New Model's once regular pay had deteriorated into sporadic and uncertain disbursements and its religious diversity had become the focus of bitter dispute in pulpit and press. Soldiers disbanded in the localities or voluntarily withdrawing from service found themselves the objects of judicial retribution directly related to their wartime activities. Unsubstantiated reports of soldiers hanged at assizes for commandeering horses were matched by petitions to the House of Lords from officers imprisoned for debt. The decision at Westminster to reorganize the New Model brought these issues, as well as Parliament's continued neglect of widows and maimed soldiers, to the fore. Modeling their activity upon the petitions of London citizens to the Common Council, the soldiers drafted a petition to be presented to Sir Thomas Fairfax. Holles's declaration against the petition and charges against the officers involved left the Army without a means of remedying their material grievances. Moreover, the denial of their right to petition, a right basic to Englishmen and not denied the City or groups of county inhabitants, led to an examination of Parliament's care for its loyal soldiers. From within the ranks agitators were selected to present the soldiers' fears to their officers, whereas Councils of War provided the officers with an opportunity to prepare a vindication of the Army's conduct. Material grievances soon gave way to generalized demands for the recognition of the Army's service and the soldiers' rights as citizens of the nation. Continued recruitment for the Irish venture came to be seen as an attempt to divide the Army and prevent the recognition of its legitimate complaints.

The initial agitation for the redress of material greivances was thus replaced by demands for the vindication of the Army's honor. Small misunderstandings burgeoned into symbolic confrontations and the declaration of March 30 and the examination of Army officers in the House of Commons replaced arrears and indemnity as the central contentions between Army and Parliament. By mid-

Conclusion

May, as the House of Commons worked to resolve the material complaints expressed in the soldiers' March Petition, new regimental petitions revealed that the controversy was now focused upon the actions taken by Holles's party at Westminster. The enemies whom the Army feared would become their judges were no longer royalists and neutrals, but the members of faction and interest in the Houses of Parliament. The decision to disband the Army in the midst of its agitation finally split the officer corps along religious and political lines. For both supporters and opponents of Holles's party the Irish venture became a test of allegiance. Almost one-third of the Army's officers above the rank of lieutenant left service by June 1647, thereby cementing the commitment of those who opposed the venture and unifying the Army ideologically. The order for disbandment was stoutly resisted both in a resolution of the officers at the Council of War and in a mutiny of the first regiment ordered to be mustered out.

The radicalization of the Army and its refusal to disband was immediately succeeded by political action. Fearing the designs of Holles's party and his Scottish and City allies, a contingent of New Model troops seized Charles at Holmby House with the intention of bringing him to Army headquarters. The Army's demands for redress of its grievances were succeeded by threats of armed invasion of London and finally the impeachment of Holles and ten of his party supporters. The Army's emergence as a political force was justified as an attempt to eradicate faction and interest from politics at Westminster – to restore a "free Parliament." This was exactly the goal of the citizens of London who opposed the Army's action and demanded that Parliament meet force with force. In this atmosphere parliamentary politics collapsed under the competing pressures upon the Houses at Westminster. The Army, the reformadoes who crowded the City and demanded the payment of their own arrears, and the City government, intent upon preserving the powers of its Militia Committee and protecting itself from invasion, all forced Parliament to vote the satisfaction of their conflicting demands. A narrowly averted confrontation in mid-June was succeeded by the ultimate crisis in July. The Army's impeachment of the eleven members of Holles's party and its insistence upon the reconstitution of the London Militia Committee temporarily stiffened resolve in the City. Reformadoes and apprentices, whose own desires were sacrificed to

283

Army demands, invaded the two Houses of Parliament and forced the recall of recent votes. The two speakers and large parts of both Houses fled Westminster for protection in the Army, and the New Model troops marched on London to restore the members and the privileges of Parliament.

The struggle between Army and City over the privileges of Parliament symbolized the institution's loss of power and prestige. Each outside pressure group came to see Parliament only as the party of its members who pursued its particular aims, identifying its opponents as men of faction and interest. This was neither cant, rationalization, nor sheer insanity. The holistic notion of the political process dictated that Parliament could not leave unredressed the grievances of loyal subjects. The rise of party at Westminster was seen as the predominance of special interest against the pursuit of the public good. The parliamentary political process had been overcome by force, but force used to restore an old concept of political order. As adversary politics had replaced consensus, so radical politics succeeded the parliamentary way.

It is, then, no longer paradoxical that the rise of the New Model Army was both the mainspring of revolution and the force that deterred more radical change. The self-conscious, almost painful entrance of the soldiery into political affairs was decisive in shaping subsequent events. On the one hand, the conflict that began between King and Parliament was escalated by the Army's participation in efforts at settlement. By its claim to represent the people, ambiguous though it was, the Army insisted upon safeguards against tyranny that included restrictions upon Parliament as well as the monarchy. Despite its intentions, the Army's actions undermined Parliament, both by questioning the motives of its members and by revealing the weakness of its authority. Yet, on the other hand, the Army's commitment to constitutional and parliamentary government uprooted the programs for radical reconstruction that blossomed alongside the soldiers' agitation. The necessity of maintaining the forms of legitimacy delimited the bounds of experimentation. The goals sought in 1647 were those to which the Army leadership adhered in the succeeding decade.

The Army's rise transmuted the political situation that had

existed at war's end. Holles's long-term plan for eliminating the areas of dispute between King and Parliament was, of course, shattered by the soldiers' actions. Whatever Holles's miscalculations were, he was firmly in touch with the upsurge of war weariness and renewed royalist sentiment and, even allowing for Charles's unerring ability to stymie settlement, he was leading the nation on a course which could have ended in peace. The Army's intervention foreclosed this opportunity and permanently altered the circumstances that had brought it about. First, further fragmentation of the parliamentary cause fed the King's appetite for playing ends against the middle. It cannot be to the Army leaders' credit that they believed they could be honest broker to an accord with a monarch thrice revealed as perfidious. In this effort, they achieved no more success than had Holles. But the Army held another mediative position, one that had more lasting consequences than their role between King and Parliament. As Holles stood middle ground between rigid Presbyterians and crypto-royalists, so did the Army occupy the widening space between the political Independents in Parliament and the London radicals.

There can be no doubt but that the Army's rise gave new life to the diverse groups of Londoners who had, almost since the outbreak of war, agitated for far-reaching religious and political change.[1] Holles's rule had marked the low point in the radicals' fortunes: their appeals to the Common Council had been rejected; a crackdown against "heresy" (using powers designed to suppress Catholics) had threatened their worship; their petitionary campaign, like the Army's, had been aborted and some of the petitioners arrested; and finally, at the height of the confrontation between Army and Parliament, they were identified as a "fifth column" and a crowd of them attempting to present a petition to the Common Council were brutally assaulted by cavalry forces of the London militia.[2] Moreover, as the weight of the powers arrayed against them grew, the once-united radical movement split apart, squabbling first over political tactics, but soon revealing deep theological discord, fissures over belief and practice that not even the invective of their enemies could overcome. The emergence of the Army gave the radicals a new focus for their causes. Within the Army's regiments there was support for the Londoners' religious diversity and, encompassed by its emerging ideology – the defense of justice and the liberty of the subject – protection for oppressed citizens. Although the Army adopted few of the radicals' programs, it could not ignore their appeals.

Indeed, the Army's assault upon parliamentary politics reinvigorated the analyses of authority and legitimacy that, with the notable exceptions of Lilburne and Overton, had been muted in the first months of 1647. These focused upon Parliament and many of them adopted the Army's own language, which stressed the growth of "faction and interest." "If there be any statute that is against the welfare and safety of the people, it is better broke than kept," wrote the author of "A Vindication of the Army," in defending the soldiers' refusal to disband.[3] "There is no privilege of the House of Commons that must stand in competition with the safety of the people" was the premise that led another anonymous pamphleteer to urge the suspension of the eleven members.[4] The author of "Reformation with the Heels Upward" proposed "that the just privileges of Parliament may be by Declaration made manifest... and the Kingdom not enslaved by an unknown and unlimited privilege."[5] The echoes of the Army's programs are unmistakable and the logic of its defense of its disobedience to Parliament irreparably eroded all institutional authority.

Most importantly for the future, the Army's program, thus justified, was achieved through the threat and use of force. The pressing need, at every step of its activism, for decisive responses; the self-righteousness and justice of its cause; even, eventually, the belief that it acted on behalf of the nation were irrestible inducements to bring into the political system the one thing that it could not accommodate. The disbandment mutinies, the seizure of the King, the impeachment of the eleven members, all escalated the conflict between Parliament and the Army and elicited similar responses from reformadoes and the London Militia Committee. Cromwell, for one, was continually distressed by the eagerness of some Army members to intervene with might at each turn of events. Yet he too sanctioned the first steps on the road to London, the studied advances and withdrawals of Army headquarters that eliminated parliamentary alternatives. The Army had not begun the assault on parliamentary politics, but, like so much else, it carried it to new heights. The events of the summer of 1647 were more than an adumbration to Pride's Purge and the execution of the King.

Conclusion

Yet the nature of the Army's rise, its limited goals of achieving material security and a vindication of its honor – the soldiers' insistence that they were not meddling in affairs of state – restricted the nature of the reforms that the Army would sanction. Until the very end, City leaders believed they faced a mutiny for pay: reports of the Army's advance at the end of July assured the government that the soldiers were coming to seize the City's treasure. Historians continue to characterize the Army's actions as a "revolt" rather than as a process of radicalization that resulted in a political movement.[6] Fear, distrust, misapprehension: all were critical components in the Army's rise, but they are not its defining characteristics. The soldiers' entrance into politics was carefully articulated and each new manifesto, like a litany, began with the rejection of the March Petition and added the successive violations of the Army's rights and reputation; actions were restrained and particular grievances frequently moderated to maintain unity; and although fired with passion, only the disbandment mutiny at Chelmsford and Joyce's seizure of the King were spontaneous, undisciplined actions – not until the demonstration at Burford would the Army's radicalization threaten to degenerate into revolt.

It is deeply significant that the process of radicalization began with an appeal for arrears and indemnity. These were issues that both united the soldiery at the lowest level of self-interest and provided the clearest evidence of potential injustice once concerns were generalized. The soldiers' subsequent focus on rights and liberties developed within this unequivocal context. As their right to their pay and freedom from judicial harassment were incontestable, and as they existed independently from all ideological persuasions, the soldiers needed little prodding to translate this violation of their just rights into a potentially perpetual tyranny. The threat to their safety, financial and physical, was a wellspring from which the Army could constantly replenish its ardor and which generated its insistence upon fundamental safeguards. Because their political intervention derived from such tangible grievances, the soldiers never doubted the justness of their actions. Even without the psychological preconditioning of self-confidence and righteousness that came with their triumph, and beyond the chiliasm of the "saints" among them, officers and soldiers naturally expected reward, rather than punishment, for their faithful service.

That the first challenge to the soldiers' expectations came in the rejection of a petition elevated a potential mutiny for pay into an ideological conflict. Not only were their requests unquestionably just, but the method used to attain them was both lawful and moderate. The soldiers had readily accepted the suggestion of their officers that the petition be presented to Fairfax and that he have a free hand in eliminating anything offensive. Its contents had been trimmed to those grievances shared by the whole Army. Thus its rejection, before it was even presented to Fairfax or Parliament, was stunning. The right of redress of grievances by petition was one of the fundamental liberties of Englishmen that the war had been fought to defend. The threat to the Army's security implicit in the neglect of the soldiers' material condition was compounded by the rejection of their right to petition. When this threat was combined with efforts to divide the Army into separate contingents, the soldiery was quick to conclude that an active conspiracy to deprive them of their rights was underway. Forced to its own devices, the Army responded not with aimless violence or bitter acquiescence, but with an organized appeal to their field commanders in the House of Commons through the first agitators of the regiments. Rapidly, material issues were superseded by those of the Army's honor.

In defense of their rights and reputation the soldiery had begun to organize itself. But, as with the desires expressed in their March Petition, the selection of agitators was sanctioned only to secure those things that pertained to them as soldiers. As their actions became more extraordinary, especially in the context of the omnipresent fear of mutiny, the soldiers became committed to demonstrating their legitimacy. This meant, first, gaining the trust of their officers who, though sharing the men's grievances, were also responsible for their discipline. The selection of officer agitators and the preparation of the regimental statements in May greatly aided this process. As Parliament had sent its Commissioners to investigate distempers, the soldiery was intent upon demonstrating its orderliness, while at the same time expressing its discontents. Despite the high tempers caused by subscriptions to the Irish venture, the May rendezvous took place without incident. Additionally, the soldiers legitimized their actions by avoiding political issues in which they had intense interest as individuals but only marginal concern as an Army. Chief among these were the reinstitution of the covenant and conformity to the new church establishment as tests of office.

Conclusion

By such self-restraint the soldiery intended to demonstrate to Parliament and nation the injustice they had suffered.

Self-restraint also aided the unity necessary to delay recruitment for Ireland until after the redress of grievances. The attempt of Parliament to divide the soldiery, both in plans for future service and into proponents and opponents of the Irish service, was countered by intense efforts to keep the men together. Ensign Nichols, the anonymous private of Cromwell's troop, and many others urged unity upon those who had agreed to go to Ireland. When the disbandment scheme was revealed, both agitators and officers immediately desired a rendezvous – the most effective means of concerted action and discipline. The turning point in the Army's radicalization was the withdrawal of the dissenting officers in early June, for even more than their material complaints, adherence to the Army's desires in the face of the order to disband provided solidarity to officers and soldiers. Throughout the summer crisis, and after it as well, unity was the Army's overriding principle and those who threatened it – the agitators in demanding a march on London in July; the radicals who produced the "Case of the Army" in October—were always on the defensive.

The quest for unity moderated the Army's radicalization and radicalism. In the first place it ensured the maintenance of discipline. Throughout April and May the contentions between supporters and opponents of the Irish venture aroused grave concern among senior officers that they were losing control of the soldiery. The danger that continued antagonism might lead to precipitous action, perhaps even a sack of London, was real. The atmosphere in the camps was supercharged by rumors and fears, compounded at every moment of crisis by the dire predictions of London radicals appealing to the soldiers for aid. The fear of insurrection was, doubtless, an important element in the decision of many officers to quit their commands, which, in turn, restored harmony to the divided regiments. In the same way, the shared goals of leaders and followers, after the refusal to disband, blunted the potential for class antagonism by smoothing over the enormous disparity between the arrears of officers and soldiers. When Parliament attempted to entice New Modelers to London with offers of back pay it was a matter of great pride to the soldiery that their officers risked considerable sums to maintain the Army's unity. Finally, solidarity demanded unanimity in action, a factor that at first brought men like Cromwell into line with the soldiers' undertakings, but that later inhibited demands for marches to London. The deliberative apparatus that the Army created, the Committee of Officers and the General Council all served to maintain the Army's unity.

As with their actions, the Army's ideology was both a limiting and liberating force. Its fundamental tenet was opposition to "faction and interest," a belief in the public good. In its struggle with the King Parliament had reasserted the doctrine of *salus populi suprema lex*, and this, in its contestation with Parliament, the Army revived. In its most narrow sense, "private interest" was merely corruption and self-aggrandizement, expressed by the soldiers in charges of embezzlement and pluralism. Similarly, the safety of the people could mean little more than the soldiers' arrears and indemnity. Slogans and catchphrases do not readily reveal the bounds that men set upon their behavior. The Army intervened in the nation's affairs to defend "the fundamental rights of free born Englishmen," by no means a hollow notion, but one that also justified the actions of royalists, levellers, and clubmen. The reformadoes who listed to oppose the New Model also claimed that they had not been members of a "mere mercenary Army," and the numerous participants in the assault on Parliament acted in defense of its freedom.[7] Revolutions are spawned by competing visions of justice.

The Army's commitment to public good – to the commonwealth – could be seen not only in its efforts to free Parliament, but also in the subordination of its own private ends. Although the soldiers' protested against religious persecution and hoped for accommodation, they never sought an alteration of church government. No other issue had been so emphasized by Army detractors, who had predicted since the New Model's creation that the soldiers would enforce a limitless toleration. This the Army denied, not only in its manifestos but in all its actions. The harmonious diversity of religious beliefs within the ranks may have served as an example for the common good, but it never was intended as a blueprint for the nation. At no point during its radicalization does it appear that the Army saw itself heir to the rich dissident tradition that linked Lollards to Marian exiles to the New England way. Religious radicalism may explain some of the soldiers' self-confidence and enthusiasm but its transcendent character is irreconcilable with the

Conclusion

constitutional limitations the soldiers placed upon their action. One by one the religious extremists defected from the Army, precisely because of its secular domination.

If religious radicalism was only an incidental precondition to the Army's ideology and radicalization, other long-term developments had more direct impact. Chief among these were the expansion of political participation, both directly through the erosion of exclusionary property qualifications and the multiplication of offices in the localities; the increase of literacy, particularly in urban areas and among apprentices and servants; and the growth of a legal consciousness that assumed an impartial equity. The soldiers' politicization was remarkably sophisticated, their manifestos mature, and their sense of justice white hot. It was this inbred belief in their rights and liberties, fertilized by the traditions of centuries and the events of 1647, that motivated the soldiery. Like all revolutionary bodies, their aspirations were as noble as their hopes were utopian.

NOTES

CHAPTER I. THE PARLIAMENTARY CAUSE

1 C. H. Firth and F. Rait, eds., *Acts and Ordinances of the Inter-regnum*, 3 vols. (London, 1911), I, 14.
2 Conrad Russell, "Parliament and the King's Finances," in Conrad S. R. Russell, ed., *The Origins of the English Civil War* (London, 1973), p. 114.
3 Russell, p. 111; J. S. Morrill, *The Revolt of the Provinces: Conservatives and Radicals in the English Civil War 1630–50* (London, 1976), pp. 17ff.
4 Perez Zagorin, *The Court and the Country* (New York, 1969); Valerie Pearl, *London and the Outbreak of the Puritan Revolution* (London, 1960).
5 Brian Manning, "Neutrals and Neutralism in the English Civil War," D.Phil. diss., Oxford University, 1957, Chapter 2.
6 David Underdown, *Somerset in the Civil War and Interregnum* (Newton Abbott, 1973); Alvan Everitt, *The Community of Kent and the Great Rebellion* (Leicester, 1966); Manning, "Neutrals and Neutralism"; J. S. Morrill, *Cheshire 1630–60* (Oxford, 1974), pp. 31–74.
7 D. Brunton and D. H. Pennington, *Members of the Long Parliament* (London, 1954); M. F. Keeler, *The Long Parliament* (Philadelphia, 1954); David Underdown, *Pride's Purge* (Oxford, 1971).
8 Manning, p. 357.
9 Morrill, *The Revolt;* Underdown, *Somerset.*
10 Firth and Rait, I, 14.
11 B.L. Sloan Mss. 4,957, fol. 24r. This same precedent is cross-referenced under statutes, fol. 32r.
12 B.L. Add. Mss. 19,398, fol. 155.
13 *C.S.P.D. 1645–7*, p. 155.
14 Juxon, Dr. Williams' Library, Mss. 24.50, fol. 73.
15 E. 339 (12), "The Humble Acknowledgement and Petition of Divers Inhabitants of London."
16 Bodl. Clarendon Mss., vol. 29, fol. 165.
17 Rushworth, VI, 446.
18 Rushworth, VI, 587.

19 E. 1084 (11), William Prynne, "Minors No Senators."
20 C. S. Sims, ed., "Policies in Parliament," *Huntington Library Quarterly* 15 (1951), 51. There were, of course, occasional violations of this rule, but as late as 1644 D'Ewes still found them rare enough to be recorded in his journal. B.L. Harl. Mss. 166, fol. 153.
21 Sims, p. 51.
22 Ibid., p. 47.
23 William Hakewill, "The Manner of Holding Parliaments" (London, 1641), unpaginated.
24 *L.J.*, 7, 131, 134–5. In May 1646, when the Commons demanded the peers' reasons for the rejection of a bill, they expressed a similar practice: "Such a negative answer they hold not to be usual in the proceedings of Parliament; for if one House may give a negative answer without any reasons offered, the other House may adhere without giving any reasons for the same; and so the Houses will have no clear understanding of the grounds of each other's resolutions." *L.J.*, 8, 314.
25 J. E. Neale, *The Elizabethan House of Commons* (London, 1953), p. 338.
26 B.L. Add. Mss. 26,644, fol. 13, "The Passage of a Bill Through Parliament."
27 Sims, p. 50.
28 Wallace Notestein, *The House of Commons, 1604–10* (New Haven, Conn., 1971), p. 441.
29 C. S. Sims, ed., "The Speaker of the House of Commons," *American Historical Review* 45 (1939), 92.
30 Ibid., 94.
31 That opposition appeared in Caroline Parliaments is too obvious to comment upon. But, in light of Dr. Hirst's comments, it must be reiterated that opposition was achieved despite the structure of parliamentary politics. It was understood, even by the oppositionists, as illegitimate (though necessary) behavior and their efforts to deny the implications of their actions offer a far more realistic context for studying "opposition" than the simple assumption that political activity differs little over the centuries. D. M. Hirst, "Unanimity in the Commons, Aristocratic Intrigues and the Origins of the English Civil War," *Journal of Modern History* 50 (1978), esp. 57 n. 11.
32 Hakewill, "The Manner of Holding Parliaments."
33 Sims, "The Speaker of the House of Commons," 95.
34 Ibid.
35 Sims, "Policies in Parliament," 53.
36 E. 1084 (11), William Prynne, "Minors No Senators."
37 M. A. Kishlansky, "The Emergence of Adversary Politics in the

Long Parliament," *Journal of Modern History* 49 (December, 1977), 617–40.

38 *Oxford English Dictionary*, s.v. "party"; Bulstrode Whitelocke, *Memorials of English Affairs*, 4 vols. (London, 1853), II, 146; Edmund Ludlow, *The Memoirs of Edmund Ludlow*, ed. C. H. Firth, 2 vols. (Oxford, 1894), I, 141; Juxon, Dr. Williams' Library, Mss. 24.50, fol. 106; Robert Baillie, *The Letters and Journals of Robert Baillie*, ed. David Laing, 3 vols. (Edinburgh, 1841–2), II, 336.

39 Baillie, II, 410.

40 *The Journal of Sir Simonds D'Ewes*, ed. Wilson Coates (New Haven, Conn., 1942), p. 233. I owe this reference to C. S. R. Russell.

41 Clement Walker, "The Mystery of the Two Juntoes," in *Select Tracts Relating to the Civil Wars in England*, ed. F. Maseres (London, 1815), I, 333.

42 Ludlow, I, 147; Whitelocke's "Annals," B.L. Add. Mss. 37,344, fol. 4; Sir William Waller, *Vindication of the Conduct and Character of Sir William Waller* (London, 1793), p. 225. Prynne, writing in 1646, assessed: "There are greater differences, distractions between the King and Parliament, and more laboring to make parties in the House to serve ends (if possible) than in any former age." E. 1084, "Minors No Senators," p. 14.

43 Dr. Hirst's belief that the redefinition of "party" could only have occurred if some adherent proudly proclaimed himself a "party" member is logically fallacious. By the same reasoning there was no innovation in religion because none of the disputants would admit to being an innovator. Marchmont Needham, a most acute observer of political developments, was convinced of the emergence of political parties by May 1647. His mordant analysis, E. 392 (13), "The Case of the Kingdom Stated According to the Proper Interests of the Several Parties Engaged," accepts the structural change by which parties developed. Needham's tract drew predictable criticism – "What can be more carnal than to tell the citizens they cannot flourish unless they mind only their peculiar interest" – in the anonymous "Anti-Machiavell or Honesty Against Policy: An Answer to the Case of the Kingdom Stated," E. 396 (16). Hirst, 55.

44 Rushworth, I, preface; quoted in R. C. Richardson, *The Debate on the English Revolution* (London, 1977), p. 16. "Ingenuous": honest.

45 Lucy Hutchinson, *The Memoirs of Colonel Hutchinson* (London, 1973), p. 166; my italics.

46 Walker, p. 334; "Every Parliament man ought to vote according to his own judgment, not another's only, and it is very dangerous for others to vote with such and such persons only in the House, and to make their votes the sole ground of their concurrent Ay or No is

the highway to faction." E. 1084 (11), William Prynne, "Minors No Senators," p. 14.
47 Holles, p. 250.
48 Hutchinson, pp. 7, 166.
49 Clarke Papers, I, 178.
50 *O.P.H.*, 16, 151.
51 A. S. P. Woodhouse, *Puritanism and Liberty* (London, 1938), p. 31.
52 Waller, pp. 9, 12–13.
53 D'Ewes, B.L. Harl. Mss. 166, fol. 196.
54 See Everitt for a case study that focuses on the county committee.
55 The county-committee records provide a useful focus for studying the localities but suggest a more coherent administration than in fact occurred.
56 The difficulties the county committee of Buckinghamshire had with Sir Samuel Luke is one well-documented example. See especially Luke, pp. 337–8.
57 J. S. Morrill, "Mutiny and Discontent in English Provincial Armies 1645–47," *Past and Present* 56 (1972), 49–74.
58 For a considered study see Clive Holmes, *The Eastern Association* (Cambridge, 1974).
59 Firth and Rait, I, 291.
60 Ibid., I, 413–16.
61 Ibid., I, 376, 398–400.
62 S. R. Gardiner, ed., *Constitutional Documents of the Puritan Revolution* (Oxford, 1906), p. 267.
63 For varying theories about the committee's composition see Wallace Notestein, "The Creation of the Committee of Both Kingdoms," *American Historical Review* 17 (1912); J. H. Hexter, "The Rise of the Independent Party," Ph.D. diss., Harvard University, 1936; Lawrence Kaplan, *Religion and Politics During the English Civil War* (New York, 1976); Michael Mahony, "The Presbyterian Party in the English Civil War," D.Phil. diss., Oxford University, 1973.
64 The four Commons' military commanders were Cromwell, Haselrig, Stapleton, and Waller. All the other commoners on the committee had legal training. Essex, Manchester, Warwick, and Northumberland among the peers on the committee were also military leaders.
65 *C.J.*, 3, 408.
66 *C.J.*, 3, 437.
67 Firth and Rait, I, 398–400.
68 Rejection of Gardiner's war-party – peace-party division implies no support for Hexter's trinity of war party – middle group – peace

party. J. H. Hexter, *The Reign of King Pym* (Cambridge, Mass., 1941). Both assume far too rigid a structure of groupings within the House of Commons. C. M. Williams's estimation of no more than a handful of consistent supporters of either "party" is much nearer the mark. C. M. Williams, "Henry Marten," D.Phil. diss., Oxford University, 1954. See also M. A. Kishlansky, "The Emergence of Adversary Politics in the Long Parliament," *Journal of Modern History* 49 (1977), 617–18.

CHAPTER 2. THE CREATION OF THE NEW MODEL ARMY

1 Speaker Lenthall to the Committee at Norwich, February 24, 1645. B.L. Add. Mss. 19,398, fol. 155.
2 E. 6 (7), Thomas Hill, "The Season for England's Self-Reflection."
3 Baillie, II, 501.
4 Whitacre, B.L. Add. Mss. 31,116, fol. 154; D'Ewes, B.L. Harl. Mss. 166, fols. 105–6.
5 *C.S.P.D. 1644–5*, p. 21; D'Ewes, B.L. Harl. Mss. 166, fol. 129.
6 Baillie, II, 247.
7 D'Ewes, B.L. Harl. Mss. 166, fol. 181.
8 *C.J.*, 3, 718.
9 *C.S.P.D. 1644–5*, p. 152; D'Ewes, B.L. Harl. Mss. 166, fol. 156; Whitacre, B.L. Add. Mss. 31,116, fol. 176, *C.S.P.D. 1644–45*, p. 152.
10 B.L. Loan 29/123/Misc. 31. This document, missing since the breakup of the Duke of Manchester's library, is the Earl's defense against the charges of Cromwell and Waller. Rushworth's account of Manchester's defense is seriously distorted and reliance upon it has led A. N. B. Cotton to conclude erroneously that Manchester took the offensive against Cromwell. "Cromwell and the Self-Denying Ordinance," *History* 62 (June, 1977), 211–31.
11 *C.J.*, 3, 704, 713–14; Whitacre, B.L. Add. Mss. 31,116, fol. 178.
12 Whitacre, B.L. Add. Mss. 31,116, fol. 178.
13 *C.J.* 3, 718. This sequence of events is more likely than the one commonly followed from Rushworth, VI, 4. Tate had been appointed to present a report to the Committee of the Whole and that was the most logical time for him to present his motion for debate. Cromwell's speech, which all accounts agree followed Tate's, spoke directly to the self-denying ordinance rather than to a general diatribe against "pride and covetousness." When the House reconvened after the Committee of the Whole, Tate would have had to present his motion formally, and this was when Vane offered his second. This makes clear, as all observers recalled, that the motion was Tate's and not a spontaneous suggestion of Cromwell's.

14 Abbot, I, 314.
15 Ibid. The possibility that Abbott has incorrectly dated Cromwell's second and third speeches on the self-denying ordinance is strong. Most likely the second speech came on the 17th and the third on the 19th. For a fuller discussion see M. A. Kishlansky, "The Emergence of Radical Politics in the English Revolution" (Ph.D. diss., Brown University, 1977), pp. 103–4 n. 9.
16 Rushworth, VI, 4.
17 *C.J.*, 4, 718; Whitacre, B.L. Add. Mss. 31,116, fol. 178.
18 B.L. Sloane Mss. 1,519, fol. 37. Juxon's comment was similar: " 'tis a very strange piece of providence being but now so bedeviled that wise men know not what to say or do or could see to the end of it." Juxon, Dr. Williams' Library, Mss. 24.50, fol. 33.
19 E. 21 (11), *Weekly Intelligencer*, no. 84, December 3–10, 1644; E. 21 (17), *Scottish Dove*, no. 60, December 6–13.
20 Baillie, II, 247.
21 Juxon, Dr. Williams' Library, Mss. 24.50, fol. 39.
22 Whitacre, B.L. Add. Mss. 31,116, fol. 174; *C.J.*, 3, 695; Whitelocke, *Memorials*, I, 355; G. E. Aylmer, "Place Bills and the Separation of Powers," *Transactions of the Royal Historical Society* 5 ser., 15 (1965), 45–69.
23 *C.J.*, 3, 669, 679.
24 *C.J.*, 3, 699.
25 *C.J.*, 3, 699, 703.
26 *C.S.P.D. 1644–5*, p. 145.
27 Ibid., p. 171; *C.J.*, 3, 717; Whitacre, B.L. Add. Mss. 21,116, fol. 178.
28 E. 22 (10), Simeon Ashe, "A True Relation of the Most Chief Occurrences," p. 12.
29 E. 18 (13), "The Six Secondary Causes of the Spinning Out of This Unnatural War."
30 Gardiner, *Great Civil War* II, 90–1. As always, Gardiner is preoccupied with Cromwell's role in these events and thus overlooks their background.
31 Clarendon, III, 456–7.
32 *C.J.*, 3, 721.
33 Whitacre, B.L. Add. Mss. 31,116, fol. 180; *C.J.*, 3, 726.
34 *C.J.*, 3, 726. The question was that Essex be excepted.
No   100   Vane and Evelyn (Wilts.)
Yea   93   Holles and Stapleton
35 Whitacre, B.L. Add. Mss. 31,116, fol. 180; *C.J.*, 3, 726.
36 Immediately after the passage of the ordinance on the 19th a committee was appointed to consider the individual financial losses involved. *C.J.*, 3, 729.

37 Whitelocke, *Memorials*, I, 353–5; Abbott, I, 316.
38 *C.J.*, 3, 727. All three were presbyterians, Hill and Marshall moderate and Sedgwick staunch. Interestingly they all had close ties to the Earl of Warwick, whose attitude toward unity and reform may have been different from his opposition to self-denial. See B. Donagan, "The Clerical Patronage of Robert Rich, Second Earl of Warwick 1619–42," *Proceedings of the American Philosophical Society* 120 (1976), 388–419.
39 Clarendon, III, 456.
40 Ibid., III, 457.
41 *C.J.*, 3, 728.
42 Luke, p. 414.
43 Whitacre, B.L. Add. Mss. 31,116, fol. 181. It should be noted that D'Ewes's diary has a gap from December 2 to February 11.
44 *L.J.*, 7, 112.
45 *L.J.*, 7, 115, 117.
46 *L.J.*, 7, 127.
47 *L.J.*, 7, 129; D'Ewes, B.L. Harl. Mss. 166, fol. 173.
48 *L.J.*, 7, 131.
49 Ibid.
50 *L.J.*, 7, 132–5.
51 *C.S.P.D. 1644–5*, pp. 182, 186, 188.
52 The role of the Scots Army has often been misunderstood, leading to the conclusion that they were denied employment in the New Model on religious grounds alone. L. Kaplan, *Religion and Politics During the English Revolution* (New York, 1976), pp. 112, 122.
53 *C.S.P.D. 1644–5*, p. 203.
54 Ibid., p. 197.
55 Ibid., pp. 199–200.
56 Ibid., p. 205.
57 Ibid.
58 Robert Bell, ed., *Memorials of the Civil War: Comprising the Correspondence of the Fairfax Family*, 2 vols. (London, 1849), I, 143.
59 See the enlarged assessments for the Eastern Association, C. H. Firth and F. Rait, eds., *Acts and Ordinances of the Interregnum*, 3 vols. (London, 1911), I, 368; and the London and Middlesex assessment, I, 398–9. These are weekly assessments, to be multiplied by four to arrive at the New Model rates that appear in I, 614–15.
60 *C.S.P.D. 1644–5*, p. 205.
61 Whitacre, B.L. Add. Mss. 31,116, fol. 185. This claim was at best ambiguous. By trimming manpower and eliminating the overlapping command structure the New Model would theoretically save £15,574 per month. But by narrowing its base of operation Parlia-

ment was forced to enlarge the northern and western forces. See Kishlansky, p. 80.

62 *C.J.*, 4, 16, 18.

63 *C.J.*, 4, 26.

64 Whitacre, B.L. Add. Mss. 31,116, fol. 188.

65 Ibid.

66 *C.J.*, 4, 26.

67 Ibid.

68 *Mercurius Aulicus*, January 12, 1645.

69 J. H. Hexter, "The Rise of the Independent Party," (Ph.D. diss., Harvard University, 1936), p. 340. In explaining the passage of the self-denying ordinance Hexter postulated: "To bamboozle a considerable faction is a real feat; Vane bamboozled a nation."

70 *L.J.*, 7, 159, 165, 166.

71 *L.J.*, 7, 165.

72 *L.J.*, 7, 169; 175.

73 *L.J.*, 7, 192.

74 *C.J.*, 4, 42–3; Whitacre, B.L. Mss. 31,116, fol. 191.

75 Whitacre, B.L. Add. Mss. 31,116, fol. 191; *C.J.*, 4, 44; Luke, pp. 438–9. The compromise on soldiers taking the covenant presented a humorous dilemma. Because many soldiers were pressed, they could escape service by refusing the covenant. The two Houses closed this loophole by not appointing a specific time for common soldiers to take the covenant. *L.J.*, 7, 192 (incorrectly paginated, follows p. 189).

76 Luke, p. 140.

77 *L.J.*, 7, 204–6.

78 *C.J.*, 4, 54. Sir Thomas Fairfax, *A Short Memorial*, in F. Maseres, ed., *Select Tracts Relating to the Civil Wars in England*, 2 vols. (London, 1815), II, 442.

79 Bell, *Fairfax Correspondence*, I, 161; H.L.R.O. Nalson Mss. (photocopy), vol. 8, fol. 133.

80 *C.J.*, 4, 63.

81 *C.J.*, 4, 42.

82 *C.J.*, 4, 51.

83 Ibid.

84 Common Council Journal, vol. 40, fol. 125; *C.J.*, 4, 71.

85 The Commons debates were on February 28, March 1, and March 3. None of these sessions lasted past 2 o'clock in the afternoon: D'Ewes, B.L. Harl. Mss. 166, fols. 180–1.

86 D'Ewes, B.L. Harl. Mss. 166, fol. 180.

87 Ibid., fols. 180–1; Whitacre, B.L. Add. Mss. 31,116, fol. 196.

88 *C.J.*, 4, 64.

89 H.L.R.O. Nalson Mss. (photocopy), vol. 8, fol. 133. This list, which Essex emended, has not survived, although the changes made in the Lords' list to his regiments are probably identical to his own.

90 The list appears in H.L.R.O. Main Papers, February–March 1645, fols. 145–7. Pickering was to be replaced by Lord Robartes's Lieutenant Colonel, William Hunter; Montague by Colonel William Herbert; Rainsborough by Colonel William Ogleby; and Okey by Colonel Mill.

91 These occurred in the regiments of Aldriche, Fortescue, and Ingoldsby. All are marked in this manner on the list, and other replacements, not marked, may have followed this principle as well.

92 Bethell and Packer may also have been excluded on religious grounds. See Clive Holmes, *The Eastern Association in the English Civil War* (London, 1974), pp. 201–2.

93 H.L.R.O. Main Papers, February–March 1645, fol. 147; S.P. 28/29.

94 *C.S.P.D. 1644–5*, p. 155.

95 Much of the hard evidence for such a balancing comes in 1647 when the Army split over the Irish venture and obedience to parliamentary commands. See Chapter 7. One cannot argue that because a man exhibited presbyterian leanings in 1647 that he had held them as early as 1645. But the list of New Model colonels who were presbyterians in 1647 is impressive: Butler, Graves, Fortescue, Harley, Pye, Rossiter, Sheffield, and perhaps even Fairfax and Skippon.

96 After the disaster at Lostwithiel Essex's infantry was rearmed and reclothed. It and Manchester's horse were supplied in February 1645. *C.J.*, 4, 42.

97 H.L.R.O. Main Papers, February–March 1645, fol. 145.

98 *C.J.*, 4, 76; D'Ewes, B.L. Harl. Mss. 166, fol. 183.

99 *C.J.*, 4, 75, 76. This was highly unusual, as Whitelocke noted: "a course not formerly used and of too much haste for a parliamentary way." Whitelocke, *Memorials*, I, 410; D'Ewes, B.L. Harl. Mss. 166, fol. 183.

100 Whitacre, B.L. Add. Mss. 31,116, fol. 198; *C.J.*, 4, 77; *L.J.*, 7, 276.

101 *L.J.*, 7, 277.

102 "It was alleged that there was a general order that 'no proxy should be made use of'; of which question was made." *L.J.*, 7, 277. Dissents were entered by the Earls of Essex, Manchester, Denbigh, Bolingbroke, Rutland, and Stamford and Lords Bruce, Maynard, Berkeley, and Grey of Warke.

103 The full clause was: "Preserving the safety of His Majesty's person, in the preservation and defense of the true Protestant religion,

the defense of the Parliament, and the conservation of this realm and the subjects thereof in peace, from all unlawful violence, oppression, and force, howsoever countenanced by any pretended commission or authority from His Majesty, or otherwise."

104 *L.J.*, 7, 288. The Lords who had favored the "new modeling" were the Earls of Salisbury, Nottingham, and Pembroke, Viscount Say and Sele, and Lords North and Wharton. Those opposed were the Earls of Manchester, Denbigh, and Stamford and Lords Grey and Willoughby.

105 *C.J.*, 4, 93.

106 *L.J.*, 7, 292.

107 *L.J.*, 7, 293.

108 The three absentees were the Earl of Suffolk and Lords Grey and Berkeley. D'Ewes, B.L. Harl. Mss. 166, fol. 197.

109 *L.J.*, 7, 299–300.

110 *L.J.*, 7, 302.

111 It seems likely that the Scottish officers resigned en masse. On March 3 the Scottish Commissioners had requested that the Lords exercise careful control over the officers of the New Model, suggesting that experienced commanders not be discharged and young ones not included. In the end the Lords had no control over the list and this may have caused the Scots to withdraw, especially because many of the Lords' additions were Scotsmen. *L.J.* 7, 261. On April 16 the Scottish Commissioners submitted a petition for the payment of the arrears of all four of the colonels who had not taken their commands, as well as for a number of other officers. Bodl. Tanner Mss., vol. 60, fol. 03. On that same day Sir William Waller informed the House of Commons that Holborn and Middleton had resigned, making clear that the Commissioners knew of the resignations beforehand and may have ordered them. D'Ewes, B.L. Harl. Mss. 166, fol. 201. The author of *Vindiciae Veritatis* stressed that "it is true there were some able and experienced commanders of the Scots who did very good service and if they would have stayed and kept their commands it was that which was desired." E. 811 (2), p. 108.

112 Bodl. Tanner Mss., vol. 60, fols. 33–4. Aldriche was a religious presbyterian. H.L.R.O. Main Papers, May 1647.

113 B.M. Sloane Mss. 1519, fol. 112.

114 *C.J.*, 4, 136.

115 In 1647 Harley and Butler would prove strong supporters of Holles's party, whereas Waller and Hammond would remain with the Army.

116 Whitelocke, *Memorials*, I, 418; Luke, p. 244.
117 Luke, p. 244; Rushworth, VI, 17; Bodl. Tanner Mss., vol. 60, fol. 73.
118 E. 273 (3), *London Post*, no. 27, March 11, 1645.

CHAPTER 3. THE TRIUMPH OF THE NEW MODEL ARMY

 1 *C.S.P.D. 1645–7*, p. 155.
 2 Luke, p. 207.
 3 Bodl. Tanner Mss., vol. 60, fol. 214.
 4 E. 292 (3), *Moderate Intelligencer*, no. 18, June 26–July 3, 1645.
 5 Whitacre, B.L. Add. Mss. 31,116, fol. 215; D'Ewes, B.L. Harl. Mss. 166, fol. 218.
 6 *C.S.P.D. 1644–5*, p. 441.
 7 *L.J.*, 7, 391.
 8 Ibid.
 9 *C.J.*, 4, 132; *L.J.*, 7, 357; Whitacre, B.L. Add. Mss. 31,116, fol. 208.
10 Patricia Crawford, "The Savile Affair" *English Historical Review* 90 (January, 1975), 76–93. The strategy was devised to overcome the Scots' reluctance to march south rather than being "an attempt to settle the war before the Scots had the chance to march south" (p. 79).
11 *C.S.P.D. 1644–5*, p. 488; D'Ewes, B.L. Harl. Mss. 166, fol. 210; Whitacre, B.L. Add. Mss. 31,116, fol. 210. Stapleton's role in presenting the plan is of central importance.
12 Whitacre, B.L. Add. Mss. 31,116, fol. 211.
13 Ibid., fols. 211–12; D'Ewes, B.L. Harl. Mss. 166, fol. 214. Massey's appointment was planned prior to the Oxford siege but it was compatible with the new strategy. *C.S.P.D. 1644–5*, p. 459.
   English Civil War (New York, 1961), pp. 111–12.
15 D'Ewes, B.L. Harl. Mss. 166, fol. 215.
14 For an account of the siege see Austin Woolrych, *Battles of the*
16 Baillie, II, 268. Baillie's continued lamentations over the inability of the Scottish Army to contribute to the war effort makes clear that the Estates in Edinburgh, rather than the Commissioners in London, were directing military affairs.
17 Whitacre, B.L. Add. Mss. 31,116, fol. 214. For the details of Cranford's accusation see Valerie Pearl, "London Puritans and Scotch Fifth Columnists: A Mid-Seventeenth Century Phenomenon," in A. E. J. Hollaender and W. Kellaway, eds., *Studies in London History* (London, 1969).
18 On June 4 Miles Corbett was accused of having advance knowledge of a design to betray Leicester, although the allegations were

not subsequently substantiated. D'Ewes, B.L. Harl. Mss. 166, fols. 214–15.

19 Whitacre, B.L. Add. Mss. 31,116, fols. 214–15; D'Ewes, B.L. Harl. Mss. 166, fol. 218; C.J., 4, 172.

20 D'Ewes claimed that Cranford received bail "because he is a strong Presbyterian and many in the House regard the accusation as a plot of the Independents against him." D'Ewes, B.L. Harl. Mss. 166, fol. 218.

21 Whitacre, B.L. Add. Mss. 31,116, fol. 214; D'Ewes, B.L. Harl. Mss. 166, fol. 218; C.J., 4, 172.

22 Pearl, pp. 324ff.

23 Savile communicated only with Say and Lady Temple. Vane and St. John were informed of the progress of the negotiations by Say. B.L. Add. Mss. 32.093, fol. 211.

24 Crawford, p. 79.

25 The meeting at Essex House has been related only by Whitelocke. He narrates that he and John Maynard were called there and in the presence of the Scottish Commissioners, the Earl of Essex, Holles, Stapleton, and some others, told of a plan to impeach Cromwell as an incendiary. Whitelocke and Maynard were then asked for the English legal definition of "incendiary." They gave it and pointed out that it differed from the Scots' use of the term. From their answer it was concluded that Cromwell could not be so charged. This incident is generally thought to imply that an alliance had already been made between the Scots and the "presbyterians." A more plausible explanation, however, is that Whitelocke and Maynard were called in not to join the plot, but to demonstrate that impartial legal opinion would oppose it. Essex and Holles would certainly have known this and must have staged the charade to dissuade the Scots from acting unilaterally. It is unlikely, as L. Kaplan asserts that the Scots restrained Holles and Stapleton; *Politics and Religion During the English Revolution* (New York, 1976), p. 85. Whitelocke, *Memorials*, I, 343–8.

26 Crawford, pp. 83–4.

27 This committee was appointed on July 4. It had twenty-seven members, including members of both factions. Whitacre, B.L. Add. Mss. 31,116, fol. 221.

28 Ibid., fols. 218, 222; C.J., 4, 195.

29 Baillie, II, 487–92. The authenticity of these letters remains in doubt.

30 C.J., 4, 214.

31 D'Ewes, B.L. Harl. Mss. 166, fol. 243.

32 Whitelocke's Annals, B.L. Add. Mss. 37,343, fol. 397.
33 Ibid.
34 Ibid., fol. 405.
35 Ibid., fol. 398.
36 Ibid., fol. 395.
37 Ibid., fols. 398–9.
38 The decision to lay the matter aside was not a decision to settle it in favor of Holles and Whitelocke. (Crawford, p. 88.) Motions to exonerate or convict the two were defeated and both Whitacre and D'Ewes recorded that the decision was to table the business. Yonge, who suggests an outcome more favorable to Holles and Whitelocke, left the House in the early afternoon (as did D'Ewes, who returned to hear the conclusion) and missed most of the debate. He obviously heard its resolution from a supporter of the two. Whitacre, B.L. Add. Mss. 31,116, fol. 222; D'Ewes, B.L. Harl. Mss. 166, fol. 243; Yonge, B.L. Add. Mss. 18,780, fol. 82r.
39 This bizarre incident, to which Stamford offered little defense, was was first brought before the House of Commons in May. Whitacre, B.L. Add. Mss. 31,116, fols. 211–12.
40 Cranford's punishment was a fine of £2,000, £500 to each of the M.P.s he had charged. Whitacre, B.L. Add. Mss. 31,116, fol. 221.
41 Holles received leave to go to the country for two months on July 29. D'Ewes, B.L. Harl. Mss. 166, fol. 249. Whitelocke received leave on August 5. D'Ewes, B.L. Harl. Mss. 166, fol. 250.
42 Joshua Sprigge, *Anglia Rediviva* (London, 1647), p. 122. Although these divisions of the Army were the most important ones, occasionally other regiments or brigades were detached for separate service. For example, in December 1645 Colonel Thomas Rainsborough's infantry regiment was sent to Abingdon (*C.S.P.D. 1645–7*, p. 263). After the capture of Bristol Major General Skippon's regiment was left there under the command of Colonel John Birch, who was an itinerant parliamentary officer. J. and T. W. Webb, eds., *Military Memoir of Colonel John Birch* (London, Camden Society, 1873), p. 22.
43 *C.S.P.D. 1644–5*, pp. 578, 581.
44 Lists of council members appear in *L.J.* 7, 421, and Rushworth, VI, 68.
45 Luke, p. 317; *L.J.*, 7, 421.
46 The single exception was the letter the Council of War sent to the Scottish Army after Montrose's victory at Kilsyth. Rushworth, VI, 68; Sprigge, p. 96.
47 The pay of cavalry regiments by troop enables us to identify changes in the officer corps with precision. As the infantry was

paid by regiment, changes among their officers are more difficult to establish. Two lists of Army officers survive for the period between its creation and the end of the war in 1646. H.L.R.O. Main Papers, January 1645, and Sprigge, *Anglia Rediviva*. This latter list is reprinted by E. Peacock in *Army Lists of Roundheads and Cavaliers* (London, 1863). Neither list is reliable: both contain errors and confuse officers with the same or similar names. Generally better, but not entirely accurate, is C. H. Firth and G. Davies, *Regimental History of Cromwell's Army*, 2 vols. (Oxford, 1940). The best source for identifying army officers is the administrative volumes in S.P. 28.

48 For Whalley's regiment see B.L. Harl. Mss. 427.

49 They were Captains Samuel Barry, Thomas Bush, William Guilliams, John Hoskins, Walter Perry, and Captain Selby.

50 B.L. Harl. Mss. 427; Captains William Bough and William Dendy.

51 Pickering died at Antre and Lloyd at Taunton.

52 Herbert was originally selected by the House of Lords as an alternative to Montague. His appointment as a replacement is a sure indication that the "Independents" were not in control of Army selection at Westminster.

53 Whitacre, B.L. Add. Mss. 31,116, fol. 248; Weldon later returned to Kent, where he remained active throughout the war. See Alan Everitt, *The Community of Kent and the Great Rebellion, 1640–60* (London, 1966).

54 An indication of Montague's parliamentary participation was that he took the covenant at the first possible opportunity after his election, on October 29, 1645. *C.J.*, 4, 326.

55 E. 25 (18), *Parliamentary Scout*, no. 83, January 10–17, 1645.

56 Lieutenant colonels Ralph Cottesworth, Severinus Durfey, John Francis, Oliver Ingoldsby, and Jeffrey Richbell; Major John Done.

57 For Bland see S.P. 28/44/215.

58 B.L. Harl. Mss. 427. Although Firth contended that vacancies in the Army were usually filled by merit rather than strict seniority, his examples are mostly drawn from the 1650s. C. H. Firth, *Cromwell's Army* (London, 1921), p. 49.

59 B.L. Add. Mss. 18,976, fol. 205. Other examples of efforts by prominent M.P.s to gain places in the Army for friends or relations are B.L. Sloane Mss. 1,519 fols. 93, 110; B.L. Loan 29/27, Sir Robert Harley to Fairfax and Cromwell.

60 Sprigge, p. 19.

61 *C.J.*, 4, 415. Of the colonels and majors in the New Model, Philip Twisleton, Nathaniel Rich, Charles Fleetwood, Edward Pickering, Thomas Harrison, and Matthew Tomlinson were listed in 1642 as

"Gentlemen of the Lifeguard who had money to buy horses, saddles and scarfs, at the cost of £18." B.L. Add. Mss. 25,460.

62 E. 309 (11), *Moderate Intelligencer*, no. 37, November 6–13, 1645.

63 *C.S.P.D. 1645–7*, pp. 351; *C.S.P.D. 1644–5*, p. 464.

64 Whitelocke, *Memorials*, I, 428.

65 Luke, p. 284.

66 Ibid., p. 311.

67 E. 309 (25), *Moderate Intelligencer*, no. 38, November 13–20, 1645.

68 The indemnity problem had received attention before it became an issue in 1647. In December 1645 the House of Lords ordered "that it be reported to both Houses to declare their pleasure concerning such officers serving the Parliament as have executed the commands of their superior officers, in pressing of carriages, taking horses or other services for the Army against whom actions are now brought." *L.J.*, 8, 46.

69 Firth, *Cromwell's Army*, pp. 276–310.

70 E. 327 (4), *Continuation of Special and Remarkable Passages*, no. 24, February 27–March 6, 1646.

71 E. 313 (21), *Moderate Intelligencer*, no. 42, December 18–25, 1645.

72 Baillie, II, 265.

73 B.L. Add. Mss. 19,398, fols. 162–3, 177, 185, 198. See also Godfrey Davies, "Documents Illustrating the First Civil War," *Journal of Modern History* 3, (1931), 64–71.

74 Bodl. Carte Mss., vol. 95, fols. 88–93. These examples come from 1643.

75 Among other paradoxes relating to the assessment, Robert Scawen's report to the Commons in December 1645 pinpointed two specific categories of persons behind in their assessments: M.P.s and New Model officers. The importance of either group may have been largely symbolic but the insistence that officers pay their assessments suggests that their financial resources may have been better than many have supposed. Whitacre, B.L. Add. Mss. 31,116, fol. 250.

76 Sprigge, p. 127.

77 *H.M.C. Portland*, I, 267.

78 Both Gardiner, *Great Civil War*, III, 39–43, and I. Gentles, "The Arrears of Pay of the Parliamentary Army at the End of the First Civil War," *Bulletin of the Institute of Historical Research* 48 (1975), 52–63, have relied on aggregate figures and have assumed that the Army would have received full pay.

79 The difficulties in analyzing the pay warrants have been discussed in my dissertation, pp. 171–6. Two regiments have been excluded

from this analysis, Fairfax's and Fortescue's. See M. A. Kishlansky, "The Emergence of Radical Politics in the English Revolution" (Ph.D. diss., Brown University, 1977), p. 172.

80 An adequate sample of these arrears claims can be found in S.P. 28/59/26, 28/57/309, 28/59/210, 28/48/248. Kishlansky, p. 173.

81 For the method employed in calculating regimental disbursements see Kishlansky, p. 174. An important correction to the cavalry figures given in Chart II, p. 175, can now be made. The regiments of Fairfax, Ireton, and Whalley were paid in December 1645, reducing their aggregate arrears by twenty-eight days and the length of time they went unpaid to twenty-eight days. S.P. 28/33/385, 424–438.

82 Alnwick Castle, Duke of Northumberland Mss. 51, fol. 2. Even after receiving no pay in September, some soldiers were less than indigent.

83 Thus when the Scottish officers petitioned for their arrears in 1645 they claimed to have lent money to their troops and were thus hard pressed to return to Scotland. Yonge, B.L. Add. Mss. 18,780, fol. 7.

84 Half pay for free quarter was deducted by an ordinance of December 24, 1647. S.P. 28/57/309. This can be seen in the arrears claims of various individual troopers like private Ralph Fidgeon of Captain Gardiner's troop in Colonel Butler's regiment. His total arrears amounted to £34 16s. and he received £17 8s. S.P. 28/57/694. This is best observed in the distinct categories "Arrears Submitted," "Arrears Received," B.L. Harl. Mss. 427.

85 See M. A. Kishlansky, "The Sale of Crown Lands and the Spirit of the Revolution," *Economic History Review*, 2nd ser., 29 (1976), 125–30.

86 Sprigge, p. 82.

87 E. 296 (31), *The Proceedings of the Army*, no. 7, August 8–15, 1645. Besides the protest over the insufficiency of the recruits there were also complaints that most of them were the prisoners taken at Naseby. E. 262 (44), *Perfect Occurrences*, no. 33, August 8–15, 1645.

88 Sir Thomas Fairfax, *A Short Memorial*, in F. Maseres, ed., *Select Tracts Relating to the Civil Wars in England*, 2 vols. (London, 1815), II, 443.

89 E. 301 (4), "Mr. Peters' Report from Bristol." *C.S.P.D. 1645–7*, p. 170; *C.J.*, 4, 267, 299.

90 *L.J.*, 7, 700.

91 *C.S.P.D. 1645–7*, p. 268; *C.J.*, 4, 369.

92 E. 320 (18), *Perfect Occurrences*, no. 6, January 30–February 6, 1646.

93 Bodl. Tanner Mss., vol. 60, fol. 214.
94 *H.M.C. Portland*, I, 242.
95 E. 295 (7), *Moderate Intelligencer*, no. 23, July 31–August 7, 1645.
96 See for example, E. 282 (10), *Moderate Intelligencer*, no. 10, May 1–8, 1645.
97 S.P. 28/140/pt. 7; B.L. Add. Mss. 19,398, fol. 161.
98 E. 304 (12), "A Copy of Lieutenant-General Cromwell's Letter in Taking Basing."
99 Sprigge, p. 326; Gardiner, *Great Civil War*, II, 312.
100 S.P. 28/38/400. Leo Solt, *Saints in Arms* (Stanford, 1959), p. 9, inexplicably claims Peter enlisted as an Army chaplain in 1644. R. P. Stearns clearly shows that he was occupied with other commissions at that time. The Strenuous Puritan (Urbana, Ill., 1954), p. 225ff.
101 E. 336 (1), *Weekly Intelligencer*, no. 147, April 28–May 5, 1646.
102 Ram's sermon to the troops before Newark on March 27, 1646, reveals no traces of radical religion. Among other things, Ram exhorted his audience that soldiers should be content with their wages. "That a soldier should be content with a little; food and raiment is enough." Robert Ram, "Sermon at Balderton" (1646), p. 20.
103 Solt, p. 9, n. 13. Solt seems uncertain about Erbury's New Model service. His pay warrants show that he served in Ingoldsby's regiment as a chaplain from August 17, 1646 to January 4, 1647. Thereafter he was chaplain in Lambert's regiment. S.P. 28/45/269. One other curious aspect of the "radical" chaplains Solt identifies is that they were all appointed not to the New Model, but to the old armies. Although he puts the best face on it, William Haller arrives at much the same conclusion. W. Haller, "The Word of God in the New Model Army," *Church History* 19 (1950), 17.
104 E. 372 (22), "A Just Apology for an Abused Army."
105 E. 286 (12), *True Informer*, no. 6, May 31, 1645; *C.J.*, 4, 139.
106 Richard Baxter's *Reliquiae*, M. Sylvester, ed. (London, 1696), is not a good guide to the Army's religious diversity, for Baxter's brief service was with Whalley's regiment.
107 E. 401 (24), "Vox Militaris."
108 Firth and Rait, I, 677.
109 *Mercurius Aulicus*, April 28, 1645.
110 Baillie, II, 504.
111 E. 401 (24), "Vox Militaris."
112 E. 266 (10), *Perfect Occurrences*, no. 45, October 24–31, 1645.
113 E. 262 (44), *Perfect Occurrences*, no. 33, August 8–15, 1645.

114 Rushworth, VI, 74.
115 Holles, *Memoirs of Denzil Lord Holles,* in Maseres, *Select Tracts,* I, 214–15.
116 B.L. Add. Mss. 21,506, letter 41; David Underdown, "Party Management in the Recruiter Elections 1645–48," *English Historical Review* 83 (April 1968), 245–6.
117 Underdown, 248. Underdown has not demonstrated New Model interference in elections, although it is clear from his research that the Army systematically intercepted correspondence (p. 255).

CHAPTER 4. THE ASSAULT ON PARLIAMENTARY POLITICS

1 Juxon, Dr. Williams' Library, Mss. 24.50, fol. 73.
2 The publication of Charles's captured correspondence, E. 292 (27), "The King's Cabinet Opened," and that of Digby taken at Sherborne, E. 329 (15), "The Lord George Digby's Cabinet," dissuaded many parliamentarians from entering into a new round of negotiations.
3 *C.J.,* 4, 513–14.
4 Common Council Journal, vol. 40, fols. 151–3; *C.J.,* 4, 348.
5 Perez Zagorin, *The Court and the Country* (New York, 1969), pp. 223–4ff; Valerie Pearl, *London and the Outbreak of the Puritan Revolution* (Oxford, 1960), p. 4. The distinction between official City petitions and petitions of groups of citizens is an important one.
6 Common Council Journal, vol. 40, fol. 131.
7 D'Ewes, B.L. Harl. Mss. 166, fol. 216.
8 *C.J.,* 4, 163.
9 Juxon, Dr. Williams' Library, Mss. 24.50, fol. 45.
10 *C.J.,* 4, 280.
11 E. 302 (19); in Thomason's hand.
12 *C.J.,* 4, 319; *L.J.,* 7, 660.
13 Whitacre, B.L. Add. Mss. 31,116, fol. 240.
14 Common Council Journal, vol. 40, fol. 148. The objections were: (1) the parties to choose the elders were not named; (2) the number of elders was not expressed; (3) the qualifications of the elders were not determined; (4) their powers not established; and (5) the duration of their appointments not set.
15 Common Council Journal, vol. 40, fol. 148.
16 Ibid., fol. 150.
17 *C.J.,* 4, 348.
18 Ibid., Whitacre, B.L. Add. Mss. 31,116, fol. 244.

19 Juxon, Dr. Williams' Library, Mss. 24.50, fol. 54.
20 Ibid., fol. 56; E. 314 (3), *Mercurius Civicus*, no. 136, December 24– January 1, 1645/46.
21 Common Council Journal, vol. 40, fol. 160; Jukon, Dr. Williams' Library, Mss. 24.50, fol. 56.
22 E. 327 (5), "Religious Covenanting Directed."
23 Common Council Journal, vol. 40, fol. 161; E. 314 (21), *Moderate Intelligencer*, no. 42, December 18–25, 1645.
24 *C.J.*, 4, 407.
25 Ibid.
26 *L.J.*, 8, 104.
27 *L.J.*, 8, 105.
28 *C.J.*, 4, 407.
29 The letter was reported to the Commons by Francis Allen, who was both an M.P. and a common councillor. For the controversy over his report see M. A. Kishlansky, "The Emergence of Radical Politics in the English Revolution" (Ph.D. diss., Brown University, 1977), pp. 245–6.
30 Parliament's establishment of the lay Commissioners is detailed in *O.P.H.*, 14, 285–6.
31 Common Council Journal, vol. 40, fol. 174.
32 Juxon, Dr. Williams' Library, Mss. 24.50, fols. 65–6.
33 *L.J.*, 7, 714; 8, 104.
34 Juxon, Dr. Williams' Library, Mss. 24.50, fol. 66. As all notice of this petition had been expunged from the journals of both Houses and, with the exception of the original petition from the citizens, from the Common Council Journal as well, Juxon's account is the only source for details of the petition, its reception by the two Houses, and the subsequent meeting at the Common Council.
35 Juxon, Dr. Williams' Library, Mss. 24.50, fol. 66.
36 Ibid.
37 Ibid.
38 Ibid.
39 Ibid.
40 Ibid.
41 Ibid., fol. 67.
42 Ibid.
43 Bodl. Tanner Mss. vol. 60, fol. 554, entitled "Heads of a speech to be given at Common Council March 14," is the only other reference to the meeting held in the City on March 16. The heads were more sharply focused toward reasserting parliamentary privileges but the decision about what statements were to be stressed was explicitly left to those appointed to manage the conference.

44 Common Council Journal, vol. 40, fol. 176.
45 Juxon, Dr. Williams' Library, Mss. 24.50, fol. 71. "The City also has taken some courage, and are again in the way to remonstrate all their grievances, not only for the matter of the church, but of the state." Baillie, II, 367–8.
46 Juxon, Dr. Williams' Library, Mss. 24.50, fol. 71.
47 Ibid., fol. 78.
48 Ibid.
49 Ibid.
50 Ibid.
51 Ibid., fol. 79.
52 *C.J.*, 4, 555.
53 Common Council Journal, vol. 40, fols. 179–80.
54 Whitacre, B.L. Add. Mss. 31,116, fol. 271.
55 *C.J.*, 4, 555–6.
56 *L.J.*, 8, 332–34.
57 *L.J.*, 8, 331.
58 *L.J.*, 8, 332. The protesters were the Earls of Northumberland, Pembroke, Kent, Salisbury, and Denbigh, Viscount Say and Sele, and Lords Wharton, Grey, Howard, and Montague.
59 *L.J.*, 8, 334.
60 Juxon, Dr. Williams' Library, Mss. 24.50, fol. 108.
61 Bodl. Tanner Mss., vol. 60, fol. 554.
62 Juxon, Dr. Williams' Library, Mss. 24.50, fol. 78; E. 509 (5), *Perfect Diurnal*, no. 147, May 18–25, 1646.
63 Juxon, Dr. Williams' Library, Mss. 24.50, fol. 78.
64 Ibid., fol. 79.
65 E. 339 (12), "The Humble Acknowledgement and Petition of Divers Inhabitants of London." See also E. 339 (14), *Weekly Account*, no. 23, May 27–June 3, 1646.
66 E. 340 (5), "The Interest of England Maintained."
67 E. 341 (5), "A Glass for Weak-Eyed Citizens."
68 E. 339 (12), "Humble Acknowledgement"; Common Council Journal, vol. 40, fol. 183.
69 E. 343 (11), "A Remonstrance of Many Thousand Citizens," reprinted in D. M. Wolfe, *Leveller Manifestoes of the Puritan Revolution* (New York, 1967).
70 Wolfe, *Leveller Manifestoes*, pp. 120–1.
71 E. 309 (11), *Moderate Intelligencer*, no. 37, November 6–13, 1645.
72 Wallace Notestein, "The Establishment of the Committee of Both Kingdoms," *American Historical Review* 17 (1912), 477–95.
73 Baillie, II, 268.
74 Ibid., II, 343.

75 Ibid.
76 *L.J.*, 7, 442–3.
77 *L.J.*, 8, 36; 45.
78 *O.P.H.*, 14, 172.
79 *L.J.*, 8, 188.
80 A complete list of Scottish objections to the propositions is in Bodl. Tanner Mss., vol. 60, fols. 562–5.
81 Whitacre, B.L. Add. Mss. 31,116, fol. 273.
82 *O.P.H.*, 14, 260.
83 Baillie, II, 336.
84 E. 294 (14), Thomas Coleman, "Hopes Deferred and Dashed."
85 E. 294 (12), Robert Baillie, "Errors and Induration."
86 E. 317 (5), Robert Baillie, *A Dissuasive from the Errors of the Time.*
87 Baillie, II, 342.
88 Ibid., II, 365, 342.
89 Ibid., II, 352.
90 Juxon, Dr. Williams' Library, Mss. 24.50, fol. 47. See also Kishlansky, pp. 198–200.
91 Buchanan's connection with the Scottish representatives is elucidated in one of Baillie's letters to Scotland. "Mr. Buchanan is gone to a place safe enough: if he comes among you, he is a man worthy of great honor for many good services." Baillie, II, 367. In October 1645 Buchanan had written a preface to the publication of several papers from the Scottish Commissioners. E. 305 (1).
92 David Buchanan, "A Short and True Relation" (1645).
93 E. 314 (15), David Buchanan, "An Explanation of Some Truths"; E. 1.179 (5), "Truth Its Manifest."
94 E. 314 (15), "An Explanation of Some Truths," p. 37.
95 E. 811 (2), "Vindiciae Veritatis," p. 22.
96 Baillie, II, 327.
97 Ibid., II, 361.
98 Ibid., II, 337.
99 Ibid., II, 352.
100 H. W. Meikle, ed., *Correspondence of the Scots Commissioners in London* (Edinburgh, 1917), p. 157.
101 Baillie, II, 352–3.
102 Ibid., II, 358.
103 Ibid., II, 358–9.
104 Ibid., II, 359.
105 E. 333 (1), "Some Papers of the Commissioners of Scotland."
106 *O.P.H.*, 14, 321.
107 *C.J.*, 4, 507.

108 *C.J.*, 4, 510.
109 Baillie, II, 367.
110 Meikle, p. 174.
111 *C.J.*, 4, 513.
112 *C.J.*, 4, 513–14.
113 *C.J.*, 4, 513.
114 Ibid.

CHAPTER 5. THE COLLAPSE OF PARLIAMENTARY POLITICS

1 E. 399 (12), "The Humble Acknowledgement and Petition of Divers Inhabitants of London."
2 Sir William Waller, *Vindication of the Character and Conduct of Sir William Waller* (London, 1793), p. 7.
3 Whitacre, B.L. Add. Mss. 31,116, fol. 277.
4 Henry Cary, ed., *Memorials of the Great Civil War 1642–52*, 2 vols. (London, 1842), I, 30.
5 *L.J.*, 8, 460.
6 *C.J.*, 4, 644. This issue was sufficiently controversial to cause a close division.
   Yea 130 Holles and Earle
   No   102 Haselrig and Evelyn (Wilts.)
7 *C.J.*, 4, 644.
8 Whitacre, B.L. Add. Mss. 31,116, fol. 281; M. Stieg, ed., *The Diary of John Harington M.P. 1646–53* (Old Woking, Surrey, Somerset Record Society, 74, 1977), p. 32.
9 Whitacre, B.L. Add. Mss. 31,116, fol. 281; *C.J.*, 4, 649, 650.
10 *C.J.*, 4, 659.
   Yea 140 Holles and Stapleton
   No   101 Haselrig and Evelyn (Wilts.)
11 Harington, p. 34.
12 *C.J.*, 4, 663.
   No   112 Holles and Sir William Lewes
   Yea 102 Haselrig and Evelyn (Wilts.)
13 *C.J.*, 4, 599.
14 D'Ewes, B.L. Harl. Mss. 166, fols. 209, 255.
15 *L.J.*, 8, 442.
16 *C.J.*, 4, 629.
17 Bodl. Tanner Mss., vol. 59, fols. 547–9. The exact breakdown of payments on sequestered estates was: September–December 1644, £17,640; January–December 1645, £10,600; January–September 1646, £44,659.
18 D'Ewes, B.L. Harl. Mss. 166, fol. 177.

19 C.J., 4, 620; 625; 623; L.J., 8, 440; 454.
20 Juxon astutely added, "but wherein God overrules and has unexpectedly ruined them so as never to rise again. And by this same way Henry VIII took to destroy monasteries by selling them to persons of all sorts and so to interest the whole Kingdom in the business." Juxon, Dr. Williams' Library, Mss. 24.50, fol. 88.
21 Common Council Journal, vol. 40, fol. 191.
22 Whitacre, B.L. Add. Mss. 31,116, fol. 283. Besides the sale of choice church estates the City financiers had obtained another goal they had long sought: retroactive interest for loans made in the early years of the war. They proposed a scheme in which investors could double an original loan they had made and receive interest at 8 percent for the entire sum. Although it was protested that "those who had parted with all for Parliament should be neglected and others who lent of their superfluity should be largely paid," this was another concession to which Holles had agreed in order to ensure City finance. Harington, p. 35.
23 C.J., 4, 665.
Yea   105   Haselrig and Evelyn (Wilts.)
No   100   Holles and Stapleton
As the ordinance for the sale of delinquents' estates could not be passed through the Lords, the ordinance for the City loan continued to use the excise and the bishops' lands as security. In the event, the bishops' lands yielded £200,000 in somewhat less than a month.
24 L.J., 8, 474.
25 The ordinance for the Associations to be continued and granted half their excise had languished in the Upper House since July. L.J., 8, 447. On September 3 the Lords agreed to the ordinance with the alteration that the Lord-Lieutenants would act in place of the county committees.
26 After a month's delay on the Commons' order to continue the treasurers at war for six months the Lords finally passed the bill on September 17, extended the treasurers for only two weeks. L.J., 8, 493.
27 L.J., 8, 543.
28 On September 11 the Lords "after long debate" amended the ordinance so that the Common Council could decide on receipts from either the excise or the bishops' lands. In this way they hoped to persuade the City not to press for the total sale of the episcopal estates. When the Commons refused their amendment the Lords quickly gave in. L.J., 8, 486, 489–90.
29 L.J., 8, 514, 515.

30 The ordinance was finally endorsed on November 17. C. H. Firth
and F. Rait, eds., *Acts and Ordinances of the Interregnum*, 3 vols.
(London, 1911), I, 887–904.
31 *C.J.*, 4, 632. The passions aroused by this debate were manifested
in two separate charges. John Gurdon claimed that the attempt to
divide the New Model was instigated by the Scots, a charge that
infuriated Holles. In return, Holles accused the New Model of
having cashiered presbyterian officers, a claim that Cromwell countered with the facts. Harington, p. 30.
32 Harington, p. 30; Whitacre, B.L. Add. Mss. 31,116, fol. 279.
33 C. H. Firth, ed., *The Memoirs of Edmund Ludlow*, 2 vols. (Oxford, 1894), I, 142.
34 *C.J.*, 4, 625, 634, 640.
35 *C.J.*, 4, 630; E. 511 (29), *Perfect Diurnal*, no. 158, August 3–10.
36 Bodl. Tanner Mss., vol. 59, fol. 566; E. 513 (20), *Perfect Diurnal*,
no. 169, October 19–26, 1646; Bodl. Rawlinson Mss., A. 258, fol.
35.
37 B.L. Loan 29/122/Misc. 24. The conditions outlined by Massey's
officers were strikingly similar to those that the New Model would
propose when Irish service was offered to them. See Chapter 7.
38 E. 337 (18), *Moderate Intelligencer*, no. 62, May 7–14, 1646. Although this comment was offered earlier in a different context, the
Intelligencer echoed these sentiments in September when the fate
of the armies became a focus of concern. "... employ them for
recovering our own and friends abroad, and for the same monies
they are like to cost for departure or discharge." E. 353 (18),
Moderate Intelligencer, no. 79, September 3–10, 1646.
39 *C.J.*, 4, 618; 623; 628; *L.J.*, 8, 454; 456–7; 478.
40 *C.J.*, 4, 687; Whitacre, B.L. Add. Mss. 31,116, fol. 285. That this
vote again reflected anti-Scottish feeling is revealed by Harington's
single comment on the debate: "The Scots will not depart except
our Army stand firm; terrible clouds hang over us and will fall on
us." Harington, p. 42.
41 *C.J.*, 4, 713.
Yea 57 Evelyn (Wilts.) and Livesay
No   56 Harley and Cromwell
42 *L.J.*, 8, 425.
43 *L.J.*, 8, 460.
44 *L.J.*, 8, 530–1. The Earl of Lincoln and Lord Willoughby drafted
this letter and the Earls of Manchester, Denbigh, Kent, and Nottingham and Lord Wharton entered dissents against it.
45 *C.J.*, 4, 697.
46 Ibid. See Fairfax's letter, *L.J.*, 8, 544.

47 *L.J.*, 8, 563.
48 *L.J.*, 8, 548. For the identity of the anti-innovatory peers and their activities see Chapter 6, p. 146–7.
49 *C.J.*, 4, 672.
50 Ibid. This order, however, countermanded the agreement with the Scots that they would be consulted as well.
51 *C.J.*, 4, 672–3.
52 *L.J.*, 8, 499–500. The afternoon session began at four o'clock and those absent from the morning debate were the Earls of Rutland and Middlesex and Lords North and Howard. This is a significant example of the separate aims of Holles's party and the anti-innovatory Lords. See Chapter 6.
53 *C.J.*, 4, 622.
54 *C.J.*, 4, 673.
55 *C.J.*, 4, 690.
56 *C.J.*, 4, 680; Whitacre, B.L. Add. Mss. 31,116, fol. 285. The practical problems of appointing new Commissioners nullified the intentention of the Houses to dispose of the seal. Lords and Commons disputed both the number of commissioners and the merits of the individuals nominated until the commission granted to the former Commissioners lapsed. The seal was then placed in the hands of the Speakers, where it remained for the rest of the year.
57 Whitacre, B.L. Add. Mss. 31,116, fol. 289.
58 On May 26 the Upper House had its highest attendance of the year and on August 13 its lowest. *L.J.*, 8, 331, 463.
59 The Earl of Manchester, "temporary speaker" since 1645, received his most recent quarterly continuation on July 22. *L.J.*, 8, 437.
60 *H.M.C.*, vol. 3, 4th report, part I, Denbigh Mss., p. 268.
61 *L.J.*, 8, 405. The conflict began with the publication of "The Just Man in Bonds," E. 342 (2).
62 *L.J.*, 8, 432.
63 For Lilburne's own account see E. 341 (12), "The Freeman's Freedom Vindicated."
64 *L.J.*, 8, 432. The fine was £2,000 and the prison sentence, finally rendered in September, was seven years. *L.J.*, 8, 494.
65 *L.J.*, 8, 427; 669 f. 10 (67).
66 E. 346 (8). The pamphlet was examined in the Upper House on August 4. *L.J.*, 8, 451.
67 *L.J.*, 8, 457.
68 E. 353 (17); *L.J.*, 8, 491.
69 See Chapter 6.
70 *L.J.*, 8, 405.
71 *L.J.*, 8, 442; 447.

72 *L.J.*, 8, 442.

73 *L.J.*, 8, 457.

74 *L.J.*, 8, 467.

75 *L.J.*, 8, 443.

76 *C.J.*, 4, 620; 682.

77 *L.J.*, 8, 481.

78 *L.J.*, 8, 481.

79 *L.J.*, 8, 485.

80 *C.J.*, 4, 625, 604, 617.

81 *L.J.*, 8, 416, 425; *C.J.*, 4, 598.

82 *C.J.*, 4, 604.

83 *C.J.*, 4, 621.

84 *C.J.*, 4, 671; Harington, p. 37.

85 *C.J.*, 4, 685; Harington, p. 41.

86 Whitacre, B.L. Add. Mss. 31,116, fol. 285; *C.J.*, 4, 686.

87 *C.J.*, 4, 697.

88 *L.J.*, 8, 485.

89 *C.J.*, 4, 665.

90 *C.J.*, 4, 665.

    Yea 82 Trevor and Stapleton

    No   64 Wentworth and Cromwell

91 *C.J.*, 4, 666–7.

92 *C.J.*, 4, 666–7; *L.J.*, 8, 493.

93 *L.J.*, 8, 489, 501.

94 *L.J.*, 8, 542; Harington, p. 46.

95 E. 353 (21), "A Remonstrance of the Kirk of Scotland."

96 E. 360 (12), "Some Papers Given In by the Scots Commissioners."

97 Whitacre, B.L. Add. Mss. 31,116, fols. 290–1; *C.J.*, 4, 730. The question was whether the words "Lords and" were to remain.

    No   110 Haselrig and Evelyn (Wilts.)

    Yea 90 Holles and Stapleton

    Harington, p. 46.

98 *C.J.*, 4, 730.

99 All divisions recorded in the Commons have been counted with the exception of those in which divisions to put the question were resolved in the affirmative and the question was put. In such cases only the division on the issue has been recorded.

100 *C.J.*, 4, 508, 511, 529.

101 *C.J.*, 4, 471.

102 *C.J.*, 4, 521, 588.

103 In February there were six committees appointed, in March thirteen, in April twelve, in May seventeen, in June eighteen, and in July nineteen. For a study of committees and their procedure in

a later period see William Bidwell, "The Committees and Legislation of the Rump Parliament, 1648–1653: A Quantitative Study" (Ph.D. diss., University of Rochester, 1977), chapter 2.

104 A fuller list of the twenty-five M.P.s who sat on at least twenty committees in this period contains: Nathaniel Fiennes (41), Henry Marten (40), Denzil Holles (39), John Glyn (36), Edmund Prideaux (35), Sir Henry Vane, Jr. (34), Samuel Brown (34), Sir John Evelyn of Wiltshire (34), Sir Arthur Haselrig (34), Bulstrode Whitelocke (32), Oliver St. John (31), Sir Philip Stapleton (31), Francis Allen (31), John Lisle (29), Sir William Lewes (28), Gilbert Gerrard (28), Sir Thomas Widdrington (27), John Selden (26), Sir Peter Wentworth (24), John Maynard (22), Alexander Rigby (22), Denis Bond (22), Robert Reynolds (21), Sir William Waller (20), and William Ball (20).

105 *C.J.*, 4, 399, 423.

106 *C.J.*, 4, 428, 444, 462, 478–9, 490, 518, 523.

107 January 7, *C.J.*, 4, 399; March 26, *C.J.*, 4, 491; June 1, *C.J.*, 4, 560; April 21, *C.J.*, 4, 518.

108 July 10, *C.J.*, 4, 613; July 11, *C.J.*, 4, 615.

109 *C.J.*, 4, 549, 601.

110 *C.J.*, 4, 400; Whitacre, B.L., Add. Mss. 31,116, fol. 253.

111 Whitacre, B.L. Add. Mss. 31,116, fol. 253.

112 *C.J.*, 4, 426.

113 *C.J.*, 4, 426; Harington noted other changes in the procedures of the grand committees or Committee of the Whole House, Harington, pp. 16, 41.

114 *C.J.*, 4, 506.

115 May 11, *C.J.*, 4, 542.

116 Twice on September 1, *C.J.*, 4, 659; September 10, *C.J.*, 4, 665; November 18, *C.J.*, 4, 725; and November 28, *C.J.*, 4, 730.

117 Holles and Stapleton: *C.J.*, 4, 659, 665, 672, 677, 725, 730; *C.J.*, 5, 10, 33. Haselrig and Evelyn (Wilts.): *C.J.*, 4, 659, 663, 665, 687, 725, 730, *C.J.*, 5, 12, 24, 25, 27, 30.

118 *C.J.*, 4, 662, 676, 691, 700, 707, 722, 736, *C.J.*, 5, 11, 12.

119 *C.J.*, 4, 659; Harington, p. 34.

120 *C.J.*, 4, 660; Harington, p. 34.

121 *C.J.*, 4, 662, 663, 665, 666, 667.

122 *C.J.*, 4, 671; Harington, p. 37.

123 *C.J.*, 4, 672–3.

124 *C.J.*, 4, 674–7.

125 *C.J.*, 4, 677.

126 *C.J.*, 4, 672.

127 *C.J.*, 4, 679, 688.

128 *C.J.*, 4, 680–8.
129 Whitacre, B.L. Add. Mss. 31,116, fol. 285; Harington, p. 42. The vote on the question had been carried by Stapleton and Lewes over Cromwell and Haselrig 55–54. But on the issue the vote with the same tellers was 56–54 against the ballot box.
130 *C.J.*, 4, 658, 676, 680.
131 *C.J.*, 4, 675.
132 *C.J.*, 4, 697, 700, 707.
133 *C.J.*, 4, 722, 726.
134 *C.J.*, 5, 10, 30.
135 *C.J.*, 5, 10.

CHAPTER 6. THE REIGN OF PARTIES

1 Bodl. Clarendon Mss., vol. 29, fol. 165.
2 See M. A. Kishlansky, "The Emergence of Adversary Politics in the Long Parliament," *Journal of Modern History*, 49 (December, 1977), 617–40.
3 This is the unsupported assertion of J. R. MacCormack, *Revolutionary Politics in the Long Parliament* (Cambridge, Mass., 1973), p. 129. For the correct analysis see D. E. Underdown, "Honest Radicals in the Counties 1642–9," in *Puritans and Revolutionaries*, ed. D. Pennington and K. V. Thomas (Oxford, 1978), pp. 193–4.
4 *L.J.*, 8, 644.
5 *L.J.*, 8, 646; *C.J.*, 5, 45.
6 *C.J.*, 5, 52; "and then the ordinance was, upon the question, recommitted, upon the whole debate thereupon had this day, in the House to consider and bring in instructions for the Committee."
7 *L.J.*, 8, 677–8.
8 *L.J.*, 8, 678.
9 *L.J.*, 8, 695–6.
10 Whitacre, B.L. Add. Mss. 31,116, fol. 300.
11 *C.J.*, 5, 73.
12 *C.J.*, 5, 71–2. Among the Commons' findings was that a number of Lords had received large sums of money from the Goldsmiths' Hall Committee as reparations for their losses during the war.
13 *L.J.*, 8, 708.
14 *C.J.*, 5, 53; *L.J.*, 8, 676, 677; Whitacre, B.L. Add. Mss. 31,116, fol. 297. This refusal to give conference preceded by two days the refusal to give conference on the Army. On this occasion the votes for a conference were equal. The controversy over the keeping of the Great Seal was complicated by other matters beyond the conflict between the Houses. See D. E. Underdown, "Party Manage-

319

ment in the Recruiter Elections 1645–48," *English Historical Review* 83 (April, 1968), 253–4.

15 *C.J.*, 5, 49.

16 *C.J.*, 5, 56. Robert Reynolds and Robert Scawen managed the conference that presented these arguments to the Lords on January 18.

17 *L.J.*, 9, 57. The monthly assessments lapsed in November 1646, although collection of arrears continued.

18 *L.J.*, 8, 688.

19 *L.J.*, 8, 686.

20 *C.J.*, 5, 85.

21 Ibid.

22 Common Council Journal, vol. 40, fols. 200–4.

23 *L.J.*, 9, 19.

24 *L.J.*, 9, 71.

25 Juxon, Dr. Williams' Library, Mss. 24.50, fol. 96. The Lords responded not only to the City's December petition, but to all of their former representations. Manchester informed the delegation that the peers "have commanded me to give hearty thanks upon the whole matter of petitions presented by you . . . and to let you know that they will take the particulars of your petitions unto the speedy consideration."

26 *L.J.*, 9, 43.

27 *L.J.*, 9, 70. It is unknown whether the Lords actually divided, that is, whether one side left the House or physically distinguished themselves in some other way.

28 Another procedural novelty occurred in the Upper House shortly after the first divisions. On March 17 the Lords debated the readmission of the Earls of Bedford, Clare, and Holland. Unwilling to decide the issue, the majority of peers voted to refuse a second reading to the bill. This generated further confusion and a vote was taken to determine if the previous vote was equivalent to a rejection of the bill. This vote ended in a tie after a division and the appointment of tellers. The matter was postponed, indefinitely as it turned out. *L.J.*, 9, 82.

29 *C.J.*, 5, 53, 60. See also Underdown, "Party Management," pp. 253–4. Holles's intervention on the issue of the Seal conforms to Underdown's assertion that control of the Seal was a party issue. But the redrafted legislation was mostly constructed by Prideaux and Samuel Browne. On January 13 Prideaux was directed to bring the new ordinance into the House of Commons for consideration. If Holles thought Prideaux to have been an implacable party foe who had already misused the Seal in recruiter elections, it is curious

that he did not mount an effort to oust him from the preparation of the new ordinance.

30 *L.J.*, 8, 655.
31 *C.J.*, 5, 63, 73.
32 *C.J.*, 5, 72.
33 *C.J.*, 5, 76.
34 *C.J.*, 5, 56.
35 *L.J.*, 9, 57. Dissents were entered by the Earls of Northumberland, Kent, Nottingham, and Salisbury, Viscount Say and Sele, and Lords De La Warr, North, Grey, Wharton, and Howard.
36 *C.J.*, 5, 53.
37 Whitacre, B.L. Add. Mss. 31,116, fol. 297.
38 *C.J.*, 5, 61, 69; Whitacre, B.L. Add. Mss. 31,116, fols. 298–9.
39 *C.J.*, 5, 75.
40 *C.J.*, 5, 75. "£1,000 granted to Massey to pay 700 soldiers who did in a tumultuous manner petition the House." Whitacre, B.L. Add. Mss. 31,116, fol. 300.
41 *L.J.*, 9, 43.
42 *C.J.*, 5, 39, 48.
43 *C.J.*, 5, 57.
44 *C.J.*, 5, 108. This vote was carried in a division.
   Yea 84   Sir Philip Stapleton and Brian Stapleton
   No   41   Swinfin and Jenner.
45 Whitacre, B.L. Add. Mss. 31,116, fol. 300. On March 2 the Committee reported that the minimum cost to maintain the King was £100 a day. Ibid., fol. 303.
46 *C.J.*, 5, 58.
47 Whitacre, B.L. Add. Mss. 31,116, fol. 301.
48 Ibid., fol. 302; *C.J.*, 5, 89.
49 *C.J.*, 5, 90. The division was on considering the disbandment of the local forces before the disbandment of the New Model.
   No   147 Holles and Stapleton
   Yea 145 Haselrig and Evelyn (Wilts.)
50 *C.J.*, 5, 90; Whitacre, B.L. Add. Mss. 31,116, fol. 302.
51 *C.J.*, 5, 91. The division was on the question of maintaining infantry troops other than those in the garrisons.
   No   158 Holles & Stapleton
   Yea 148 Haselrig and Evelyn (Wilts.)
52 *C.J.*, 5, 98–9.
53 *C.J.*, 5, 106–7. Whitacre recorded that the debate lasted the entire day. Whitacre, B.L. Add. Mss. 31,116, fol. 303. In the newsbooks it was described as a "great debate." E. 515 (2), *Perfect Diurnal*,

no. 188, March 1–8, 1647. The division was on the question should the forces to be kept up in England be commanded by Fairfax. For the rationale of some members' votes see *H.M.C.*, vol. 4, Denbigh Mss., p. 274.

54 *C.J.*, 5, 108. Whitacre describes this debate as lasting "all day and night." Whitacre, B.L. Add. Mss. 31,116, fol. 304.

55 Abbott, I, 430. This letter is undated but clearly falls between March 11 and 19. See Lomas's note in S. L. Lomas, ed., *The Letters and Speeches of Oliver Cromwell with Elucidations by Thomas Carlyle* (London, 1904), p. 252, n. 1.

56 *C.J.*, 5, 108. The fear that malignants and former royalists would reemerge in positions of power was particularly widespread after the defeat of the King. The apprentices' petition submitted to the Commons on March 1 reemphasized the dangers of malignants who were striving "to increase differences among the well-affected." E. 515 (2), *Perfect Diurnal*, no. 188, March 1–8, 1647. To counter this danger the covenant was a test of political loyalty.

57 For an example of an accusation against a New Model trooper see the account in E. 513 (34), *Perfect Diurnal*, no. 181, January 11–18, 1647.

58 *C.J.*, 5, 69. On that day Richard Vines preached to the Commons. His sermon, "The Authors, Nature and Danger of Heresy," suggested that efforts to maintain parliamentary unity had had an adverse effect upon religion. "All men's eyes have been on Parliament, and every one saith is there no balm in Gilead? Is there no physician there? Why then is not the health of the daughter of my people recovered? And the truth is neither your diversion by sudden and difficult emergents, nor wisdom in not disobliging any party, hath been able to satisfy the Godly jealousies of many." E. 378 (29), p. 3.

59 *C.J.*, 5, 108. The division was on the question whether all who were employed in the nation's garrisons would conform to the established church.
Yea   136   Holles and Stapleton
No   108   Haselrig and Evelyn (Wilts.)

60 *C.J.*, 5, 108.
61 *C.J.*, 5, 50.
62 *C.J.*, 5, 95, 99.
63 *L.J.*, 9, 66.
64 *C.J.*, 5, 110.
65 *L.J.*, 9, 72.
66 *C.J.*, 5, 110.
67 *L.J.*, 9, 88.

68 *C.J.*, 5, 115. Fairfax believed that the Army's quartering was not an excessive burden. On March 23 he wrote to his father, "The country here doth like very well of the Army, and is very sorry that there should be any petition against them." Robert Bell, ed., *Memorials of the Civil War: Comprising the Correspondence of the Fairfax Family*, 2 vols. (London, 1848), I, 334.

69 *C.J.*, 5, 107.
70 Ibid.
71 Ibid.
72 *C.J.*, 5, 114.
73 Ibid.
74 *C.J.*, 5, 121.
75 *C.J.*, 5, 124.
76 See Chapter 7.
77 *C.J.*, 9, 122.
78 *C.J.*, 5, 127.
79 *C.J.*, 5, 128; P.R.O. S.P. 21/26/16.
80 *C.J.*, 5, 129.
81 Ibid.
82 *Gardiner, Great Civil War*, III, 229.
83 Juxon, Dr. Williams' Library, Mss. 24.50, fol. 106.
84 *L.J.*, 9, 115.
85 *L.J.*, 9, 111.
86 Bodl. Clarendon Mss., vol. 29, fol. 193, Letter of Intelligence April 15/25.
87 Clarke Papers, I, 103.
88 Haselrig's appointments as teller came on January 5, 7, 8; February 3, 17, 19; March 8, 18, 19 (counting only the division on the issue), 27 (again on the issue only); April 1, 2, 15, 27; and May 4. The record of the division of January 7 is probably confused. The division to put the question whether Sir James Harrington would be a commissioner to the King was carried 78–69, with Sir Christopher Yelverton and Robert Reynolds telling the majority. The same result, a vote of 78–69, occurred when the issue was resolved, but now Yelverton and Reynolds were said to be telling the minority. If the record of the division is correct (I have assumed the opposite), Haselrig appeared as majority teller twice between January and May.
89 Evelyn's (Wilts.) appointments as teller came on January 7, 19 (with Lewes); February 6, 17, 19, 23, 26 (with Stapleton); March 5, 8; April 1, 27; May 4, 20, 25. See below for discussion of Derby House.
90 *C.J.*, 5, 137. The actual order was approved by the House on April 8.

91 The appointment of the regiments of Rossiter and Graves to remain in England, although both were likely to be loyal to Holles,
was dictated by their unsuitability for Irish service. Rossiter's regiment remained a local Lincolnshire regiment, unlikely to leave its
county. Graves's troops were assigned to guard the King. Local
considerations may also have played a part in selecting the radical
regiments to be maintained. All three (Fairfax's, Cromwell's, and
Whalley's) had been drawn from the Eastern Association, where
they were presumably to be stationed in the scheme for the standing Army.

92 Henry Cary, ed., *Memorials of the Great Civil War 1642–52*, 2 vols.
(London, 1842), I, 183–5. The letter to Rossiter is subscribed "j.c."
in the copy printed by Cary and "H." in the letter found in the
Tanner Mss., vol. 58, fol. 18. Neither readily identifies a senior officer in Rossiter's regiment.

93 M. Stieg, ed., *The Diary of John Harington, M.P.* (Old Woking,
Surrey, Somerset Record Society Publications, 74, 1977), p. 47;
C.J., 5, 131.

94 *C.J.*, 5, 133; Harington, p. 47. On April 8 the Derby House Committee offered Skippon the post, "knowing your power and influence upon that Army." P.R.O. S.P. 21/27/8.

95 *C.J.*, 5, 137.

96 *C.J.*, 5, 138, 140–1.

97 *C.J.*, 4, 694; Karl S. Bottigheimer, *English Money and Irish Land*
(Oxford, 1970), pp. 102–3.

98 *C.J.*, 4, 694.

99 *C.J.*, 4, 690, 694.

100 The contrasting labels given to this committee hint at the Lords'
objections to its powers. On October 29, 1646 the peers sent a message to the Commons to have instructions prepared for Lord Lisle
by "the members of both Houses that are of the Committee of
Both Kingdoms." *L.J.*, 8, 550. On receiving this vote the Commons
decreed "that this House does agree with the Lords, that it be referred to the Committee of Lords and Commons at Derby House."
C.J., 4, 709. But when the Lords recorded this vote on October 30
they noted that the Commons had agreed to refer the instructions
"to the members of both Houses that are of the Committee of
Both Kingdoms." *L.J.*, 8, 550. The distinction was the difference
between the Commons' additions of its seven members and the
originally constituted Committee of Both Kingdoms.

101 In the period between March 1 and July 31 Haselrig attended four
times; Cromwell not at all; Nathaniel Fiennes eight times, and Sir

Henry Vane, Jr., between five and eleven. Holles attended thirty-one sessions and Stapleton twenty-eight. P.R.O. S.P. 21/26.

102 *C.J.*, 5, 95; *L.J.*, 9, 33. Despite the Lords' refusal, Reynolds began sitting on the Committee February 22. P.R.O. S.P. 21/26.

103 *L.J.*, 9, 33.

104 *L.J.*, 9, 111.

105 *L.J.*, 9, 86. Whether these votes resulted from the Goldsmiths' Hall controversy, a new controversy over the regulation of the University of Oxford, or from the composition of the Derby House Committee is unknown.

106 *C.J.*, 5, 135. Holles could not make this report himself for he had never been approved a member of the Derby House Committee by the Lords.

107 *L.J.*, 9, 127. From their appointment these peers dominated attendance by Lords at Derby House. P.R.O. S.P. 21/26.

108 *C.J.*, 5, 134, 144.

109 *C.J.*, 5, 135, 138, 139.

110 *C.J.*, 5, 143.

111 *C.J.*, 5, 177; P.R.O. S.P. 21/26/40.

112 P.R.O. S.P. 21/26. Pierrepont did not resume sitting at Derby House until August 11.

113 See Chapter 1, p. 23. Also M. A. Kishlansky, "The Emergence of Radical Politics in the English Revolution" (Ph.D. diss., Brown University, 1977), Chapter 2.

114 Holles was added to the committee appointed to prepare the declaration against tumultuous soldiers on February 9. *C.J.*, 5, 82.

115 *C.J.*, 5, 143, 151.

116 *C.J.*, 5, 132, 119.

117 The debate over the appointment of commanders for the Irish expedition aroused such passion that "Holles and Colonel Ireton delated as like to fight a duel." Harington, p. 47. The Commons ordered their reconciliation. *C.J.*, 5, 133. On May 27 the House divided on appointing Francis Rivett to a post in Wiltshire. Holles and Stapleton were present both at the debate and at the time the question was put. Neither appeared in the division and the speaker directed them to give their votes. Stapleton voted yea and Holles no. *C.J.*, 5, 187. In March there were ten divisions and seven committees; in April twelve divisions and eight committees; and in May fourteen divisions and ten committees.

118 *C.J.*, 5, 133.

119 *C.J.*, 5, 133, 132.

120 Common Council Journal, vol. 40, fol. 212; *C.J.*, 5, 134.

121 Common Council Journal, vol. 40, fol. 212.

122 *L.J.*, 9, 131; *C.J.*, 5, 143.

123 *C.J.*, 5, 145; *L.J.*, 9, 143.

124 Common Council Journal, vol. 40, fol. 213.

125 Ibid., fol. 217a.

126 *C.J.*, 5, 148.

127 *L.J.*, 9, 150; the division was 10–6, with Lords Wharton and Willoughby acting as tellers.

128 *L.J.*, 9, 161.

129 Ibid.

130 *L.J.*, 9, 164; *C.J.*, 5, 159.

131 Common Council Journal, vol. 40, fol. 216.

132 Harington, p. 51.

133 *C.J.*, 5, 163, 166. The course for the indigent citizens was finally resolved on May 27. On May 6 the Commons had ordered £10,000 charged upon Goldsmiths' Hall "for the relief of such poor indigent persons as both Houses shall think fit." *C.J.*, 5, 164. Whether this money was ever raised or disbursed is unknown. After the Common Council requested its annual grant of £20,000 for the maintenance of its militia, the Commons ordered £12,000 for the City militia and £18,000 for poor citizens who had lent money to the parliamentary cause. This totaled the £30,000 the City had originally requested. *C.J.*, 5, 188.

134 P.R.O. S.P. 28/350/pt. 2. This is a record of all subscriptions to the £200,000 loan. Although many subscribers are easily identified with Holles's majority or with traditional Irish interests, Colonel Edmund Ludlow and John Boys were also among those who advanced money.

135 *C.J.*, 5, 161. The purgation of political or religious Independents from the Militia Committee (of which there were few) was accompanied by their exclusion from Common Council committees, and in two extreme cases, from the council itself. See Valerie Pearl, "London's Counter-Revolution," in G. E. Aylmer, ed., *The Interregnum: The Quest for Settlement* (London, 1972), pp. 44 ff. Juxon, Dr. Williams' Library, Mss. 24.50, fol. 108.

136 Cary, I, 194–8.

137 Ibid., 196.

138 *L.J.*, 9, 114. Whether these colonels actually intended to go to Ireland is impossible to ascertain. The Londoner who sent news to the Army headquarters believed that these subscribers would not themselves go to Ireland but only "mean to drive their men to it." Clarke Mss., vol. 41, fol. 3. But of the five officers named, two – Jackson and Sheffield – certainly intended to fight in Ireland.

139 *L.J.*, 9, 134, 153. P.R.O. S.P. 21/27/16.
140 Cary, I, 191.
141 *L.J.*, 9, 153.
142 Ibid.; G. E. Cokayne, *Complete Peerage.*
143 *C.J.*, 5, 176.
144 Harington, p. 53.
145 *L.J.*, 9, 152.
146 *C.J.*, 5, 155. "Whether the Lords may send such a message to this House in respect of the privilege of this House in the matter of money."
147 *C.J.*, 5, 155.
 Yea 114 Stapleton and Glyn
 No   78   Haselrig and Livesay
148 *C.J.*, 5, 173.
149 *C.J.*, 5, 160, 174; *L.J.*, 9, 201. The Lords read this bill three times in the same session and passed it.
150 *C.J.*, 5, 188. For a discussion of the indemnity problem see J. S. Morrill, "The Army Revolt of 1647," in *Britain and the Netherlands*, A. C. Duke and C. A. Tamse, eds. (The Hague, 1977), VI, 54–78.
151 *C.J.*, 5, 176.
 Yea 139 Lewes and Grimston
 No   100 Mildmay and Wentworth
152 Cary, I, 216.
153 Harington, p. 53.
154 *C.J.*, 5, 181.
155 *C.J.*, 5, 183; P.R.O. S.P. 21/26/62–6.
156 *C.J.*, 5, 192; P.R.O. S.P. 21/26/62–6.
157 *C.J.*, 5, 184.
158 *C.J.*, 5, 191.
159 *L.J.*, 9, 222.
160 P.R.O. S.P. 21/26/41.
161 See M. A. Kishlansky, "The Army and the Levellers: The Roads to Putney," *Historical Journal* (forthcoming).

CHAPTER 7. THE RISE OF THE NEW MODEL ARMY

1 Rushworth, VI, 446.
2 E. 290 (5), *Scottish Dove*, no. 88, June 20–7, 1645.
3 Rushworth, VI, 88.
4 Holles, "Memoirs of Denzil Lord Holles," in F. Maseres, ed., *Select Tracts Relating to the Civil Wars in England*, 2 vols. (London, 1815), I, 201.
5 *H.M.C. Portland*, III, 156; Bodl. Clarendon Mss., vol. 29, fol. 195;

J. S. Morrill, "The Army Revolt of 1647," in *Britain and the Netherlands*, A. C. Duke and C. A. Tamse, eds. (The Hague, 1977), VI, 54–78; M. A. Kishlansky, "The Army and the Levellers: The Roads to Putney," *Historical Journal* (forthcoming); I. Gentles, "Arrears of Pay and Ideology in the Army Revolt of 1647," in B. Bond and I. Roy, eds., *War and Society* (London, 1976), I, 44–66, arrives at the same conclusion but must be used with great care.

6 *L.J.*, 9, 164.

7 B.L. Loan 29/122/Misc. 16.

8 E. 511 (29), *Perfect Diurnal*, no. 158, August 3–10, 1646.

9 *C.J.*, 4, 513.

10 Whitelocke, *Memorials*, II, 118.

11 P.R.O. S.P. 28/39.

12 Henry Cary, ed., *Memorials of the Great Civil War 1642–52*, 2 vols. (London, 1842), I, 197.

13 P.R.O. S.P. 28/39/41.

14 Ibid., 28/38.

15 Ibid., 28/39.

16 Ibid., 28/38–9.

17 Ibid., 28/40.

18 Ibid., 28/41.

19 Ibid., 28/41, 44.

20 This is contrary to the assertion of Gentles, "Arrears of Pay of the Parliamentary Armies at the End of the First Civil War," *Bulletin of the Institute of Historical Research* 48 (1975), 52–63.

21 *C.J.*, 5, 53. In the first six months of 1647 the Army received a portion of its pay in every month but May. In that month Parliament had planned to disband the Army and use the monthly pay for the soldiers' severance.

22 *L.J.*, 8, 438.

23 E. 515 (3), *Perfect Diurnal*, no. 189, March 8–15; J. S. Morrill, "The Army Revolt of 1647." The papers of the indemnity committee (S.P. 24), which Morrill has used so fruitfully, pose problems in discussing the New Model. A survey of the cases heard by the Committee in 1647 failed to turn up any New Model members. It is undeniable that perception of how others were treated fed the soldiers' apprehensions (although not in this early period, for the Committee's work did not begin until June), but it is also true that arrangements for the New Model were never as haphazard as they were for other parliamentary soldiers.

24 Bodl. Tanner Mss., vol. 59, fol. 792. The Committee of Suffolk to Speaker Lenthall, March 4, 1647.

25 Alan Everitt, *The Community of Kent and the Great Rebellion* (Leicester, 1966), pp. 150–1. Everitt attributes Sedley's arrest to the local friction between the sheriff and Sir Anthony Weldon. Added to the local dimension was the fact that three orders from Westminster had prohibited the prosecution of soldiers for acts committed during the war.

26 E. 413 (17), "The Copy of a Letter Sent to His Excellency Sir Thomas Fairfax from Major Francis White."

27 Cary, I, 233–4.

28 J. S. Morrill, *Cheshire 1630–60* (Oxford, 1974), pp. 192–8; Everitt, pp. 219–30.

29 *O.P.H.*, 15, 222.

30 *L.J.*, 9, 71–2.

31 See Chapter 6.

32 *L.J.*, 9, 112–13; *C.J.*, 5, 127. Sir William Waller has left an extensive, if colored, account of this commission in his *Vindication of the Character and Conduct of Sir William Waller* (London, 1793), pp. 44–50.

33 *L.J.*, 9, 113.

34 Ibid.

35 Waller, *Vindication*, p. 51.

36 Ibid., p. 52.

37 *C.J.*, 5, 127.

38 E. 515 (4), *Perfect Diurnal*, no. 190, March 15–22, 1647.

39 The Large Petition was brought to the attention of the House of Commons on March 15 by an unnamed informant. It was given over for examination to a committee chaired by Colonel Edward Leigh. See M. A. Kishlansky, "The Army and the Levellers."

40 *L.J.*, 9, 82.

41 Gardiner, *Great Civil War*, III, 256.

42 William Haller, ed., *Tracts on Liberty in the Puritan Revolution*, 3 vols. (New York, 1934), III, 405. See Morrill, "Army Revolt."

43 Haller, *Tracts*, III, 405.

44 *O.P.H.*, 15, 342–4.

45 Waller, *Vindication*, p. 51.

46 Rushworth, VI, 445.

47 Rushworth, VI, 447.

48 *L.J.*, 9, 114.

49 Clarke Papers, I, 2. The letter from the Army preserved both in the Clarke Mss. and in Rushworth's *Collections* speaks only of seventeen subscribers for the Irish service rather than the twenty-nine whose names appear on the papers submitted to the Houses of

Parliament. There is no explanation for this discrepancy, although some of those whose names appear on this initial list would later claim that their signatures were forged.

50 Bodl. Tanner Mss., vol. 58, fol. 59. The Parliamentary Commissioners to Sir Thomas Fairfax, April 19, 1647.
51 Clarke Papers, I, 6–7.
52 Ibid., I, 6.
53 Waller, *Vindication*, p. 81.
54 Clarke Papers, I, 8.
55 Ibid., I, 7.
56 Ibid., I, 12–13.
57 Ibid., I, 13–14; Waller, *Vindication*, p. 91.
58 Clarke Papers, I, 14; B.L. Loan 29/175. The dispute over Lilburne's command became part of the Commissioners' investigation into obstructions to the Irish service.
59 Clarke Papers, I, 16.
60 *H.M.C. Portland*, I, 418.
61 E. 409 (25), "A Declaration of the Engagements, Remonstrances, Desires and Resolutions . . . ," p. 3.
62 Clarke Papers, I, 10.
63 Ibid., I, 16–17.
64 *H.M.C. Portland*, III, 156.
65 Clarke Papers, I, 424, "Colonel Wogan's Narrative."
66 Ibid., I, 7–8.
67 Waller, *Vindication*, p. 87. "We gave free entertainment to all that made us a rational proposition; and to spur them on the better by hopes of preferment. . . ."
68 Waller, *Vindication*, p. 87; Cary, I, 197.
69 *C.J.*, 5, 133, 137, 141.
70 *C.J.*, 5, 173, 181.
71 E. 384 (11), "A New Found Strategem."
72 Holles, *Memoirs*, I, 236.
73 Rushworth, VI, 448.
74 E. 515 (7), *Perfect Diurnal*, no. 193, April 5–12, 1647.
75 E. 384 (11), "A New Found Strategem." B.L. Loan 29/123/misc. 35. The examination of the printing of this pamphlet did not make great progress.
76 Rushworth, VI, 448.
77 Cary, I, 204.
78 William Walwyn, "Walwyn's Just Defense," in William Haller and Godfrey Davies, eds., *The Leveller Tracts 1647–53* (New York, 1944), p. 357.
79 See p. 173.

80 "The Vindication of the Officers of the Army under Sir Thomas Fairfax," in Rushworth, VI, 469ff.
81 E. 515 (4), *Perfect Diurnal,* no. 190, March 15–22, 1647. The *Diurnal* contains the first mention of the Army's petition and places the agitation in Rich's regiment. This is borne out by John Wildman, who, in castigating Cromwell and Ireton for their conduct during the petitioning campaign, accused them of using "their creatures to suppress the soldiers' first most innocent and modest petition. Colonel Rich sent several orders to some officers to prevent subscriptions of that petition." John Wildman, "Putney Projects," quoted in Clarke Papers, I, xx.
82 *O.P.H.,* 15, 343. For a brief time Army members believed that it was this clause that had offended Parliament. In the "Vindication of the Officers" they wrote, "for the particular intimation that the Royal assent may be desired, we never intended it to lessen your authority; but since you have by offering the propositions, judged the desiring the King's assent convenient." Rushworth, VI, 470.
83 Clarke Papers, I, 66.
84 E. 515 (4), *Perfect Diurnal,* no. 190, March 15–22, 1647; "And we proceeded at this time with the greatest care and caution we could of giving the least offense, intending not to present our petition to this honorable House, but with the approbation and mediation of his Excellency. . . ." "Vindication of the Officers," Rushworth, VI, 469.
85 Rushworth, VI, 446.
86 Clarke Papers, I, 11; E. 515 (9), *Perfect Diurnal,* no. 195, April 19–26, 1647.
87 Rushworth, VI, 461; Clarke Papers, I, 11.
88 Clarke Papers, I, 17.
89 B.L. Loan 29/175/52–3. This account demonstrates both the initiative of the common soldiers and the misinformation that was spread during the crisis. The trooper from Cromwell's regiment believed Whalley's regiment would be sent to Ireland.
90 Bodl. Tanner Mss., vol. 58, fol. 141.
91 Rushworth, VI, 468.
92 Ibid.; E. 515 (10), *Perfect Diurnal,* no. 196, April 26–May 3, 1647.
93 B.L. Loan 29/175/50.
94 Waller, *Vindication,* pp. 92–3. The imprisonment of Ensign Nichols was soon to become a *cause célèbre* within the Army. Nichols was arrested by Major Francis Dormer for distributing the March Petition among the companies Dormer was reorganizing for the Irish service. His pockets were searched and his papers taken from him. The Commissioners brought Nichols to London without informing

Fairfax, who had, for reasons of health, left the Army's headquarters. Nichols was granted £2 from the Army's discretionary funds to defray the cost of his imprisonment. The Army later claimed that Nichols's rights had been violated and Fairfax's powers denigrated by these actions. Juxon, Dr. Williams' Library, Mss. 24.50, fol. 107; B.L. Loan 29/175; William Clarke's Accounts, Chequers Mss. 782, fol. 50; Clarke Mss., vol. 41, fol. 106.

95 On the opposition by Cromwell and Ireton see Firth's discussion in Clarke Papers, I, xix–xx; and Abbott, I, 434.

96 It is generally assumed that these were the "radical" cavalry regiments. In fact, they were all the cavalry regiments with the exception of Rossiter's, stationed in Lincolnshire, and those of Pye and Graves, which were at Holmby. For this common misrepresentation see I. Gentles,"Arrears of Pay and Ideology," 48.

97 Cary, I, 203–4.

98 Rushworth, VI, 469.

99 E. 409 (25), "A Declaration of the Engagements, Remonstrances, Proposals, Desires and Resolutions ... Also Called the Army Book of Declarations," p. 9. For sources of this confusion see Don M. Wolfe, *Leveller Manifestoes of the Puritan Revolution* (New York, 1967), p. 20; H. N. Brailsford, *The Levellers and the English Revolution* (Stanford, Calif., 1961), p. 186. Neither the Second Apologie nor the more perplexing "Apology of the Common Soldiers to All Their Commission Officers" can easily be placed among the pamphlets known to have emanated from the soldiers. Their numbering seems to pair them together, and, in my judgment, they were composed in London.

100 A. S. P. Woodhouse, *Puritanism and Liberty* (New York, 1938), p. 23.

101 Clement Walker, "The History of Independency," in *Relations and Observations Historical and Politic upon the Parliament* (London, 1648), p. 34.

102 Waller, *Vindication*, pp. 112–13.

103 Geoffrey Parker, *The Army of Flanders and the Spanish Road* (Cambridge, 1972). "The military revolt departed from the pattern of the spontaneous peasant uprising. Once resolved on disobedience, the mutineers organized themselves with considerable sophistication in order to achieve their objectives. They elected leaders to govern them, followed a rational and orderly plan, and concentrated their efforts on limited and obtainable goals." (Page 187, cf. pp. 188–91, for a discussion of the *electo*.)

104 Clarendon, IV, 220. This was also the opinion of William Prynne,

First and Second Part of a Seasonable...Vindication (London, 1655): "acting more like a Parliament and supreme dictators than soldiers."
105 See pp. 173–4.
106 "Vindication of the Officers," Rushworth, VI, 469.
107 Rushworth, VI, 474; The colonels were Hewson and Okey.
108 Ibid.
109 Ibid.
110 Ibid. The notes of the examination of the agitators are preserved in Bodl. Tanner Mss., vol. 58, fol. 84.
111 Rushworth, VI, 474; Clarke Papers, I, 431.
112 Rushworth, VI, 474.
113 Rushworth, VI, 476.
114 The examination of John Powle of West Wickham, Buckinghamshire, is one example of both the pervasiveness and unreliability of these rumors. Powle was informed by one Thomas Arnold "that there is a design of Independents to make head against the Parliament while the Army is in discontent." *H.M.C. Portland*, I, 421. Similarly, it was at this time that the anonymous letter writer in Suffolk claimed that "the soldiers' quote Lilburne's books as statute Law." *H.M.C. Portland*, III, 156. The unreliability of this evidence, as well as that found in the Clarendon Mss., should be obvious. Its uncritical acceptance has, however, experienced a revival. See J. R. MacCormack, *Revolutionary Politics in the Long Parliament* (Cambridge, Mass., 1973), pp. 178ff., and Ian Gentles, "Arrears of Pay and Ideology."
115 Clarke Papers, I, 22. These rumors resulted in a clause in the statement of grievances of Colonel Lambert's regiment that read "forasmuch as we hear there was command given for surprising us in our quarters we desire the Parliament would release themselves of it by way of Declaration." Clarke Mss., vol. 41, fol. 124.
116 Rushworth, VI, 480.
117 Clarke Papers, I, 27.
118 Ibid., I, 26.
119 Ibid., I, 31.
120 Rushworth, VI, 480.
121 Ibid.
122 Ibid., VI, 485.
123 Clarke Mss., vol. 41, fols. 105–27. The returns were from the cavalry regiments of Butler, Cromwell, Fairfax, Graves, Ireton, Rich, Sheffield, and Whalley; and from the infantry regiments of Fairfax, Harley, Hewson, Lambert, Lilburne, and Waller.

124 Clarke Mss., vol. 41, fol. 126.

125 Compare the first eleven points of the three statements, Clarke Mss., vol. 41, fols. 107–11.

126 Clarke Mss., vol. 41, fols. 116–19.

127 E. 390 (26), "The Declaration of the Army," Clarke Mss., vol. 41, fols. 113, 119. Lieutenant Edmund Chillenden of Whalley's regiment and Captain John Reynolds of Cromwell's may have been two of these officer-agitators. Clarke Papers, I, 85; 426.

128 Clarke Mss., vol. 41, fol. 120.

129 "Lastly we humbly beseech the honorable House not to misapprehend anything in the forementioned agrievances but to be pleased to clothe the naked truth of them with their favorable construction and approbation." Clarke Mss., vol. 41, fol. 114.

130 Ibid., fol. 112.

131 Ibid., fol. 121.

132 Ibid., fol. 117.

133 Ibid., fol. 121–2.

134 Ibid., fols. 118, 122. The claim of Harley's regiment was that they had engaged to be "free from the yoke of episcopal tyranny" and that pressing men beyond their own light was "wholly contrary to the word of God and the best reformed churches." This phraseology, the same by which the Scots pressed for the establishment of *jure divino* presbyterianism and the erastians and independents resisted it, was losing its meaning.

135 Clarke Mss., vol. 41, fol. 109.

136 Ibid., fols. 106, 116.

137 Ibid., fols. 125, 126.

138 Ibid., fols. 125, 126, 118.

139 Ibid., fol. 106.

140 Ibid.

141 Ibid., fol. 113.

142 Ibid., fol. 121.

143 Ibid., fols. 107, 117.

144 Ibid., fol. 106.

145 Ibid., fol. 123; B.L. Loan 29/122–3. The Commissioners' examination centered on Lambert's regiment.

146 Clarke Mss., vol. 41, fol. 106.

147 Ibid., fol. 117–18.

148 Ibid., fol. 124.

149 Ibid., fol. 122.

150 Ibid., fol. 118.

151 Ibid., fol. 113.

152 Ibid., fol. 124.

153 Clarke Papers, I, 37.
154 Colonel Rich believed that this process would remove "some things not fit and impertinent and extravagant," but the intention of drawing a single statement was to stress the Army's unity. Clarke Papers, I, 63.
155 Clarke Papers, I, 37.
156 Ibid., I, 42.
157 Ibid., I, 70. The agitators also believed in the Army's essential unity. On the day following the convention, they wrote Fairfax to assure him that despite the disunity of the officers, the soldiers of the eight cavalry regiments adhered to the statement of grievances. Clarke Papers, I, 78.
158 Clarke Papers, I, 59–60. For a full list of the conflicting reports see the returns made by the Commissioners to Parliament, Clarke Papers, I, 95–9.
159 Clarke Papers, I, 55–6.
160 Ibid., I, 82.
161 Ibid., I, 35.
162 Ibid., I, 57.
163 Ibid., I, 77.
164 See Chapter 6.
165 In April, Colonel Richard Fortescue was replaced by Colonel John Barkstead. P.R.O. S.P. 28/45/268. Barkstead's succession was one of a number of replacements from outside of the Army which included Lambert and Lilburne. Although Firth attributes the appointment to Fairfax's observation of Barkstead's abilities when the Army quartered at Reading, Cromwell's hand is also apparent and may have been a more decisive factor. C. H. Firth and G. Davies, *Regimental History of Cromwell's Army* (Oxford, 1940), I, 338. Writing from London at the end of March, Cromwell added the following postscript to his letter to Fairfax: "Mr. Allen desires Colonel Baxter, sometime Governor of Reading, may be remembered. I humbly desire Colonel Overton may not be out of your remembrance." Abbott, I, 430.
166 Clarke Mss., vol. 67, fols. 3–27.
167 There are several sources for identifying those who supported the Irish venture and the parliamentary order for disbandment. The most important is the "Petition of the 100 and odd dissenting officers to the General," Clarke Mss. vol. 41, fol. 136. This petition clearly enunciates the motives of its supporters: "Their judgments guide them to believe that they ought to defend, not to divert, the proceedings of those by whose authority they were raised." Thirty-four of the fifty-one officers who withdrew from the Army signed

this document. There is also the original list of the undertakers, *L.J.*, 9, 113–14; the list of "dissenting brethren" appended to the collation of grievances given to the Commissioners on May 18, Clarke Mss., vol. 41, fols. 101–3; the changes recorded by Clarke, Clarke Mss., vol. 67, fols. 3–27; and the regimental pay warrants, P.R.O. S.P. 28/46. Firth and Davies, *Regimental History*, is unreliable and should not be accepted without verification from the foregoing sources.

168 To these limitations of evidence must be added considerations of method. Certainly the most basic calculation is the percentage of the entire officer corps that withdrew from the Army. This statistic, although revealing, masks important variations in the experiences of the individual regiments. In seven of the twenty-two regiments there were no replacements within the senior officer corps. Some of these, like Cromwell's and Lambert's, were active participants in the agitation and were united behind the Army demands. But others, like Skippon's and Rainsborough's, were engaged in missions that excluded them from participation in the Army's confrontation with Parliament.

169 The total of the senior officer corps was 175: 66 horse, 10 dragoon, and 100 foot officers. (As Fairfax held two colonelcies, he is counted only once, leaving 175.) For the purposes of calculation, and following their military experience, the dragoons are totaled with the cavalry.

170 For the sources of this information see n. 167 above. The captains who left the Army were Samuel Barry, Nicholas Bragge, William Lord Caulfield, John Farmer, Ralph Farr, Christopher Flemming, Philip Howard, Anthony Markham, Gabriel Martin, Jonas Neville, Robert Robotham, Harold, Skermager, and Edward Wogan (cavalry); John Boyce, Vincent Boyce, John Bushell, John Cope, John Denizon, Francis Dormer, Thomas Highfield, William Howard, Henry Ingoldsby, Richard Lundy, John Melvin, Francis Muskett, Charles O'Hara, Christopher Peckham, Richard Pooley, Nathaniel Short, Edward (?) Stephens, Daniel Thomas, George Weldon, Thomas Wolfe, and Arthur Yonge (infantry).

171 The unaffected cavalry regiments were those of Fairfax, Cromwell, and Whalley; and in the infantry those of Skippon, Pickering, Rainsborough, and Lambert.

172 Don M. Wolfe, *Leveller Manifestoes of the Puritan Revolution* (New York, 1944), pp. 243–6; Christopher Hill, *The World Turned Upside Down* (New York, 1972), p. 50; Firth and Davies, I, 324.

173 Clarke Mss., vol. 41, fol. 136.

174 Abbott, I, 430.
175 Firth and Davies, I, 325; For Hobson's previous service see Clive Holmes, *The Eastern Association* (Cambridge, 1974), p. 199.
176 Firth and Davies, I, 93.
177 Colonel Graves withdrew, Major Scroope remained; Colonel Pye withdrew, Major Tomlinson remained; Colonel Butler withdrew, Major Horton remained; Colonel Ireton remained, Major Sedascue withdrew; Colonel Rich remained, Major Alford withdrew; Colonel Okey remained, Major Moore withdrew. In the only regiment in which changes occurred and neither colonel nor major withdrew, Major Harrison was transferred from Fleetwood's regiment.
178 Colonel Herbert withdrew, Lieutenant Colonel Reade remained; Colonel Harley withdrew, Lieutenant Colonel Pride remained; Colonel Fortescue withdrew, Lieutenant Colonel Cobbett remained; Colonel Fairfax remained, Lieutenant Colonel Jackson withdrew; Colonel Lilburne remained, Lieutenant Colonel Kempson withdrew.

CHAPTER 8. THE EMERGENCE OF RADICAL POLITICS

1 Rushworth, VI, 587, "An Humble Remonstrance from His Excellency Sir Thomas Fairfax and the Army under His Command," June 24, 1647.
2 William Waller, *The Vindication of the Character and Conduct of Sir William Waller* (London, 1793), p. 152.
3 Ibid., pp. 152, 190.
4 Holles, "The Memoirs of Denzil Lord Holles," in F. Maseres, ed., *Select Tracts Relating to the Civil Wars in England*, 2 vols. (London, 1815), I, 248.
5 Rushworth, VI, 565, "A Declaration or Representation from his Excellency Sir Thomas Fairfax, and of the Army under His Command," June 14, 1647.
6 Robert Bell, ed., *Memorials of the Civil War: Comprising the Correspondence of the Fairfax Family*, 2 vols. (London, 1849), I, 358.
7. Juxon, Dr. Williams' Library, Mss. 24.50, fol. 109; In a petition on June 14, two groups of reformadoes claimed "that your petitioners hav[e] (not as mercenaries but as faithful and freeborn subjects) exposed their estates to ruin and their lives to all dangers for the preservation of the King, the privilege of Parliament and the liberty of the subject." H.L.R.O. Main Papers, June 1647.
8 *L.J.*, 9, 354, "A Solemn Engagement of the Citizens, etc."
9 *L.J.*, 9, 356.

10 *L.J.*, 9, 378, "A Declaration of His Excellency Sir Thomas Fairfax and the Council of War," August 3, 1647.

11 E. 409 (25), "A Declaration of the Engagements, Remonstrances, Proposals, Desires and Resolutions . . . the Army Book of Declarations," p. 53.

12 Rushworth, VI, 565, "A Declaration or Representation" June 14, 1647.

13 Rushworth, VI, 570; *L.J.*, 9, 323.

14 Rushworth, VI, 586, "An Humble Remonstrance," June 24, 1647.

15 Holles, "Memoirs," in Maseres, *Select Tracts*, I, 250; E. 397 (8), William Prynne, "A Declaration of the Officers' and the Army's Illegal Proceedings, etc."; Waller, p. 176.

16 Clement Walker, "The Mystery of the Two Juntoes," in Maseres, I, 333.

17 Rushworth, VI, 566, "A Declaration or Representation," June 14, 1647.

18 E. 396 (19), "The King's Estate at Present."

19 E. 400 (20), "A True Alarm to England."

20 *O.P.H.*, 15, 434.

21 Whitelocke, *Memorials*, II, 172.

22 E. 410 (16), Hugh Peter, "A Word for the Army and Two Words for the Kingdom."

23 *L.J.*, 9, 273; "Necessity (saith Luther) takes away and overturns all laws"; E. 398 (27), "The Army Harmless." The theme of necessity and the safety of the people pervade the tracts written in July.

24 Bell, I, 348. This is to be contrasted with the letter sent to Fairfax by the Derby House Committee, "Whereas your letter seems to imply that there are some grievances to be further presented to the Houses from the soldiers, the Houses have sat diverse days upon that business and have granted whatever they thought fit for them to grant or for the Army to desire and we doubt not but the Houses will expect a punctual obedience in their disbanding according to their orders." Derby House Committee to Sir Thomas Fairfax, May 31, 1647, P.R.O. S.P. 21/27, fol. 33.

25 Clarke Papers, I, 108–11.

26 Rushworth, VI, 498, "The Humble Petition of the Soldiers of the Army," May 29, 1647.

27 Ibid. For a variant copy with the names of the agitators from sixteen regiments see E. 409 (25), p. 16.

28 Clarke Papers, I, 109–11.

29 Henry Cary, ed., *Memorials of the Great Civil War 1642–52*, 2 vols. (London, 1842), I, 219–20; Bodl. Tanner Mss., vol. 58, fol. 129.

30 Cary, I, 221–2.

31 Rushworth, VI, 500.
32 Rushworth, VI, 499.
33 Clarke Papers, I, 104.
34 Ibid., I, 113.
35 The full story of the seizure was narrated by Lord Montague, *O.P.H.*, 15, 414–19. Joyce's letters are found in Clarke Papers, I, 118–19, and the official Army account, also Joyce's work, is printed in Rushworth VI, 513–17.
36 See Firth's brilliant deductions, Clarke Papers, I, xxiv–xxxii. His argument that Cromwell may have been informed of Joyce's expedition, but did not order it, is convincing. Also of interest is the consequence of Joyce's actions. Fairfax, most certainly, was in the dark and reacted badly to the seizure. Nevertheless, he authorized payment, on July 10, of £100 for Joyce's "extraordinary expenses," which *may* have been for the cost of the expedition. But he would not honor the obligation, privately made, that Joyce would receive the first vacant captaincy and apparently resisted the combined ministrations of Ireton and Rainsborough that Joyce be given Captain Laughton's place in Fleetwood's regiment. The seizure of the King remains a shadowy subject. William Clarke's accounts, Chequers Mss. 782, fol. 43; Clarke Mss., vol. 66, fol. 6.
37 Bell, I, 353.
38 Clarke Papers, I, 112.
39 Ibid., I, 100.
40 Ibid., I, 132.
41 Cary, I, 223.
42 Clarke Papers, I, 101; see p. 102, n. b, for Firth's attribution of this letter to Ireton.
43 *L.J.*, 9, 248; Clarke Papers, I, 122.
44 Rushworth, VI, 504.
45 Ibid. "An Humble Representation of the Dissatisfactions of the Army" is printed in Rushworth, VI, 505–10.
46 Rushworth, VI, 509.
47 Rushworth, VI, 510.
48 Rushworth, VI, 512. Gardiner's claim that this clause was inserted by Cromwell, revealing his moderating influence upon the soldiery, cannot be substantiated. It is consistent with Gardiner's belief that the soldiers were "Liburnian" radicals and that the officers damped down their revolutionary enthusiasm. But Gardiner did not make use of the regimental petitions (which Firth did not print) and so could not have known that similar expressions appeared there, without any apparent moderating influence. Gardiner, *Great Civil War*, III, 280–4.

49 Rushworth, VI, 512.
50 *C.J.*, 5, 194; *O.P.H.*, 15, 384–5. See "The Opinions and Humble Advice of the Council of War," *O.P.H.*, 15, 385–9.
51 *C.J.*, 5, 194.
52 Bodl. Clarendon Mss., vol. 29, fol. 229. Letter of Intelligence, June 3, 1647.
53 Clarke Papers, I, 116.
54 Holles, "Memoirs," in Maseres, *Select Tracts*, I, 251.
55 *C.J.*, 5, 197.
56 M. Stieg, ed., *The Diary of John Harington, M.P., 1646–53* (Old Woking, Surrey, Somerset Record Society Publications, 74, 1977), p. 55.
57 *C.J.*, 5, 197.
    Yea 154 Lord Wenman and Grimston
    No   123 Pierrepont and Haselrig
58 Whitacre, B.L. Add. Mss. 31,116, fol. 311; Harington, p. 55; *C.J.*, 5, 197.
    Yea 96 Nathaniel Fiennes and Bulkely
    No   79 Lord Herbert and Francis Gerrard
59 Whitelocke, *Memorials*, II, 151.
60 *C.J.*, 5, 197.
61 *L.J.*, 9, 232, 236; *C.J.*, 5, 198.
62 *C.J.*, 5, 200.
63 *C.J.*, 5, 199.
64 *C.J.*, 5, 201, 202, 203.
65 *L.J.*, 9, 239. The dissenting Lords, predictably, were the Earls of Stamford, Lincoln, Middlesex, and Suffolk and Lords Willoughby and Maynard. The single clause omitted in the second draft of the parliamentary explanation was "to reflect upon or lessen their authority." Compare the copies in *C.J.*, 5, 199, and *L.J.*, 9, 247.
66 *L.J.*, 9, 242.
67 *L.J.*, 9, 243.
68 *C.J.*, 5, 194.
69 *C.J.*, 5, 196; Whitelocke, *Memorials*, II, 151.
70 Juxon, Dr. Williams' Library, Mss. 24.50, fol. 109.
71 *C.J.*, 5, 201; Whitacre, B.L. Add. Mss. 31,116, fol. 311. Whitacre named Alderman Atkins, Sir Henry Vane, Sr., and Speaker Lenthall as those who were assaulted by the reformadoes.
72 *C.J.*, 5, 201; Whitacre, B.L. Add. Mss. 31,116, fol. 312.
73 *C.J.*, 5, 201. Colonel Harvey, Maynard, Massey, Stapleton, and Birch were sent out to them.
74 *L.J.*, 9, 245.
75 *C.J.*, 5, 205–6.

76 The soldiers listed their reasons for casting these officers out of the Army as: they would be privy to their counsel; they had acted counter to the rules of martial discipline; they refused to maintain the Army's just privileges; they attempted to divide the Army; and as a discouragement to others of like spirit. E. 392 (26), "A True Declaration of the Present Proceedings of the Army."

77 *C.J.*, 5, 195.

78 *C.J.*, 5, 198–9.

79 *C.J.*, 5, 200, 203.

80 Although it appeared that way to the Army, it is by no means clear that Holles was consciously attempting to build a counterforce to the New Model. First, those New Model deserters who came to London were ordered out of the City almost as soon as they arrived, and several other companies were stationed at Reading. Their usefulness in a new war was questionable in light of the refusal of the forces at Holmby to stand against Joyce's Company. Second, the reformadoes were a disorganized mob as likely to sack the City as to defend it and not all were supporters of conservative, presbyterian policies. The City government had been uneasy about their presence since March. Finally, although Holles had advocated decisive action on June 3, it was not until the Army marched toward London that any preparations for defense were made, and these were so desultory and unsuccessful that it is hard to see Holles's rather careful habits of preparation behind them. Dr. Pearl's argument, "London's Counter-Revolution," in G. E. Aylmer, ed., *The Interregnum: The Quest for Settlement* (London, 1972), p. 46, is circumstantial and open to question. Analyzing the paragraph on p. 46: the Committee of Safety was not established until the night of June 11; the Committee for Irish Affairs had been raising troops since April; as both Graves's and Pye's regiments came to the New Model intact, it is unlikely that any reformadoes had served under them; the £10,000 voted to be paid at Weavers' Hall was to send the New Model deserters to Ireland; the quarters to which the New Model deserters were assigned, on June 8, were at Worcester; these soldiers did not arrive in London until June 5 and were thus incapable of taking part in the tumults on June 4 (and probably those on the 5th as well); John Harington left London in early June to ride the western circuit.

81 Rushworth, VI, 548; E. 515 (19), *Perfect Diurnal*, no. 202, June 7–14, 1647.

82 Common Council Journal, vol. 40, fol. 218; *C.J.*, 5, 203.

83 *C.J.*, 5, 203.

84 Ibid.

85 Rushworth, VI, 549; *O.P.H.*, 15, 415.
86 Rushworth, VI, 556.
87 Ibid. The creation of the Council of the Army was one of the soldiers' demands in their Solemn Engagement. It was to be composed of "those general officers of the Army (who have concurred with the Army in the premises) with two commissioned officers and two soldiers to be chosen for each regiment." Rushworth, VI, 512. See M. A. Kishlansky, "The Army and the Levellers: The Roads to Putney," for an analysis of the role of the General Council of the Army.
88 *O.P.H.*, 15, 432–3.
89 *O.P.H.*, 15, 432–4.
90 E. 392 (7), written in Thomason's hand.
91 *C.J.*, 5, 206–7.
92 *C.J.*, 207–8; *L.J.*, 9, 255–8. The Lords suggested that the Derby House Committee be sent to consult with the City militia, but the Commons appointed a new committee for that purpose.
93 *C.J.*, 5, 208.
94 E. 515 (19), *Perfect Diurnal*, no. 202, June 7–14, 1647.
95 Common Council Journal, vol. 40, fols. 219–20.
96 E. 515 (19), *Perfect Diurnal*, no. 202, June 7–14, 1647.
97 Juxon, Dr. Williams' Library, Mss. 24.50, fol. 110.
98 Ibid.; Clarke Papers, I, 132.
99 Juxon, Dr. Williams' Library, Mss. 24.50, fol. 110; Clarke Papers, I, 133; E. 515 (19), *Perfect Diurnal*, no. 202, June 7–14, 1647; Corporation of London Record Office, Common Hall Book, vol. II, fol. 62.
100 Juxon, Dr. Williams' Library, Mss. 24.50, fol. 110; *O.P.H.*, 15, 439.
101 *O.P.H.*, 15, 438; Common Council Journal, vol. 40, fol. 221.
102 *O.P.H.*, 15, 439–40.
103 Bell, I, 354.
104 *L.J.*, 9, 263.
105 *L.J.*, 9, 261–2.
106 Cary, I, 228.
107 *O.P.H.*, 15, 450.
108 Ibid.
109 Clarke Papers, I, 134, 136. The Army's correspondent began his letter: "here hath been this day the greatest tumults and insolencies raised upon the House of Commons that ever any yet heard of."
110 Clarke Papers, I, 136.
111 *O.P.H.*, 15, 451–2.

112 Rushworth, VI, 564. "A Declaration or Representation from His Excellency . . . ," June 14, 1647.

113 Rushworth, VI, 566. "A Declaration or Representation. . . ."

114 Rushworth, VI, 564, 567, 568. "A Declaration or Representation. . . ."

115 Rushworth, VI, 567, 569–70. "A Declaration or Representation. . . ."

116 Rushworth, VI, 570–1. "The Heads of a Charge."

117 Rushworth, VI, 571. "The Heads of a Charge."

118 Rushworth, VI, 572. "A Paper Delivered to the Right Honorable Commissioners . . ."

119 C.J., 5, 213; L.J., 9, 274; Common Council Journal, vol. 40, fol. 223; C.J., 5, 217, 216.

120 C.J., 5, 237. On July 8, for example, one Cornet Arundell was examined in the House of Commons for gathering the names of reduced soldiers. There were so many of them that over 2,000 were to meet in St. James' Fields to subscribe their names.

121 Juxon, Dr. Williams' Library, Mss. 24.50, fol. 111.

122 E. 515 (24), Perfect Occurrences, no. 26, June 25–July 2, 1647.

123 C.J., 5, 217. The question was whether the listed soldiers should be be discharged.
No 76 Grimston and Tate
Yea 72 Edward Baynton and Sir Henry Mildmay
Juxon, Dr. Williams' Library, Mss. 24.50, fol. 111.

124 L.J., 9, 265; C.J., 5, 211. The question was whether the King should be given up by the Army.
Yea 146 Holles and Lisle
No 115 Livesay and Marten

125 C.J., 5, 211–15.

126 C.J., 5, 214. The question was to pay fourteen days' wages immediately and fourteen more after the Army had withdrawn twenty miles.
No 133 Lewes and Lord Cranborne
Yea 117 Bulkeley and Onslowe

127 L.J., 9, 269; C.J., 5, 211, 219.

128 C.J., 5, 215.

129 C.J., 5, 214, 219.

130 C.J., 5, 218; Whitacre, B.L. Add. Mss. 31,116, fol. 314. On June 22 Sir Robert Harley drafted a letter to someone in the Army, perhaps John Rushworth, suggesting a compromise solution: "The inquiry now, sir, is what may be a happy medicine for their reconciliation?" He suggested the payment of the soldiers' arrears, the

Army's disbandment and then its reestablishment into a force of "10 or 12,000 to remain in England . . . and go into Ireland with their own officers." Harley concluded, "if you give me encouragement I will use my best endeavors here that it may be represented to the House with most advantage. My expressions I hope are clear, my heart is by God's mercy upright herein." B.L. Loan 29/122/Misc. 16.

131 *O.P.H.*, 15, 492–3.
132 *O.P.H.*, 15, 501.
133 Ibid.
134 Rushworth, VI, 578.
135 Rushworth, VI, 585, 588, 589: "An Humble Remonstrance . . ." June 23, 1647.
136 Rushworth, VI, 591: "An Humble Remonstrance. . . ."
137 *C.J.*, 5, 222.
138 *C.J.*, 5, 223.
139 *C.J.*, 5, 225.
140 Holles, "Memoirs" in Maseres, *Select Tracts*, I, 262.
141 *C.J.*, 5, 226; 227. The House divided on the question that none could leave the Army without Fairfax's consent.
    Yea 121   Haselrig and Evelyn (Wilts.)
    No   85   Erle and Green
142 *C.J.*, 5, 229, 226. The ordinance to provide £60,000 a month on a new assessment had finally been passed by the Lords on June 23. *L.J.*, 9, 288.
143 *C.J.*, 5, 226. The Lords agreed to this order on June 29 with the single dissent of the Earl of Stamford. *L.J.*, 9, 304.
144 *O.P.H.*, 16, 27.
145 Common Council Journal, vol. 40, fols. 230–2.
146 *L.J.*, 9, 310.
147 *L.J.*, 9, 310–11.
148 Common Council Journal, vol. 40, fol. 233; *C.J.*, 5, 236.
149 Rushworth, VI, 594.
150 Bell, I, 364.
151 Rushworth, VI, 594.
152 Rushworth, VI, 594, 603. Fairfax's letter to Parliament on June 30 clearly expressed the relationship between Parliament's votes and and proximity of the Army's headquarters to London.
153 *C.J.*, 5, 227.
154 Clarke Mss., vol. 110, fols. 56–61, "Queries whether the Army ought to insist upon their charge against those persons they have accused and also see the peace of the Kingdom settled before they disband." This document was not printed by Firth.

155 Clarke Mss., vol. 110, fols. 56–7.
156 Ibid., fol. 56.
157 Ibid., fols. 58, 57.
158 Ibid., fol. 58.
159 Ibid., fol. 60.
160 *C.J.*, 5, 236. "A Particular Charge or Impeachment..." is printed in *O.P.H.*, 16, 70–92.
161 *O.P.H.*, 16, 70–3. Whitelocke's shameful conduct during these days was omitted from the printed account of his memoirs, but appears in the manuscript. The tale of his midnight flight from London and return "to my chamber in the Temple where I kept myself close, a kind of prisoner not opening the door to any, to avoid meeting with Mr. Holles and his Party," is a corrective to the sentimental assessment provided by Ruth Spalding, *The Improbable Puritan* (London, 1975). B.L. Add. Mss. 37,344, fols. 97–8.
162 *O.P.H.*, 16, 74.
163 *O.P.H.*, 16, 74–8.
164 Clarke Mss., vol. 110, fol. 57; *O.P.H.*, 16, 89.
165 *O.P.H.*, 16, 91.
166 E. 397 (8), p. 6.
167 Waller, p. 176. "One way it might look like a charge upon the eleven members; another way it resembled an arraignment of the House of Commons supposing them so weak and corrupt as to be acted by particular interests."
168 E. 398 (4), "Animadversions upon a Declaration of the Proceedings Versus the XI Members," July 13, 1647.
169 E. 397 (21), "A Clear and Full Vindication of the Late Proceedings of the Army," July 12, 1647.
170 E. 398 (22), "Certain Queries to Mr. William Prynne."
171 Rushworth, VI, 587, "An Humble Remonstrance," June 23, 1647. The Army suggested this reform "that so the Kingdom may regularly come to know who they are that perform their trust faithfully and who not."
172 Throughout this period Lilburne's influence upon the Army was, at best, negligible. See M. A. Kishlansky, "The Army and the Levellers: The Roads to Putney."
173 *O.P.H.*, 16, 30.
174 *O.P.H.*, 16, 51; Clarke Papers, I, 148.
175 Clarke Mss., vol. 110, fols. 56–7.
178 As the Army explained on July 7, "there is nothing done with effect, notwithstanding the votes of the House, to the dispersing of the reformado officers." *O.P.H.*, 16, 98–9.
179 On July 8 the Lords ordered the Derby House Committee to meet

daily and admonished the Commons' members to attend. *L.J.*, 9, 318. The decline in attendance was not precipitous, but the most active members of the Committee were no longer present. P.R.O. S.P. 21/26.

180 *O.P.H.*, 16, 99.

181 Clarke Papers, I, 152.

182 The Army complained: "and as we hear are daily listing more forces, pretending the service of Ireland." *O.P.H.*, 16, 99.

183 Clarke Papers, I, 152–6.

184 Clarke Mss., vol. 41, fol. 166. See also the agitators' response to E. 399 (2), "The petition of the Well-Affected Young Men and Apprentices."

185 *C.J.*, 5, 235.

186 *C.J.*, 5, 237.

187 *C.J.*, 5, 237, 240; *L.J.*, 9, 322. Reformadoes' arrears were also audited at Goldsmiths' Hall and Weavers' Hall. The appointment of a third location, Christ Church, was necessitated by the number of reformadoes who had entered the City by June.

188 *C.J.*, 5, 243, 252; *L.J.*, 9, 334. As these disorders took place three days before the replacement of the new Militia Committee members, that cannot have been its cause. Pearl, p. 49.

189 E. 398 (9), "The Humble Petition of Many Thousands of Young Men and Apprentices," in Rushworth VI, 614–15; Rushworth, VI, 615.

190 *C.J.*, 5, 102.

191 *O.P.H.*, 16, 108–10; E. 399 (35), "A Petition from the City of London with a Covenant."

192 *O.P.H.*, 16, 109.

193 *O.P.H.*, 16, 97–100.

194 Rushworth, VI, 610–11.

195 See "The Memoirs of Sir John Berkeley," in Maseres, *Select Tracts*, I, 355–68.

196 Clarke Papers, I, 170–3, 174.

197 It was Rainsborough who made this suggestion. Clarke Papers, I, 178–9.

198 Clarke Papers, I, 204; see E. 392 (19), "Gold Tried in the Fire," for Tulidah and his connection to Tue.

199 Clarke Papers, I, 207.

200 Ibid., I, 193.

201 Ibid., I, 182.

202 Ibid., I, 206. By the middle party Cromwell certainly meant a group of neutral M.P.s and not those whom modern historians call by that name.

203 Ibid., I, 192.
204 Ibid., I, 185.
205 Ibid., I, 202.
206 Ibid., I, 208.
207 *O.P.H.*, 16, 160–1.
208 Bell, I, 369.
209 Clarke Papers, I, 209.
210 *O.P.H.*, 16, 160–1.
211 Rushworth, VI, 630.
212 Clarke Papers, I, 216–17; *O.P.H.*, 16, 159.
213 *C.J.*, 5, 253. The question was that the Army's proposals not be considered.
   No   80   Haselrig and Evelyn (Wilts.)
   Yea   68   Irby and Tate
214 *C.J.*, 5, 254.
215 *L.J.*, 9, 349. Of the eight, two, the Earl of Lincoln and Lord Hunsdon, dissented.
216 Pearl's assertion (p. 49) that the events of July were orchestrated by the eleven members cannot be substantiated from the available evidence.
217 Juxon, Dr. Williams; Library, Mss. 24.50, fol. 112; *C.J.*, 5, 251–2.
218 *O.P.H.*, 16, 163–4.
219 *O.P.H.*, 16, 165.
220 *C.J.*, 5, 256.
221 Common Council Journal, vol. 40, fol. 235; *O.P.H.*, 16, 163–4.
222 Common Council Journal vol. 40, fols. 235–7.
223 *L.J.*, 9, 354. The Captain Farr named by Peregrine Pritty was undoubtedly Ralph Farr, a London goldsmith, and one of the dragoon officers who left New Model service. Juxon, Dr. Williams' Library, Mss. 24.50, fol. 112. Juxon claimed "the conspiracy was so strong it was cried in the streets." Two thousand signatures were gained for the engagement. E. 518 (23), *Perfect Occurrences*, no. 34, August 20–7.
224 Juxon, Dr. Williams' Library, Mss. 24.50, fol. 112.
225 *C.J.*, 5, 258.
226 *L.J.*, 9, 356: "beside that hereby the City is for the present put out of all regular posture of defense."
227 *L.J.*, 9, 356–7; *C.J.*, 5, 258.
228 *C.J.*, 5, 258.
229 *L.J.*, 9, 355.
230 Ibid.; The nine were the Earls of Manchester, Northumberland, Pembroke, Salisbury, Suffolk, and Lincoln, and Lords Howard, Willoughby, and Grey. The anti-innovatory Lords in this group

might easily have blocked the vote reconfirming the change in the militia committee if mob riots were not a greater innovation than armies. Juxon, Dr. Williams' Library, Mss. 24.50, fol. 113; Clarke Papers, I, 217–18. The best newsbook account is in E. 518 (13), *A Perfect Summary of Chief Passages in Parliament*, no. 2, July 26–August 2, 1647.

231 Juxon, Dr. Williams' Library, Mss. 24.50, fol. 113.

232 The Commons called Colonel Bellamy and Mr. Jupe into the House shortly before it was stormed. Bellamy had been the printer of the "Solemn Engagement" and was deeply involved in the campaign. See Pearl, pp. 33, 37.

233 Juxon, Dr. Williams' Library, Mss. 24.50, fol. 113. Lenthall's account of these events suggests that those opposed to the vote had the majority but the House could not divide. *O.P.H.*, 16, 196–9. E. 518 (29), *Perfect Occurrences*, no. 36, September 3–10, 1647.

234 Juxon, Dr. Williams' Library, Mss., 24.50, fols. 112–13. Pearl, pp. 33, 37.

235 Juxon, Dr. Williams' Library, Mss., 24.50, fol. 113.

236. Common Council Journal, vol. 40, fol. 240; Clarke Papers, I, 217–18.

237 Rushworth, VI, 631, 639.

238 *O.P.H.*, 16, 182.

239 *O.P.H.*, 16, 182–3.

240 *O.P.H.*, 16, 185–7.

241 Clarke Papers, I, 217–18; I follow Firth's identification of this letter.

242 *O.P.H.*, 16, 188.

243 *O.P.H.*, 16, 189.

244 Common Council Journal, vol. 40, fol. 240.

245 *Ibid.*, fol. 241.

246 *O.P.H.*, 16, 190–1; on July 29 the mayor ordered that no apprentices be allowed out of their masters' homes except on business. This was doubtless designed to demonstrate that the City government had matters well in hand. Unfortunately, the mayor's order left unfilled the ranks of the Army the Militia Committee was attempting to raise: "which [order] hath caused some obstructions to the service at present for the defense and safety of this City as that upon beat of the drum few or none hath come forth for that purpose." On July 30 the mayor's order was rescinded. Such lack of coordination may be another reason the so-called Counter-Revolution failed. Corporation of London Record Office, Common Hall Book, vol. 11, fols. 82–3.

247 Common Council Journal, vol. 40, fol. 243.

248 David Underdown, *Pride's Purge* (Oxford, 1971), p. 83.

249 *C.J.*, 5, 259.
250 *C.J.*, 5, 259–60.
251 *C.J.*, 5, 261–2.
252 *O.P.H.*, 16, 192.
253 Rushworth, VI, 647.
254 Edmund Ludlow, *The Memoirs of Edmund Ludlow*, C. H. Firth ed., 2 vols. (London, 1894), I, 207; *O.P.H.*, 16, 197.
255 Common Council Journal, vol. 40, fols. 243, 244. After an attempt to induce Skippon to take the command, which he theoretically held, Massey was put in charge of raising the City's defense. Waller and Poyntz were also prominent. Juxon, Dr. Williams' Library, Mss. 24.50, fol. 114.
256 See the Speaker's letter to Fairfax, *O.P.H.*, 16, 207–9.
257 Common Council Journal, vol. 40, fol. 250.
258 Juxon, Dr. Williams' Library, Mss. 24.50, fol. 119.
259 Ibid., fol. 118.
260 Bell, I, 349.
261 Clarke Papers, I, 213.

CONCLUSION

1 For a recent analysis of a portion of these groups see Murray Tolmie, *The Triumph of the Saints* (Cambridge, 1977).
2 M. A. Kishlansky, "The Army and the Levellers: The Roads to Putney" *Historical Journal* (forthcoming).
3 B.L. Thomason Tracts 669 f. 11, fol. 44.
4 E. 396 (1), "Reasons Why the House of Commons Ought in Justice Forthwith to Suspend the Members charged by the Army."
5 E. 399 (16).
6 Ian Gentles, "Arrears of Pay and Ideology in the Army Revolt of 1647," in Brian Bond and Ian Roy, eds., *War and Society* (London, 1976) I, 44–66. This is also the opinion of J. P. Kenyon: "no one need doubt that if the Long Parliament had settled its [the New Model's] arrears of pay and carried through its scheme of demobilization no more would have been heard of the Levellers or the Agreement of the People and very little of Oliver Cromwell." *Times Literary Supplement* (June 2, 1978), 613.
7 "Not as mercenaries, but as faithful and freeborn subjects" was the self-characterization of two groups of reformadoes who presented petitions to the Houses on June 14. This was the same day the Army issued its declaration containing the oft-quoted phrase, "we are not a mere mercenary Army." H.L.R.O. Main Papers, June 1647.

BIBLIOGRAPHY

―――――――

I. MANUSCRIPTS CITED

A. Alnwick Castle
    Manuscripts of the Duke of Northumberland, vols. 17, 51
B. Bodleian Library
    1   Carte Mss.

Vols. 79–81	Wharton Papers
83	Montreuil Correspondence
84	Sabran Correspondence
95	Miscellaneous Papers
223	Letters of Edward Montague

    2   Clarendon Mss.

Vols. 27–9	Letters of Intelligence

    3   Tanner Mss.

Vols. 58–61	1644–7

C. British Library
    1   Additional Mss.

10,114	Parliamentary Diary of John Harington
11,331–3	Correspondence of Sir William Brereton
15,903	Norfolk Papers: Letters of Alderman Atkins and Richard Harmon, M.P.
18,780	Parliamentary Diary of Walter Yonge, April–October 1645
18,979	Fairfax Correspondence
19,398	Norfolk Papers: Letters of Alderman Atkins, Mayor Tooley, and Richard Harmon, M.P.
19,399	Fairfax Correspondence
20,778	Fairfax Correspondence
21,506	Fairfax Correspondence
22,619–20	Norwich Papers
25,460	Miscellaneous Historical Documents: Gentlemen of the Earl of Essex's Lifeguard
25,465	Thomas Juxon's Journal (a partial copy)
25,708	Sir Thomas Fairfax's Memorial of the Civil War
26,641	Official Papers of the English and Scottish Commissioners
26,644–5	The Passage of a Bill Through Parliament

350

Bibliography

29,747   Rushworth Correspondence
31,116   The Parliamentary Diary of Lawrence Whitacre
32,093   Miscellaneous Papers: Holles and Savile Examinations
37,343–45   Whitelocke's Annals
46,374   Harington's Diary (copy)

2 Egerton Mss.

3514   Original Letters: Cromwell Correspondence

3 Harleian Mss.

166   Parliamentary Diary of Sir Simonds D'Ewes
252   John Rushworth's Narrative
374   Letters of Sir Simonds D'Ewes
427   An Account Book of Colonel Edward Whalley's Regiment
1,058   Rules and Orders of Parliament
1,377   Coats of Arms of the Parliamentary Army
2,315   Sir Thomas Fairfax's Memorial of the Civil War
4,619   Notes on Privileges of the House of Commons (1628)
7,001   Fairfax Correspondence

4 Sloan Mss.

1519   Miscellaneous Letters
4957   Walter Yonge, Elencus Parliamentorum

5 Portland Loan   29   Harley Papers
Boxes

15, 27, 73, 119, 122, 123, 175, 366

D. The Corporation of London Record Office
1 Common Council Journal, vol. 40, 1644–7
2 Letter Books, vol. QQ
3 Repetorium, vol. 59
4 Common Hall Book, vol. 11

E. Dr. Williams' Library, Mss. 24.50 (Thomas Juxon's Journal)

F. The House of Lords Record Office
1 Main Papers, vols. 1644–7
2 Nalson Mass. (photocopy), vols. 8, 12
3 Mss Journals: House of Lords, 1644–7

G. Worcester College Library
Clarke Mss., vols. 41, 67, 110

H. The Public Record Office
1 Exchequer Records
E 101/67/11a   Accounts of the Treasurers at War
E 351/302   Accounts of the Treasurers at War
2 Prerogative Court of Canterbury, Wills

3 State Papers
    S.P. 16   Domestic: Charles I
    S.P. 21   Domestic: Charles I
    S.P. 21/26   Day Book of the Derby House Committee
    S.P. 21/27   Letter Book of the Derby House Committee
    S.P. 28   Commonwealth Exchequer Papers
    S.P. 28/27–60 Warrants of the Parliamentary Armies 1644–9
    S.P. 28/140   New Model Army Account Books
    S.P. 28/237   Warrants of London Militia Committee
    S.P. 28/268   Committee for Arrears Account Book
    S.P. 28/252–6 Committee for Taking the Accounts of the Kingdom
    S.P. 28/350   Miscellaneous Accounts

II. PAMPHLETS AND NEWSBOOKS

A. The British Museum
  1 The Thomason Tracts: Pamphlets
    E. 3–401; 425; 506; 509–11; 513; 515–16; 518; 607; 811; 903; 1181; 1184; 669 f 9–11.
  2 The Thomason Tracts: Newsbooks
    The Citties Weekly Post
    The City Scout
    The Complete Intelligencer
    A Continuation of Certain Special and Remarkable Passages
    The Country Foot Post
    The Country Messenger
    A Diary or Exact Journal
    The Exchange Intelligencer
    The Kingdom's Weekly Intelligencer
    The London Post
    Mercurius Aulicus
    Mercurius Brittannicus
    Mercurius Civicus
    Mercurius Veridicus
    The Moderate Intelligencer
    The Moderate Messenger
    The Parliamentary Scout
    A Perfect Diurnal of Some Passages in Parliament
    Perfect Occurrences of Parliament
    Perfect Occurrences of Every Day's Journal
    Perfect Passages of Each Day's Proceedings

The Scottish Dove
The True Informer
The Weekly Account
The Weekly Postmaster
B. Houghton Library, Harvard University
    Dell, William, *Sermons and Discourses* (1652)
    Peter, Hugh, *God's Doing, Man's Duty* (1646)
    Ram, Robert, *Sermon at Balderton* (1646)
    Vicars, John, *England's Parliamentary Chronicle* (1643–6)
C. Regenstein Library, University of Chicago
    Edwards, Thomas, *Gangraena* (1646)
    Walker, Clement, *The Complete History of Independency* (1661)
D. Worcester College Library, Oxford
    Certain Considerations and Cautions by London Ministers (1646)
    The Civil Wars of the City (1645)
    A Discovery of Officers and Agitators (1647)
    England's Doleful Lamentation (1647)
    The Humble Petition of the Officers Drawn for Service in Ireland (1647)

III. PRINTED SOURCES

Abbott, W. C., ed., *The Writings and Speeches of Oliver Cromwell* (4 vols.; Cambridge Mass.: Harvard University Press, 1937–47).

Acts and Ordinances of the Interregnum, C. H. Firth and F. Rait, eds. (3 vols.; London, 1911).

Ashburnham, John, *A Narrative by John Ashburnham of His Attendance on King Charles the First* (2 vols.; London, 1830).

Baxter, Richard, *Reliquiae Baxterianae*, M. Sylvester, ed. (3 pts.; London, 1693).

Bell, Robert, ed., *Memorials of the Civil War: Comprising the Correspondence of the Fairfax Family* (2 vols.; London, 1849).

Berkely, Sir John, "The Memoirs of Sir John Berkely," in *Select Tracts Relating to the Civil Wars in England*, ed. by F. Maseres (2 vols.; London, 1815).

Blencowe, R. W., ed., *Sydney Papers* (London, 1825).

Bruce, John, ed., *The Quarrel Between the Earl of Manchester and Oliver Cromwell* (London: Camden Society Publications, new ser. 12, 1875).

Calendar of State Papers, Domestic Series 1625–65, J. Bruce, M. A. E. Green, W. D. Hamilton, eds. (43 vols.; London, 1858–97).

Bibliography

Calendar of State Papers and Manuscripts Relating to English Affairs Existing in the Archives of Venice, 1623–64, A. B. Hinds, ed. (17 vols.; London, 1912–32).

Cary, Henry, *Memorials of the Great Civil War 1642–52* (2 vols.; London, 1842).

Clarendon, Edward, Earl of, *History of the Rebellion*, W. D. Macray, ed. (6 vols.; Oxford, 1888).

State Papers Collected by Edward, Earl of Clarendon, Commencing 1621, R. Scrope and T. Monkhouse, eds. (3 vols.; Oxford, 1767–86).

The Clarke Papers, C. H. Firth, ed. (4 vols.; London: Camden Society Publications, 1891–1901).

Cokayne, G. E., ed., *The Complete Peerage* (13 vols.; London, 1910–59).

Fairfax, Sir Thomas, "A Short Memorial," in *Select Tracts Relating to the Civil Wars in England*, ed. by F. Maseres (2 vols.; London, 1815).

Gardiner, S. R., "A Letter from the Earl of Manchester on the Conduct of Cromwell," (London: Camden Society Publications, Miscellany 8, 1883).

Hanbury, Benjamin, *Historical Memorial Relating to the Independents*, (3 vols.; London, 1839–44).

Harington, John, *The Diary of John Harington M.P.*, M. Stieg, ed. (Old Woking, Surrey: Somerset Record Society Publications, 74, 1977).

Historical Manuscripts Commission, 3rd Report: Northumberland Mss.; Marquess of Bath Mass.; 4th Report: Earl of Denbigh Mss.; 6th Report: Earl of Denbigh Mss.; House of Lords Mss.; 7th Report: Earl of Denbigh Mss.; Sir Alexander Malet Mss.; G. A. Lowndes Mss.; 8th Report, pt. 2: Duke of Manchester Mss.; 9th Report: H. Chandos-Pole-Gell Mss.; 10th Report, app. VI: Braye Mss.; 11th Report, app. VI: Duke of Hamilton Mss.; 13th Report, pt. 1: Portland Mss.; 14th Report, app. II; Portland Mss.; Lord De L'Isle and Dudley Mss., vol. VI; Earl of Egmont Mss.;. Earl of Mar and Kellie Mss.; Marquess of Salisbury Mss., vols. XXII, XXIV.

Holles, Denzil, "Memorials of Denzil Lord Holles," in *Select Tracts Relating to the Civil Wars in England*, ed. by F. Maseres (2 vols.; London, 1815).

Holmes, Clive, ed., *The Suffolk Committee for Scandalous Ministers* (Ipswich: Suffolk Records Society, 13, 1970).

Hutchinson, Lucy, *Memoirs of the Life of Colonel Hutchinson*, James Sutherland, ed. (Oxford: University Press, 1973).

Bibliography

Journals of the House of Commons, 1640–66, vols. 3–5, (London, 1803).

Journals of the House of Lords, 1628–1666, vols. 6–9 (London, n.d.).

Lomas, S. L., ed., *The Letters and Speeches of Oliver Cromwell with Elucidations by Thomas Carlyle* (London, 1904).

Ludlow, Edmund, *Memoirs of Edmund Ludlow*, C. H. Firth, ed. (2 vols.; Oxford, 1894).

Meikle, H. W., *Correspondence of the Scots Commissioners in London* (Edinburgh: Roxburghe Club, 1917).

Mitchell, A. F., and Struthers, J., eds., *Minutes of the Westminster Assembly of Divines* (Edinburgh, 1874).

Montreuil, Jean de, *The Diplomatic Correspondence of Jean de Montrueil and the Brothers de Bellievre, 1645–48*, J. G. Fotheringham, ed. (2 vols.; Edinburgh, 1898–9).

The Parliamentary or Constitutional History of England (24 vols.; London, 1751–62)

Peacock, E., *Army Lists of Roundheads and Cavaliers* (London, 1863).

Peck, Francis, *Desiderata Curiosa* (London, 1779).

Rushworth, John, *Historical Collections* (8 vols.; London, 1721).

Sims, C. S., ed., "The Speaker of the House of Commons," *American Historical Review* 45 (1939), 90–5.

"Policies in Parliament," *Huntington Library Quarterly* 15 (1951), 45–58.

Sprigge, Joshua, *Anglia Rediviva*, Harry T. Moore, ed. (rpt., Gainesville, Fl.: Scholars' Facsimiles and Reprints, 1960).

Tibbutt, H. G., *The Letterbooks of Sir Samuel Luke, 1644–45* (Streatley: Bedfordshire Historical Records Society, 42, 1963).

Walker, Clement, "The Mystery of the Two Juntoes," in *Select Tracts Relating to the Civil Wars in England*, ed. by F. Maseres (2 vols.; London, 1815).

The Complete History of Independency (London, 1661).

Waller, Sir William, *The Vindication of the Character and Conduct of Sir William Waller* (London, 1793).

Webb, J., and Webb, T. W., (eds.), *The Military Memoir of Colonel John Birch* (London: Camden Society Publications, new ser. 7, 1873).

Whitelocke, Bulstrode, *Memorials of English Affairs* (4 vols.; Oxford, 1853).

IV. SECONDARY WORKS

Adair, John, *Roundhead General: A Military Biography of Sir William Waller* (London: Macdonald, 1969).

Bibliography

Aylmer, Gerald E., "Place Bills and the Separation of Powers," *Transactions of the Royal Historical Society*, 5th Ser., 15 (1965), 45–69.

"Was Oliver Cromwell a member of the Army in 1646–7 or Not?" *History* 56 (1971), pp. 183–8.

The Levellers in the English Revolution (Ithaca, N.Y.: Cornell University Press, 1975).

Bernstein, Eduard, *Cromwell and Communism* (London: George Allen and Unwin, 1930).

Berry, J., and Lee, S. G., *A Cromwellian Major-General: The Career of Colonel James Berry* (Oxford: Oxford University Press, 1938).

Bottigheimer, Karl, *English Money and Irish Land* (Oxford: Oxford University Press, 1970).

Brailsford, H. N., *The Levellers and the English Revolution* (London: Cresset Press, 1961).

Brenner, Robert, "The Civil War Politics of London's Merchant Community," *Past and Present* 58 (February 1973), 53–107.

Brunton, D., and Pennington, D. H., *The Members of the Long Parliament* (London: George Allen and Unwin, 1954).

Burne, A. H., and Young, P., *The Great Civil War* (London: Eyre and Spottiswoode, 1959).

Christianson, Paul, "From Expectation to Militance: Reformers and Babylon in the First Two Years of the Long Parliament," *Journal of Ecclesiastical History* 24 (1973), 225–44.

Coate, Mary, *Cornwall in the Great Civil War and Interregnum* (Oxford: Oxford University Press, 1933).

Cotton, A. N. B., "Cromwell and the Self-Denying Ordinance," *History* 62 (1977), 211–31.

Crawford, Patricia, "The Savile Affair," *English Historical Review* 90 (1975), 76–93.

"Charles Stuart, That Man of Blood," *Journal of British Studies* 16 (1977), 41–62.

Davies, Godfrey, "Documents Illustrating the First Civil War," *Journal of Modern History* 3 (1931), 64–71.

"The Parliamentary Army Under the Earl of Essex, 1642–45," *English Historical Review* 49 (1934), 32–54.

Dawson, W. H., *Cromwell's Understudy: The Life and Times of General John Lambert* (London: W. Hodge, 1938).

Donagan, Barbara, "The Clerical Patronage of Robert Rich, Second Earl of Warwick 1619–42," *Proceedings of the American Philosophical Society* 120, (1976), 388–419.

Everitt, Alan, ed., *Suffolk and the Great Rebellion* (Ipswich: Suffolk Records Society, 1960).

Bibliography

The Community of Kent and the Great Rebellion (Leicester: Leicester University Press, 1966).

Farnell, James E., "The Aristocracy and Leadership of Parliament in the English Civil Wars," *Journal of Modern History* 44 (1972), 79–86.

Firth, Charles H., "The Raising of the Ironsides," *Transactions of the Royal Historical Society*, new ser. 13 (1899), 17–73.

Oliver Cromwell and the Rule of the Puritans in England (New York, 1900).

Cromwell's Army (London: Methuen, 1902).

The House of Lords During the Civil War (London: Longmans Green, 1910).

"London During the Civil War," *History*, new ser. 11 (1926), 25–36.

Firth, C. H., and Davies, G., *The Regimental History of Cromwell's Army* (2 vols.; Oxford: Oxford University Press, 1940).

Fletcher, Anthony, *A County Community in Peace and War: Sussex 1600–60* (London: Longmans, 1975).

Forster, G. C. F., "County Government in Yorkshire During the Interregnum," *Northern History* 12 (1976), 84–104.

Forster, Stephen, "The Presbyterian – Independents Exorcized: A Ghost Story for Historians," *Past and Present* 44 (1969), 52–75.

Frank, Joseph, *The Levellers* (Cambridge, Mass.: Harvard University Press, 1955),

Gardiner, Samuel Rawson, *The History of the Great Civil War* (4 vols.; London: Longmans Green, 1893).

Constitutional Documents of the Puritan Revolution (Oxford, Oxford University Press, 1906).

Gentles, Ian, "The Arrears of Pay of the Parliamentary Army at the End of the First Civil War," *Bulletin of the Institute of Historical Research* 48 (1975), 52–63.

"Arrears of Pay and Ideology in the Army Revolt of 1647," in *War and Society*, ed. by B. Bond and I. Roy (London: Croom Helm, 1976), I, 44–66.

Gibb, M. A., *The Lord General: A Life of Sir Thomas Fairfax* (London: Lindsay Drummond, 1938).

Glow (Mulligan), Lotte, "The Committee-Men in the Long Parliament August 1642–December 1643," *Historical Journal* 8 (1965), 1–15.

"The Committee of Safety," *English Historical Review* 80 (1965), 289–313.

"Political Affiliations in the House of Commons After Pym's Death," *Bulletin of the Institute of Historical Research* 38, (1965), 48–70.

Bibliography

"Peace Negotiations, Politics and the Committee of Both Kingdoms, 1644–46," *Historical Journal* 12 (1969), 3–22.

"Property and Parliamentary Politics in the English Civil War, 1642–46," *Historical Studies* 16 (1975).

Godwin, William, *History of the Commonwealth of England* (4 vols.; London, 1824–8).

Haller, William, ed., *Tracts on Liberty in the Puritan Revolution* (3 vols.; New York: Columbia University Press, 1934).

The Rise of Puritanism (New York: Columbia University Press, 1938).

"The Word of God in the New Model Army," *Church History* 19 (1950), 15–33.

Liberty and Reformation in the Puritan Revolution (New York: Columbia University Press, 1955).

Haller, William, and Davies, Godfrey, eds., *The Leveller Tracts* (New York: Columbia University Press, 1944).

Hexter, J. H., "The Problem of the Presbyterian–Independents," *American Historical Review* 44 (1938–9), 22–49.

The Reign of King Pym (Cambridge, Mass.: Harvard University Press, 1941).

"Power Struggle, Parliament and Liberty in Early Stuart England," *Journal of Modern History* 50 (1978), 1–50.

Hill, Christopher, *God's Englishman* (New York: Dial Press, 1970).

The World Turned Upside Down (New York: Viking, 1972).

Hirst, Derek, "Unanimity in the Commons, Aristocratic Intrigues and the Origins of the English Civil War," *Journal of Modern History* 50 (1978), 51–71.

Holmes, Clive, "Colonel King and Lincolnshire Politics, 1642–46," *Historical Journal* 16 (1973), 451–84.

The Eastern Association (Cambridge: Cambridge University Press, 1974).

Howell, Roger, *Newcastle-upon-Tyne and the Puritan Revolution* (Oxford: Oxford University Press, 1967).

Jordan, W. K., *The Development of Religious Toleration in England* (4 vols.; Cambridge, Mass.: Harvard University Press, 1932–40).

Kaplan, Lawrence, "Presbyterians and Independents in 1643," *English Historical Review* 84 (1969), 244–56.

"The 'Plot' to Depose Charles I in 1644," *Bulletin of the Institute of Historical Research* 44 (1971), 216–23.

Politics and Religion During the English Revolution (New York: New York University Press, 1976).

Keeler, Mary F., *The Long Parliament* (Philadelphia: American Philosophical Society Memoirs, 36, 1954).

Bibliography

Ketton-Cremer, R. W., *Norfolk in the Civil War* (rpt., Hamden, Conn.: Archon Books, 1970).

King, Peter, "The Episcopate During the Civil Wars, 1642–49," *English Historical Review* 83 (1968), 523–36.

"The Reasons for the Abolition of the Book of Common Prayer in 1645," *Journal of Ecclesiastical History* 21 (1970), 327–40.

Kishlansky, Mark, "The Sale of Crown Lands and the Spirit of the Revolution," *Economic History Review*, 2nd ser. 29 (1976), 125–30.

"The Emergence of Adversary Politics in the Long Parliament," *Journal of Modern History* 49 (1977), 617–40.

"The Case of the Army Truly Stated: The Creation of the New Model Army," *Past and Present* 81 (1978), 51–75.

"The Army and the Levellers: The Roads to Putney," *Historical Journal* (forthcoming).

Liu, Tia, *Discord in Zion: The Puritan Divines and the Puritan Revolution* (The Hague: Martinus Nijhoff, 1973).

McCampbell, Alice, "The London Parish and the London Precinct, 1640–60," *Guildhall Studies in London History* 2 (1976), 107–24.

MacCormack, J. R., *Revolutionary Politics in the Long Parliament* (Cambridge, Mass.: Harvard University Press, 1973).

MacFarlane, Alan, ed., *The Diary of Ralph Josselin* (Oxford: Oxford University Press, 1976).

Malcolm, Joyce, "A King in Search of Soldiers, Charles I in 1642," *Historical Journal* 21 (1978), 251–73.

Manning, Brian, ed., *Religion, Politics and the English Civil War* (London: Edward Arnold, 1973).

The English People and the English Revolution (London: Heinemann, 1976).

Markham, Clement, *The Life of the Great Lord Fairfax* (London, 1870).

Masson, David, *The Life of John Milton* (7 vols.; London, 1859–94).

Miller, Amos, "Joseph Jane's Account of Cornwall During the Civil War," *English Historical Review* 90, (1975), 94–102

Morrill, John S., "Mutiny and Discontent in English Provincial Armies, 1645–47," *Past and Present* 56 (1972), 49–74.

Cheshire 1630–60 (Oxford: Oxford University Press, 1974).

The Revolt of the Provinces: Conservatives and Radicals in the English Civil War, 1630–50 (London: George Allen and Unwin, 1976).

"The Army Revolt of 1647," in *Britain and the Netherlands*, ed. by A. C. Duke and C. A. Tamse (The Hague: Martinus Nijhoff, 1977), VI, 54–78.

Bibliography

Morton, A. L., ed., *Freedom in Arms* (New York: International Publishers, 1975).

Neale, J. E., *The Elizabethan House of Commons* (London: Penguin, 1953).

Noble, Mark, *The Lives of the English Regicides* (2 vols.; London, 1798).

Notestein, Wallace, "The Establishment of the Committee of Both Kingdoms," *American Historical Review* 17 (1912), 477–95.

"The Winning of the Initiative by the House of Commons," *Proceedings of the British Academy* 11 (1924–5), 125–75.

The House of Commons 1604–10 (New Haven, Conn.: Yale University Press, 1971).

Nuttall, G. F., *Visible Saints: The Congregational Way 1640–60* (Oxford: Oxford University Press, 1957).

Parker, Geoffrey, *The Army of Flanders and the Spanish Road* (Cambridge: Cambridge University Press, 1972).

Paul, Robert, *The Lord Protector: Religion and Politics in the Life of Oliver Cromwell* (Grand Rapids Mich.: Eerdmans, 1955).

Pearl, Valerie, *London and the Outbreak of the Puritan Revolution* (Oxford: Oxford University Press, 1960).

"Oliver St. John and the 'Middle Group' in the Long Parliament, August 1643–May 1644," *English Historical Review* 81 (1966), 490–519.

"The 'Royal Independents' in the English Civil War," *Transactions of the Royal Historical Society*, 5th ser. 18 (1968), 69–96.

"London Puritans and Scotch Fifth Columnists," in *Essays in London History Presented to Philip Edmund Jones*, ed. by A. E. J. Hollaender and W. Kellaway (London: Hodder and Stoughton, 1969), pp. 317–31.

"London's Counter-Revolution," in *The Interregnum: The Quest for Settlement*, ed. by G. E. Aylmer (London: Macmillan, 1972), pp. 29–56.

Pease, T. C. *The Leveller Movement* (Washington, D.C.: American Historical Association 1916).

Pennington, D. H., "The Accounts of the Kingdom, 1642–49," in *Essays in Economic and Social History of Tudor and Stuart England*, ed. by F. J. Fisher (Cambridge: Cambridge University Press, 1961), pp. 182–203.

Pennington, D. H., and Roots, I., eds., *The Committee at Stafford, 1643–45* (Manchester: Manchester University Press, 1957).

Phillips, C. B., "County Committees and Local Government in Cumberland and Westmoreland, 1642–60," *Northern History* 5 (1970), 34–66.

Bibliography

Ramsey, R. W., *Henry Ireton* (London: Longmans Green, 1949).

Richardson, R. C., *The Debate on the English Revolution* (London: Methuen, 1977).

Rowe, Violet, *Sir Henry Vane the Younger* (London: Athlone Press, 1970).

Rusche, Harry, "Prophecies and Propagandas, 1641 to 1651," *English Historical Review* 84 (1969), 752–70.

Russell, Conrad, "Parliament and the King's Finances," in *The Origins of the English Civil War*, ed. by Conrad S. R. Russell (London: Macmillan, 1973), pp. 91–118.

"Parliamentary History in Perspective, 1603–29," *History* 61 (1976), 1–27.

Sanford, J. L., *Studies and Illustrations of the Great Rebellion* (London, 1858).

Schlatter, Richard, *Richard Baxter and Puritan Politics* (New Brunswick, N.J.: Rutgers University Press, 1957).

Sharpe, R. R., *London and the Kingdom* (3 vols.; London: Longmans Green, 1894–5).

Shaw, W. A., *History of the English Church During the Civil Wars and Under the Protectorate* (2 vols.; London: Longmans Green, 1900).

Simpkinson, C. H., *Thomas Harrison: Regicide and Major-General* (London: J. M. Dent, 1905).

Skinner, Quentin, "History and Ideology in the English Revolution," *Historical Journal* 8 (1965), 151–78.

Snow, Vernon, "Attendance Trends and Absenteeism in the Long Parliament," *Huntington Library Quarterly* 18 (1954–55), 301–6.

Essex, the Rebel (Lincoln: University of Nebraska Press, 1970).

Solt, Leo, *Saints in Arms* (Stanford: Stanford University Press, 1959).

Spalding, Ruth, *The Improbable Puritan: A Life of Bulstrode Whitelocke* (London: Faber and Faber, 1975).

Stearns, R. P., *The Strenuous Puritan* (Urban: University of Illinois Press, 1954).

Stevenson, David, "The Financing of the Cause of the Covenanters, 1638–51," *Scottish Historical Review* 51 (1972), 89–123.

The Scottish Revolution, 1637–44 (Newton Abbott: David and Charles, 1973).

"The Radical Party in the Kirk, 1637–45," *Journal of Ecclesiastical History* 25 (1974), 135–65.

Revolution and Counter-Revolution in Scotland (London: Royal Historical Society, 1975).

Stone, Lawrence, *The Causes of the English Revolution* (New York: Harper and Row, 1972).

Styles, Peter, "Royalist Government of Worcestershire During the

Bibliography

Civil War, 1642–46," *Transactions of the Worcestershire Archeological Society* 5 (1976), 23–40.

Taylor, J. K. G., "The Civil Government of Gloucester, 1640–46," *Transactions of the Bristol and Gloucester Archeological Society* 67 (1946–8), 59–118.

Tibbutt, H. G., *The Life and Letters of Sir Lewis Dyve, 1599–1669* (Streatley: Bedfordshire Historical Record Society, 27, 1948).

Colonel John Okey, 1606–1662 (Streatley: Bedfordshire Historical Records Society, 35, 1955).

Thomas, Keith, "The Levellers and the Franchise," in *The Interregnum: The Quest for Settlement,* ed. by G. E. Aylmer (London: Macmillan, 1972), pp. 57–78.

Thompson, Christopher, "The Origins of the Politics of the Parliamentary Middle Group," *Transactions of the Royal Historical Society,* 5th ser. 22 (1972), 71–86.

Tolmie, Murray, *The Triumph of the Saints* (Cambridge: Cambridge University Press, 1977).

Trevor-Roper, H. R., "Fast Sermons of the Long Parliament," in *Essays in British History Presented to Sir Keith Feiling,* ed. by H. R. Trevor-Roper (London: Macmillan, 1964), pp. 85–138.

Underdown, David E., "The Independents Reconsidered," *Journal of British Studies* 3 (1964), 57–84.

"The Independents Again," *Journal of British Studies* 8 (1968), 94–118.

"Party Management in the Recruiter Elections, 1645–48," *English Historical Review* 83 (1968), 235–64.

Pride's Purge: Politics in the Puritan Revolution (Oxford: Oxford University Press, 1971).

Somerset in the Civil War and Interregnum (Newton Abbott: David and Charles, 1973).

"Honest Radicals in the Counties, 1642–49," in *Puritans and Revolutionaries,* ed. by D. H. Pennington and K. V. Thomas (Oxford: Oxford University Press, 1978), pp. 186–205.

Walzer, Michael, *The Revolution of the Saints* (New York: Atheneum, 1968).

Wedgwood, C. V., *The King's War* (New York: Macmillan, 1959).

Williamson, H. Ross, *Four Stuart Portraits* (London: Evans Brothers, 1949).

Wilson, J. F., *Pulpit in Parliament* (Princeton, N.J.: Princeton University Press, 1969).

Wolfe, D. M., ed., *Leveller Manifestoes of the Puritan Revolution* (New York: Humanities Press, 1967).

362

Bibliography

Wood, A. C., "Colonel Sir Edward Rossiter," *Lincolnshire Architectural and Archeological Society* 41 (1932), 219–38.

Nottinghamshire in the Civil War (Oxford: Oxford University Press, 1937).

Woodhouse, A. S. P., *Puritanism and Liberty* (London: J. M. Dent, 1938).

Woolrych, Austin, *Battles of the Civil War* (New York: Macmillan, 1961).

Worden, A. B., *The Rump Parliament* (Cambridge: Cambridge University Press, 1974).

Worden, A. B., et al., "Presbyterians, Independents, and Puritans," *Past and Present* 47 (1970), 116–46.

Yule, George, *The Independents in the English Civil War* (Cambridge: Cambridge University Press, 1958).

"Independents and Revolutionaries," *Journal of British Studies* 7 (1968), 11–32.

"The Puritan Piety of Members of the Long Parliament," *Studies in Church History* 8 (1972), 187–94.

Zagorin, Perez, *The Court and the Country* (New York: Atheneum, 1969).

V. UNPUBLISHED WORKS

Bidwell, William, "The Committees and Legislation of the Rump Parliament, 1648–1653: "A Quantitative Study," Ph.D. diss., Univ. of Rochester, 1977.

Crummett, J. B., "The Lay Peers in Parliament, 1640–44," D. Phil. diss., Univ. of Manchester, 1972.

Dow, Frances, "The English Army and the Government of Scotland," Ph.D. diss., Univ. of York, 1976.

Gentles, Ian, "The Debentures Market and Military Purchases of Crown Land, 1649–60," Ph.D. diss., Univ. of London, 1969.

Hexter, J. H. "The Rise of the Independent Party," Ph.D. diss., Harvard Univ., 1936.

Johnson, A. M., "Buckinghamshire: A Study in County Politics," M. A. thesis, Univ. of Wales, Swansea, 1963.

Kaplan, Lawrence, "The Scots and English Civil War Politics, 1643–45," Ph.D. diss., Washington Univ., 1966.

Kirby, D. A., "The Parish of St. Stephen's Coleman Street," B. Litt. thesis, Oxford Univ., 1971.

Kishlansky, Mark, "The Emergence of Radical Politics in the English Revolution," Ph.D. diss., Brown Univ., 1977.

Bibliography

Mahony, Michael, "The Presbyterian Party in the English Civil War," D. Phil. diss., Oxford Univ., 1973.

Manning, Brian, "Neutrals and Neutralism in the English Civil War," D. Phil. diss., Oxford Univ., 1957.

Quintrell, B. W., "The Government of the County of Essex, 1603–42," Ph.D. diss., Univ. of London, 1965.

Stent, R. W., "Thomas Rainsborough and the Army Levellers," M.A. thesis, Univ. of London, 1975.

Willey, F. R., "The Independent Coalition and Changing Parliamentary Alignments," D. Phil. diss., Cambridge Univ., 1972.

Williams, C. M., "Henry Marten," D. Phil. diss., Oxford Univ., 1954.

INDEX

Index

Fairfax, Sir Thomas (*cont.*)
on New Model Army, 69, 211, 213–14
petitioned, 282, 288
politics, 73–4, 117, 125, 157, 191, 229–31, 241, 243, 252
regiment of, 176, 181, 184, 218, 220, 236
Farmer, John, 194
fasts, 18, 26, 32–3, 155, 265, 269
Fiennes, Nathaniel, 97, 132, 164
Fincher, Richard, 219, 221
Fleetwood, Charles, 61, 155, 176, 184–5, 208, 220
Foot, Sir Thomas, 87
Forbes, Alexander, 95–6
Fortescue, Richard, 63, 173–4, 192, 219
free quarter, 49, 67–8, 110, 146, 152, 183, 232, 241

Gibbs, William, 78, 80–2
Gillespie, George, 72, 95
Glyn, John, 39, 45, 83, 132, 158, 175
Goldsmiths' Hall, 111, 125–7, 145, 148, 153
Committee of, 126, 243–6, 149, 151, 168, 170–2
Gooday, Samuel, 219, 229
Goodwin, Robert, 164
Goring, Lord George, 15, 73
Graves, Robert, 162, 174, 203, 221, 236, 245
Charles I and, 230, 234
regimental arrears, 68, 184, 210, 212–13
report of, 216
retirement of, 219
Green, Giles, 151
Grey of Warke, Lord (William Grey), 172
Grimes, Mark, 216
Guildhall, 240, 265
Gurdon, John, 126, 135

Hammond, Robert, 49, 174, 190, 192, 196–7
Hammond, Thomas, 192, 196–7
Harington, John, 110, 114, 135, 172, 174, 233

Harley, Edward, 49, 68, 85, 155, 159, 162–3, 173–4, 192, 211–14, 219–21
Harrison, Thomas, 43, 155, 220
Haselrig, Sir Arthur, 60, 129, 131–3, 135, 140–2, 154, 156, 161–2, 178, 278, 280–1
Herbert, William, 63, 174, 185, 193–4, 219
Hereford, Lord (Walter Devereux), 146
Hertford, Marquis of (Thomas Seymour), 127
Hewson, John, 63, 193, 211
Hill, Roger, 20
Hill, Thomas, 26, 33, 298 n38
Hobson, Paul, 220
Holborne, James, 48–9
Holles, Denzil, 175, 176, 223, 225, 231, 234, 265
apprentices and, 259, 264
attacks on, 56–61, 131–2, 165–6, 168, 253, 276
on faction, 18, 226
financial measures of, 112–13, 116, 128, 150, 169
followers of, 20
Ireland and, 164, 173, 182, 236
leadership of, 19
New Model Army and, 154, 156–60, 162–3, 174, 179–80, 191, 197, 208, 218, 233, 243, 246, 281–2
policy and position of, 24, 32, 73–4, 102, 108, 123, 129, 140, 177–8
Scots and, 92, 110, 117–18, 133, 150–1, 277, 278, 280
strategy of, 134–5, 167, 279
Holles's party, 19, 170
emergence of, 140–2, 150, 160–1, 183
Irish venture, 283
limits of, 146, 165–6, 172–3
New Model Army and, 174, 179–82, 233, 243, 246, 252
program of, 9–10, 167, 177
radicals and, 285
reformadoes and, 237–8, 249, 264
Holmby House, 151, 168, 181, 203, 230–1, 234, 236, 238, 247, 250, 283
Horseman, John, 63
Horton, Thomas, 221

368

Index

Index

Index

Index